First Valentine's Day

BABY NAME:
_____

WHY CHOOSE HIGH-CONTRAST IMAGES?

DURING THEIR EARLY MONTHS, INFANTS DEPEND GREATLY ON THEIR VISION TO DISCOVER AND UNDERSTAND THEIR SURROUNDINGS. FROM 2 TO 14 WEEKS OF AGE, THEY SHOW A STRONG PREFERENCE FOR HIGH-CONTRAST VISUALS, WHICH ARE VITAL IN FOSTERING THEIR VISUAL STIMULATION AND SUPPORTING COGNITIVE DEVELOPMENT.

Thank You

for choosing My First Valentine's Day—a high-contrast baby book specially designed for newborns aged 0-12 months!

"REVIEW"

We'd love to hear your thoughts! Please leave us an honest review and share your experience with us—it means the world to us!

Evan Marlowe Publishing

Copyright © [2025] [Ryan Harped]

All rights reserved. No part of this book, My First Valentine's Day: High Contrast Baby Book for Newborns 0-12 Months, may be reproduced in any form without prior written permission from the publisher.

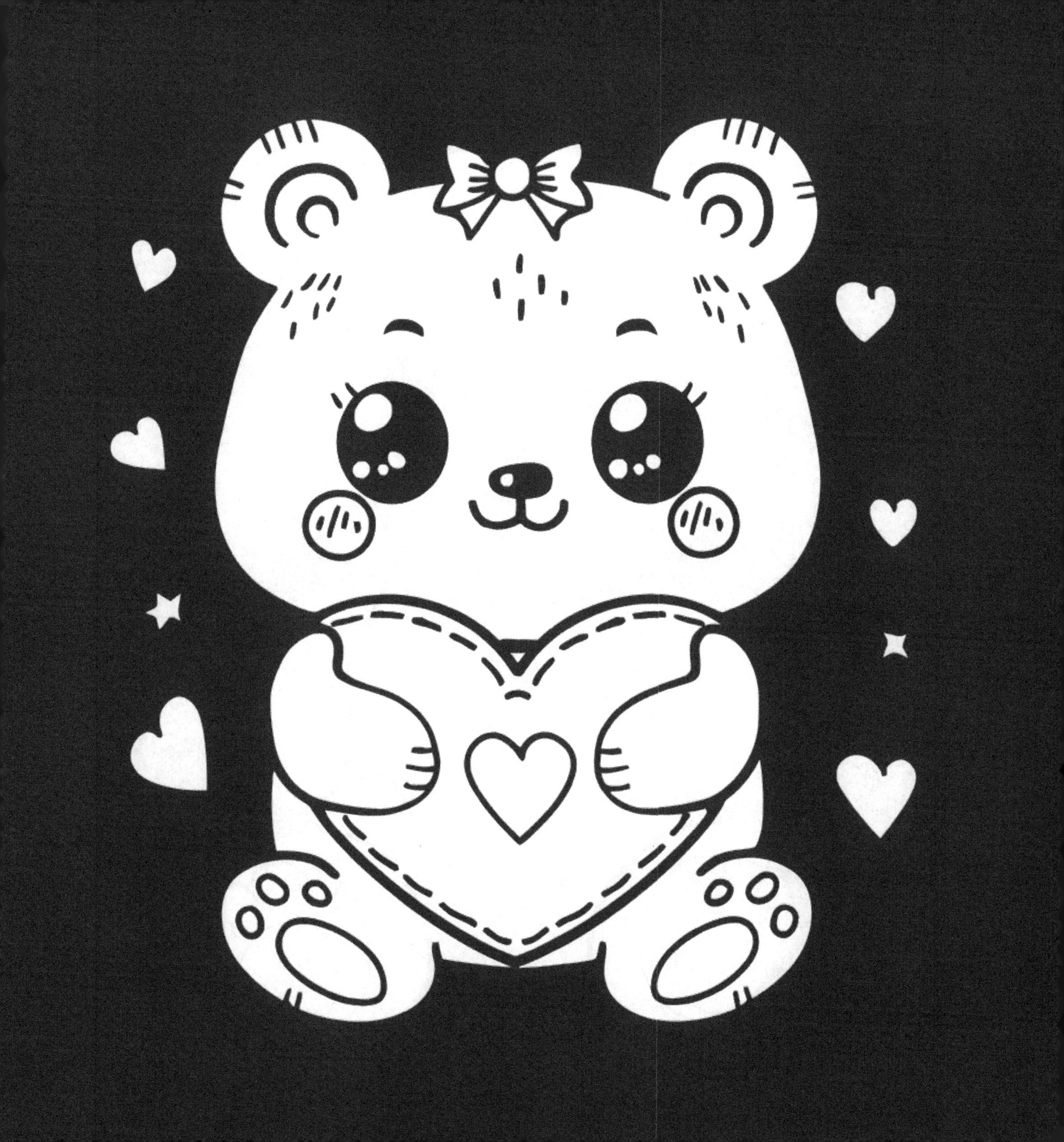

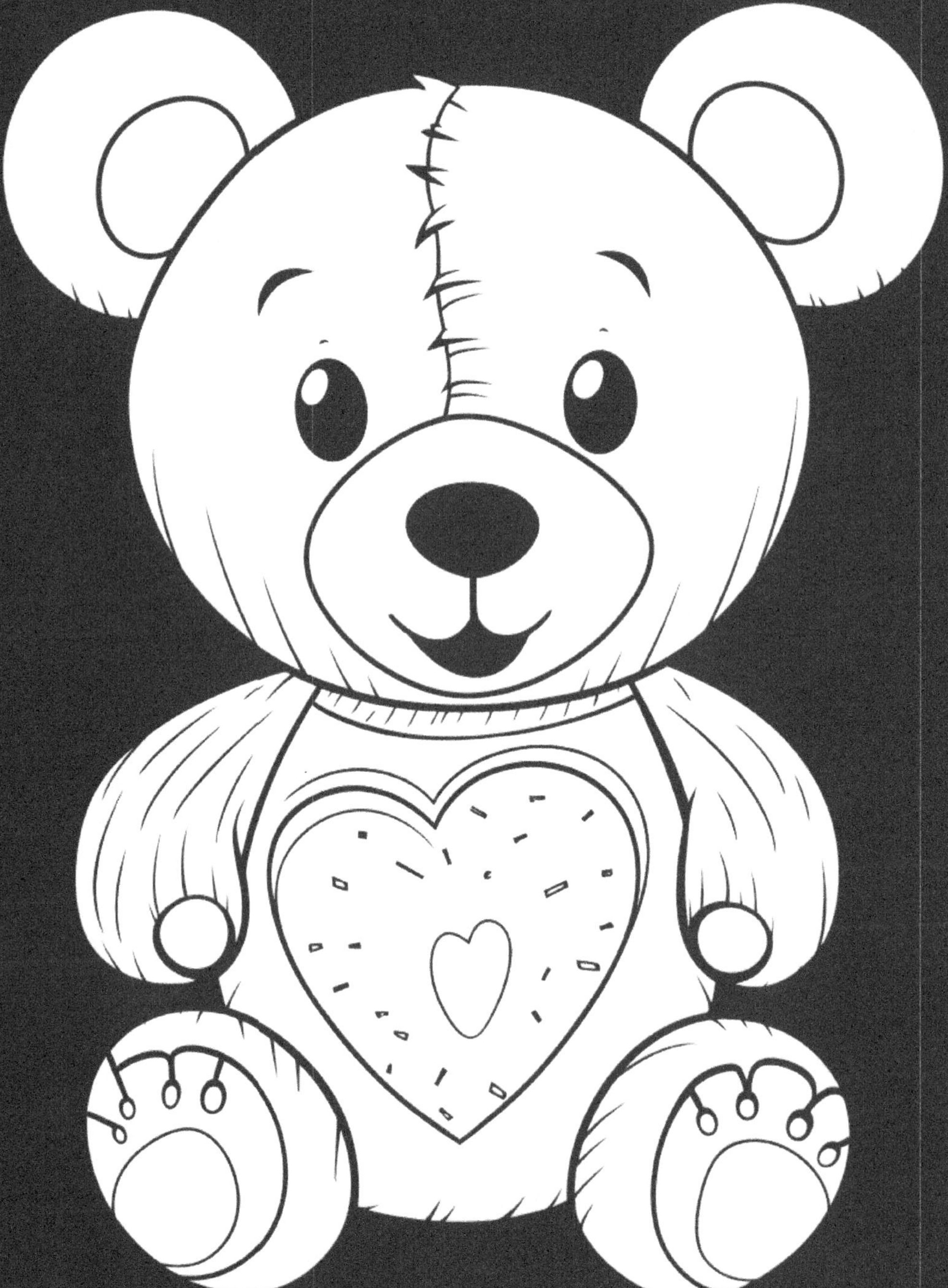

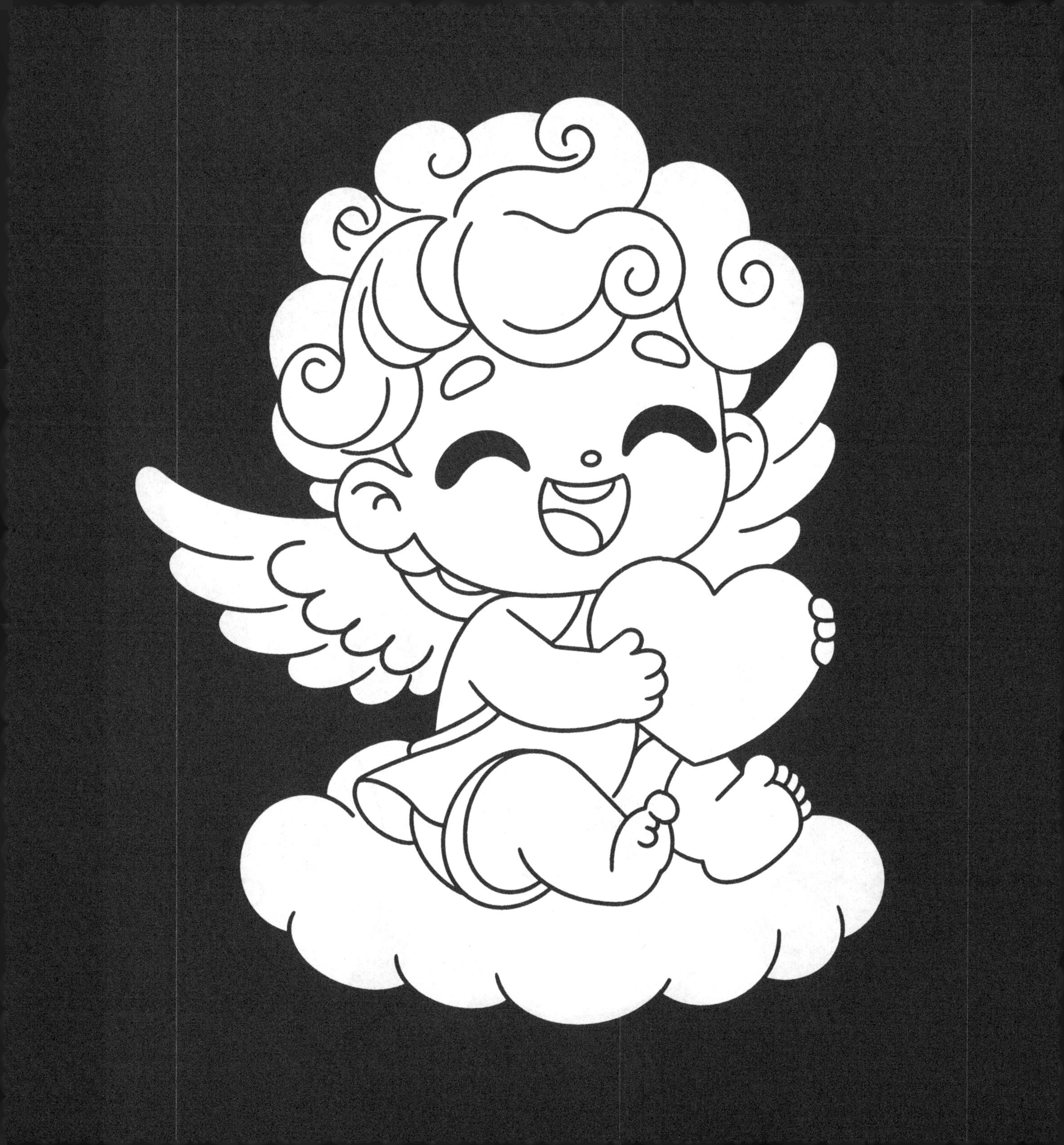

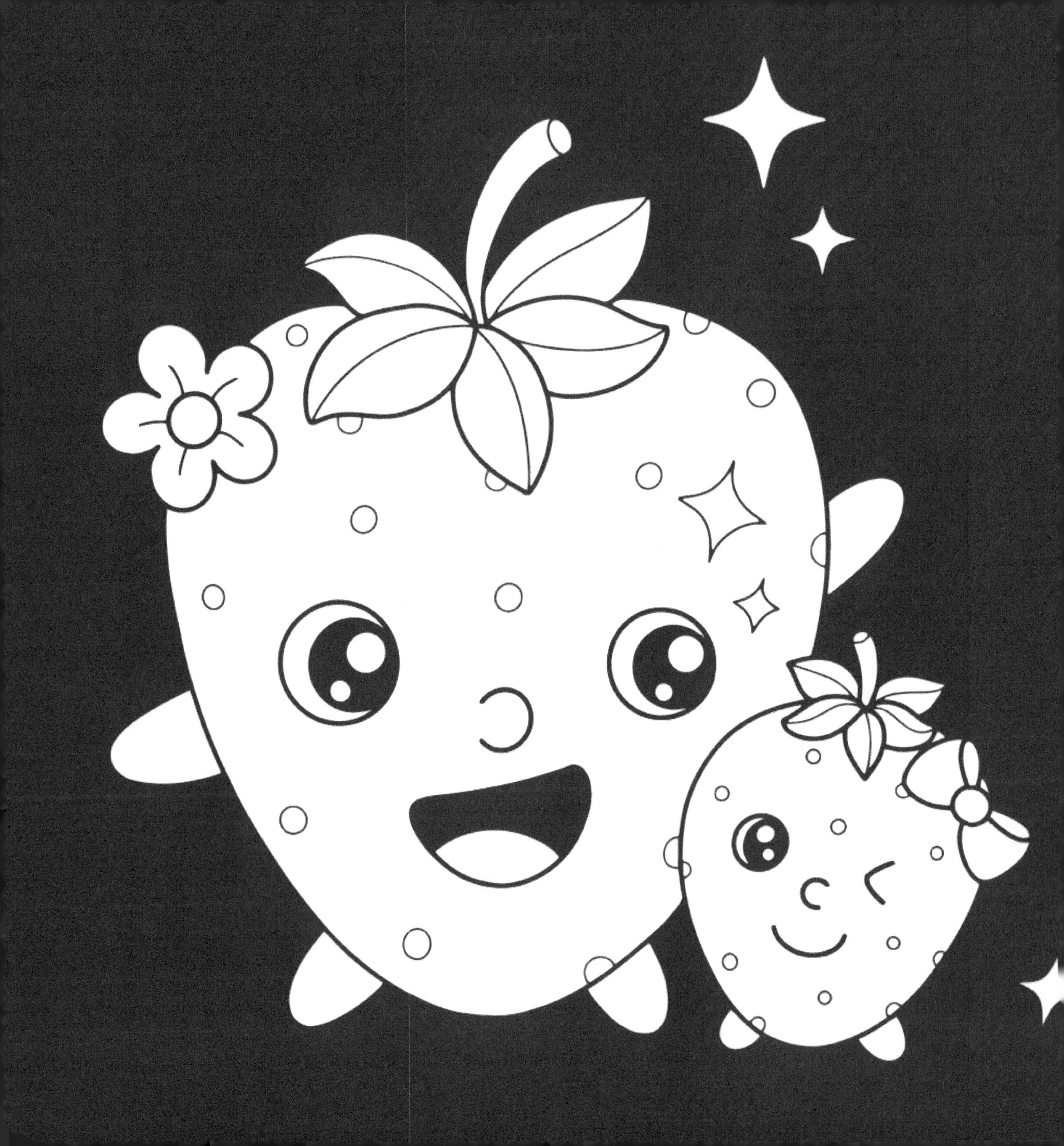

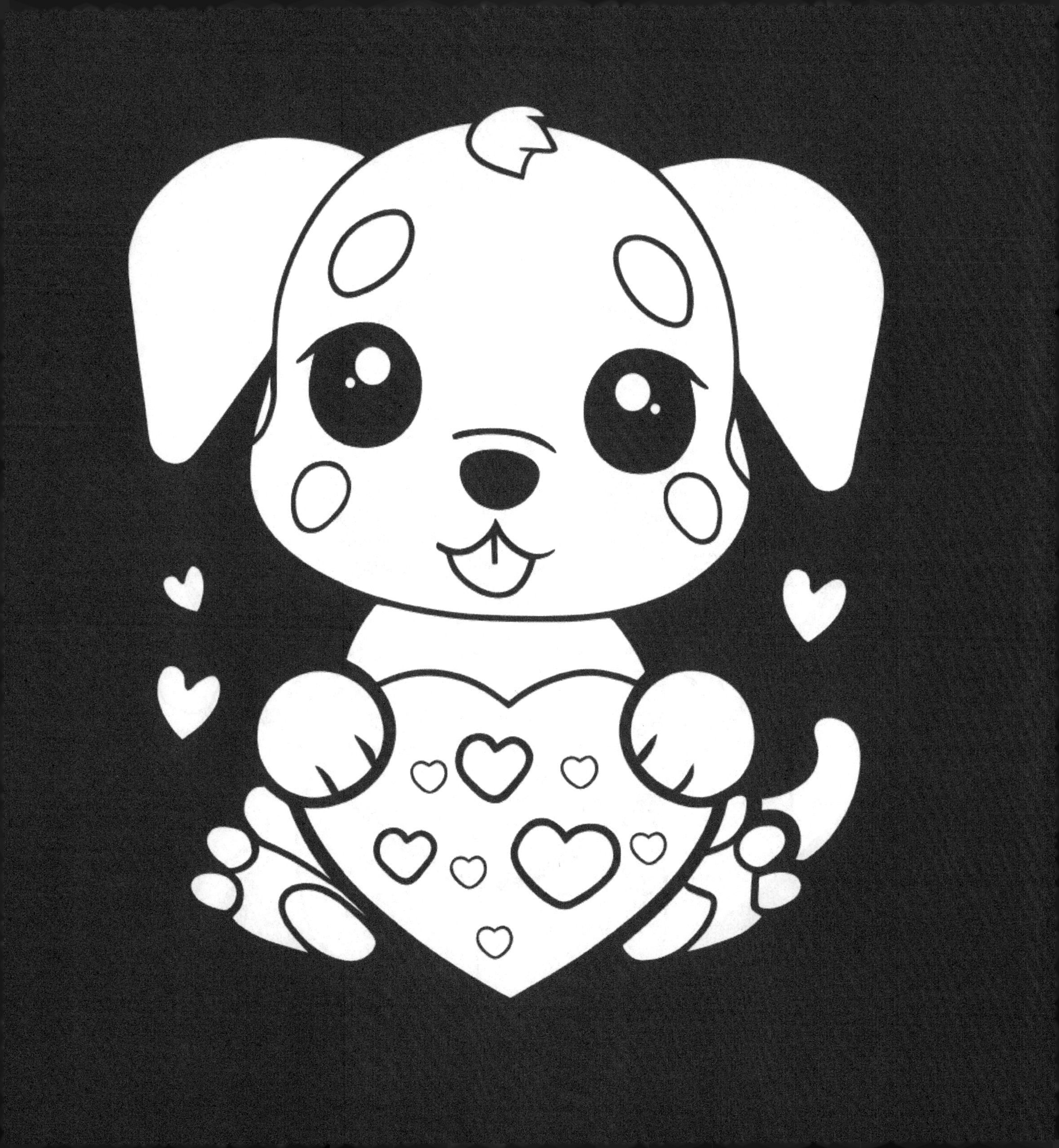

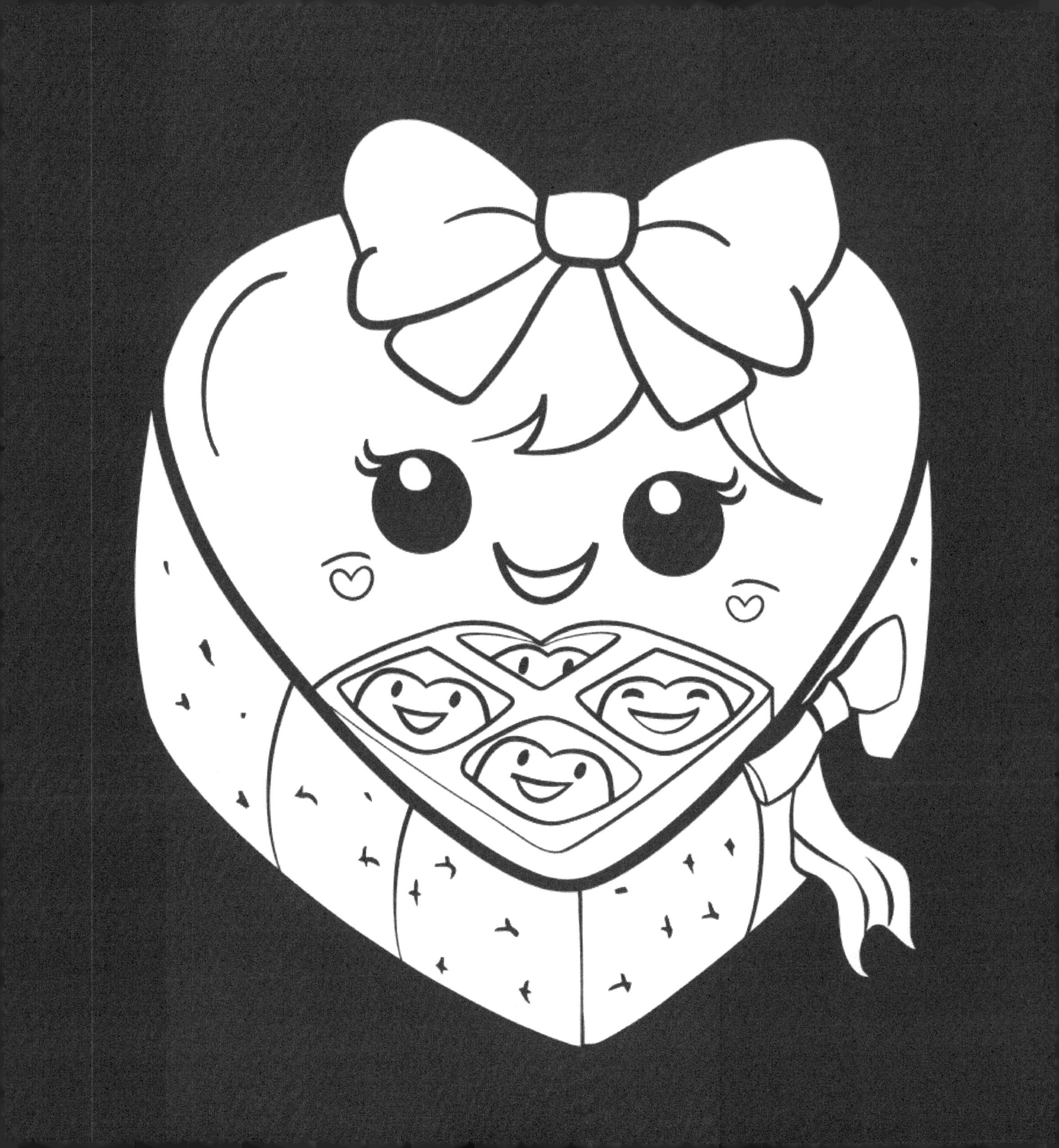

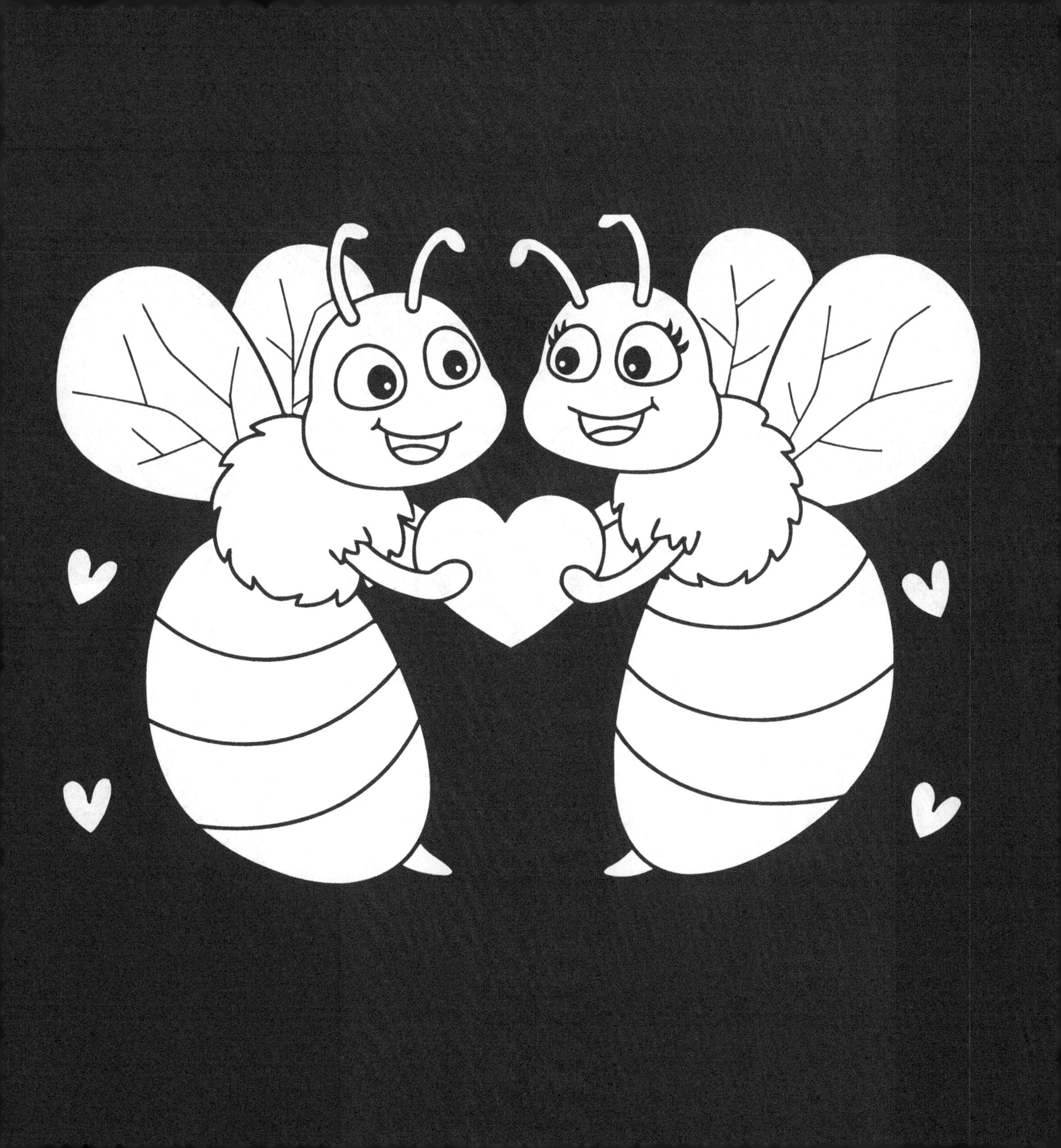

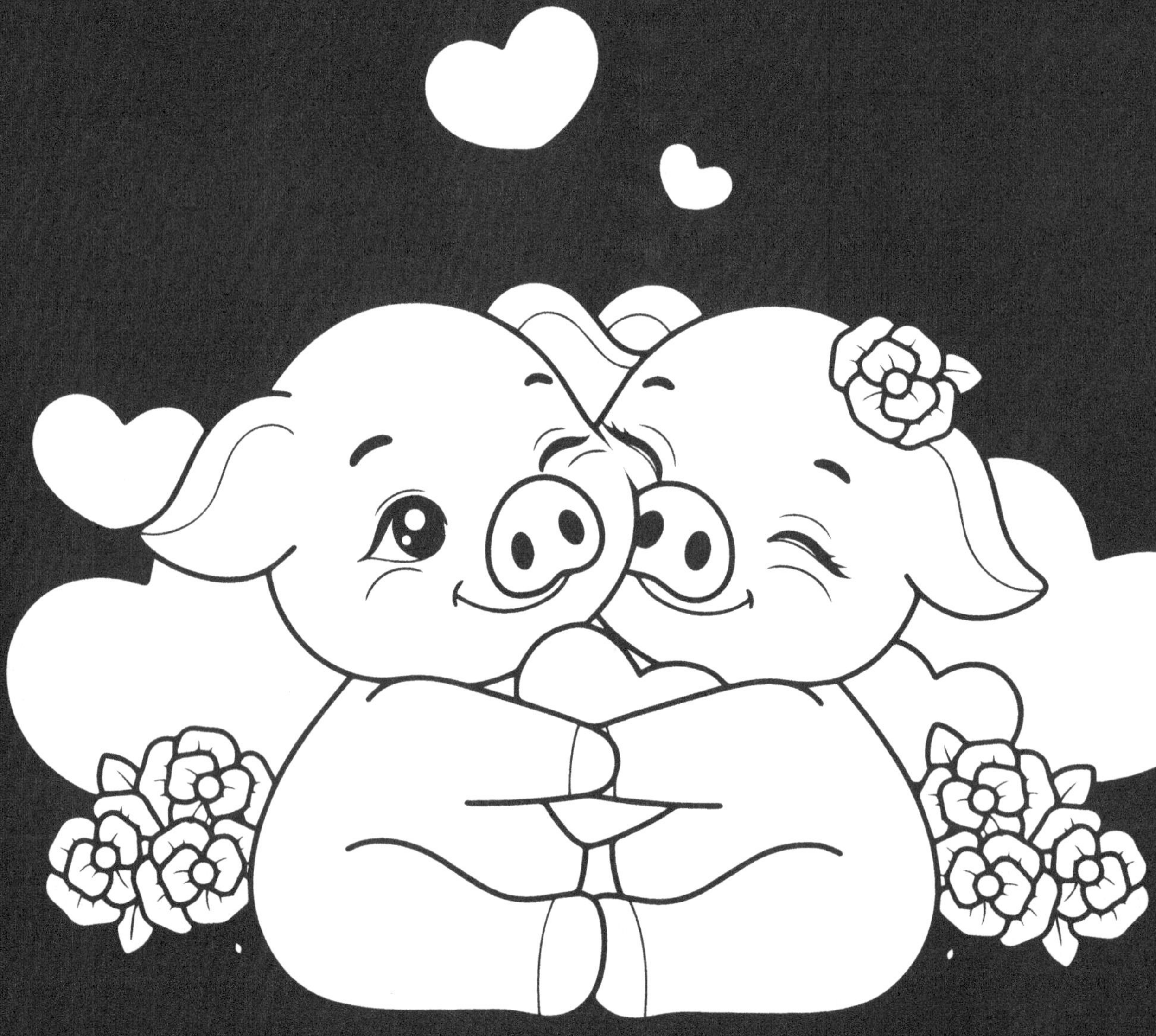

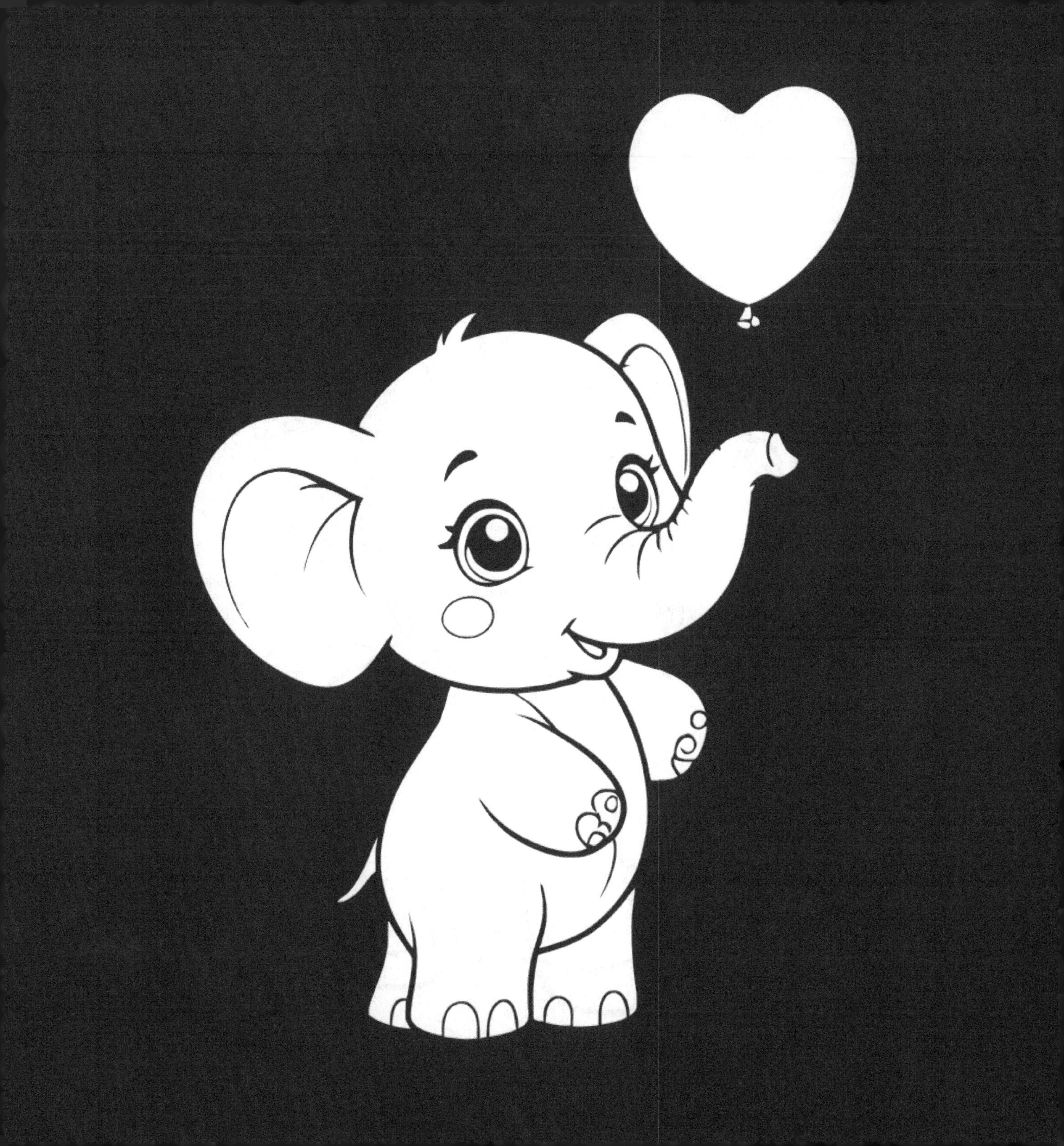

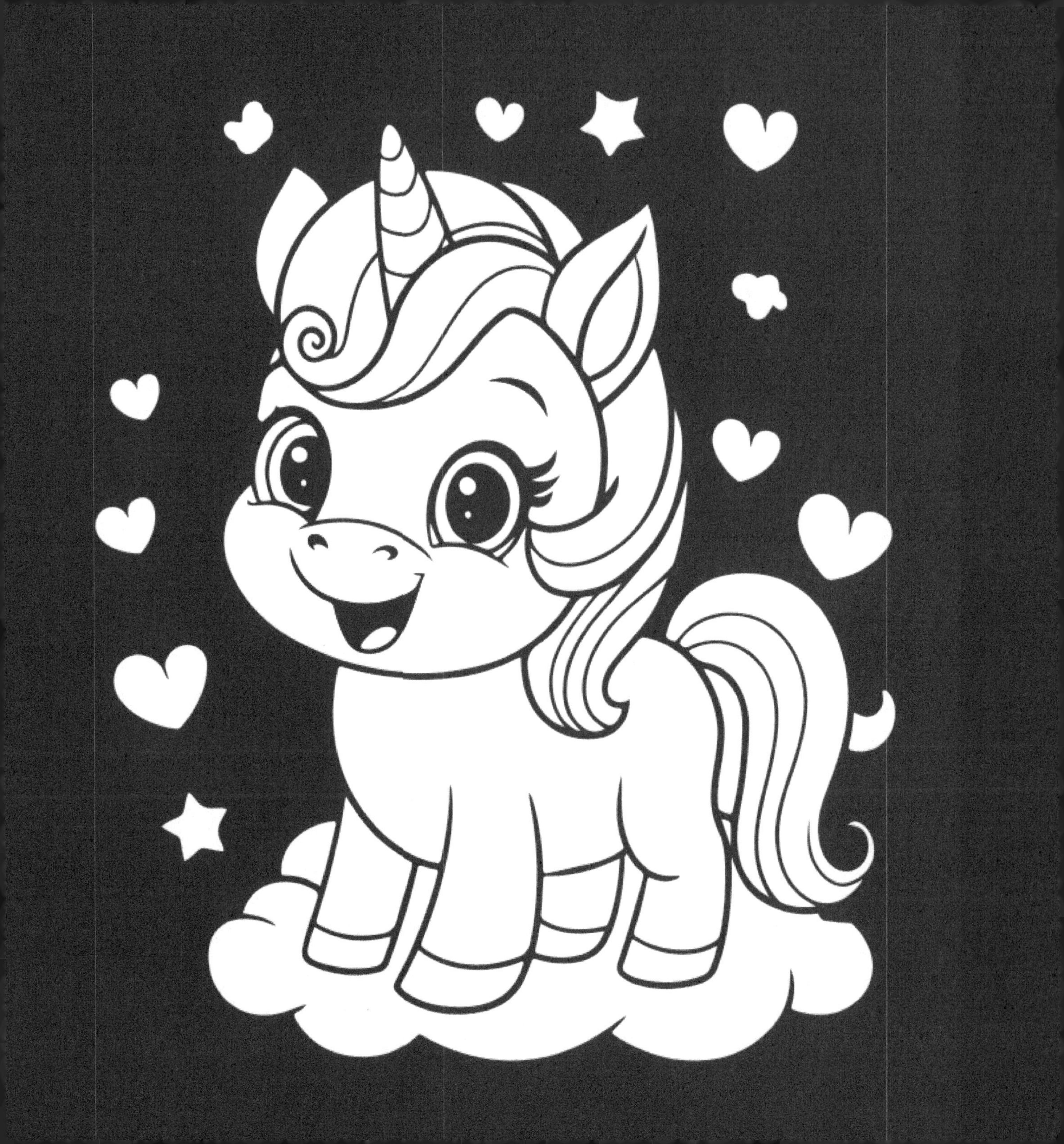

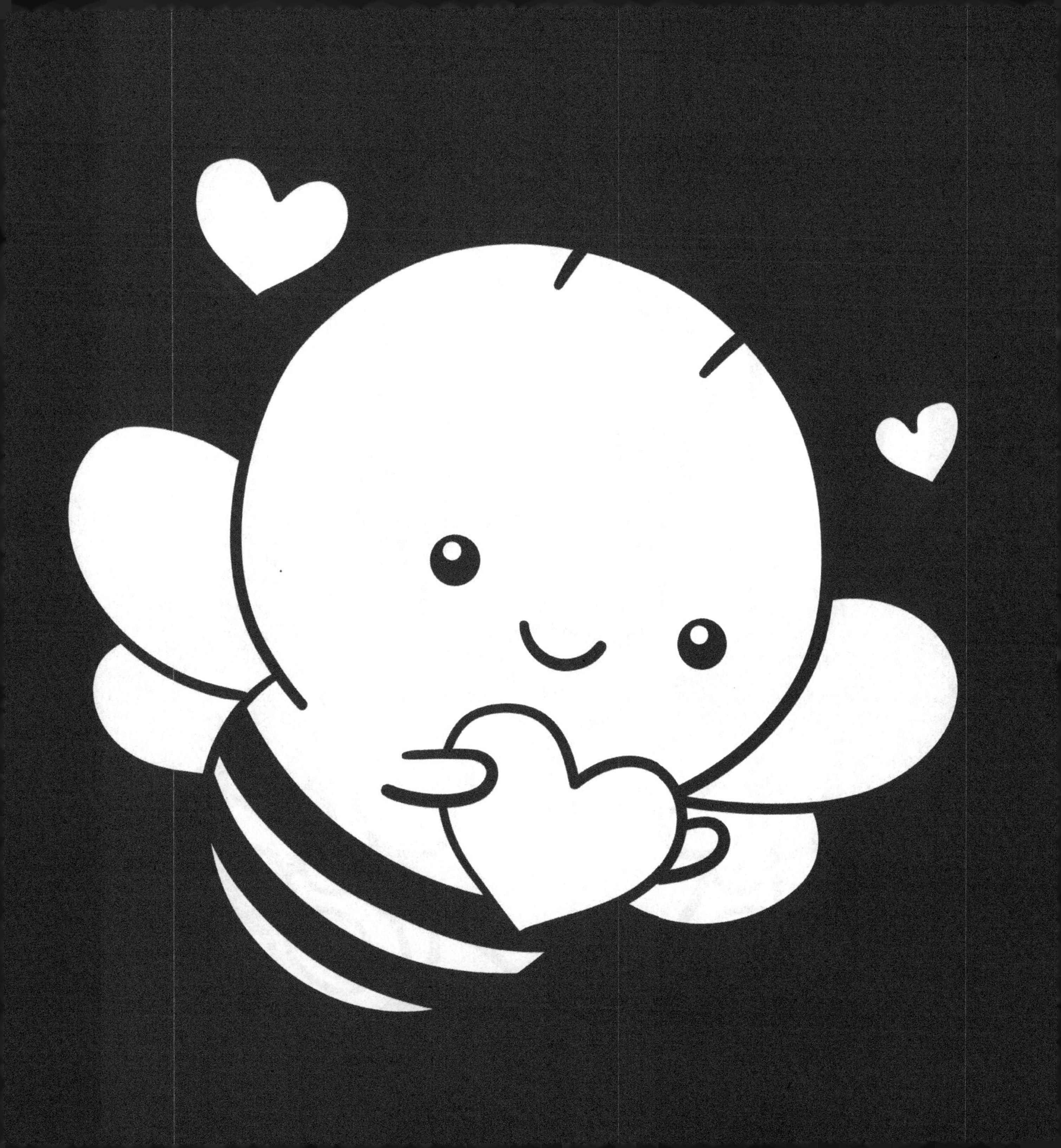

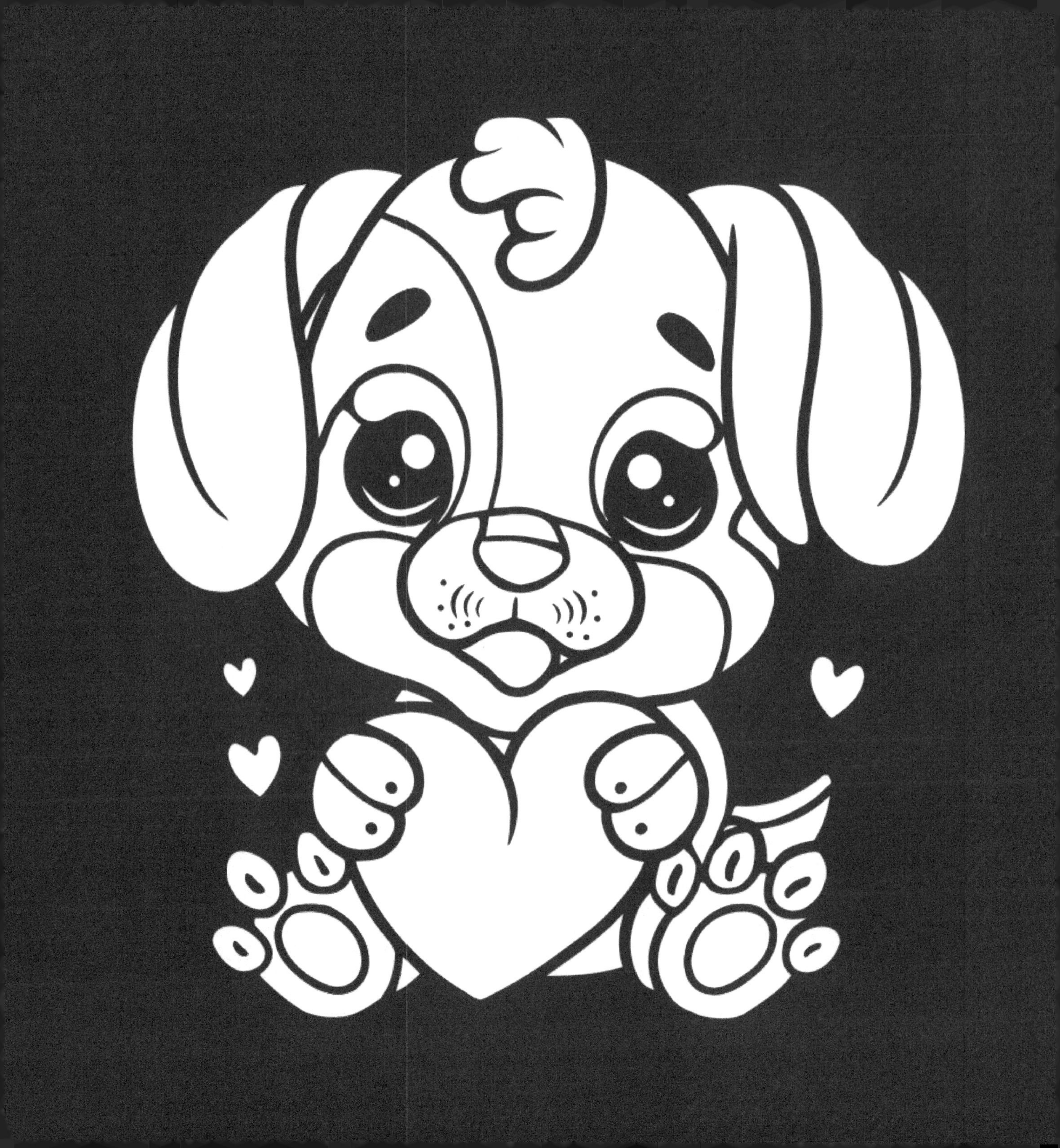

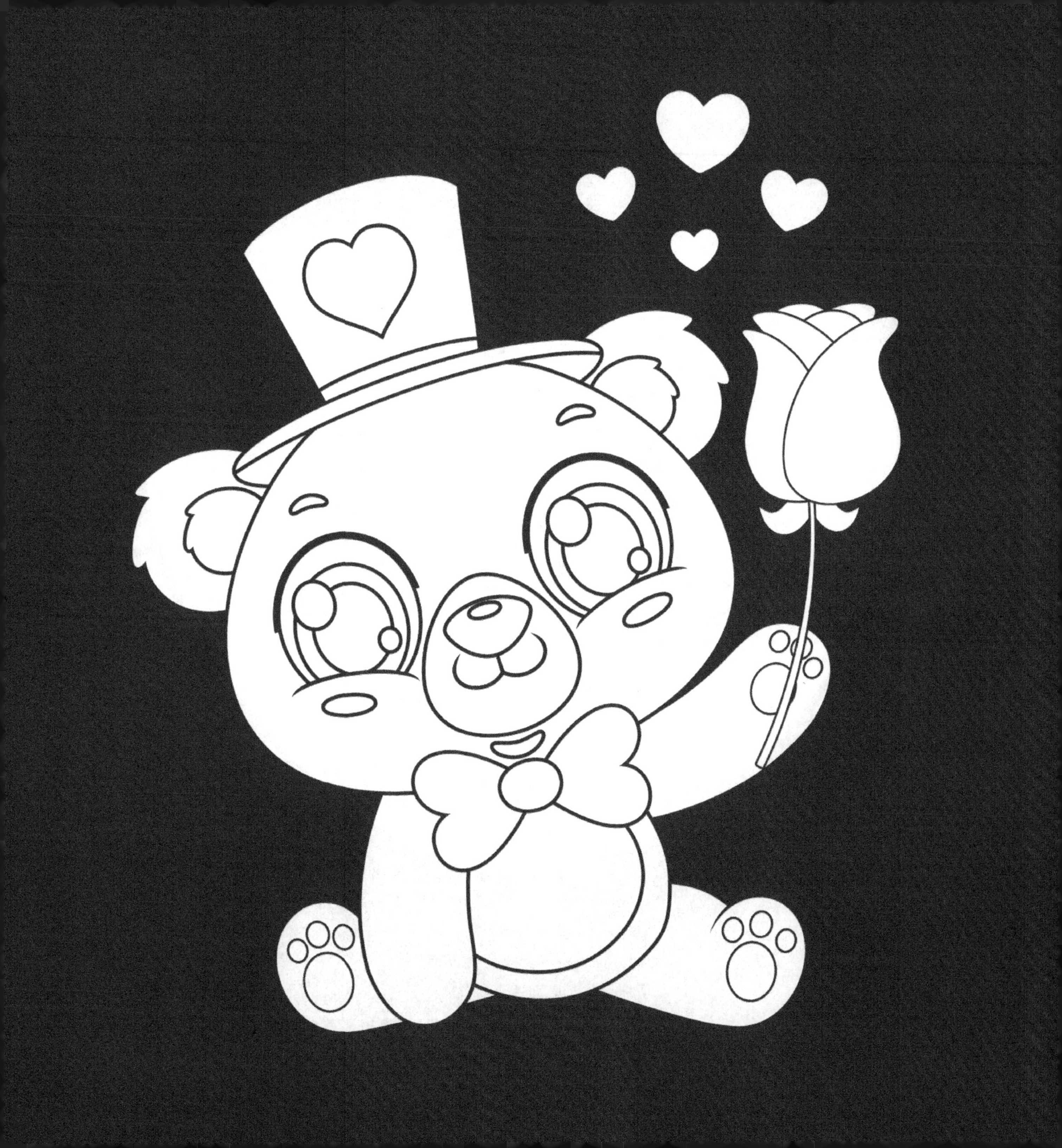

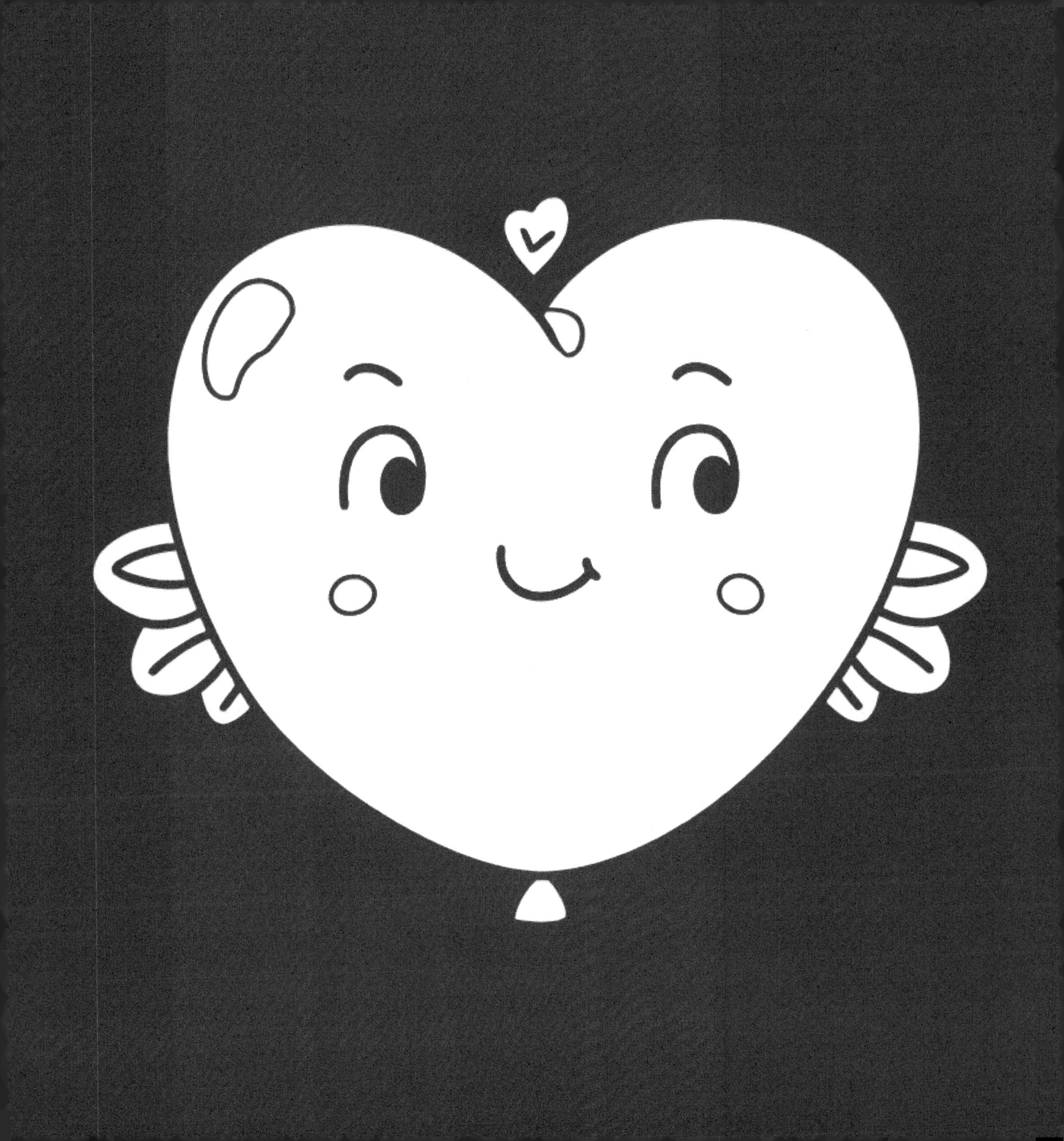

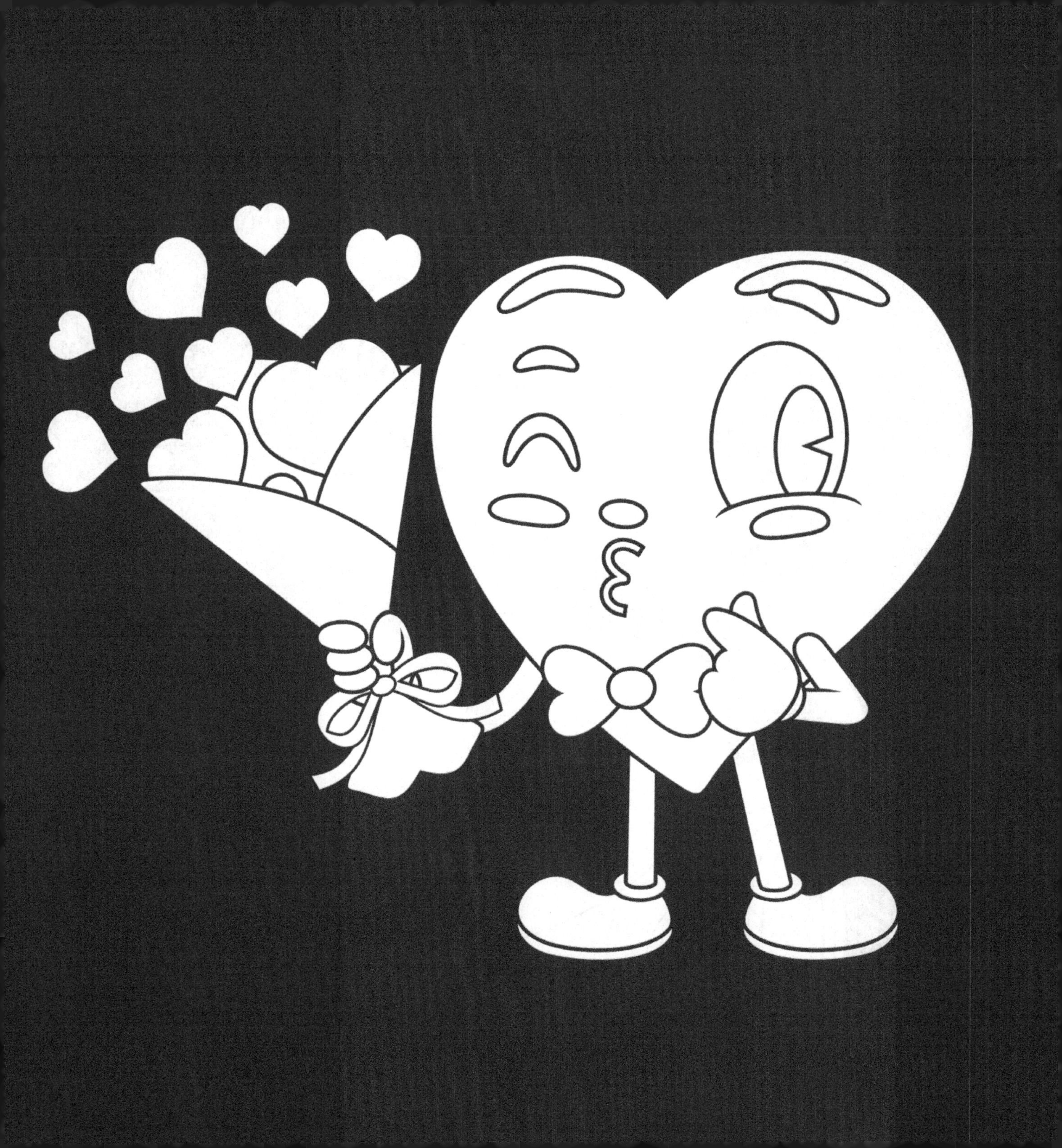

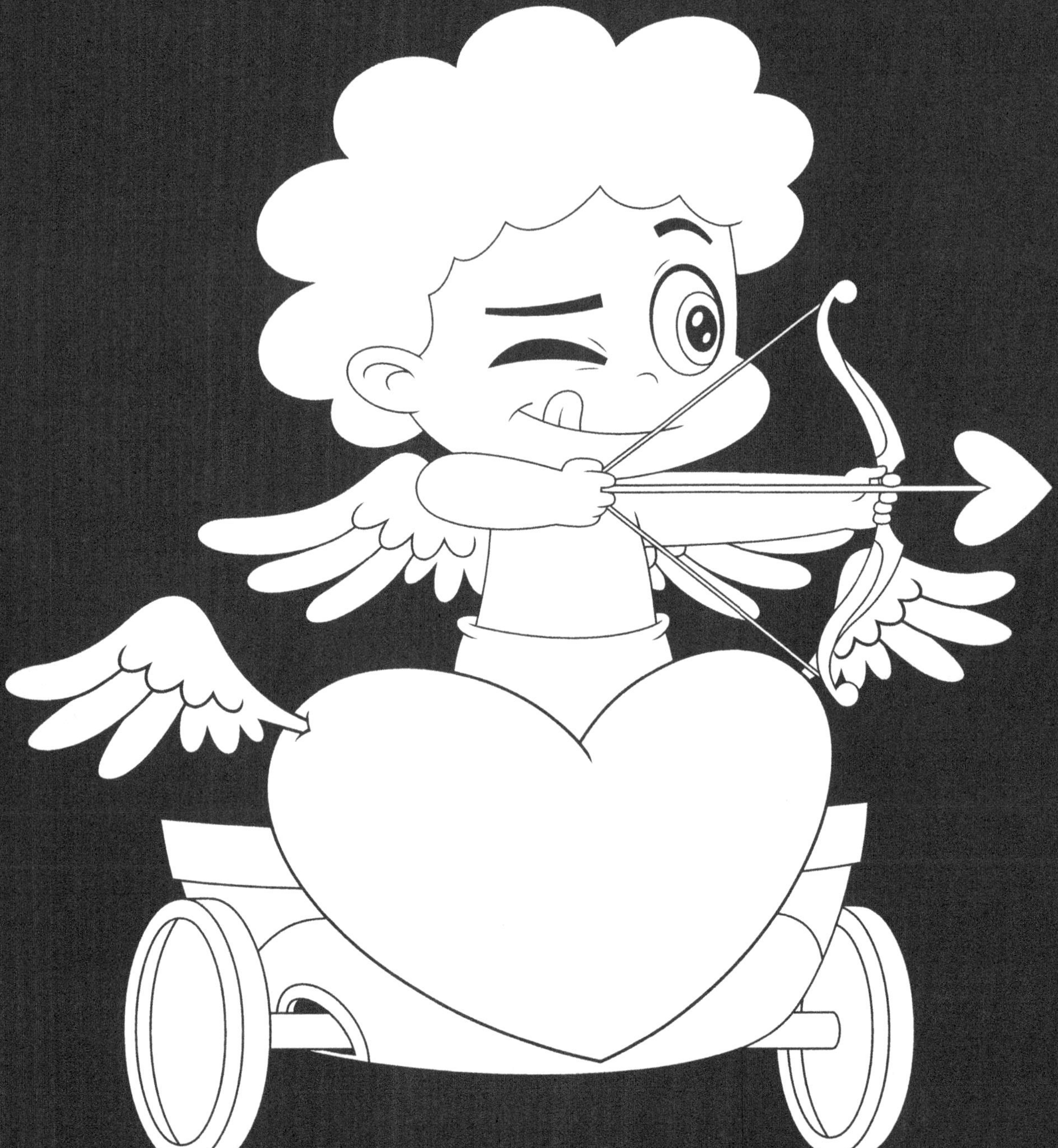

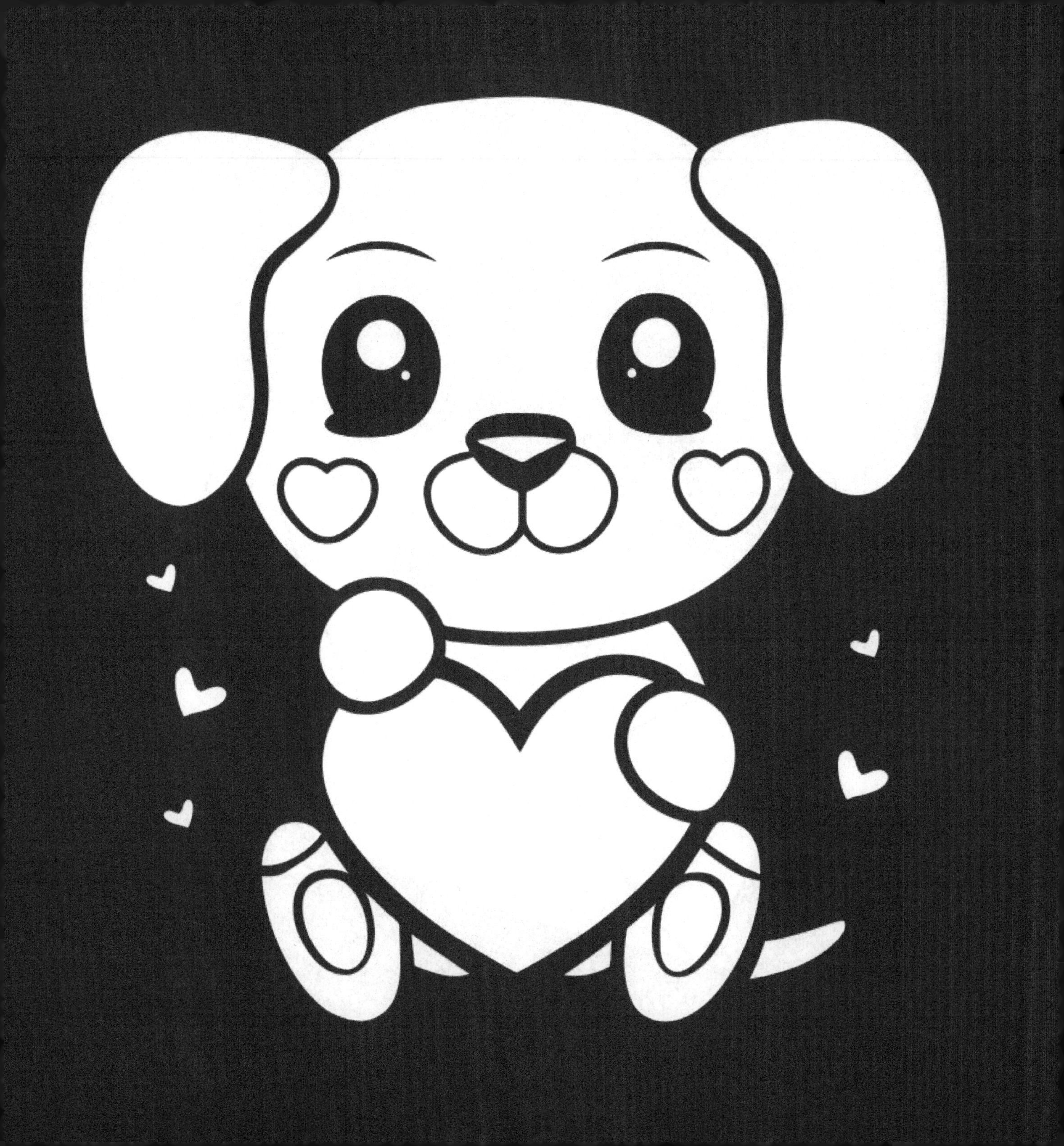

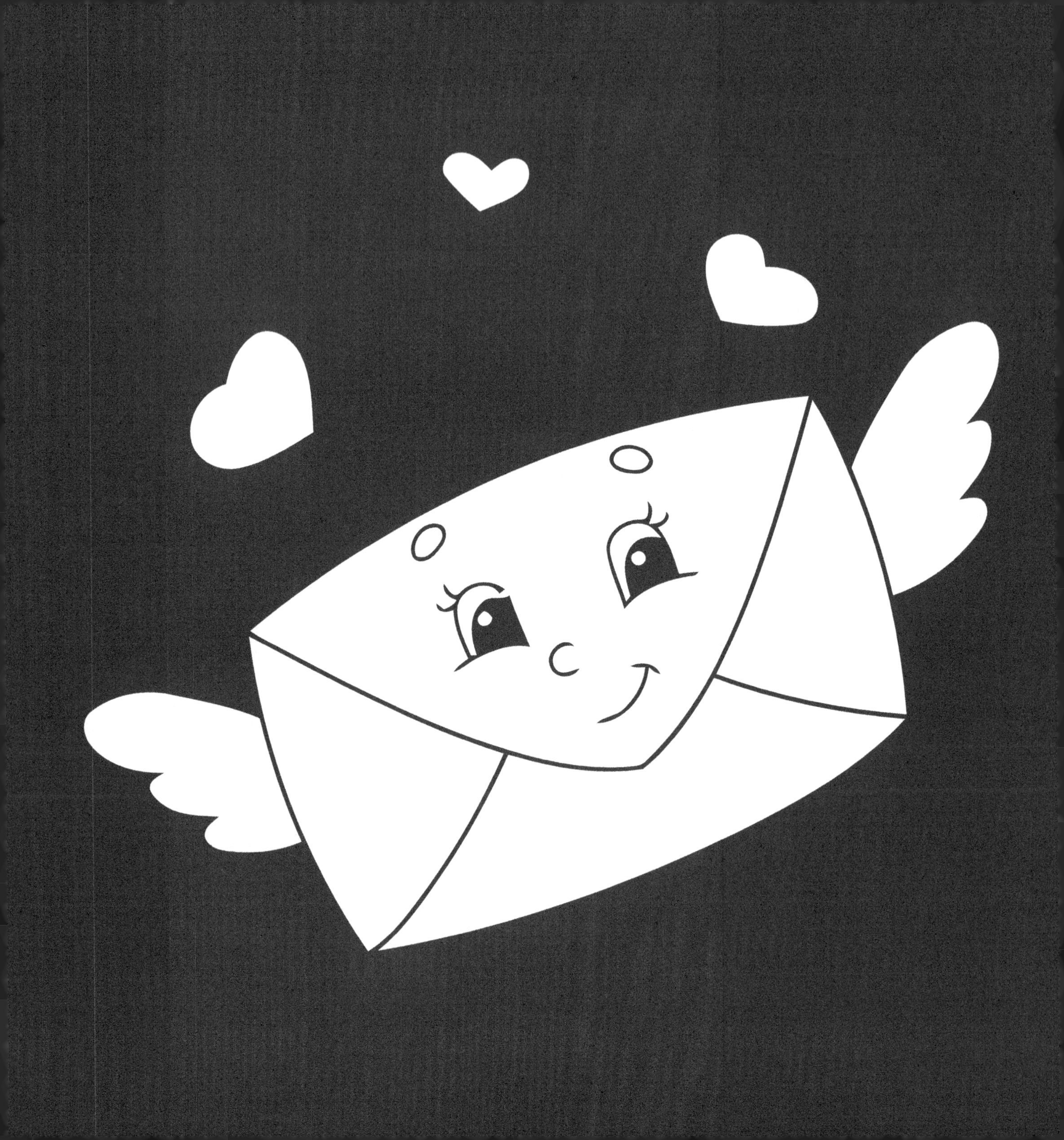

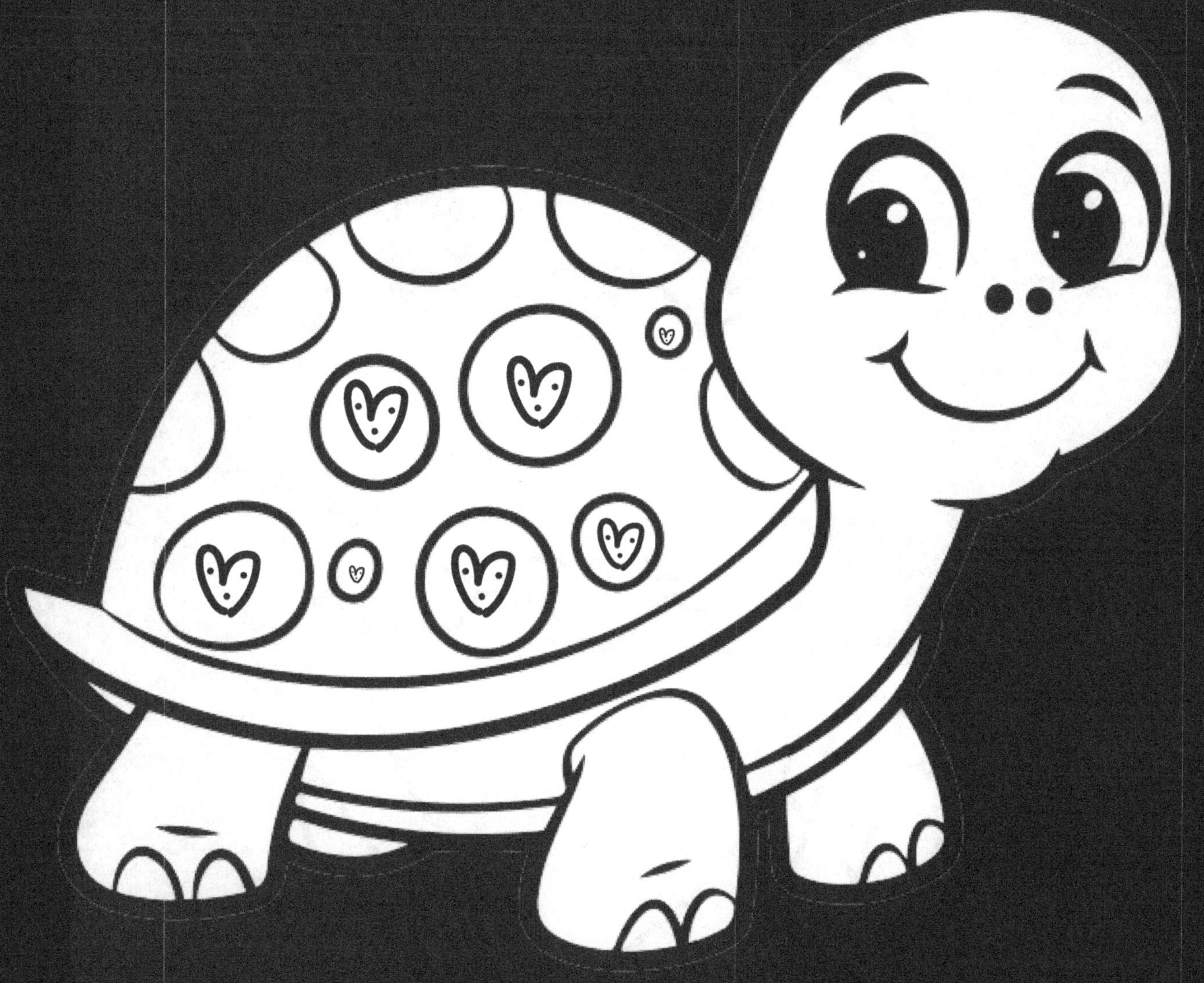

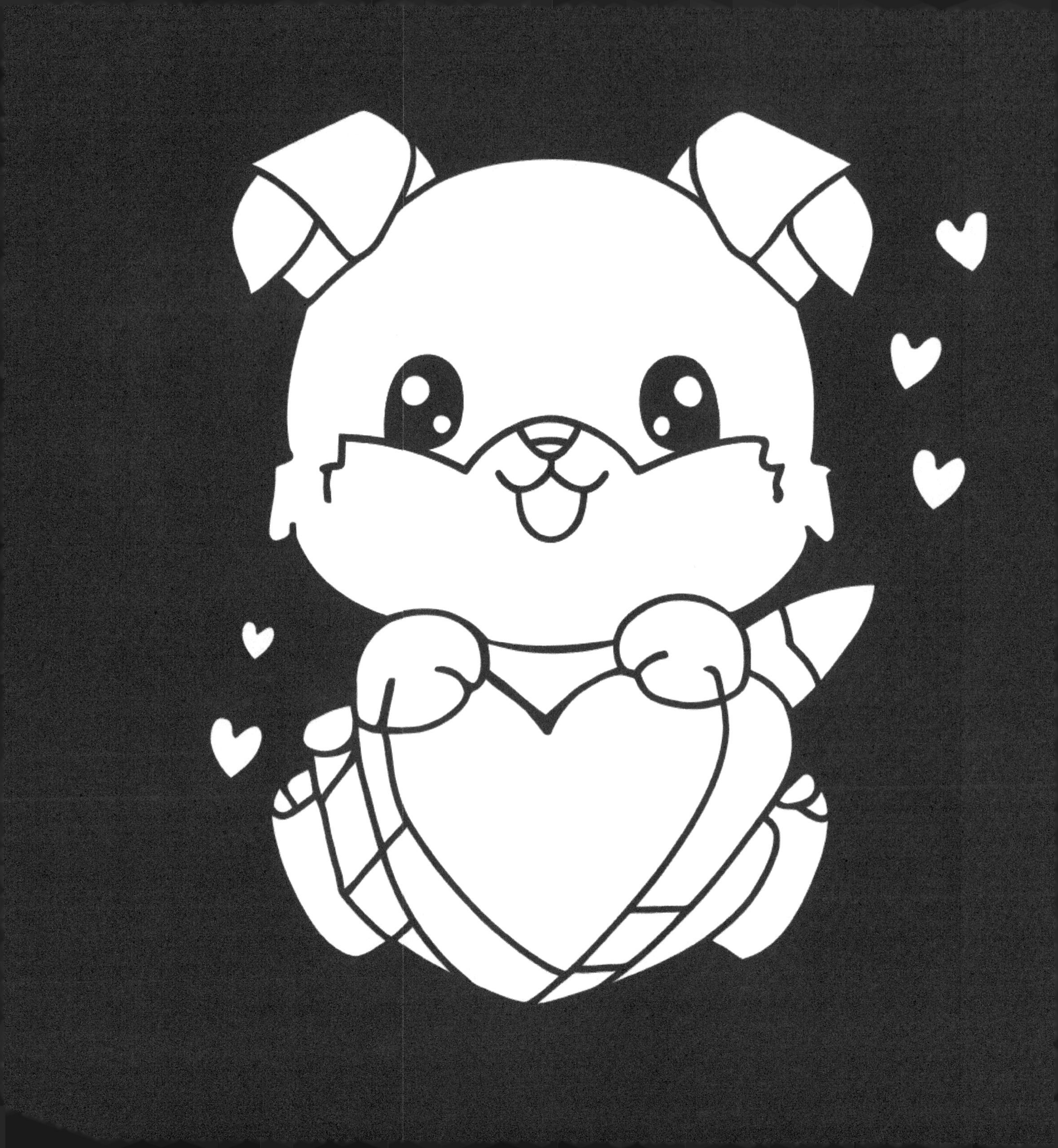

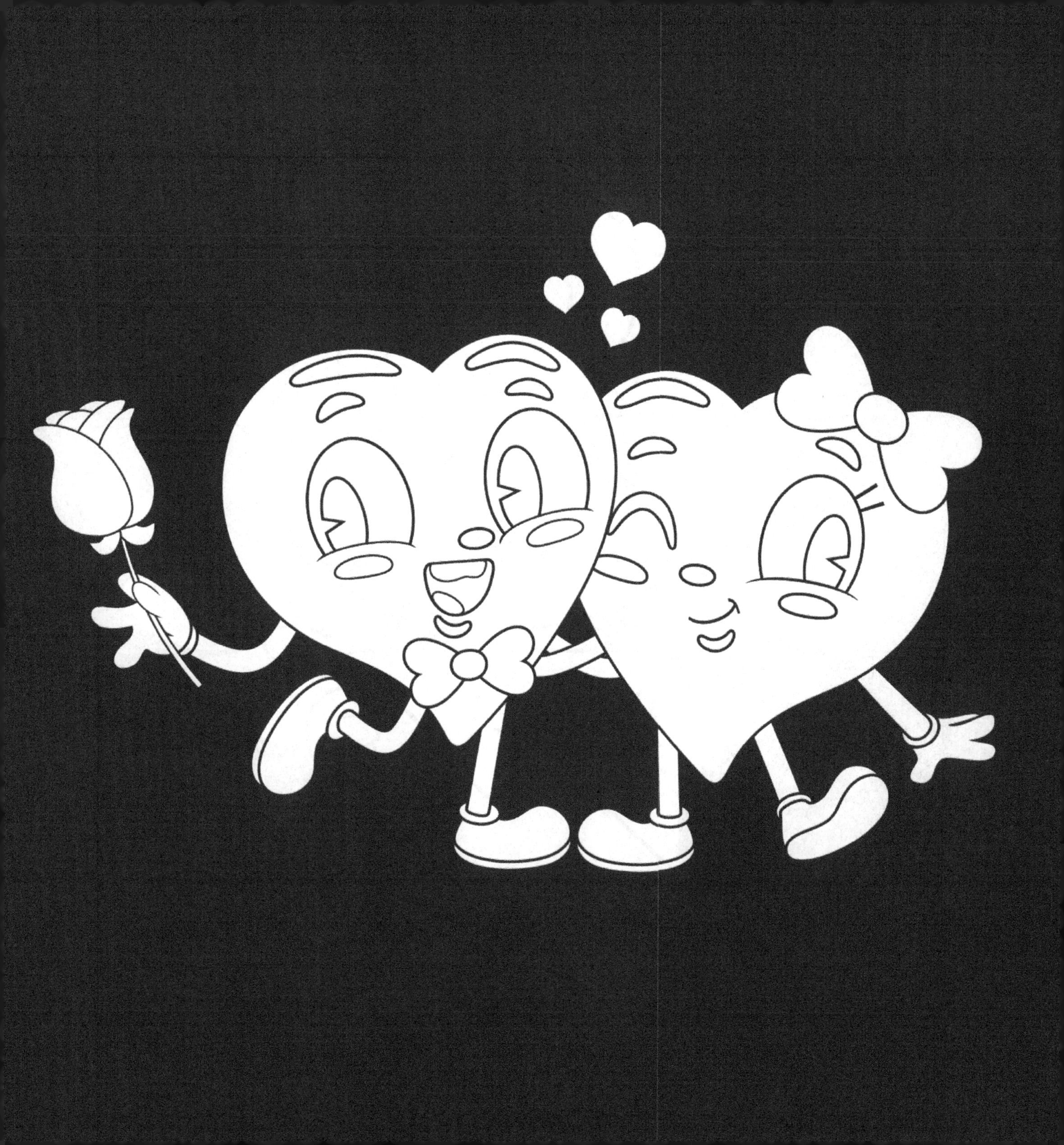

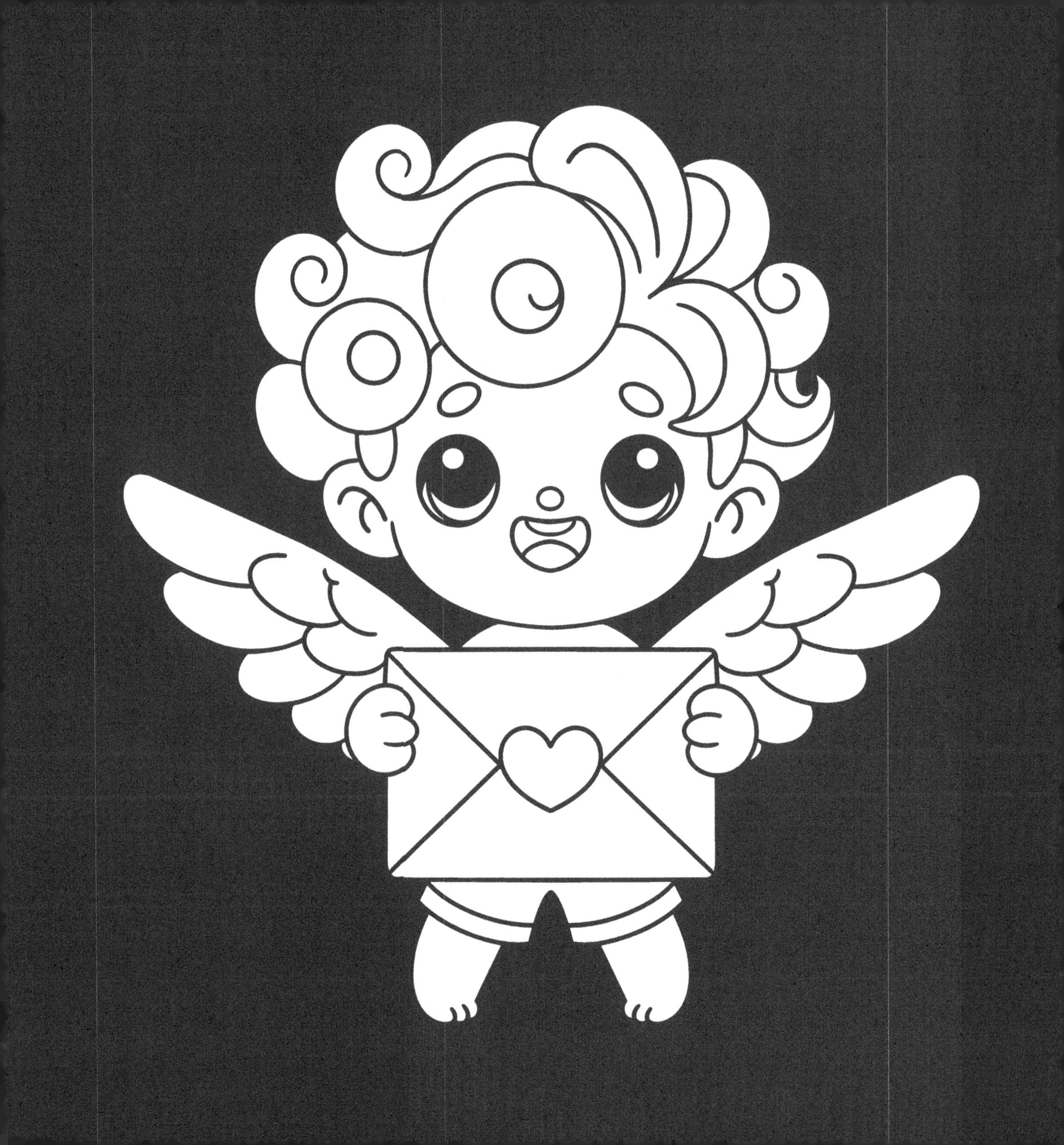

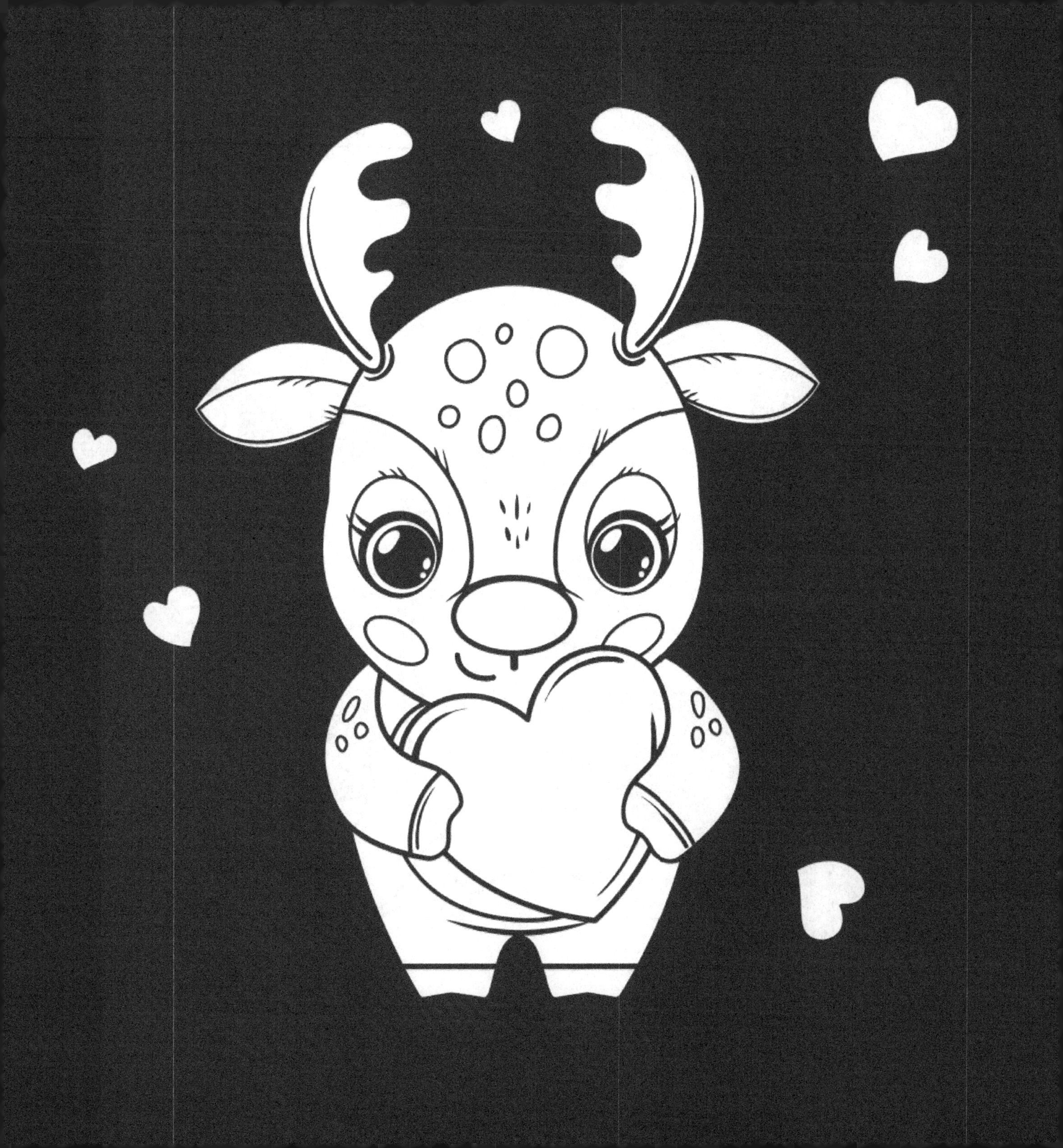

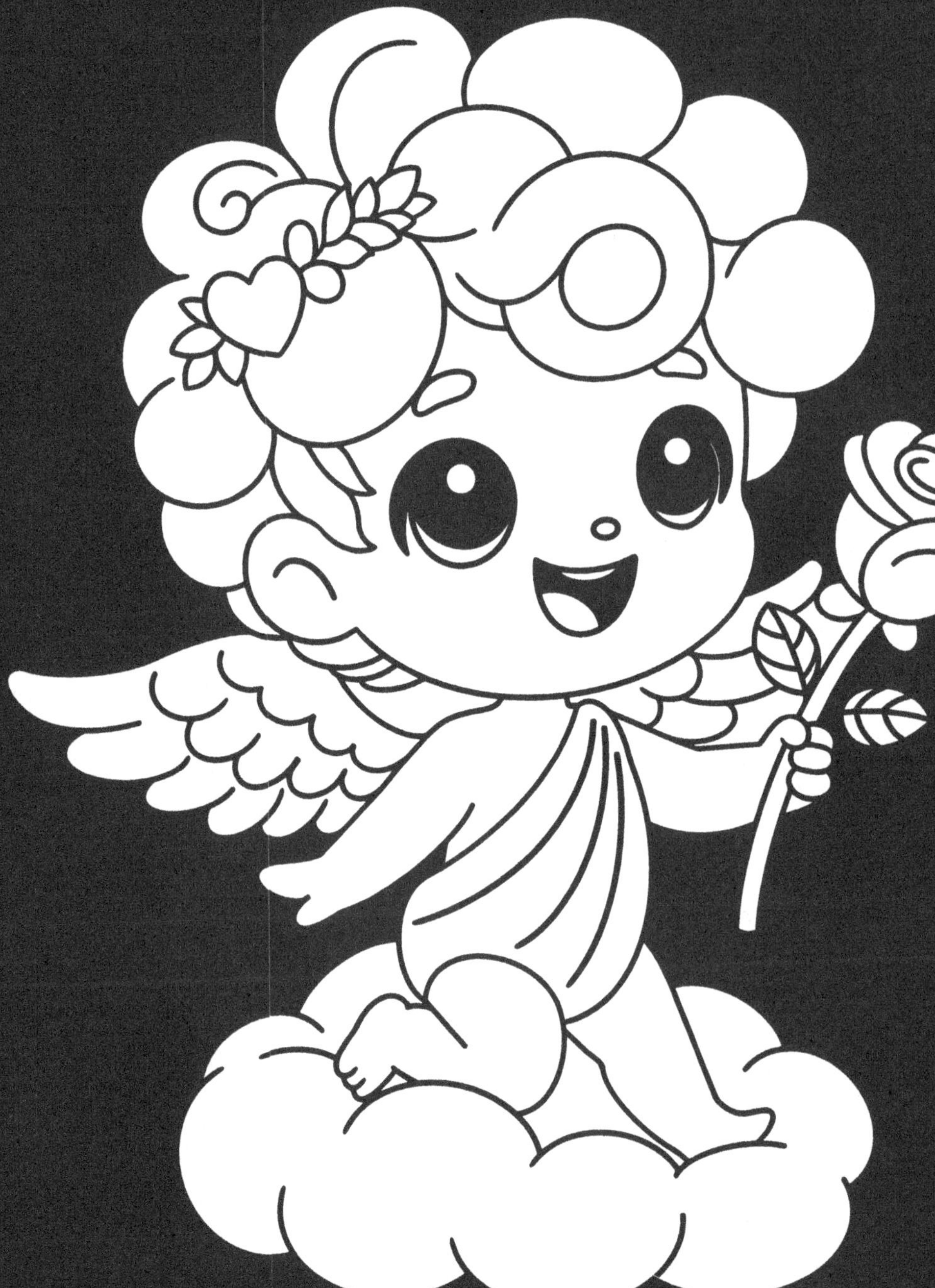

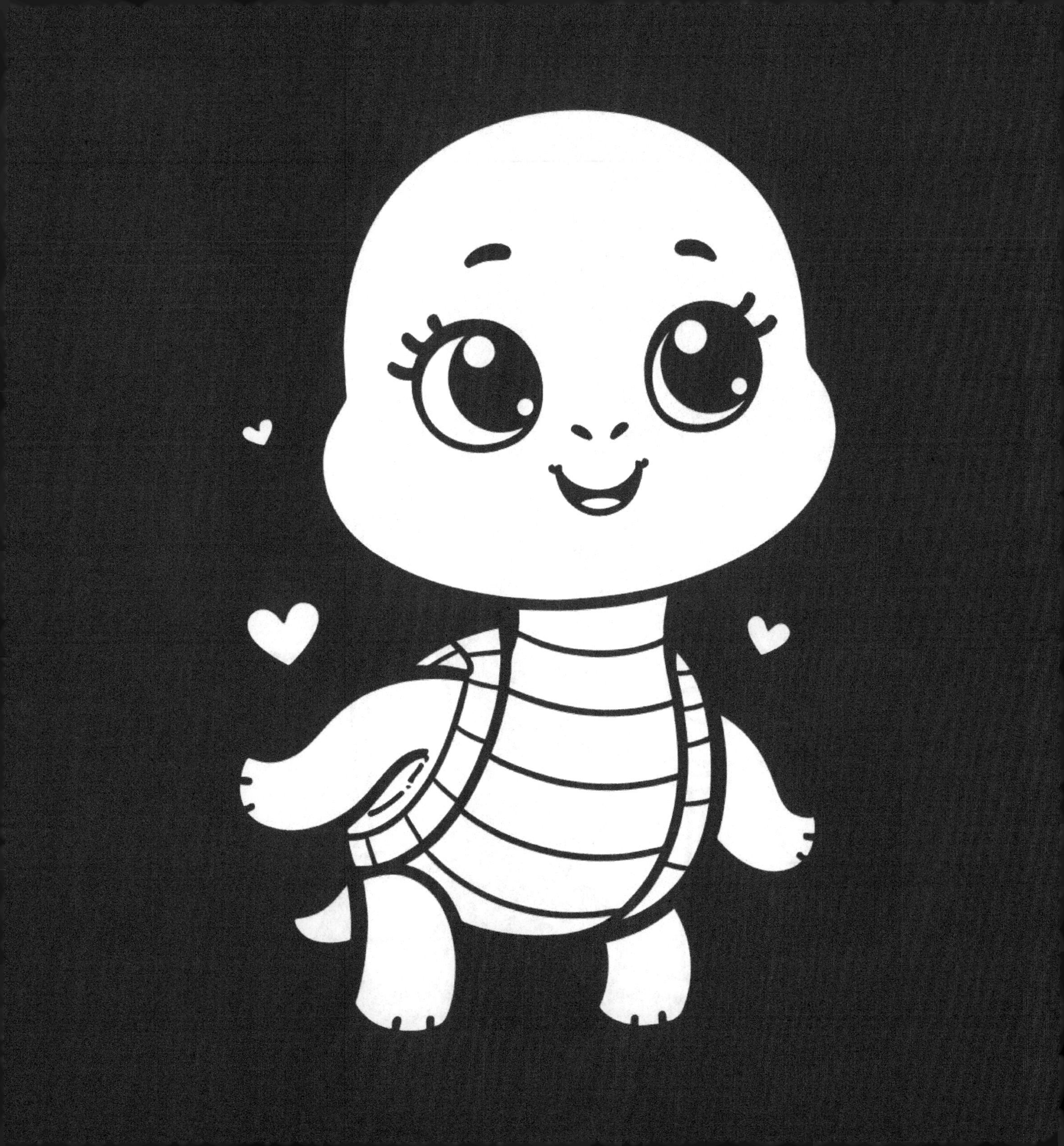

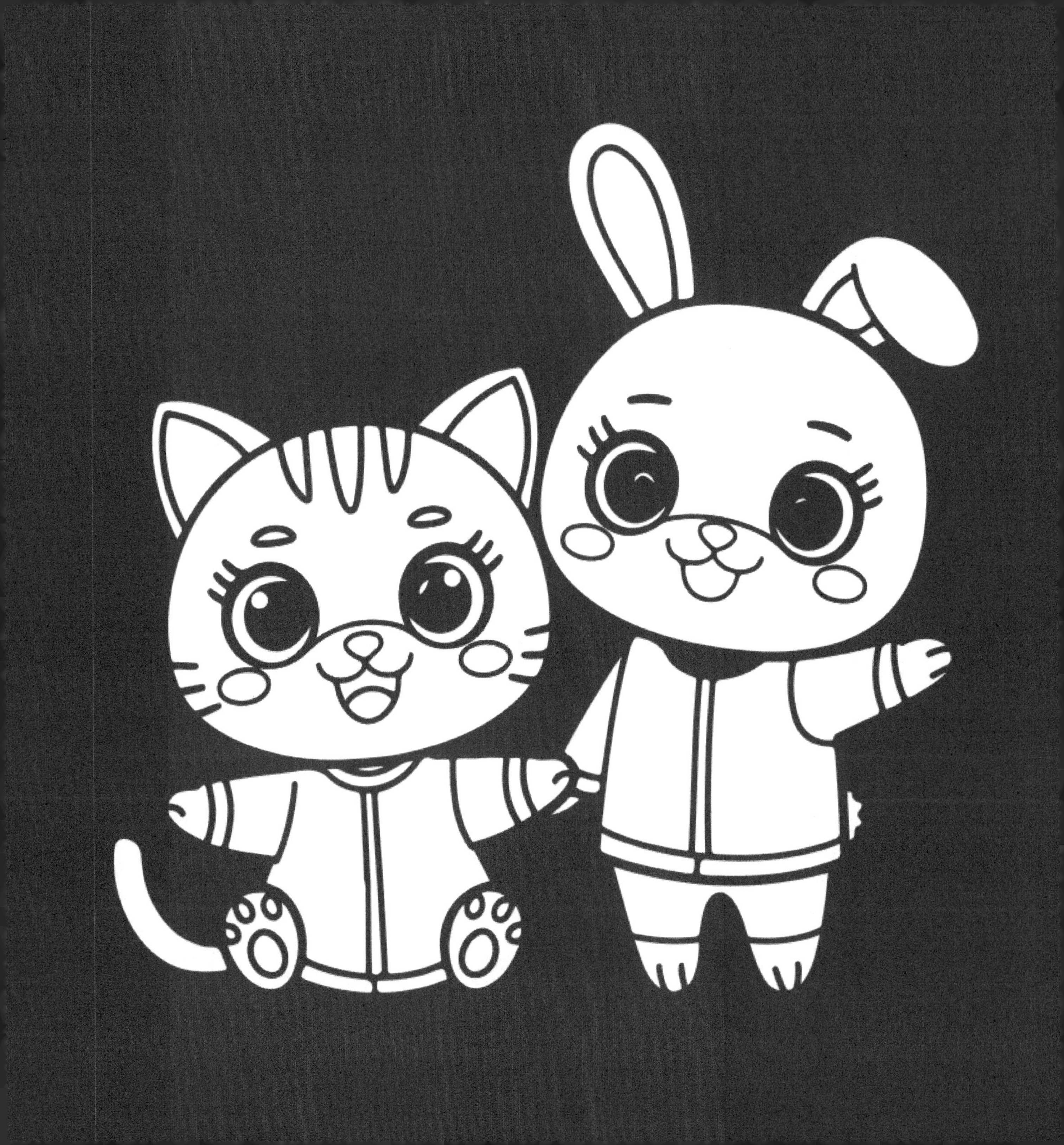

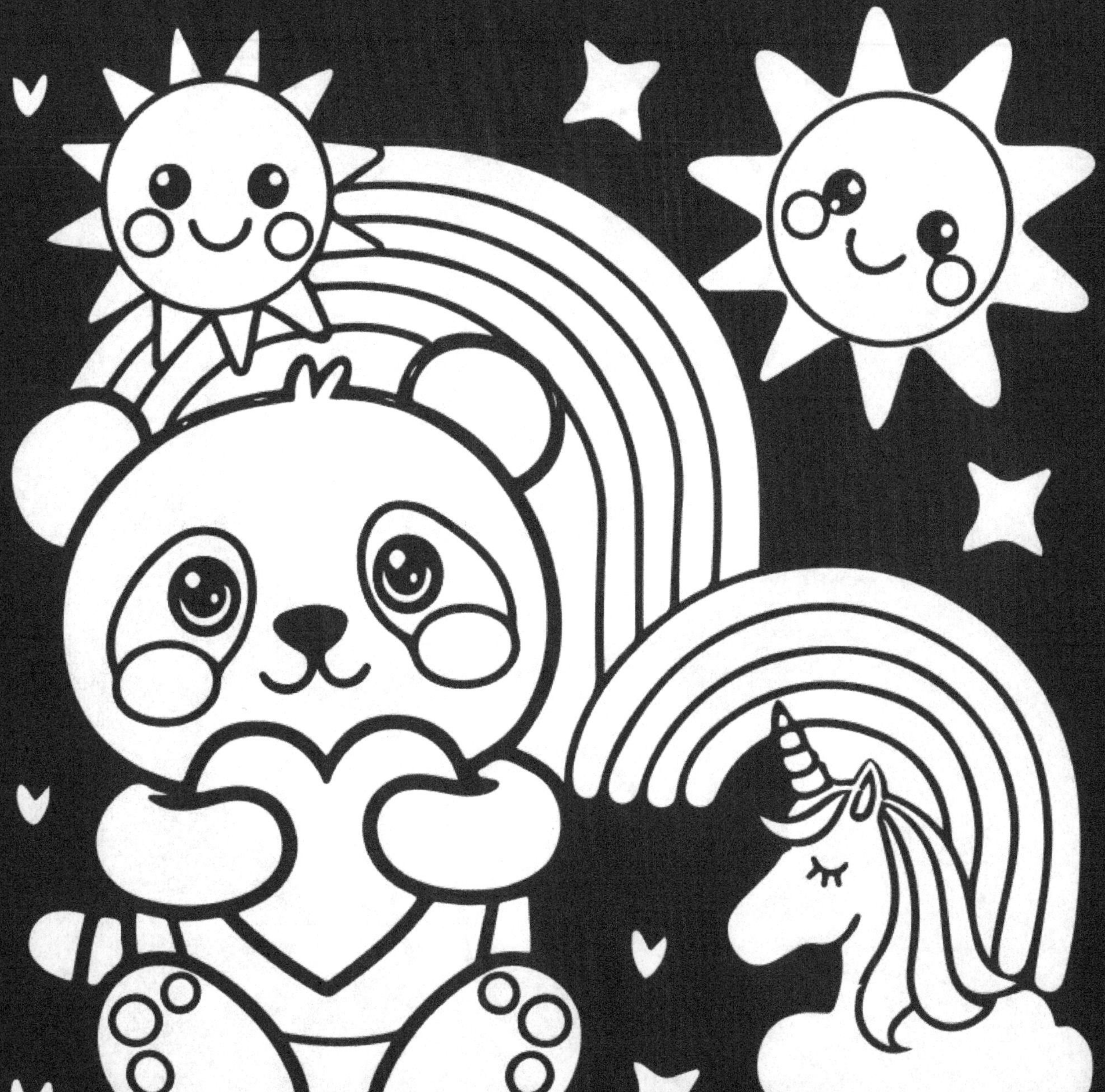

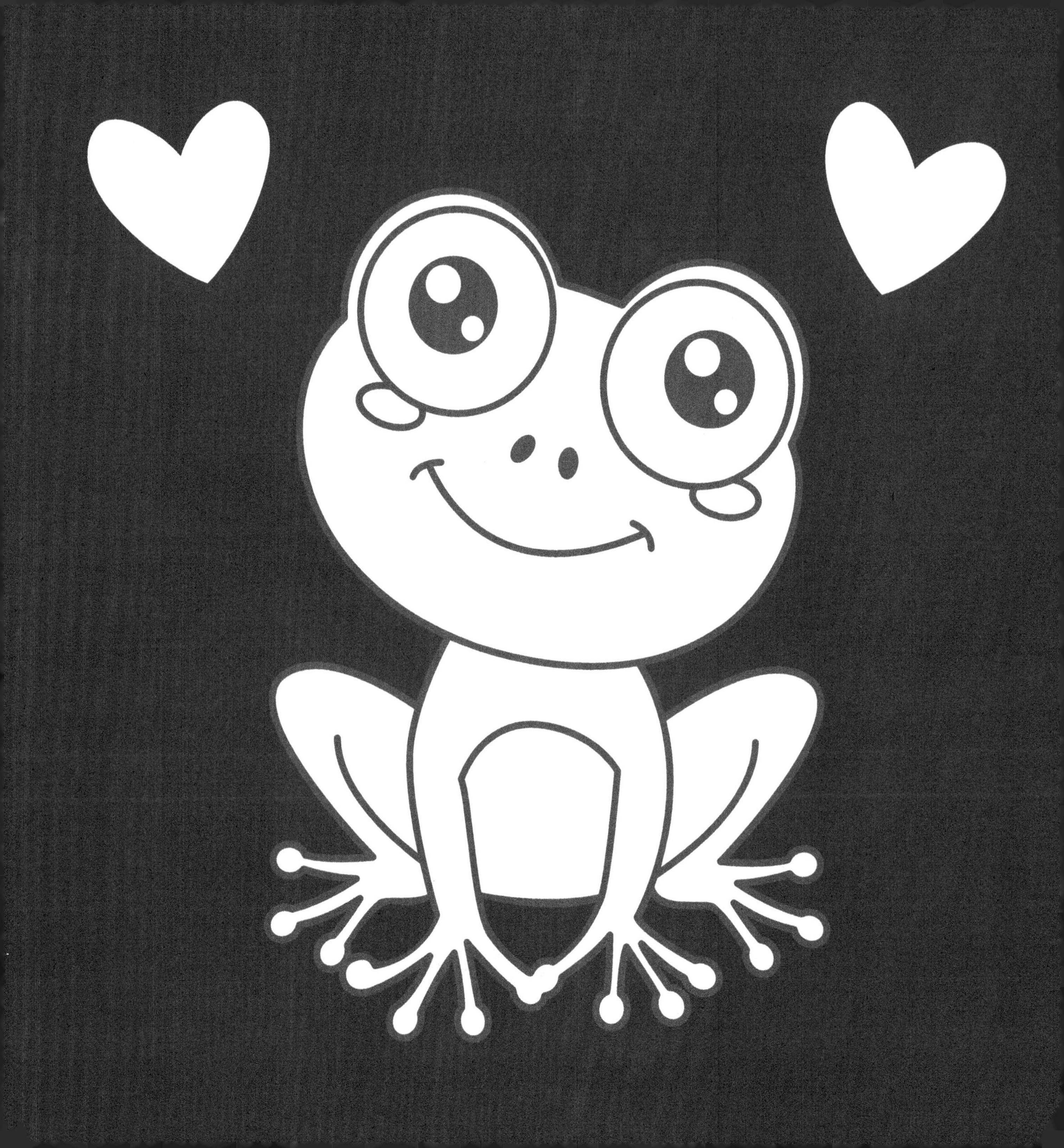

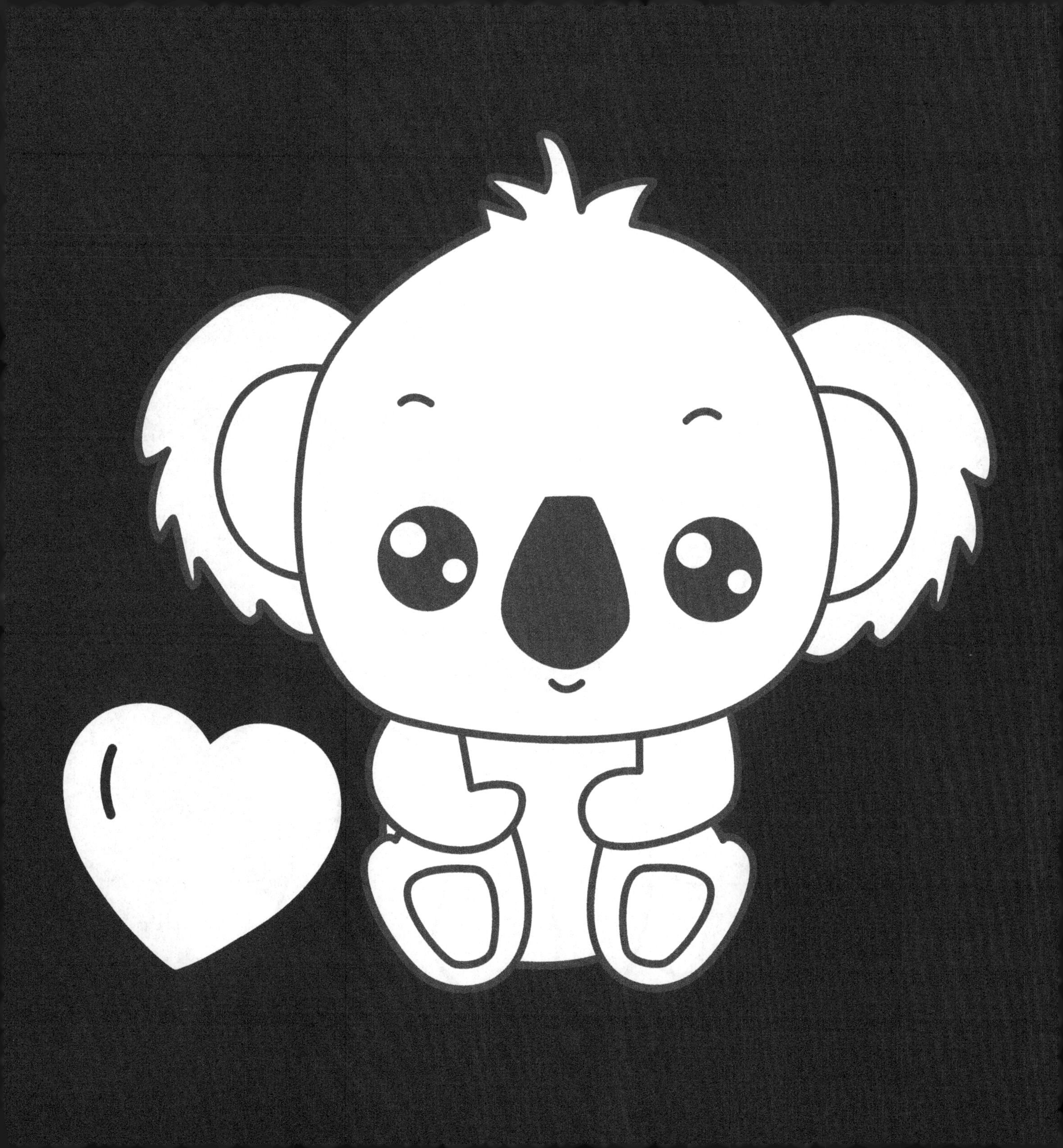

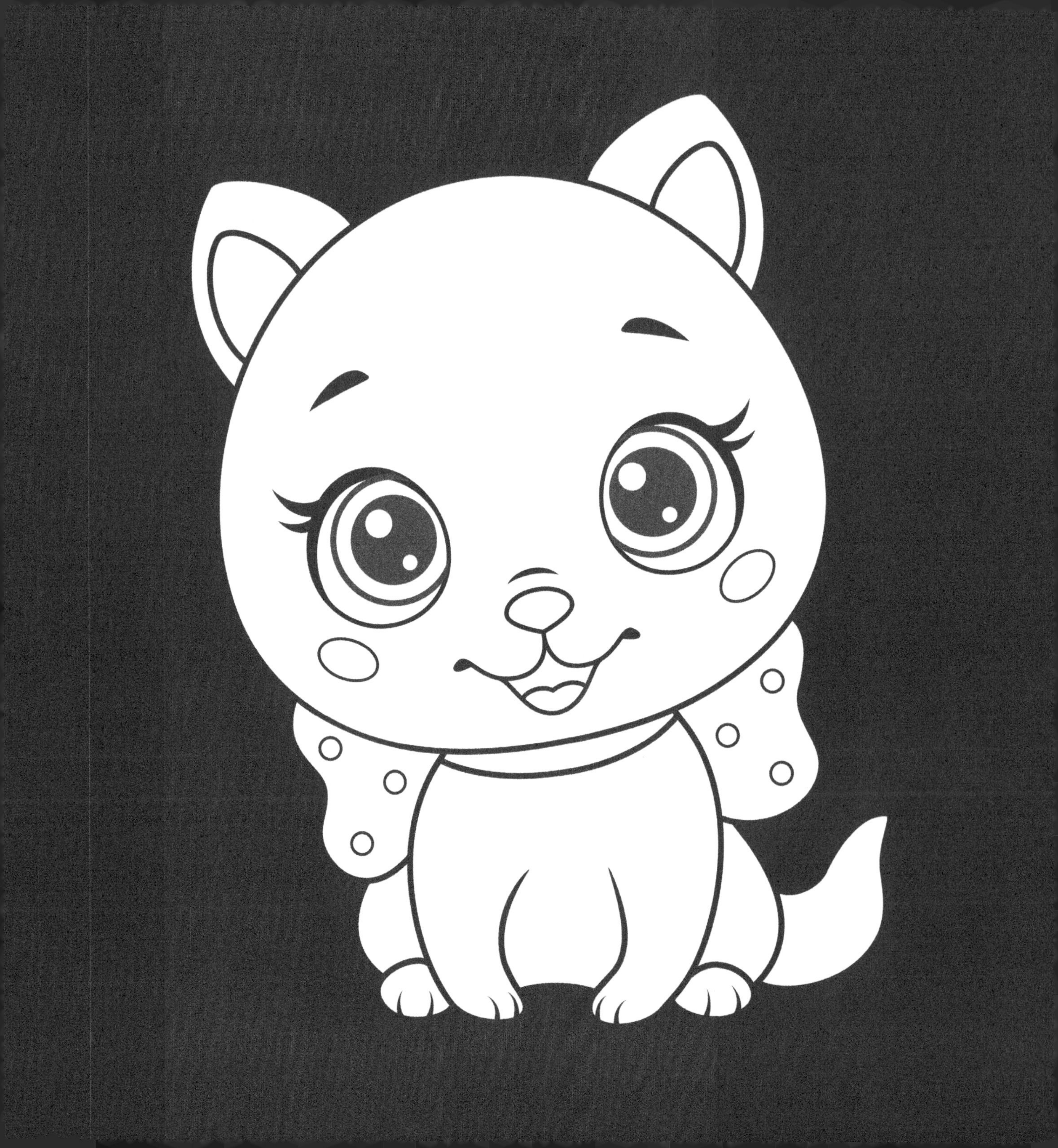

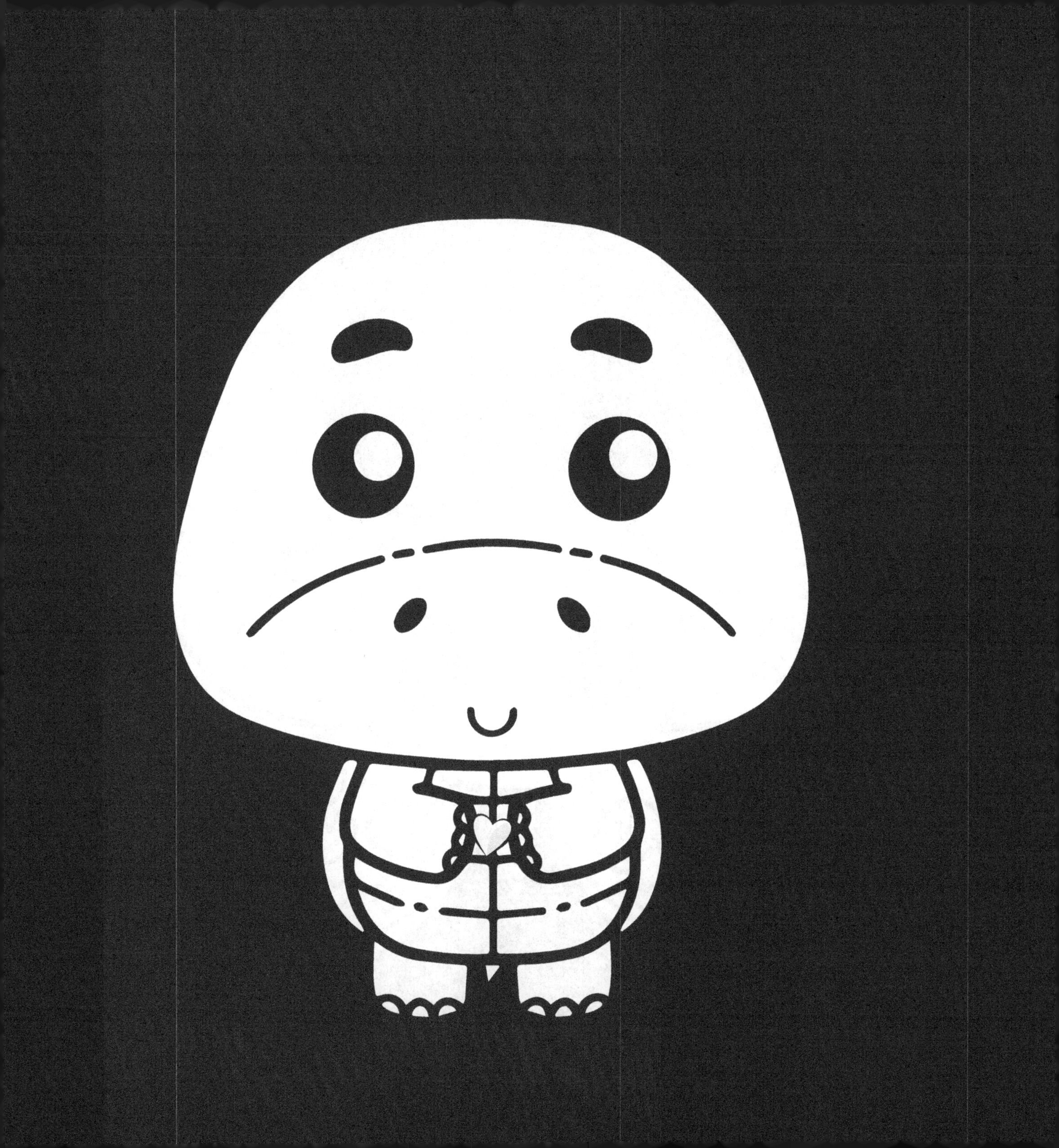

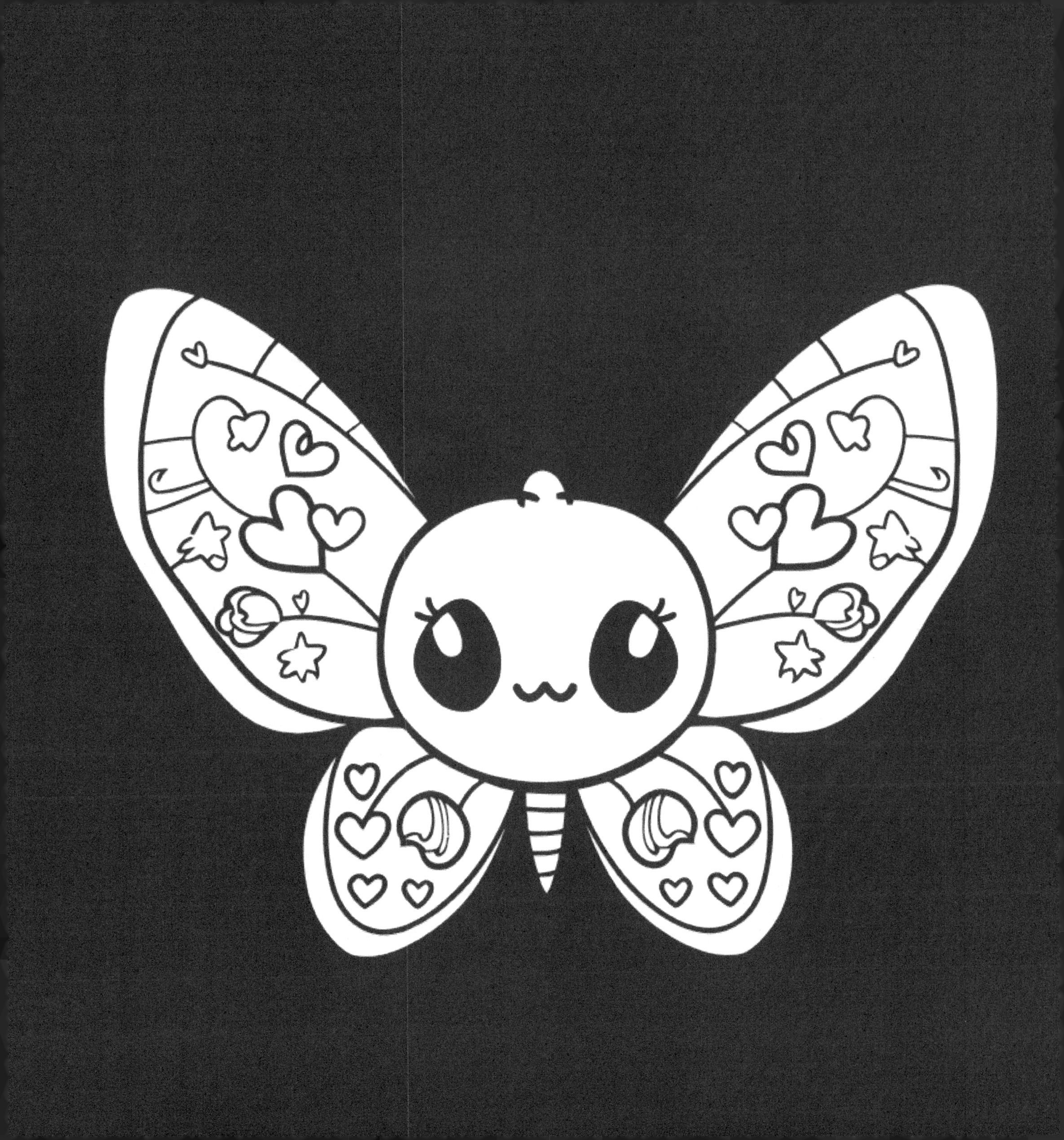

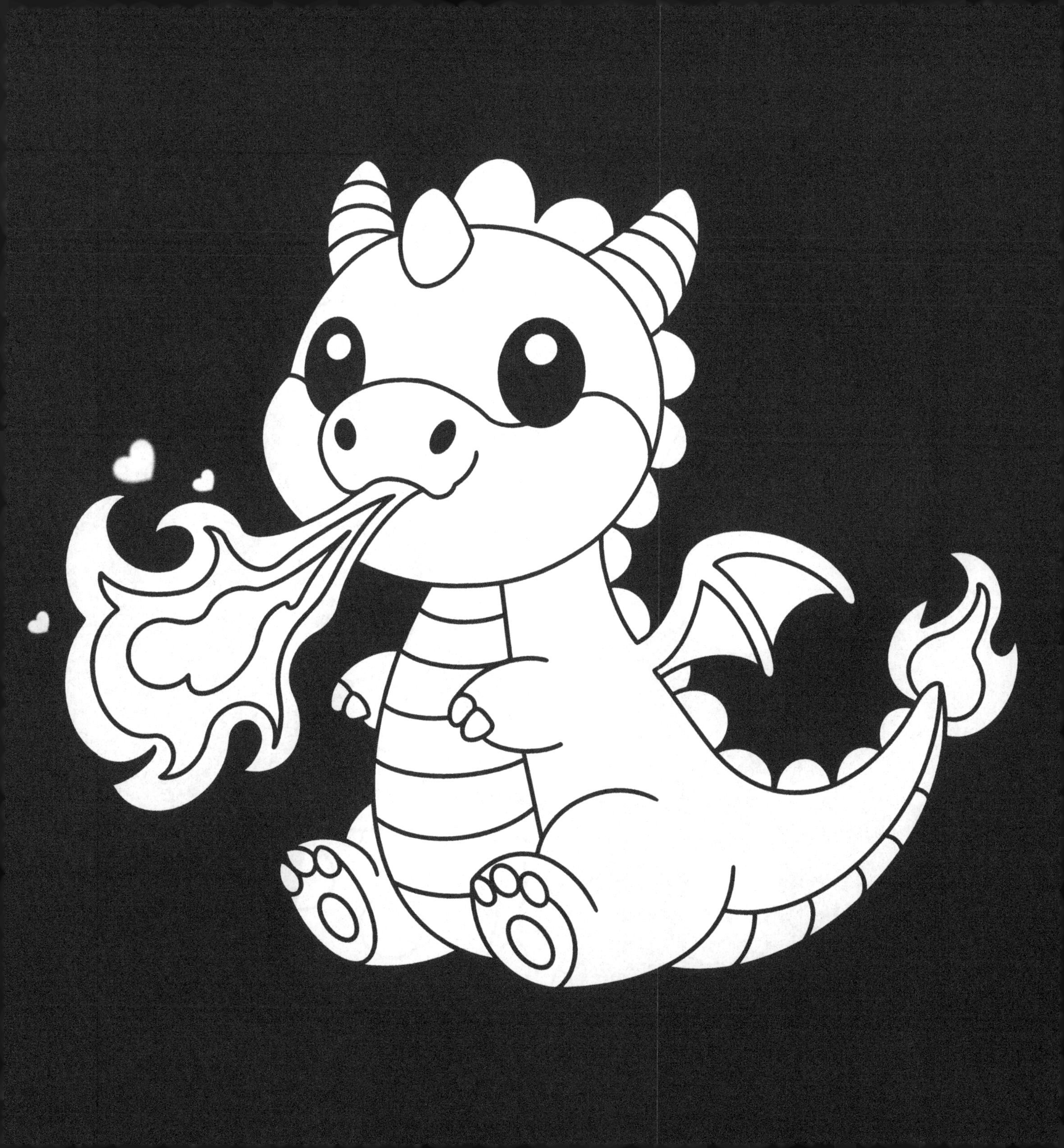

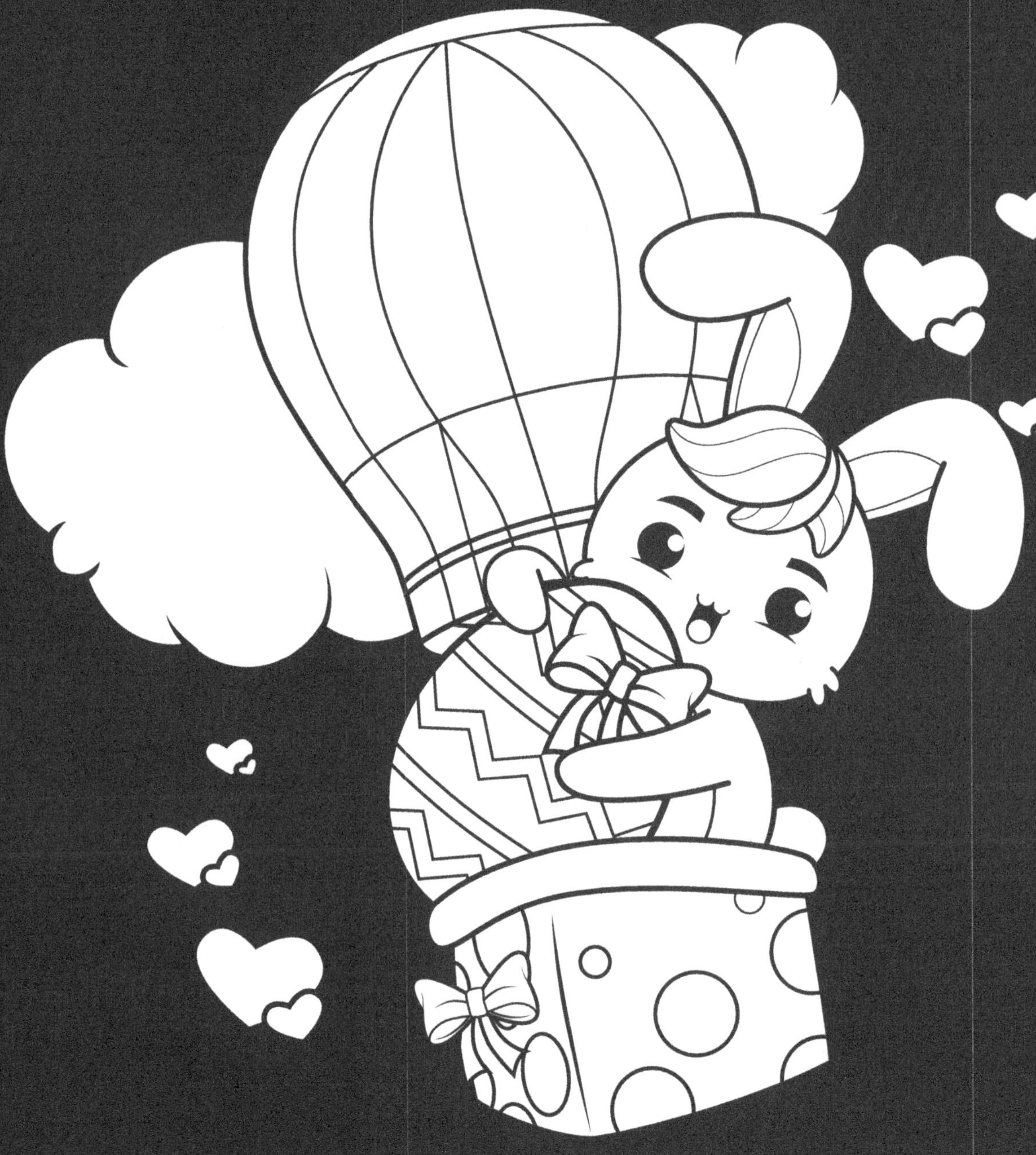

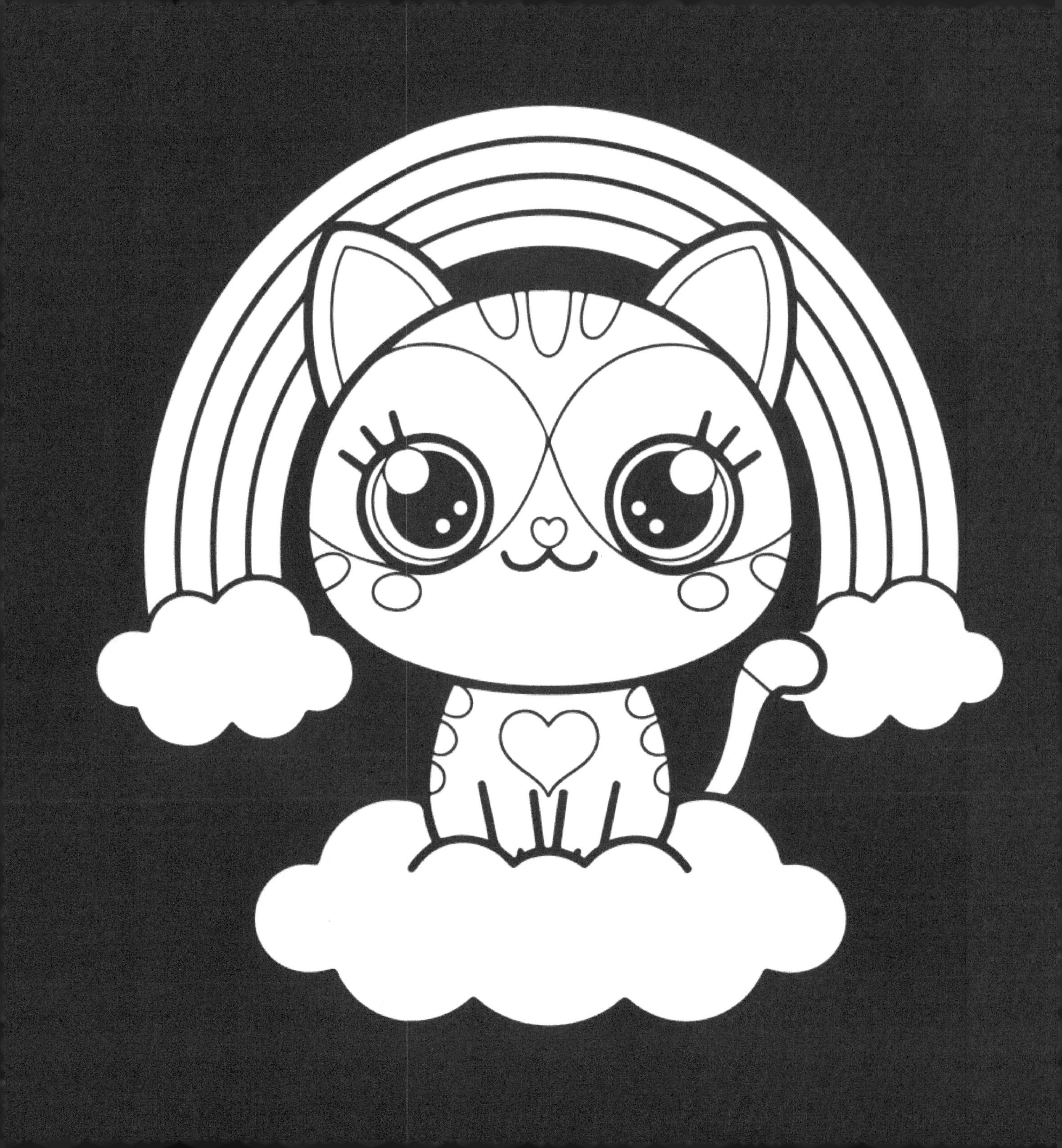

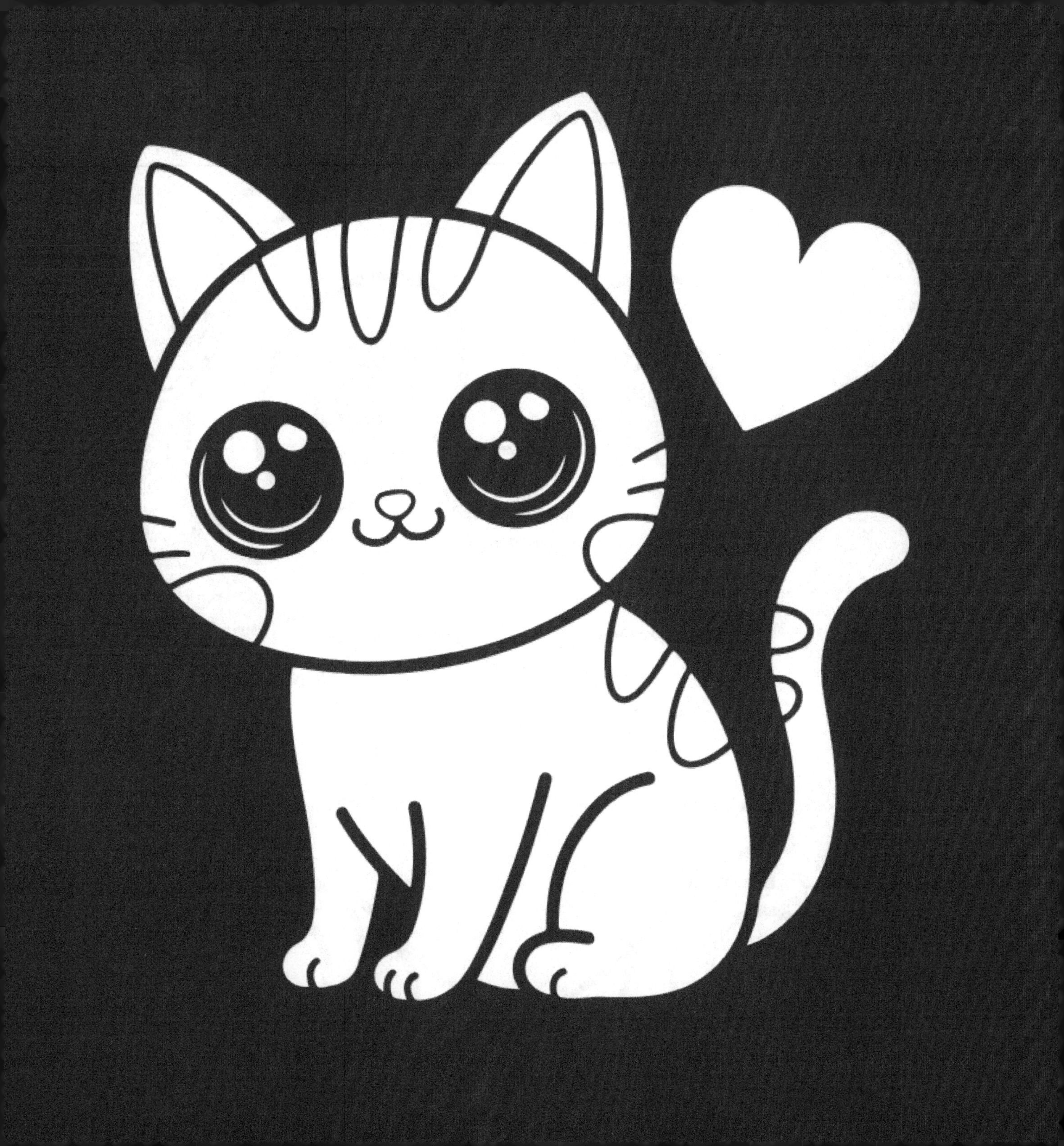

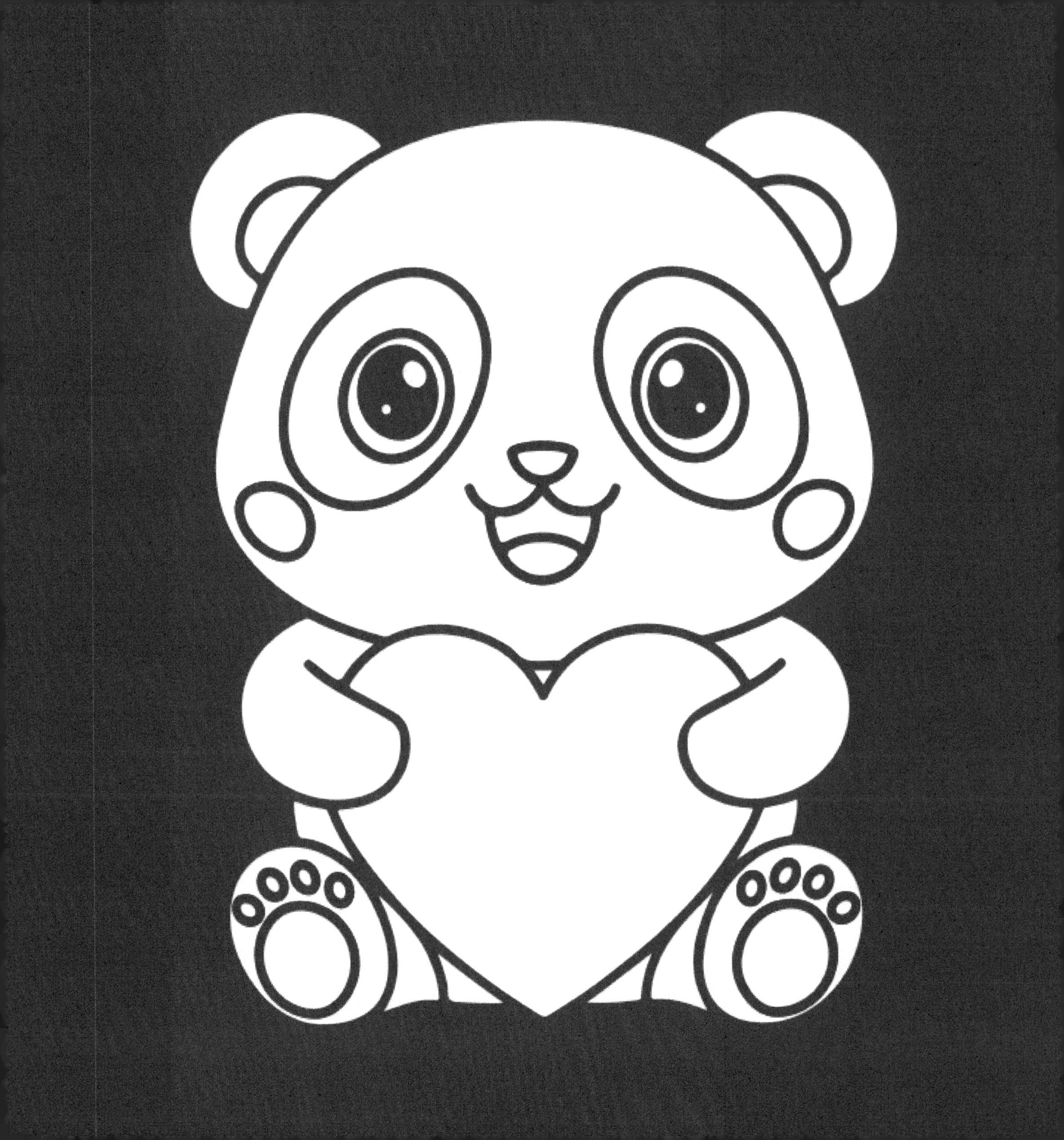

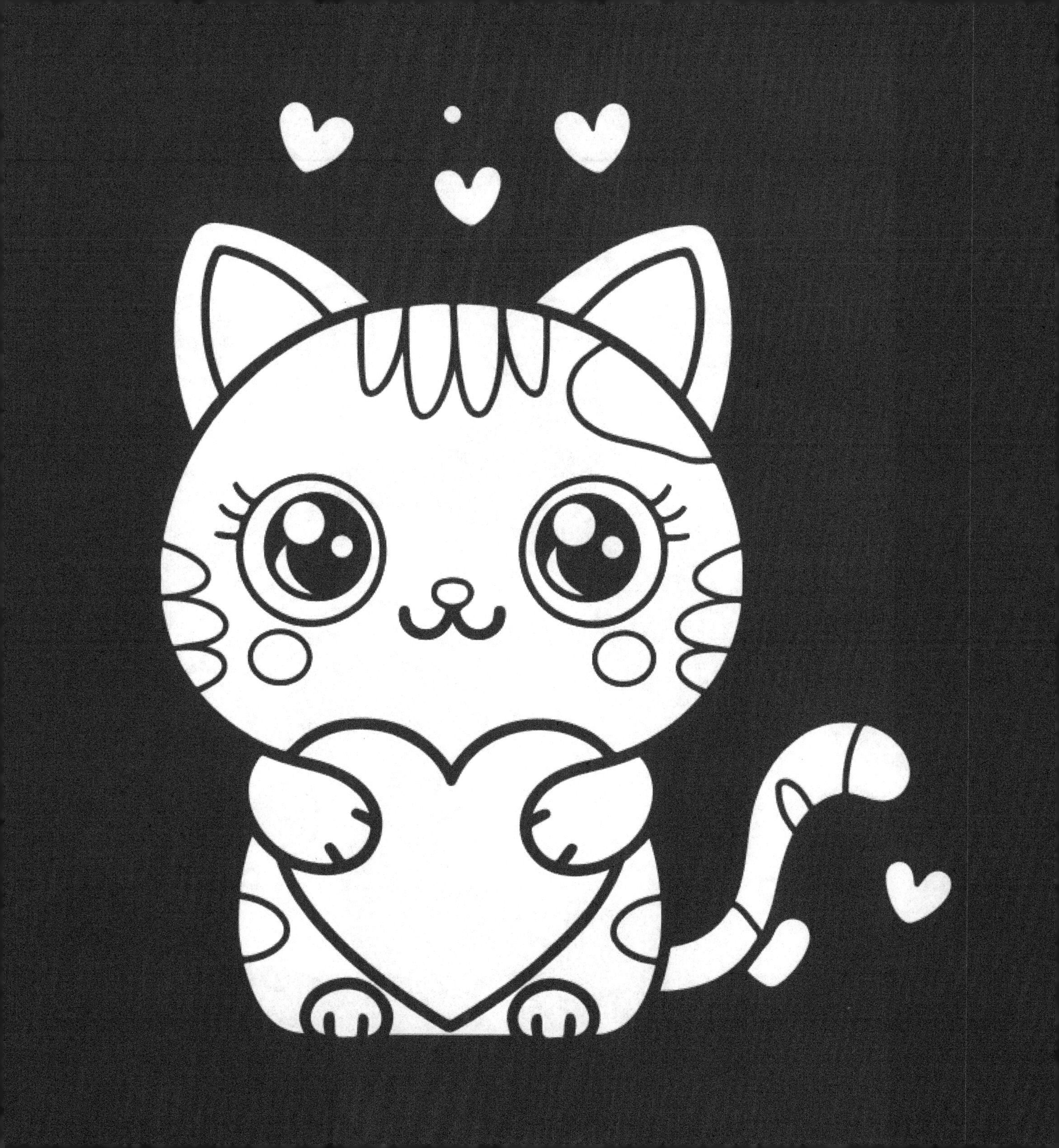

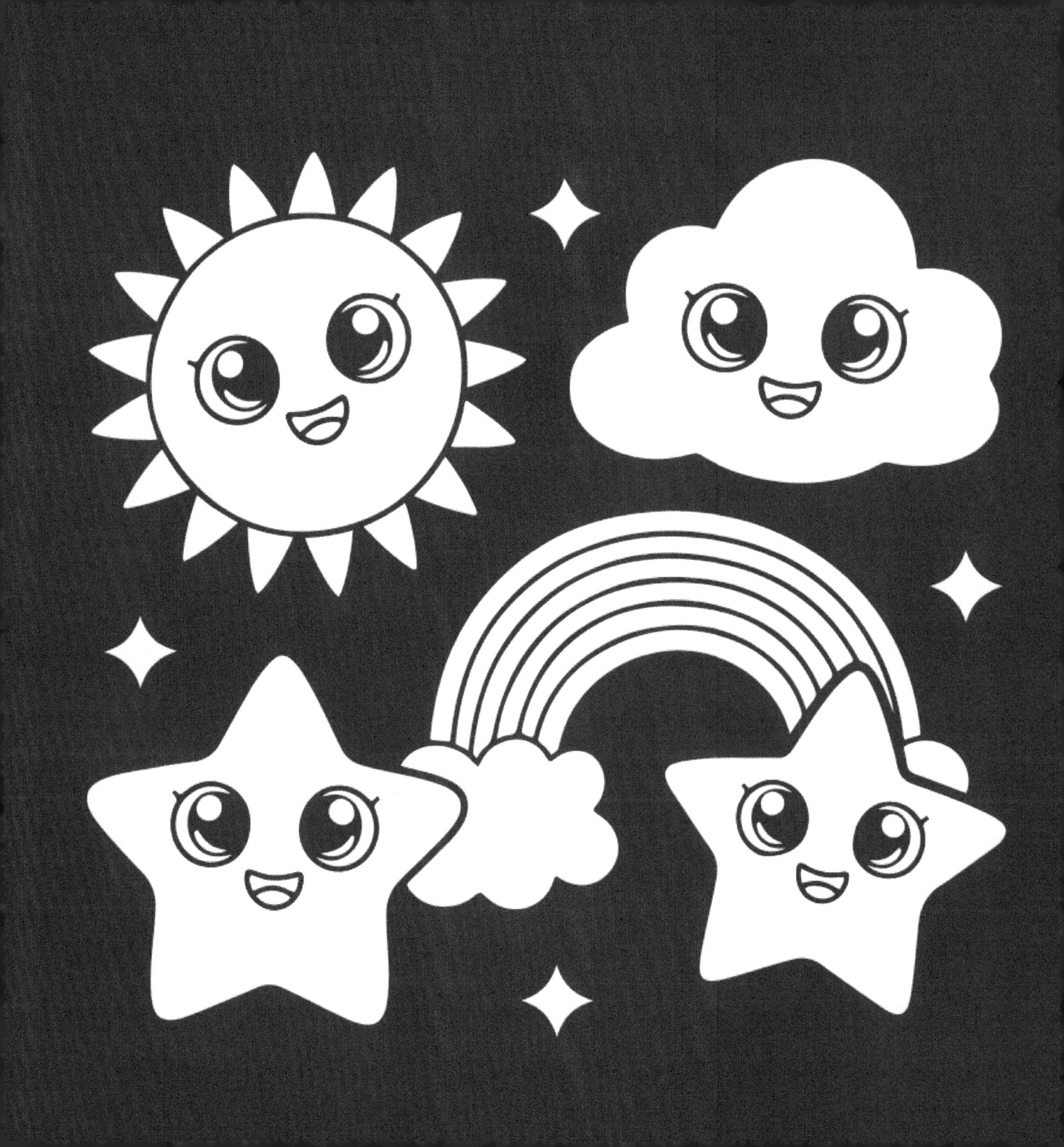

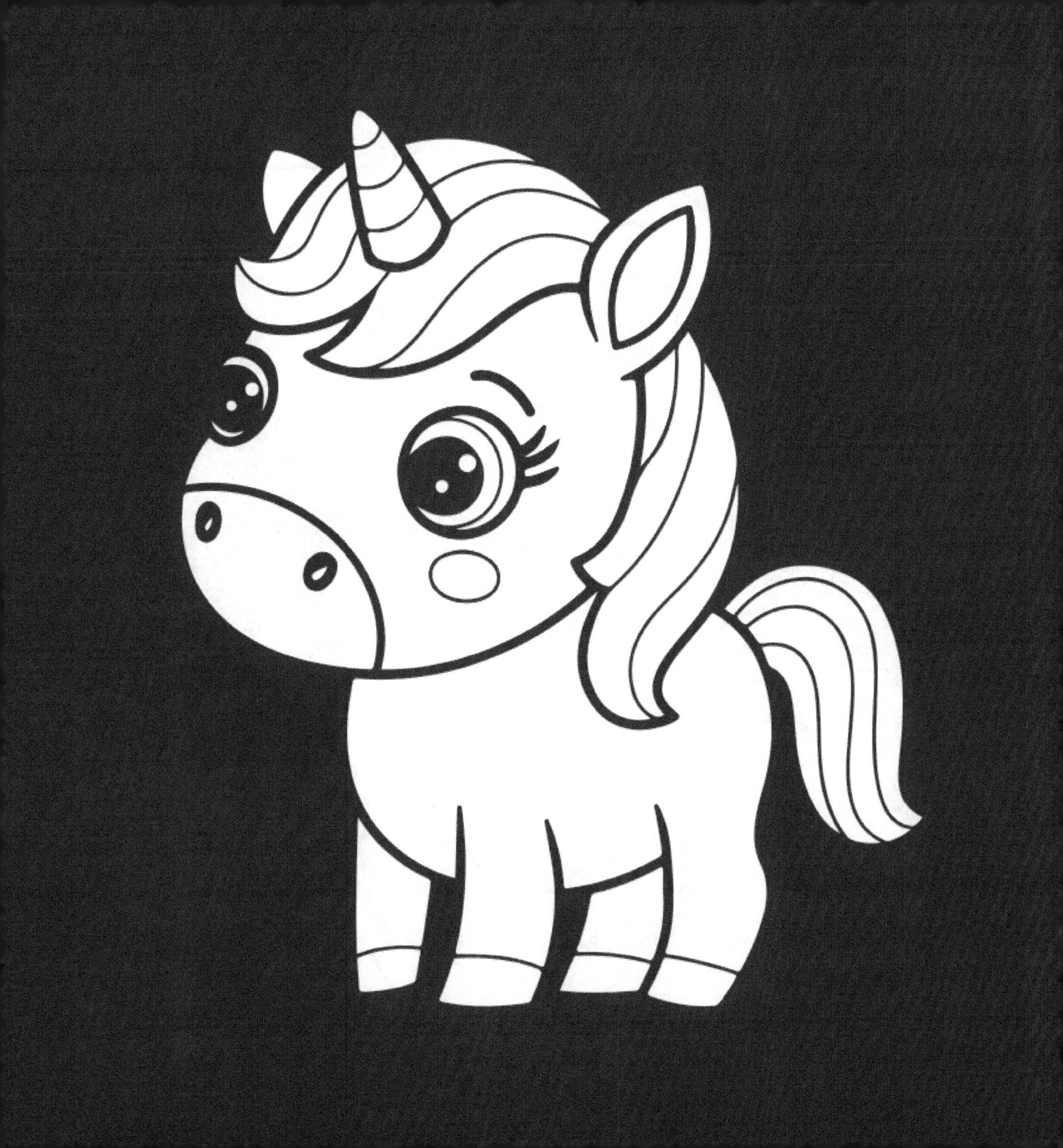

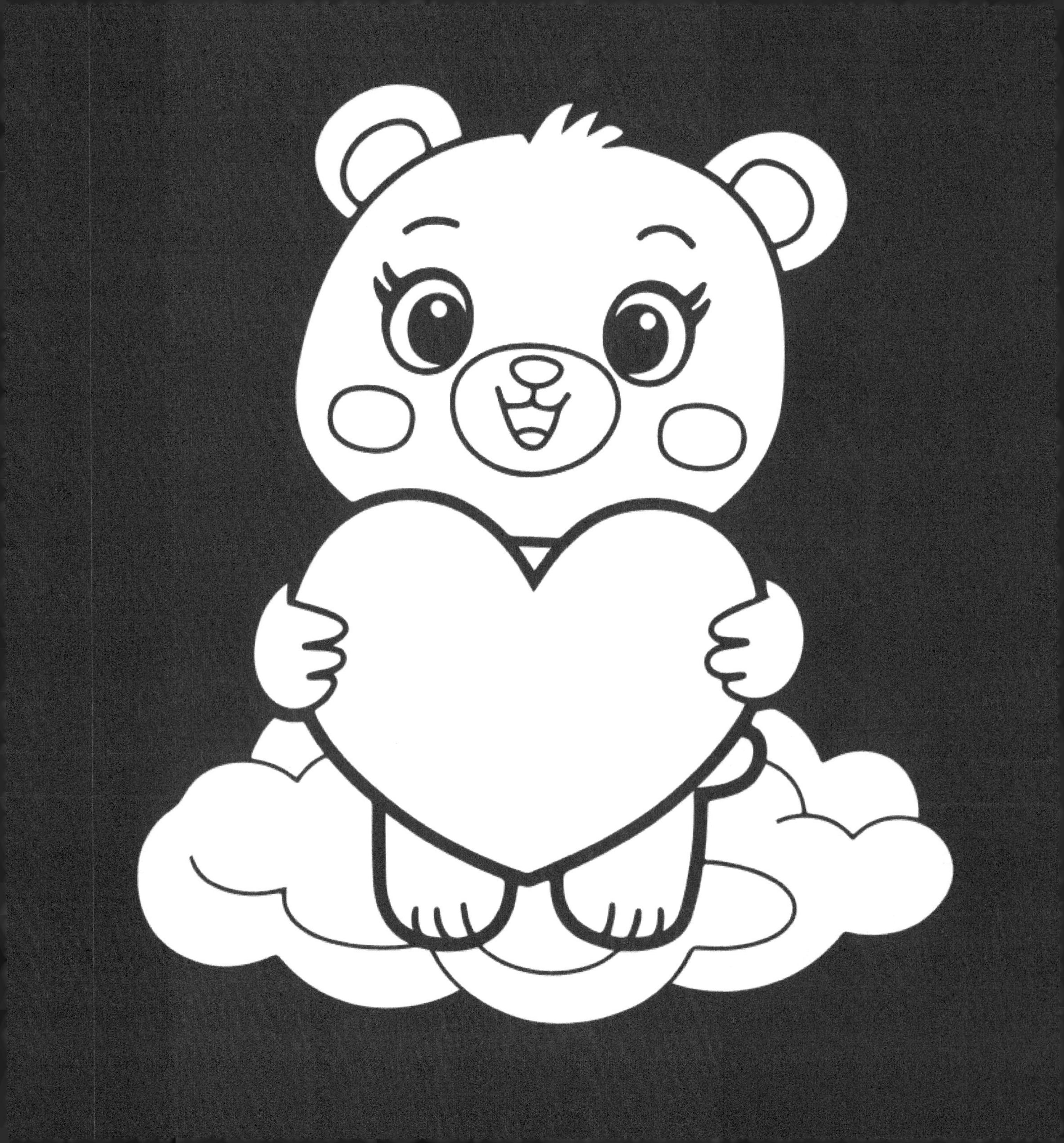

ميلا

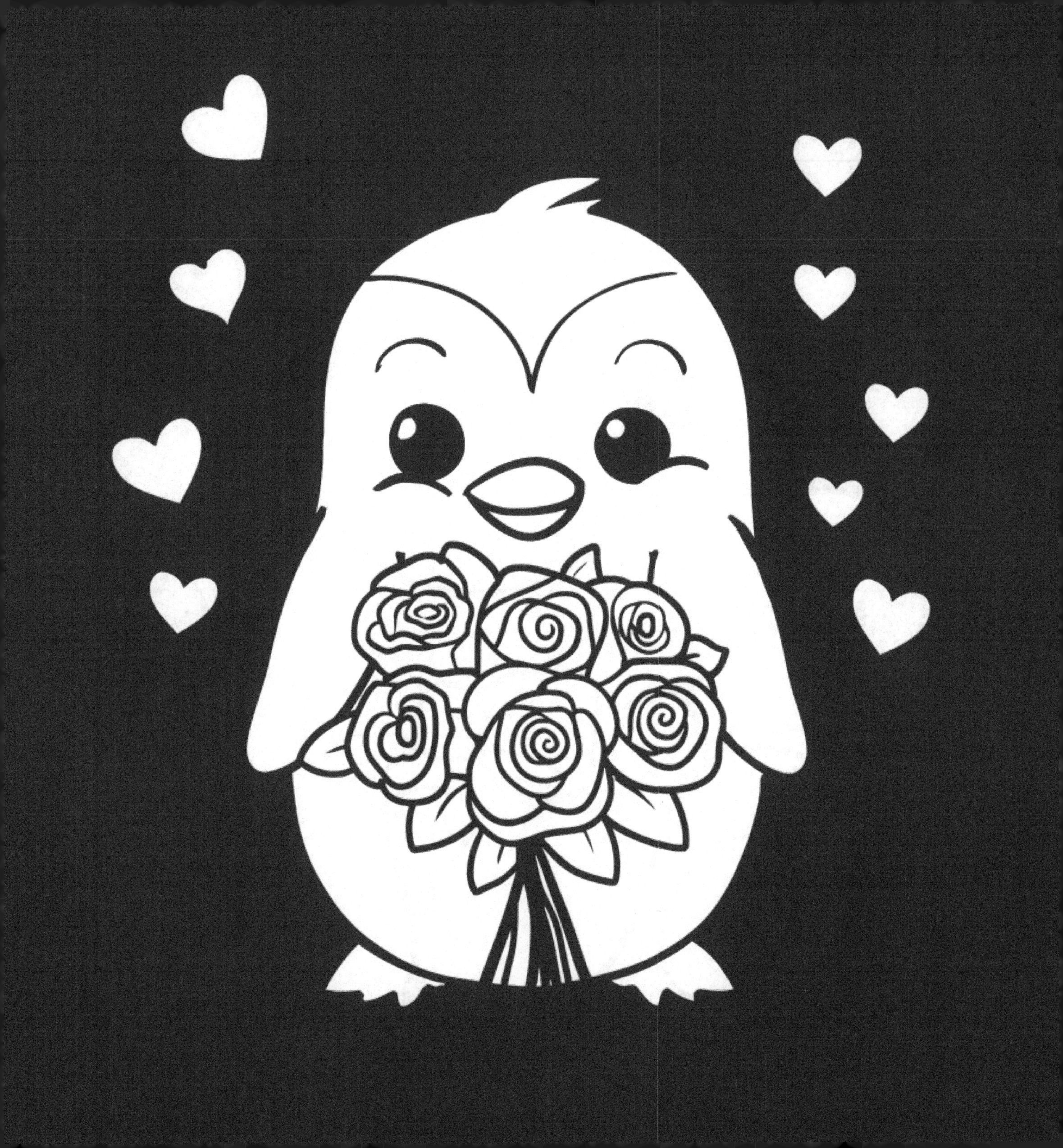

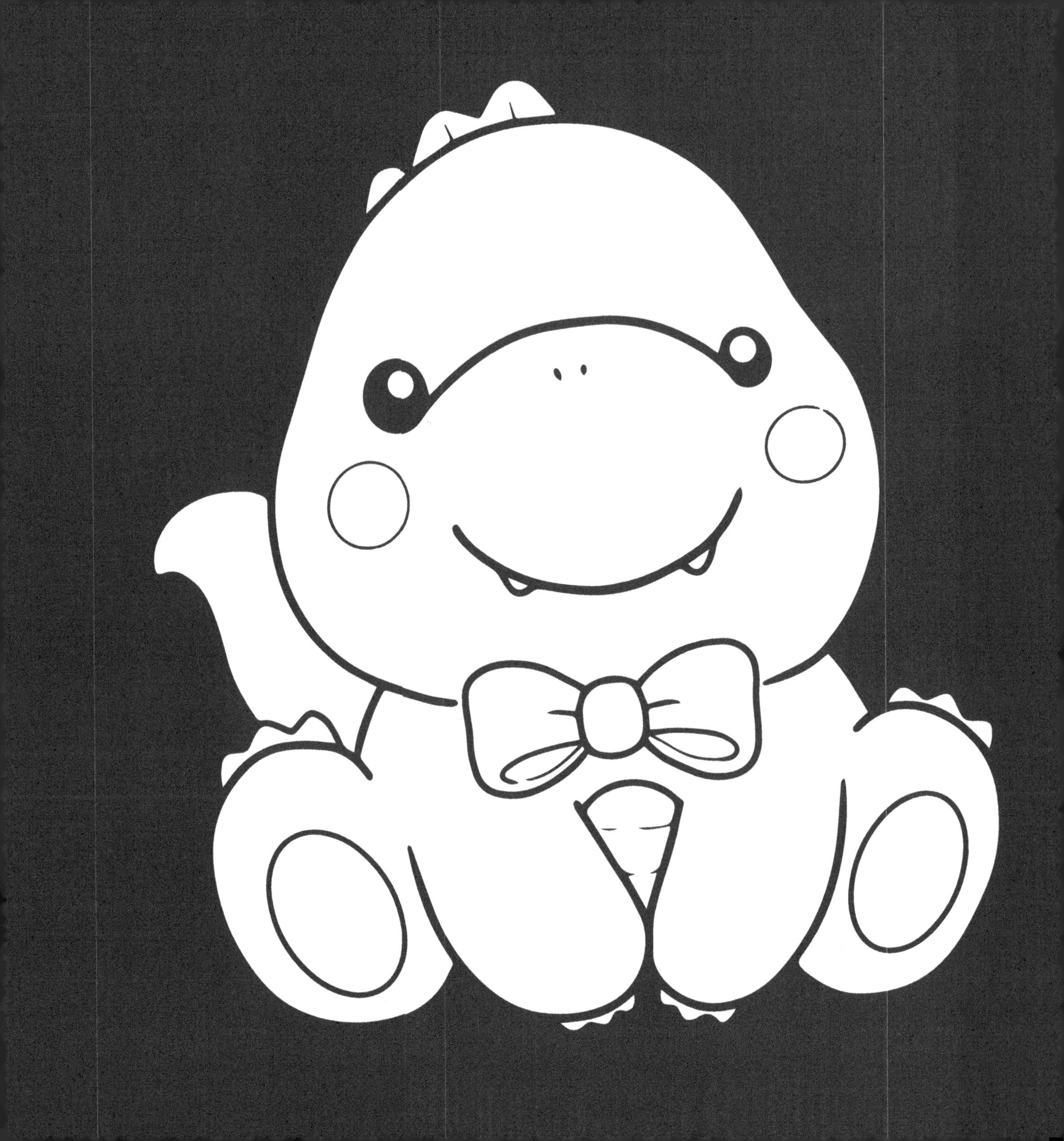

I LOVE YOU

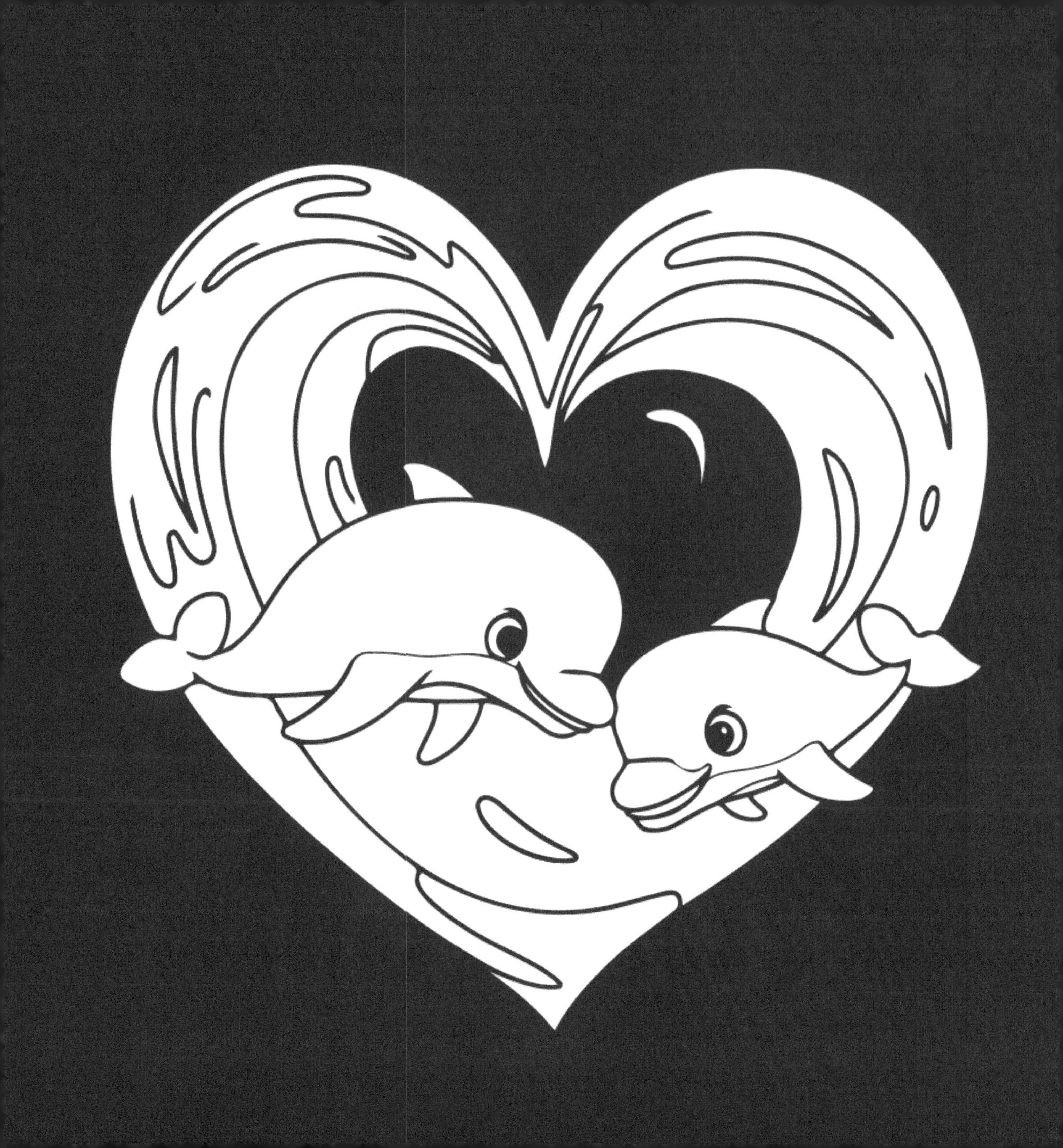

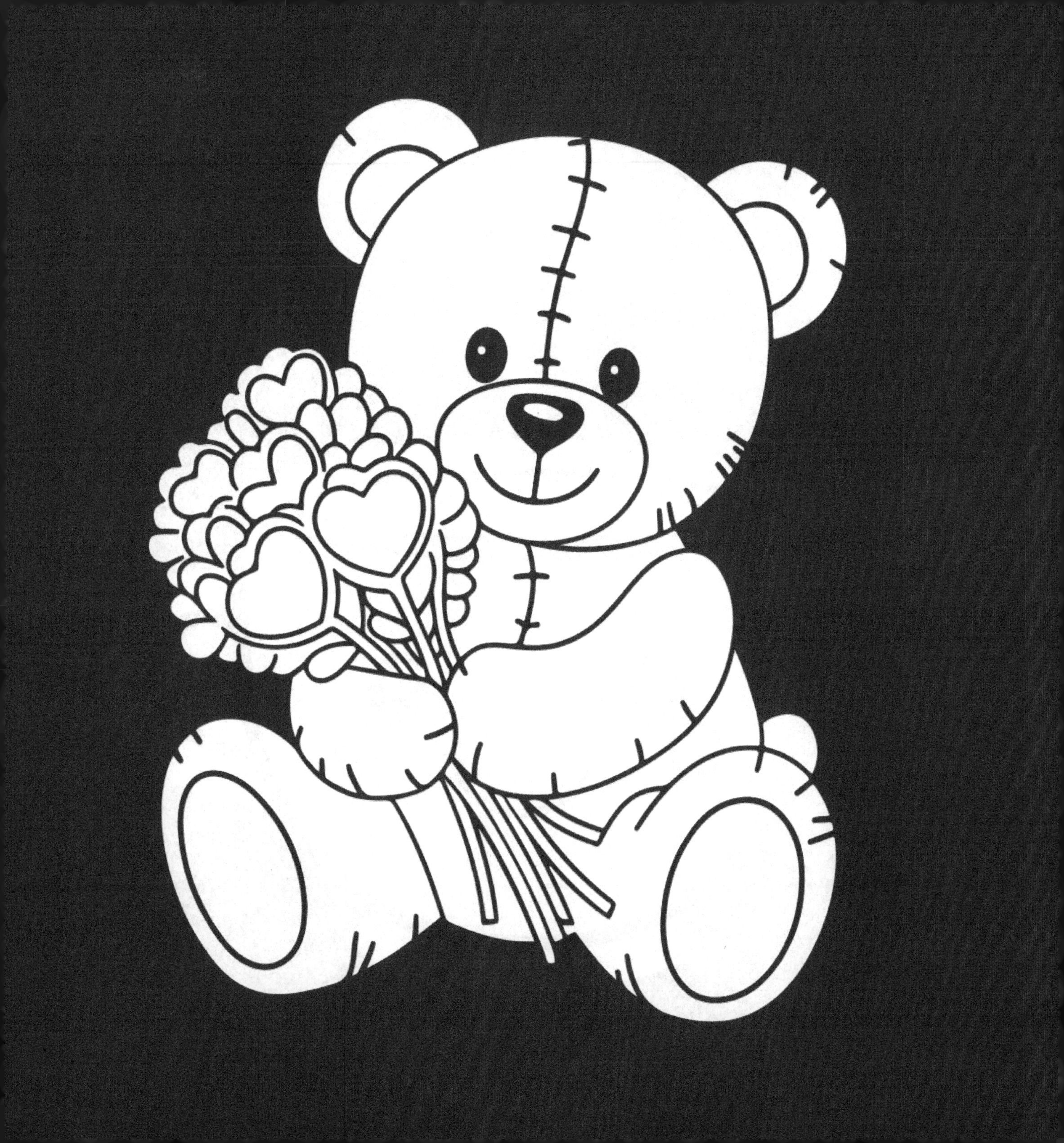

I LOVE YOU

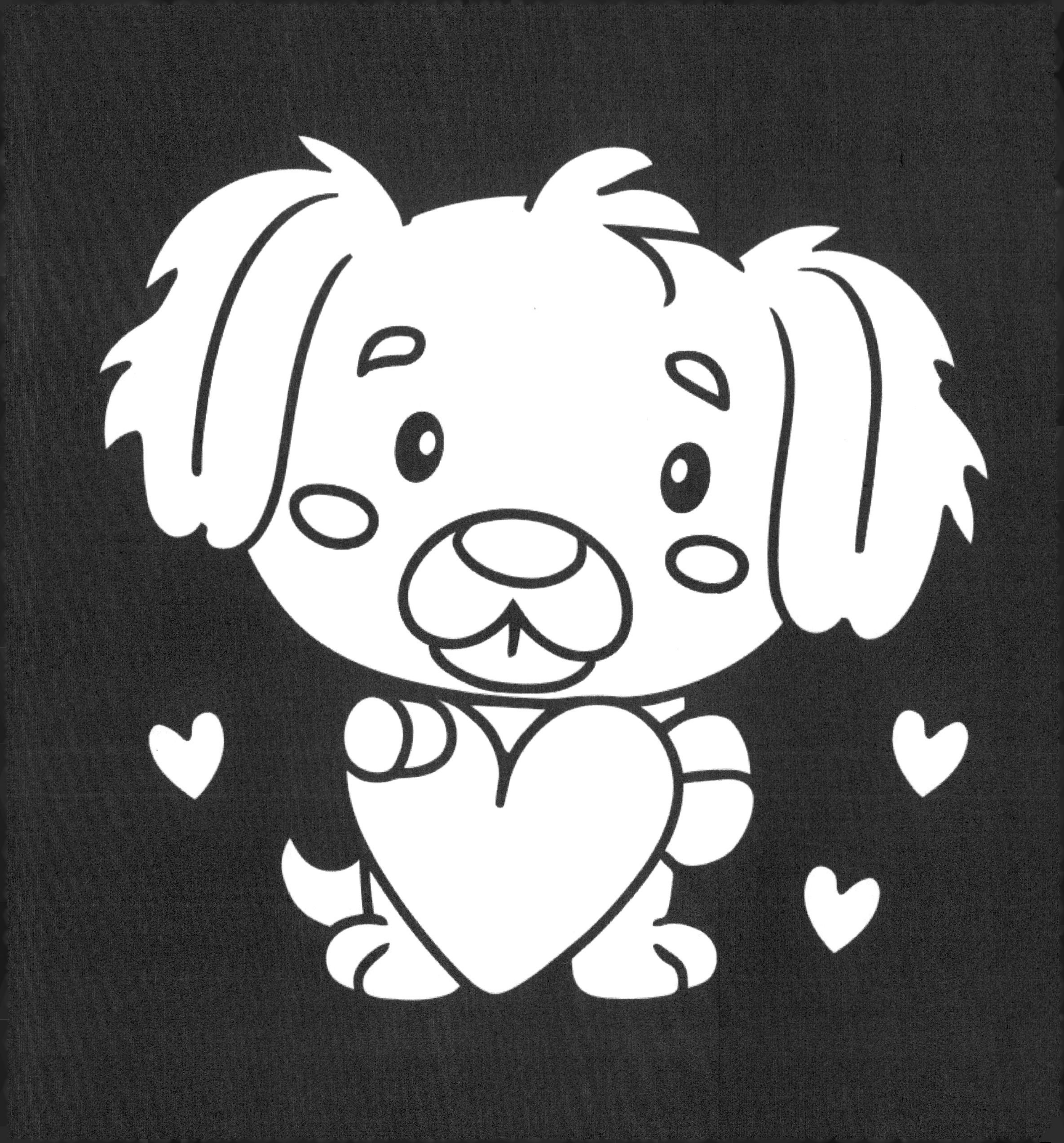

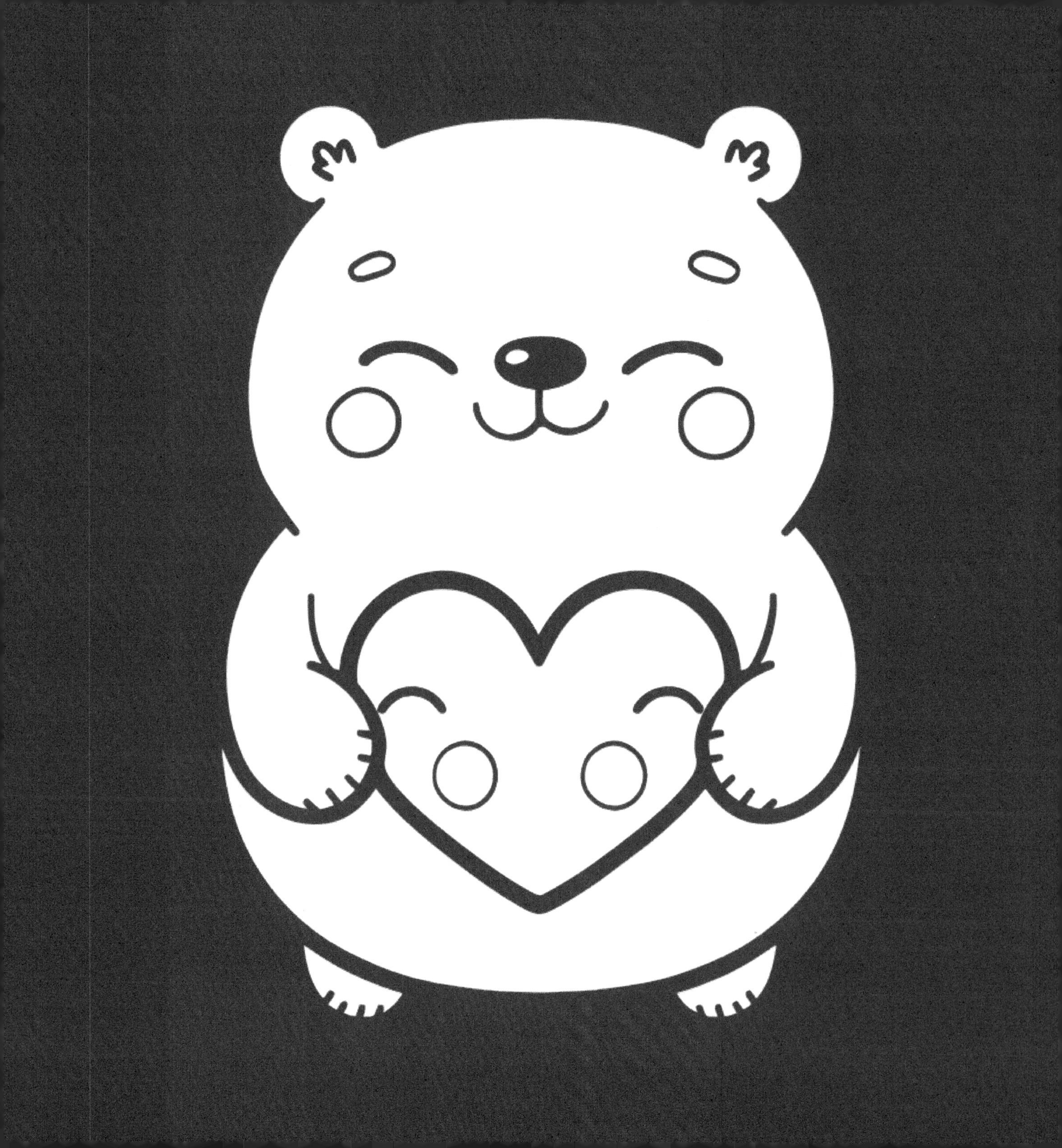

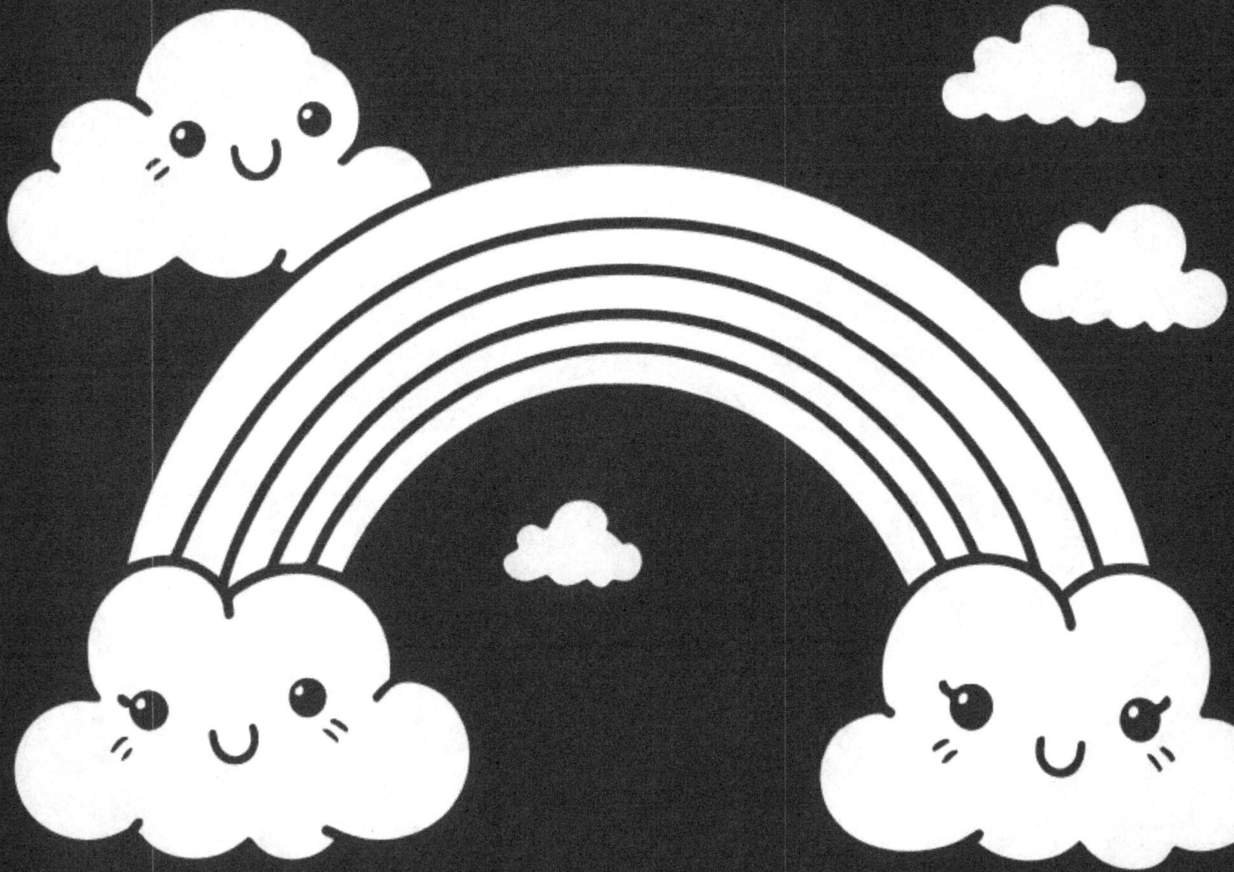

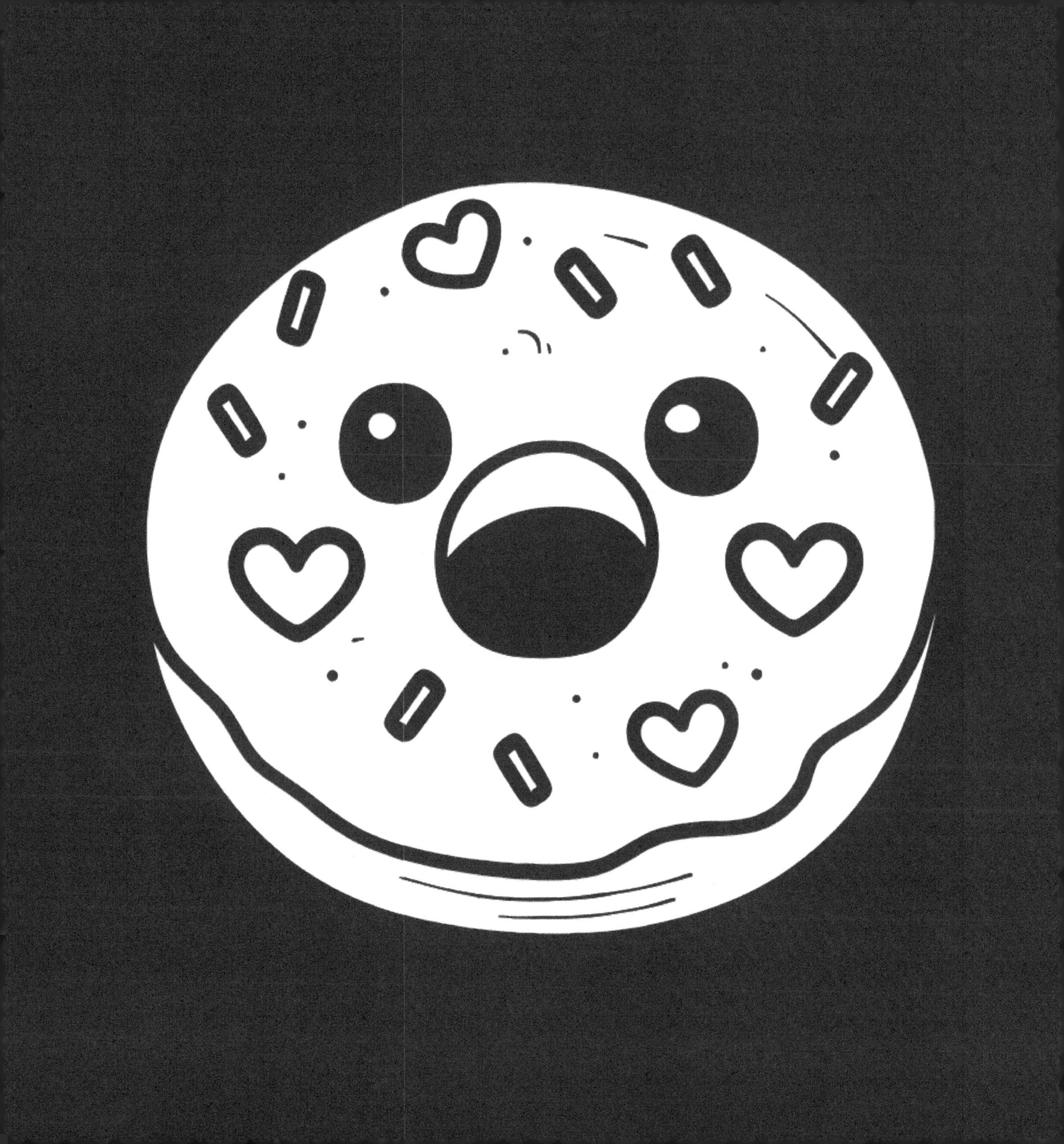

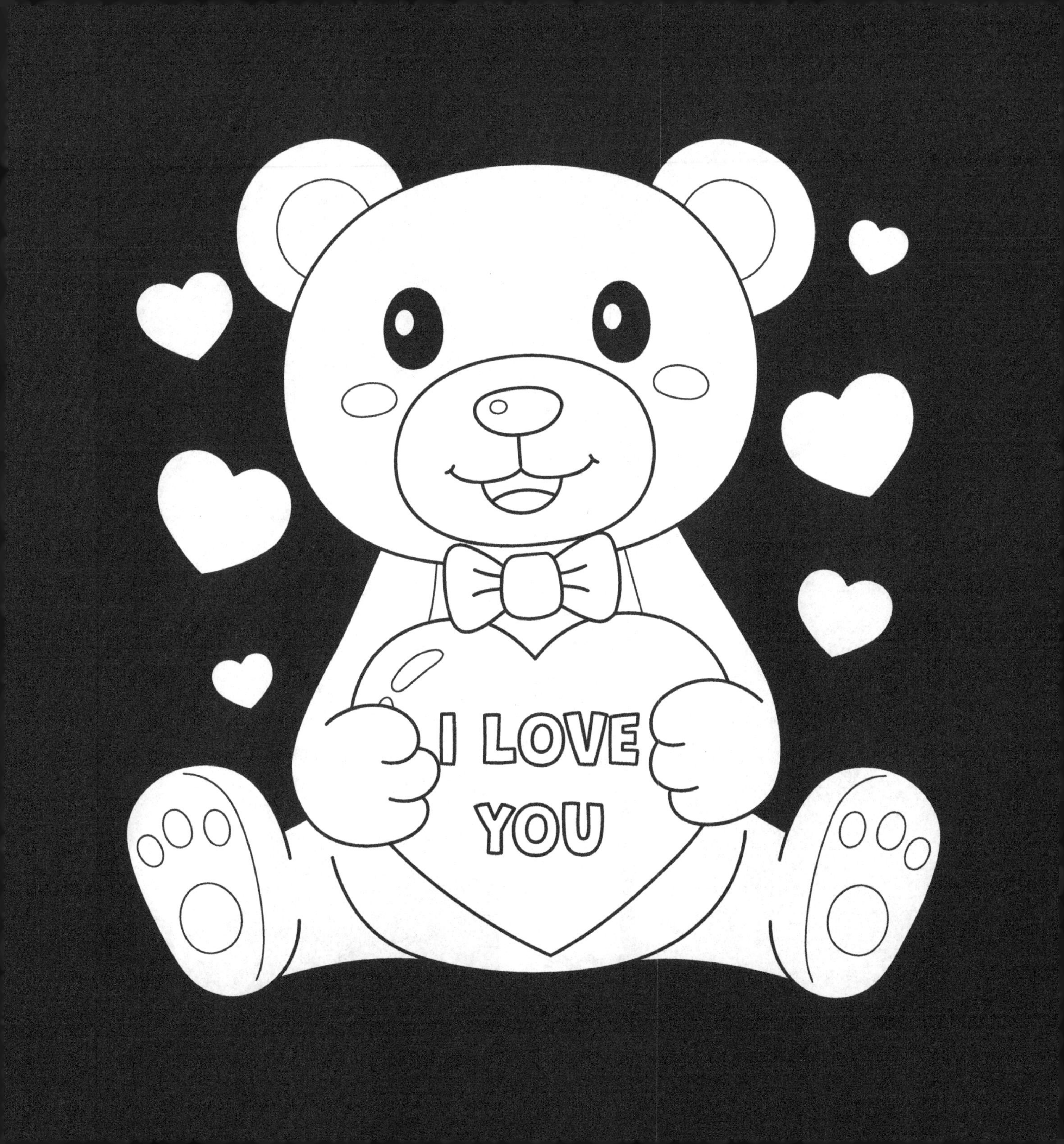
I LOVE
YOU

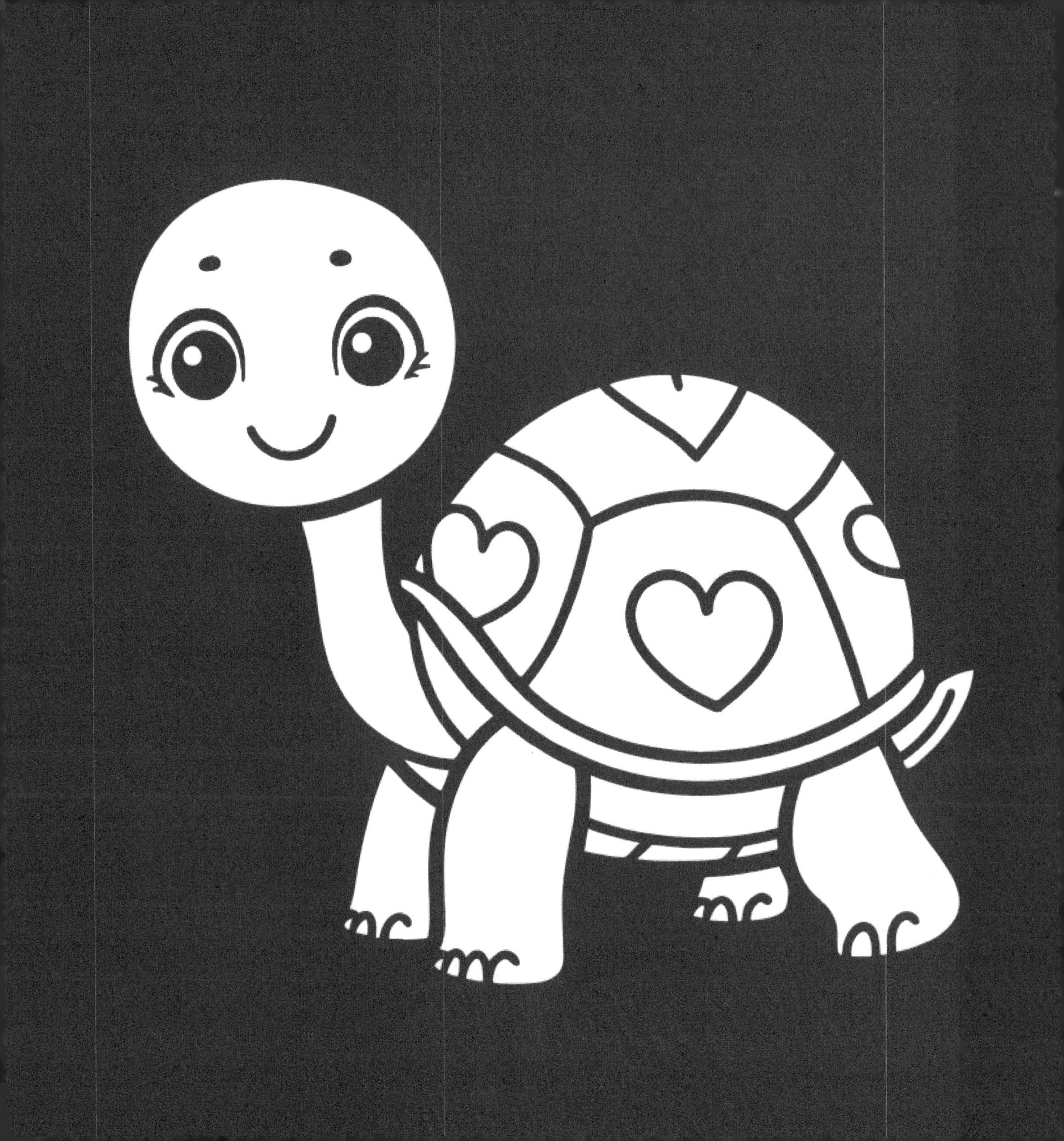

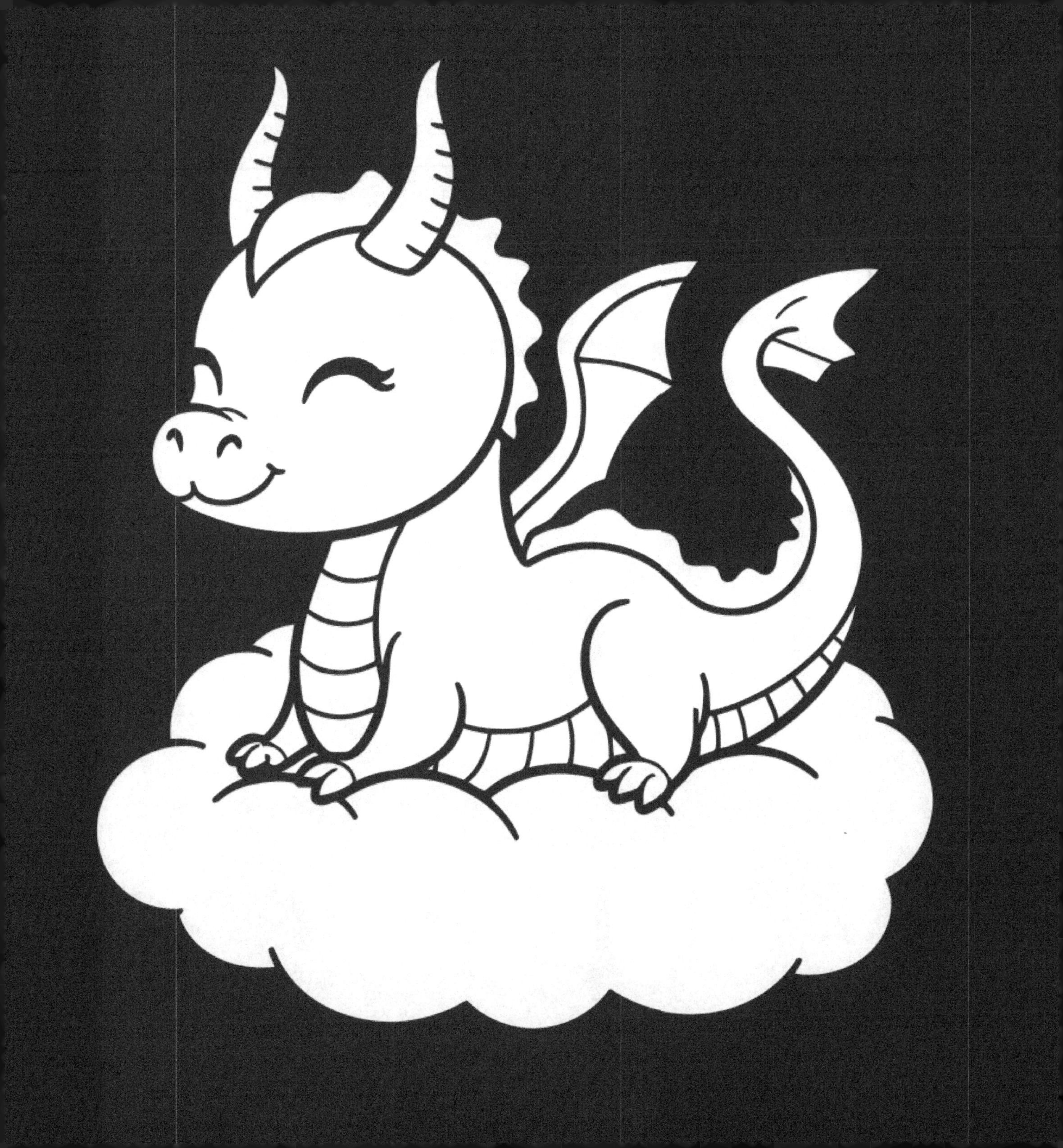

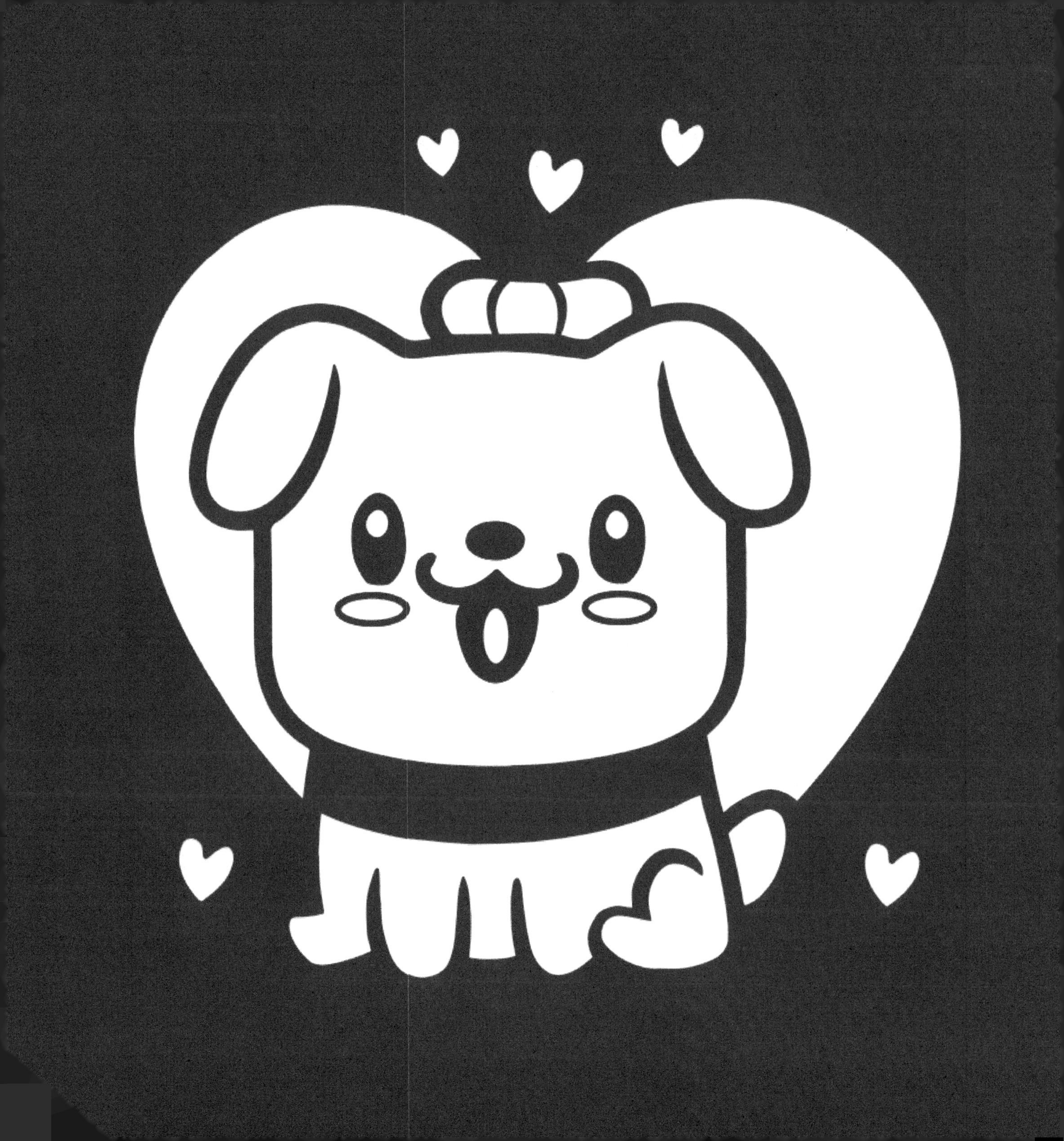

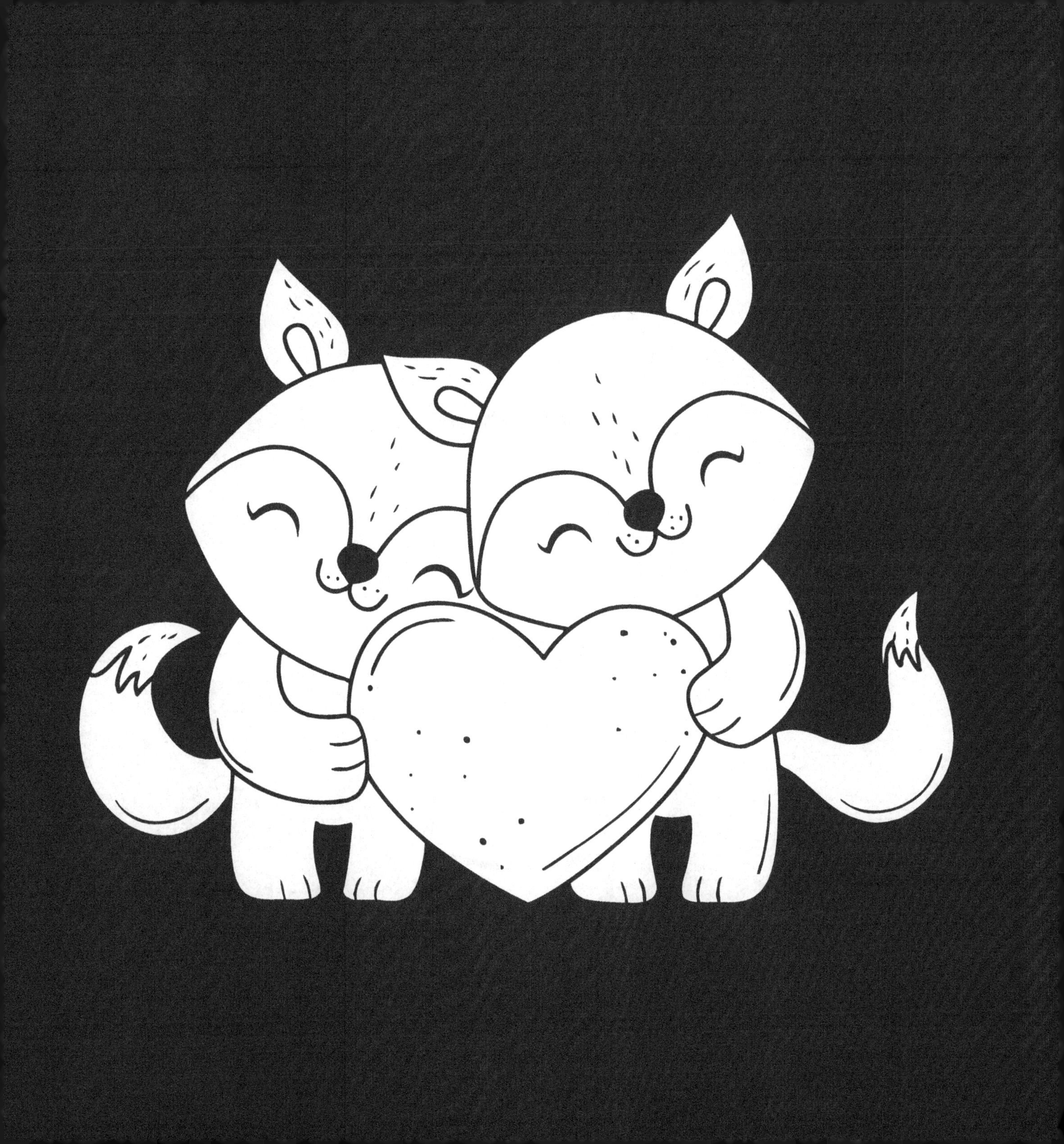

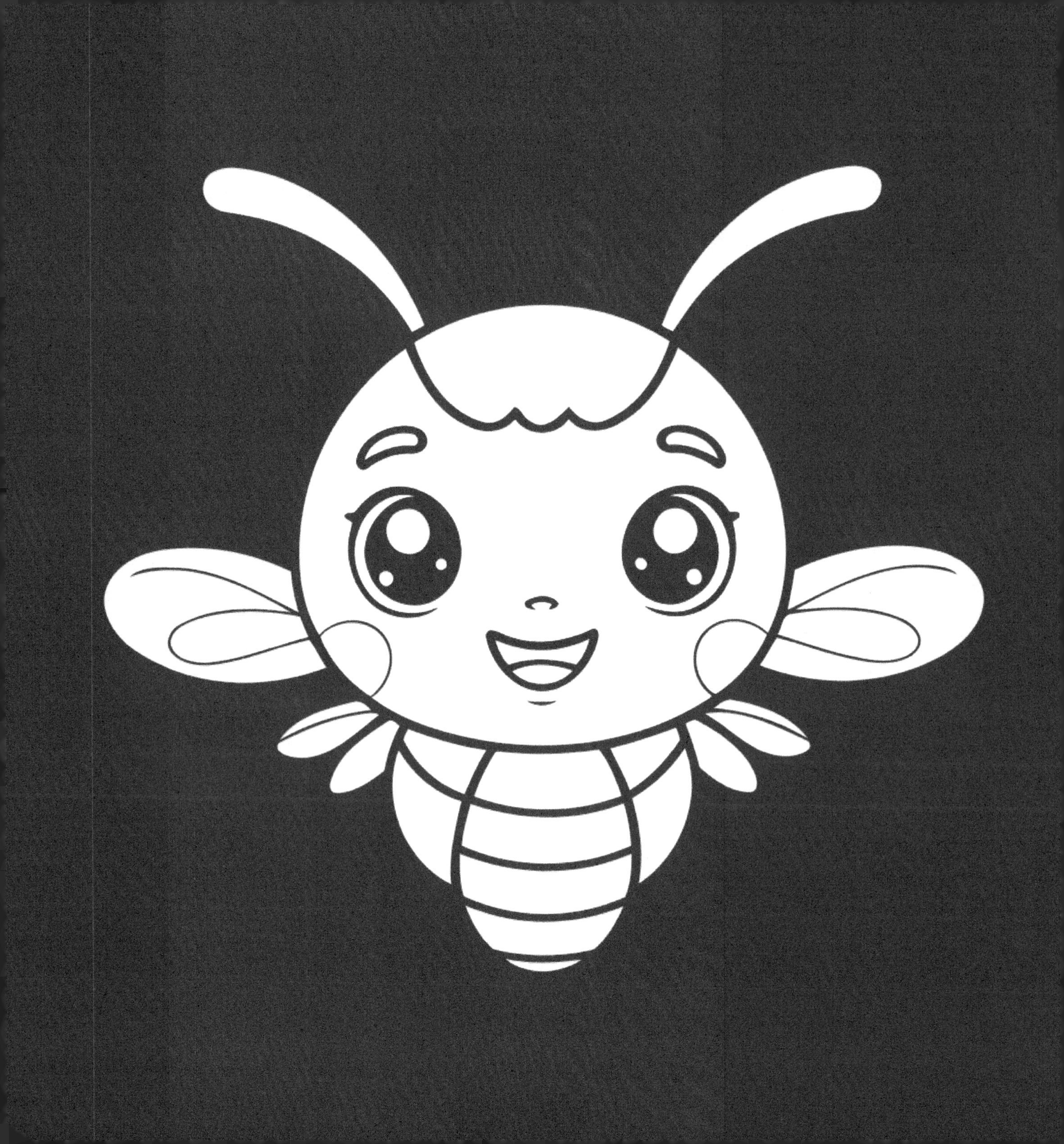

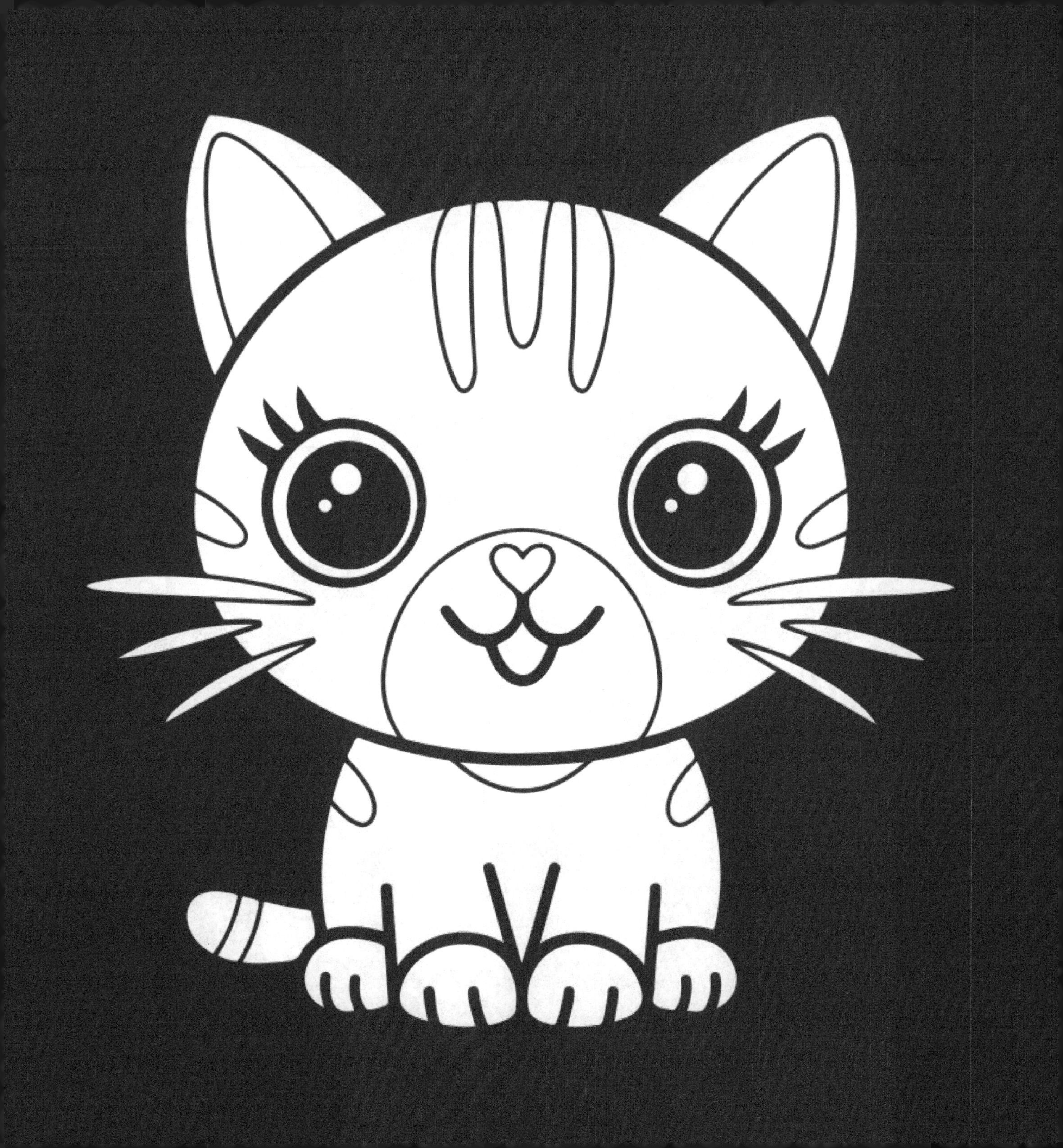

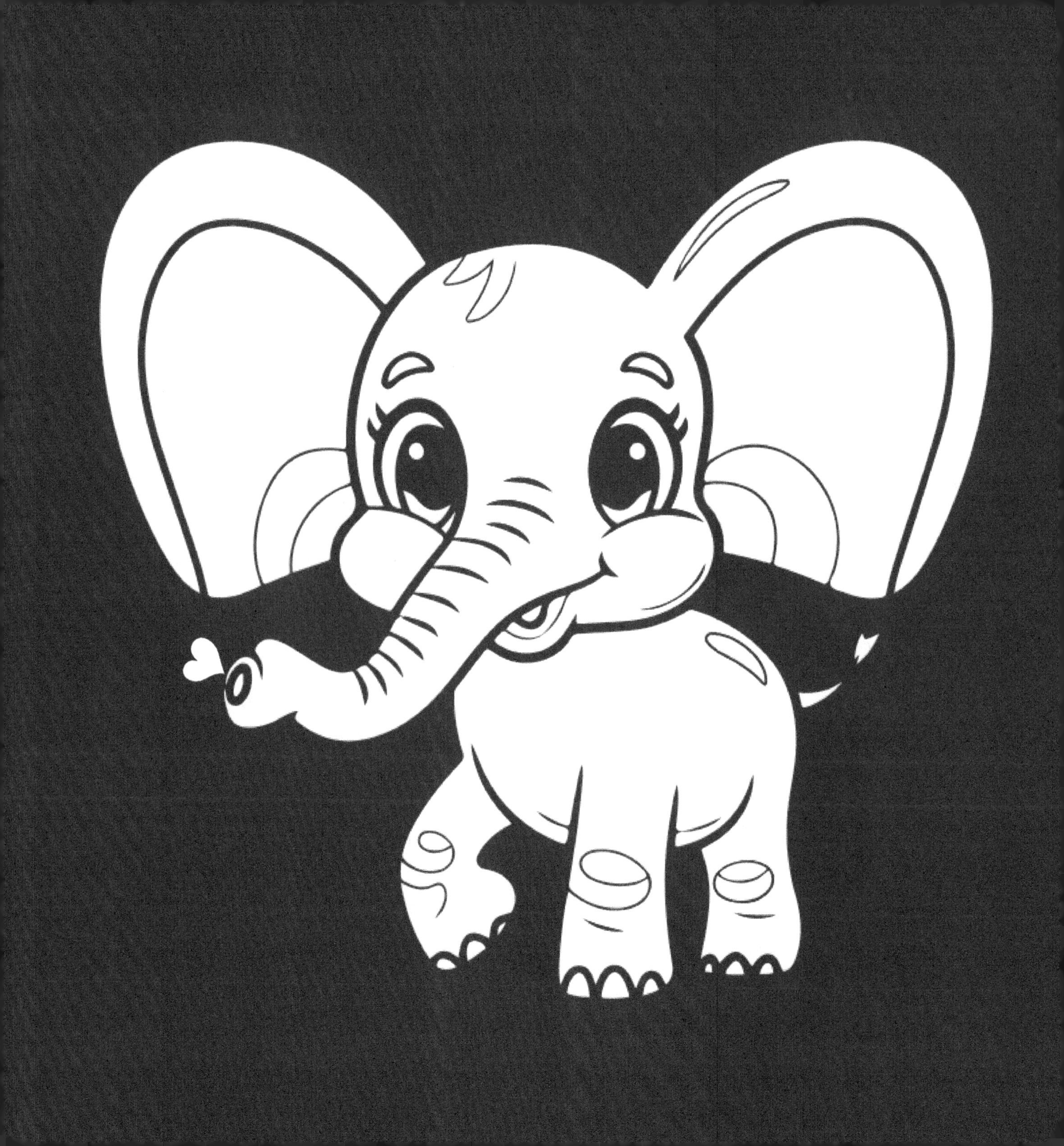

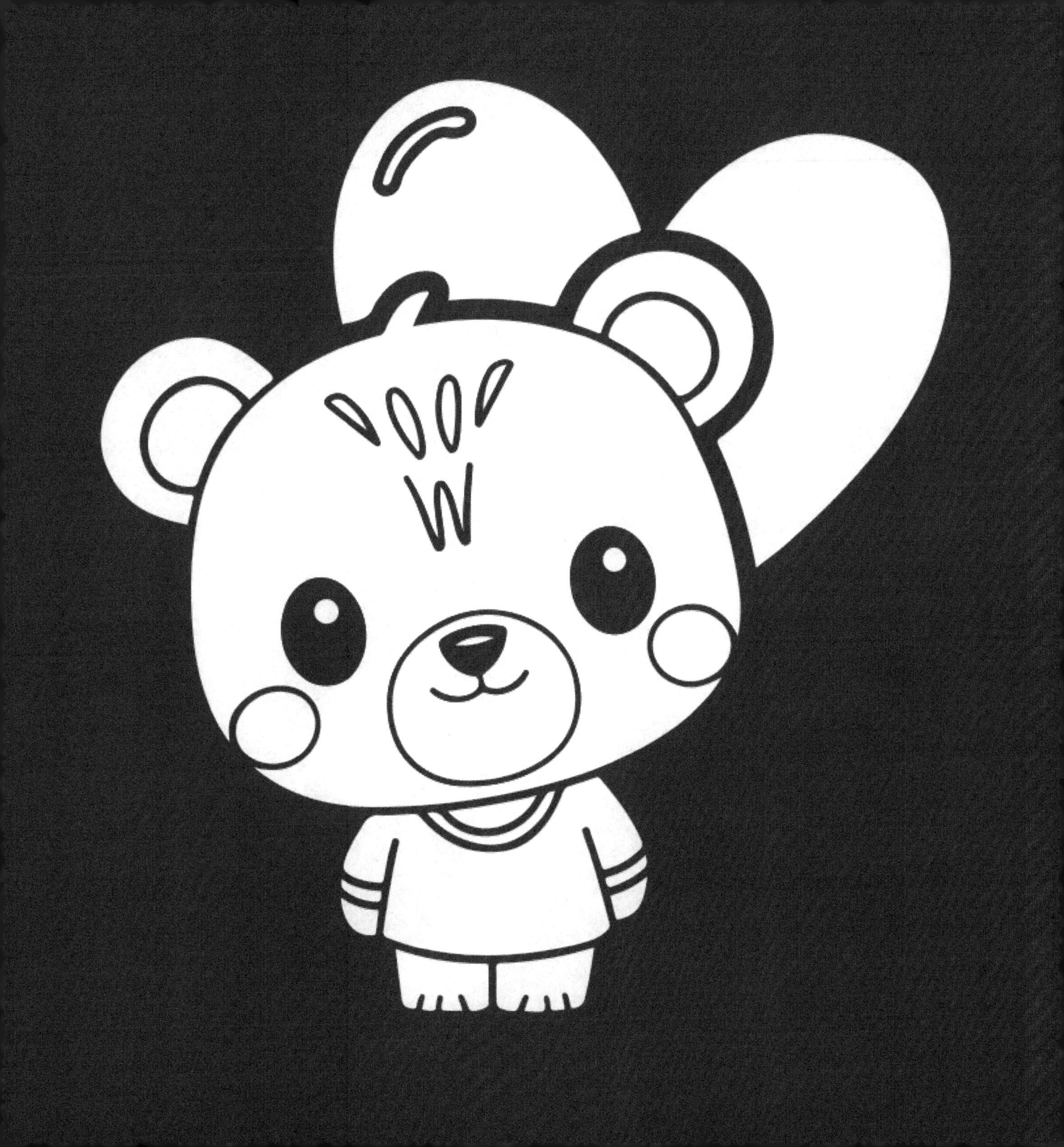

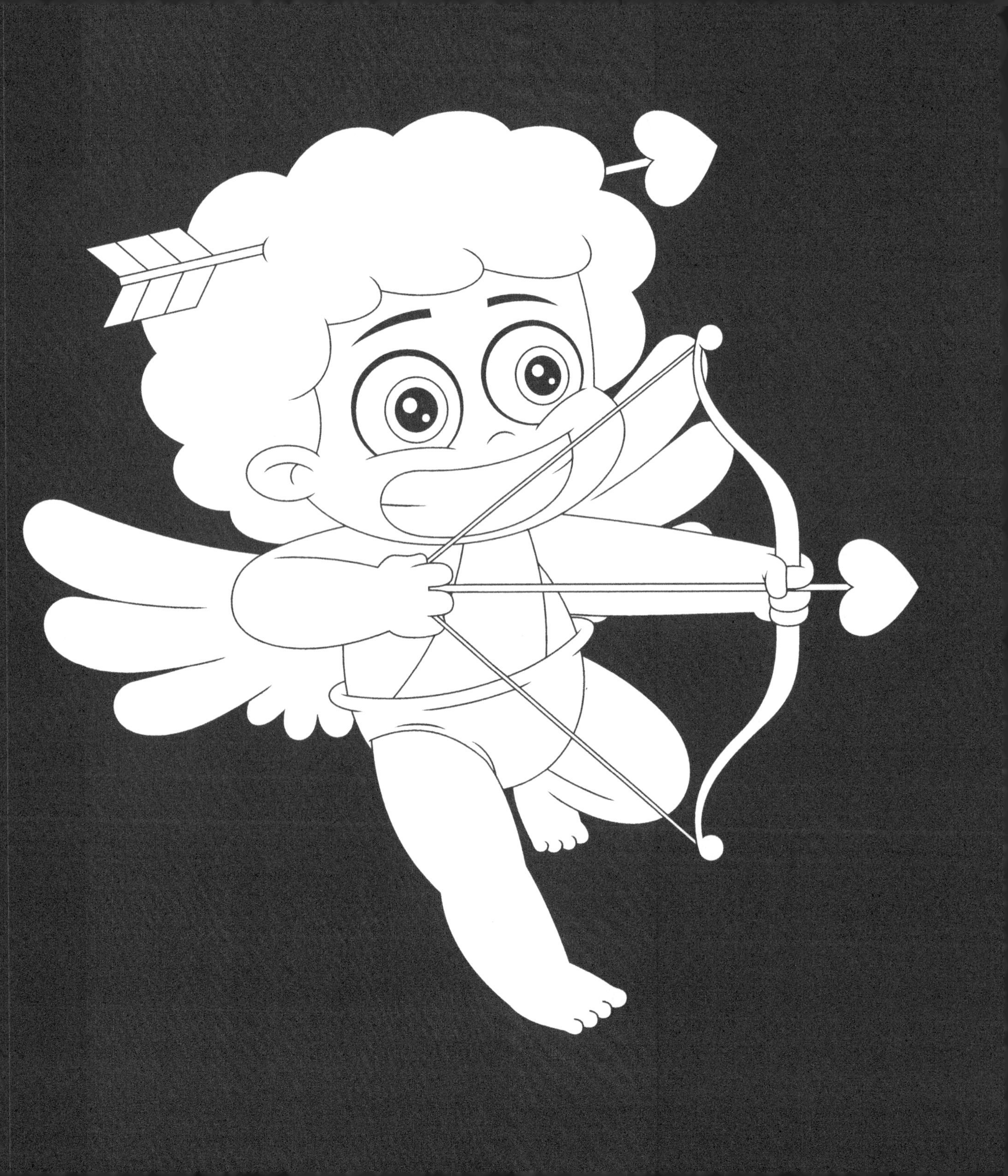

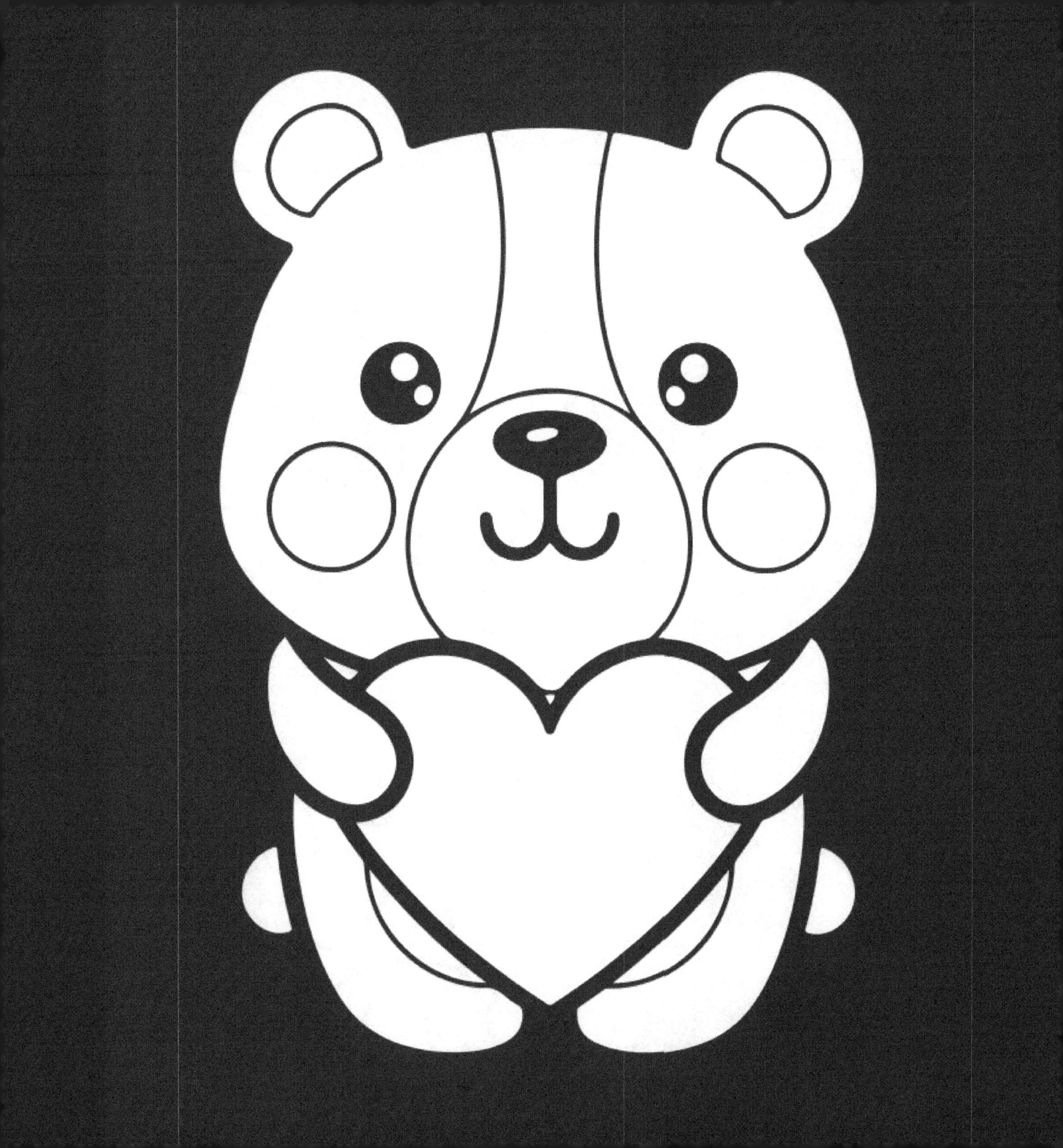

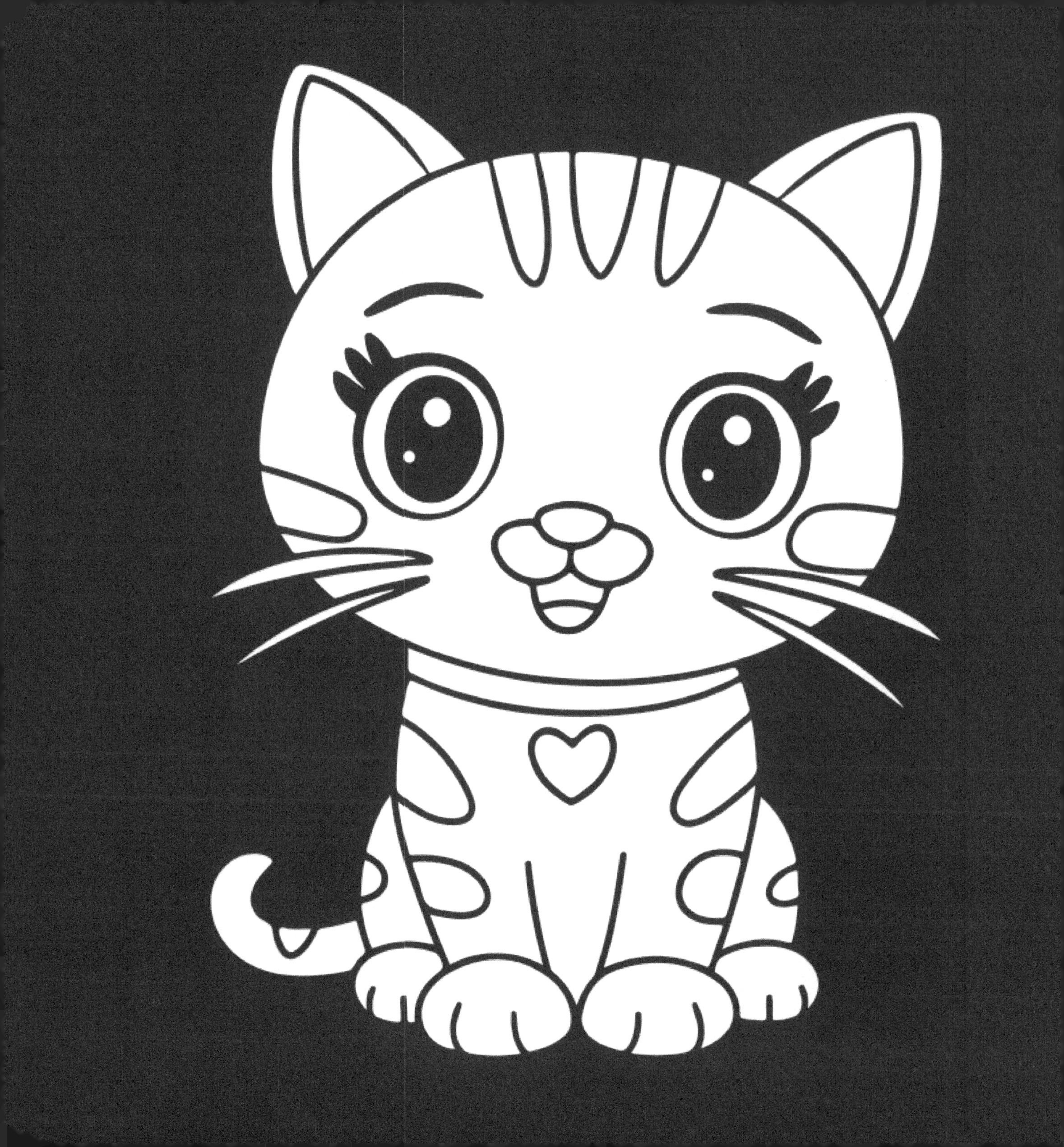

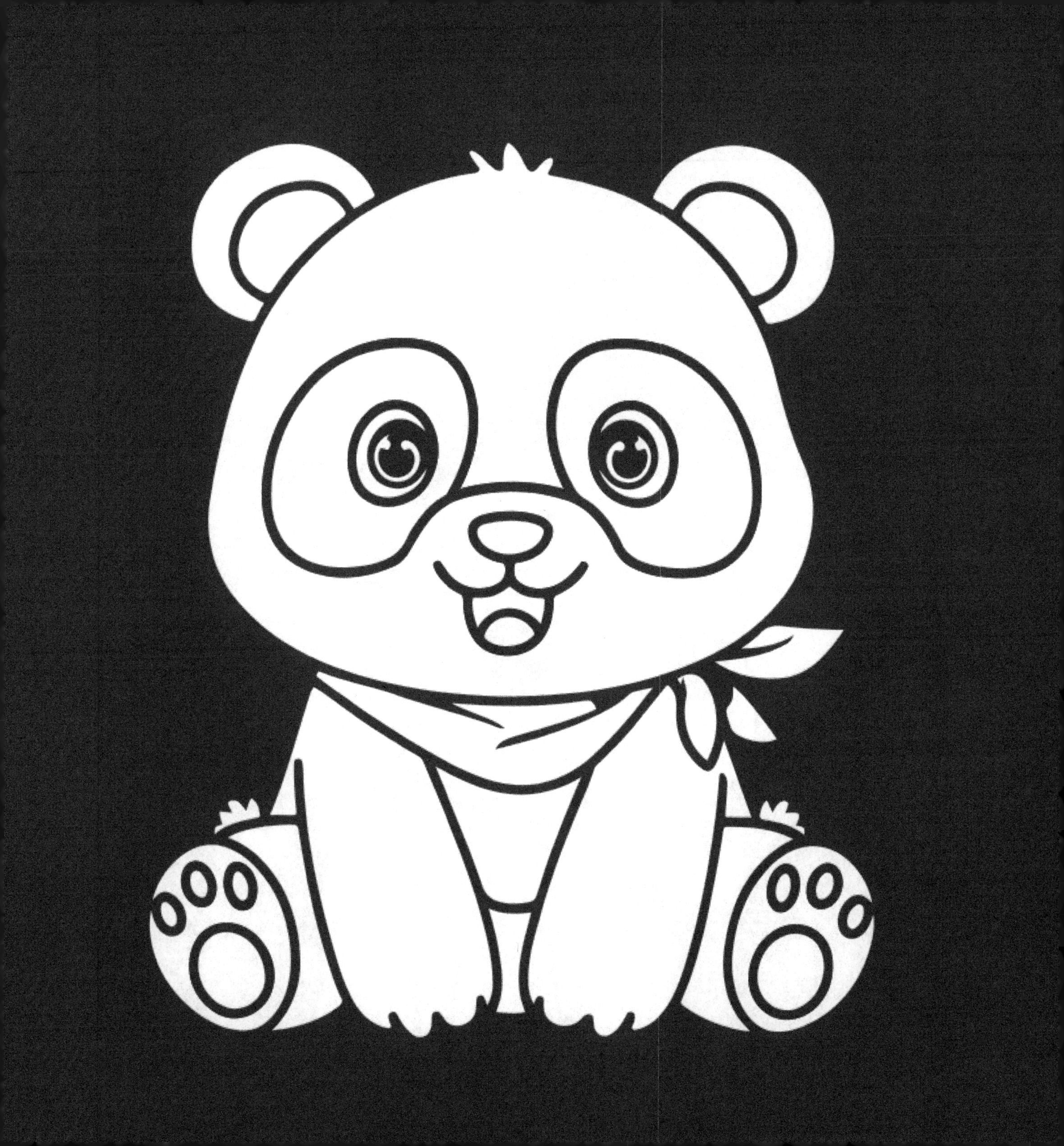

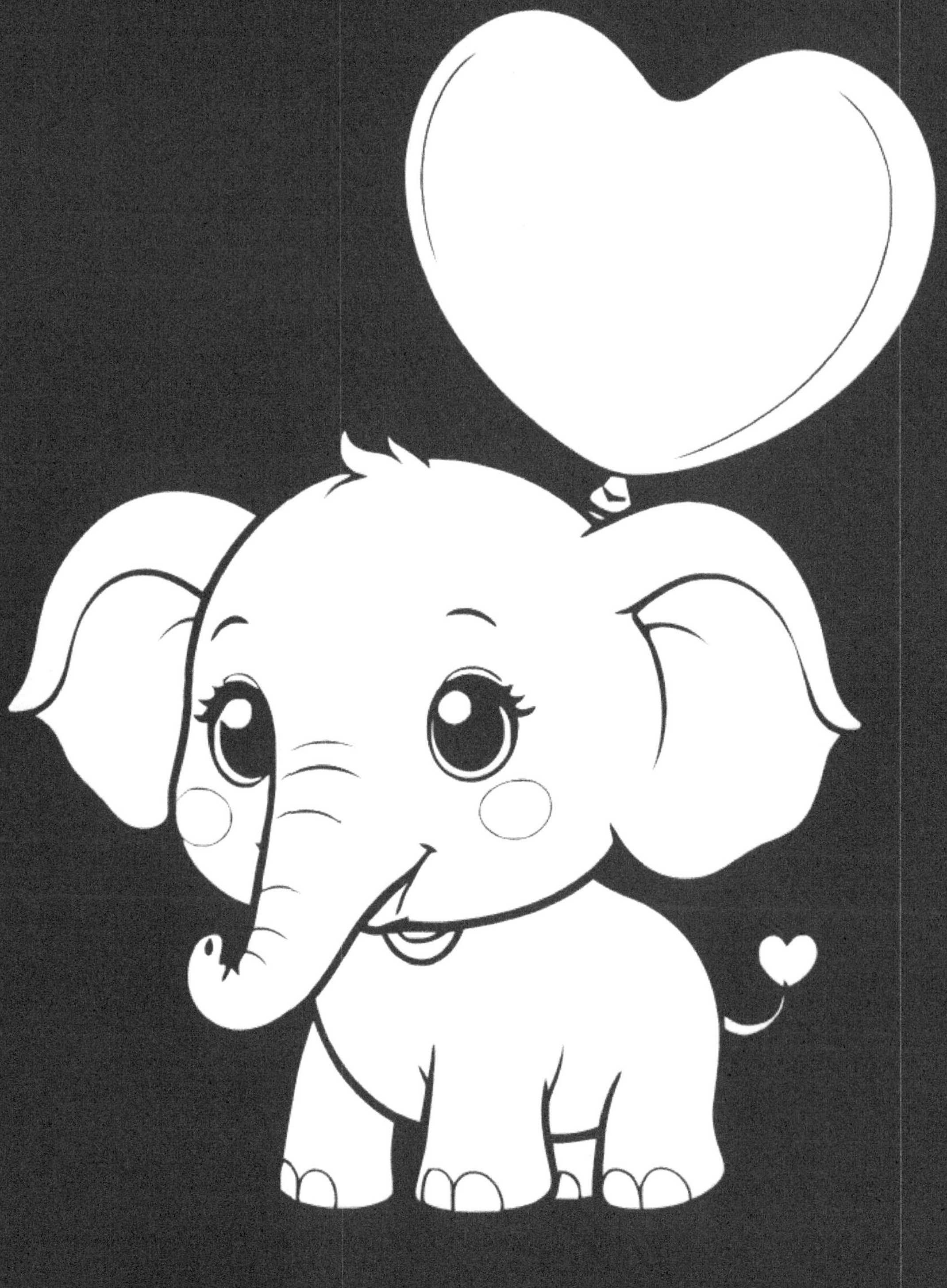

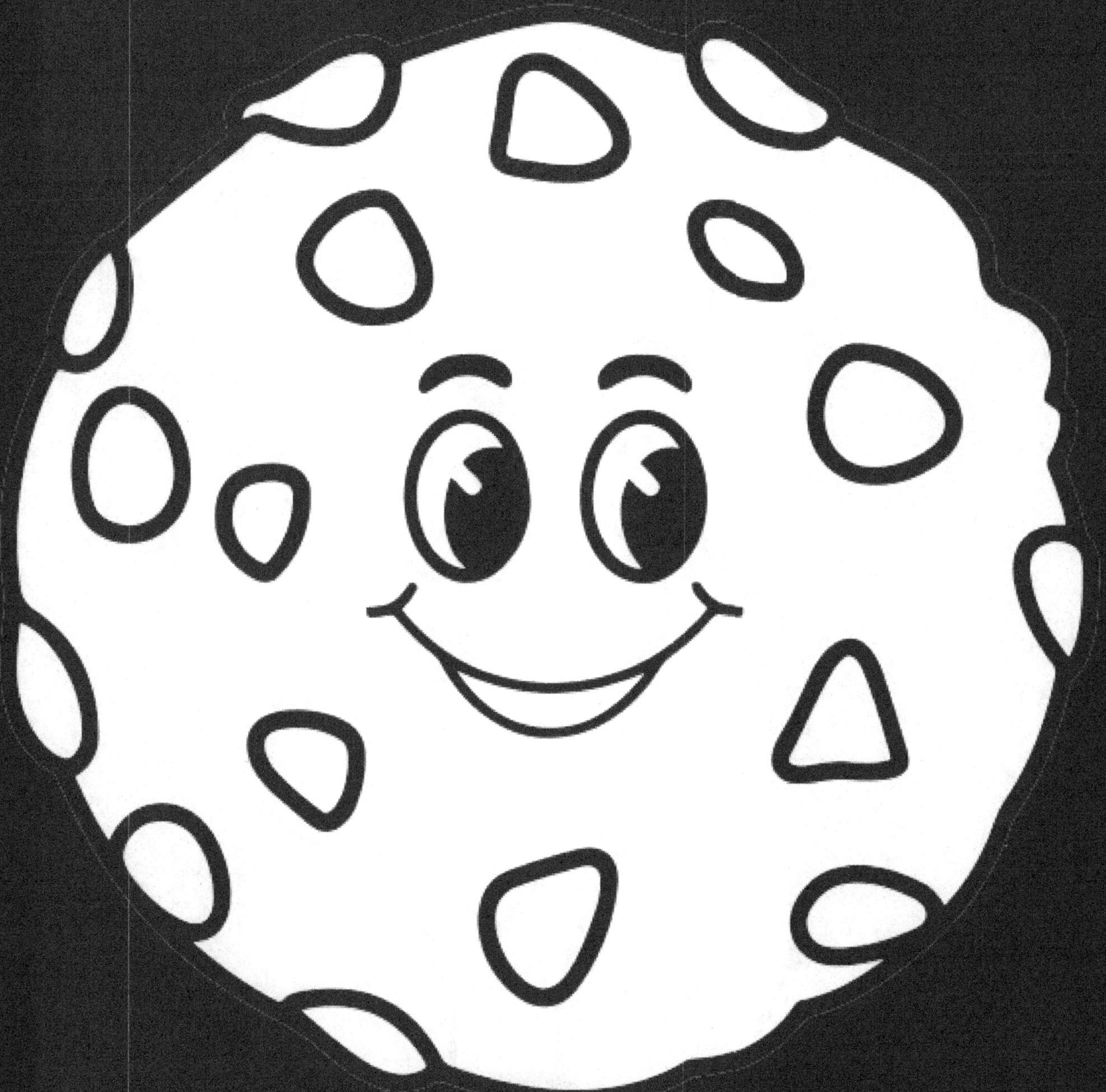

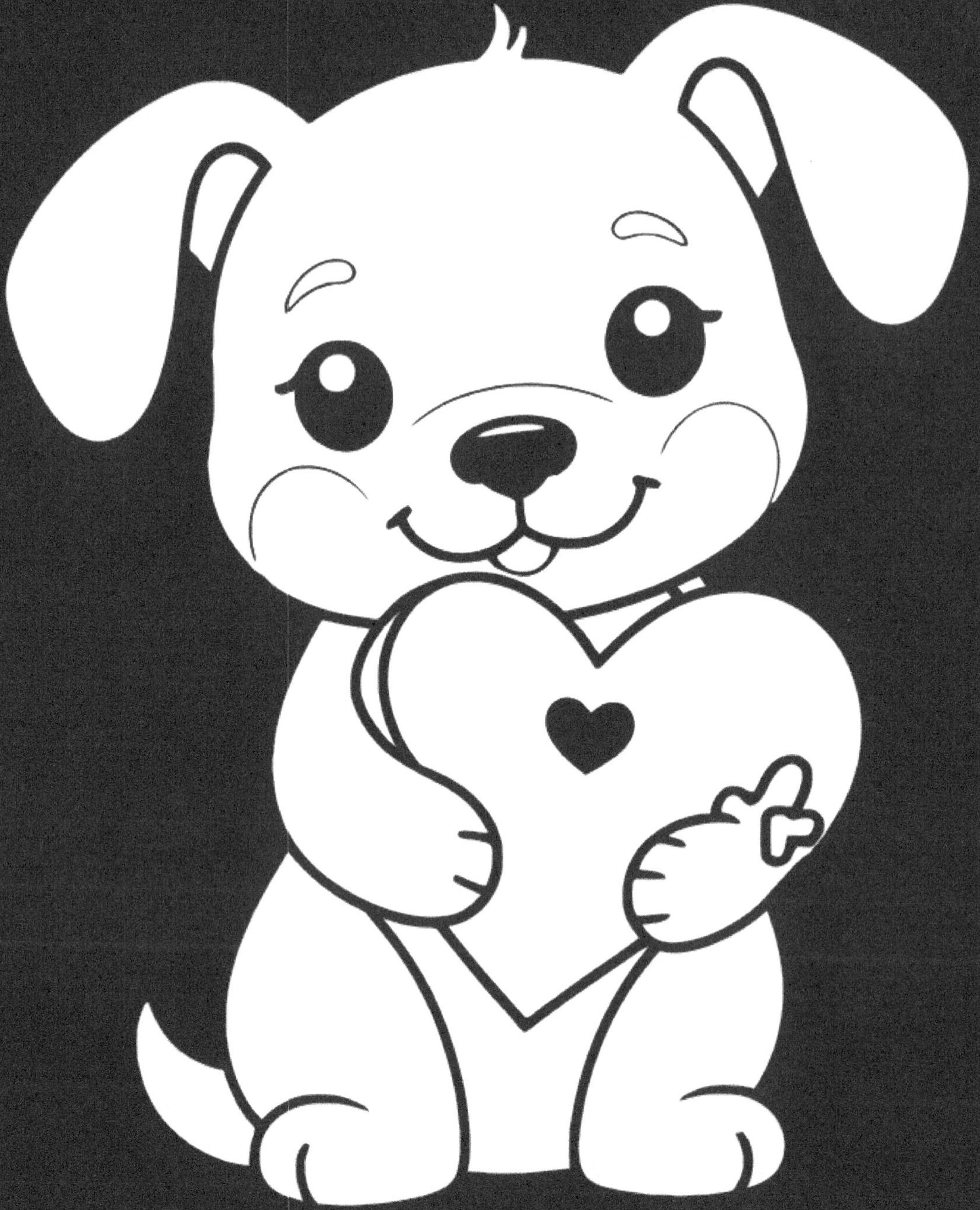

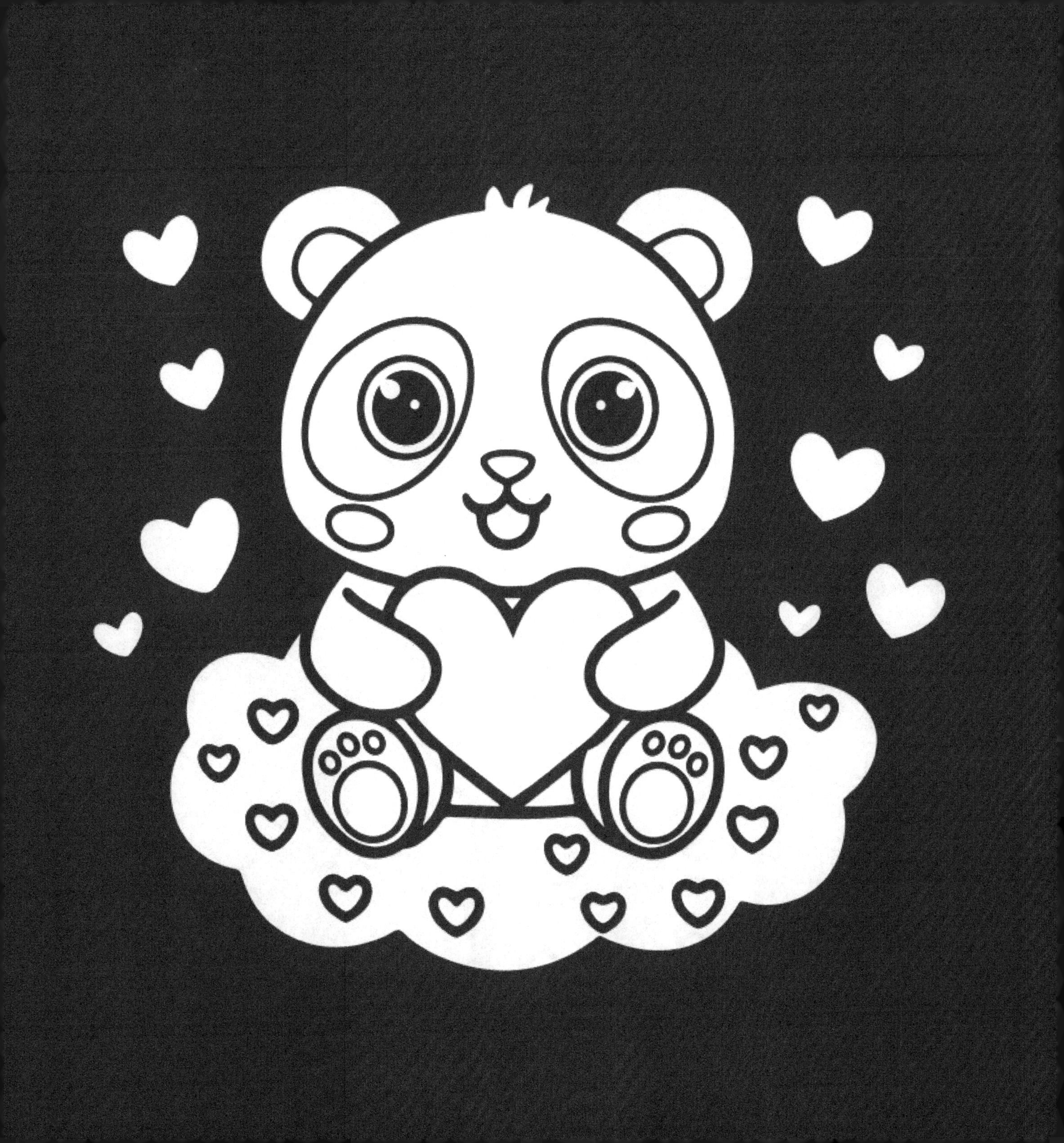

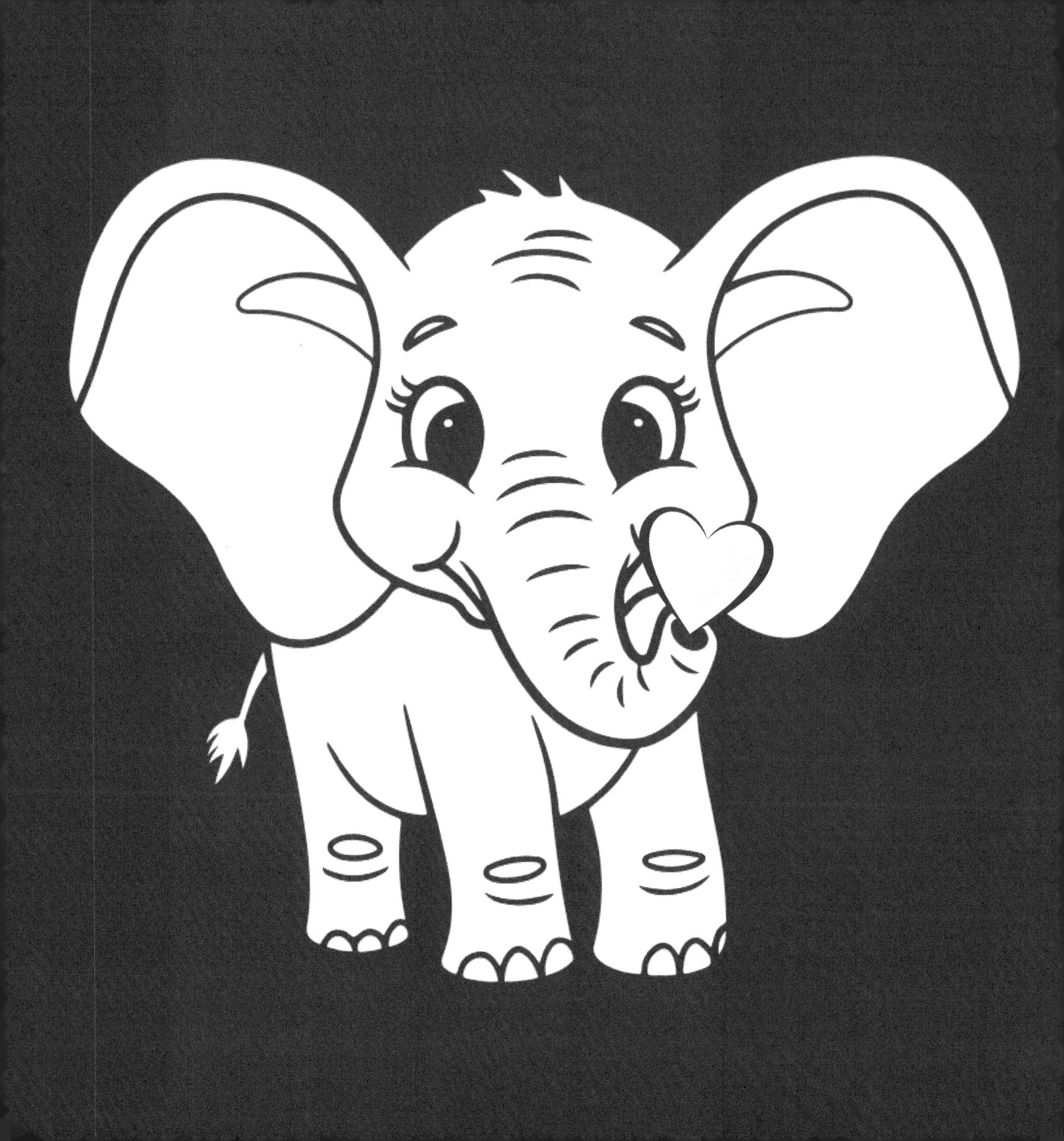

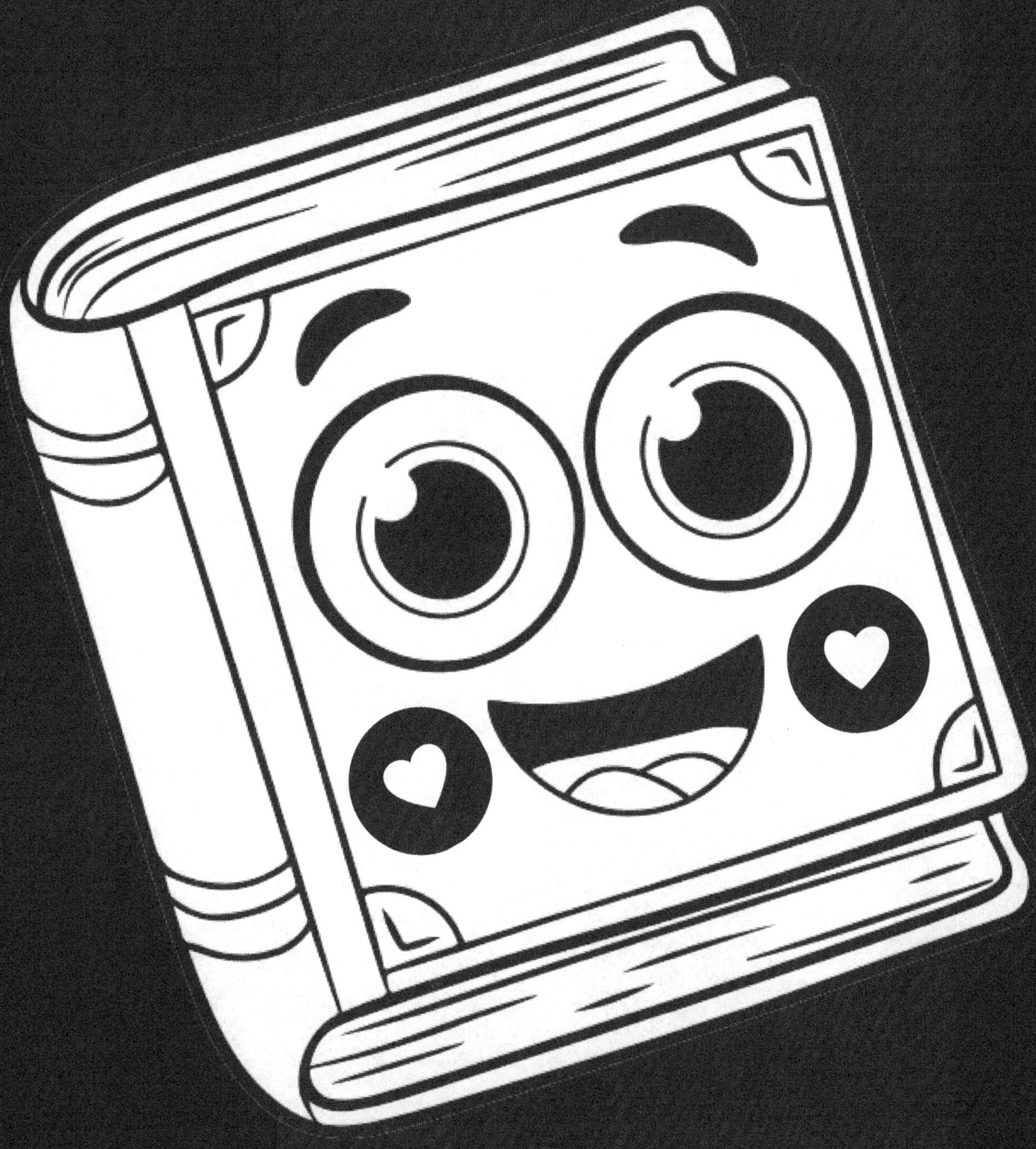

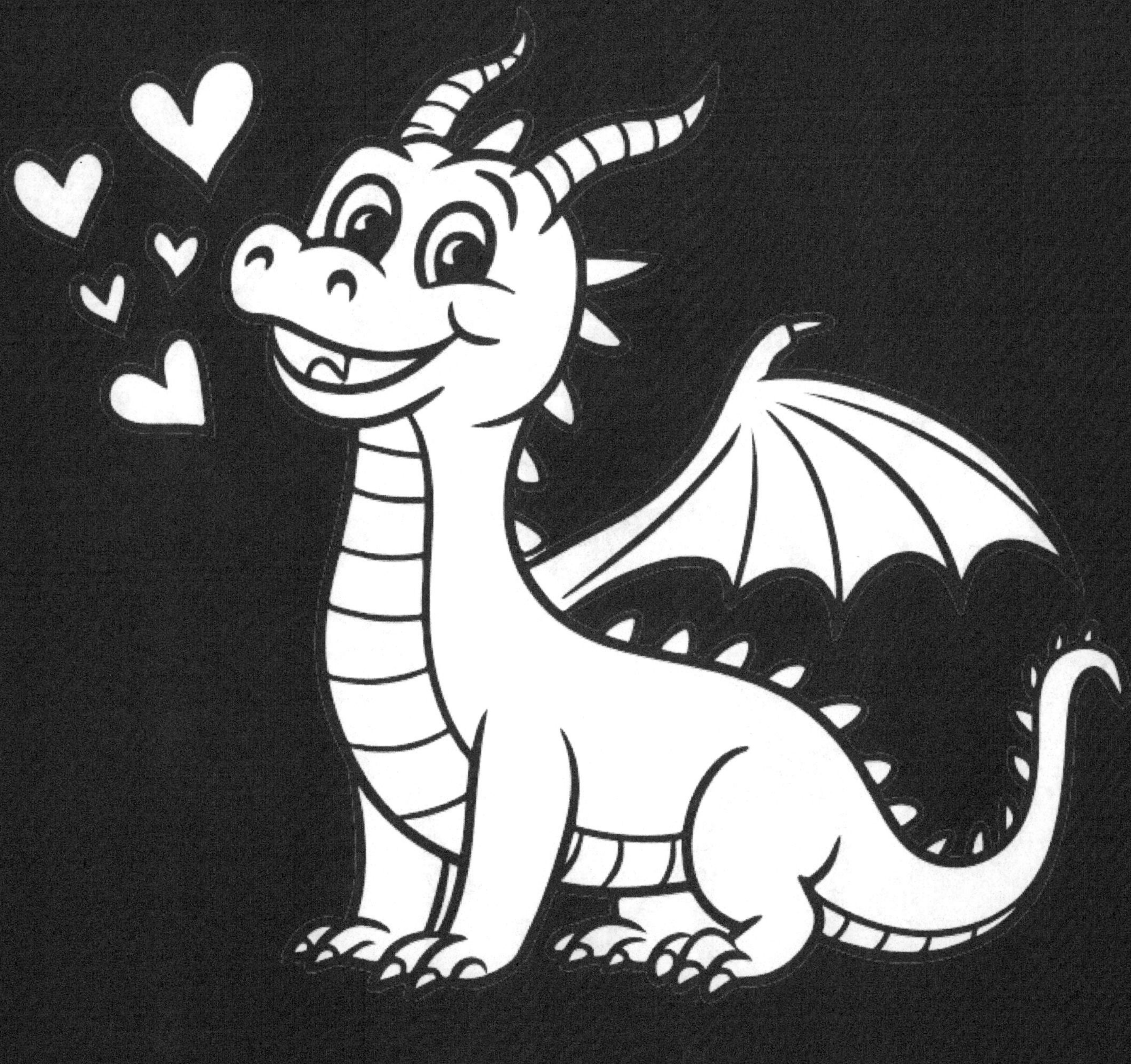

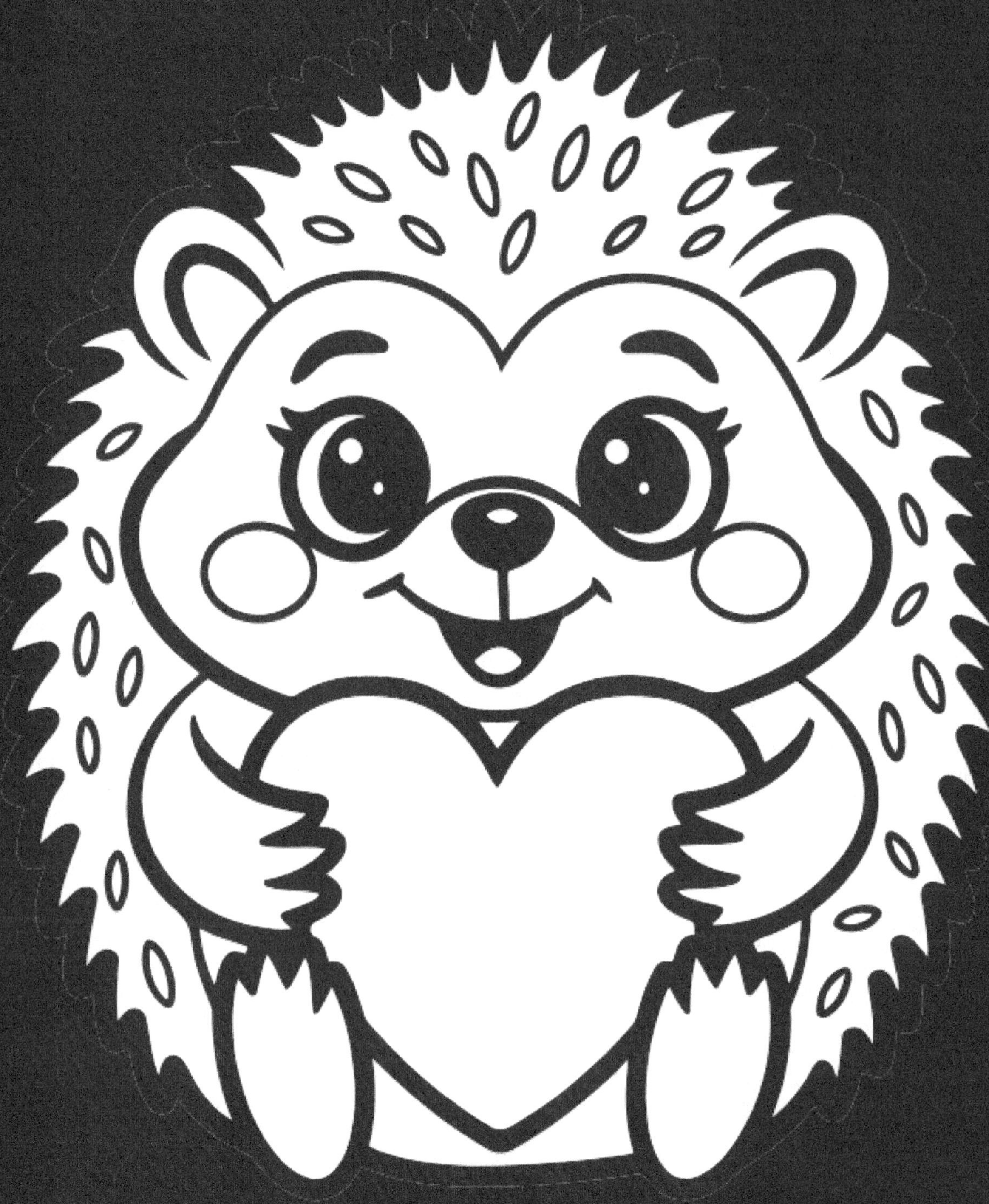

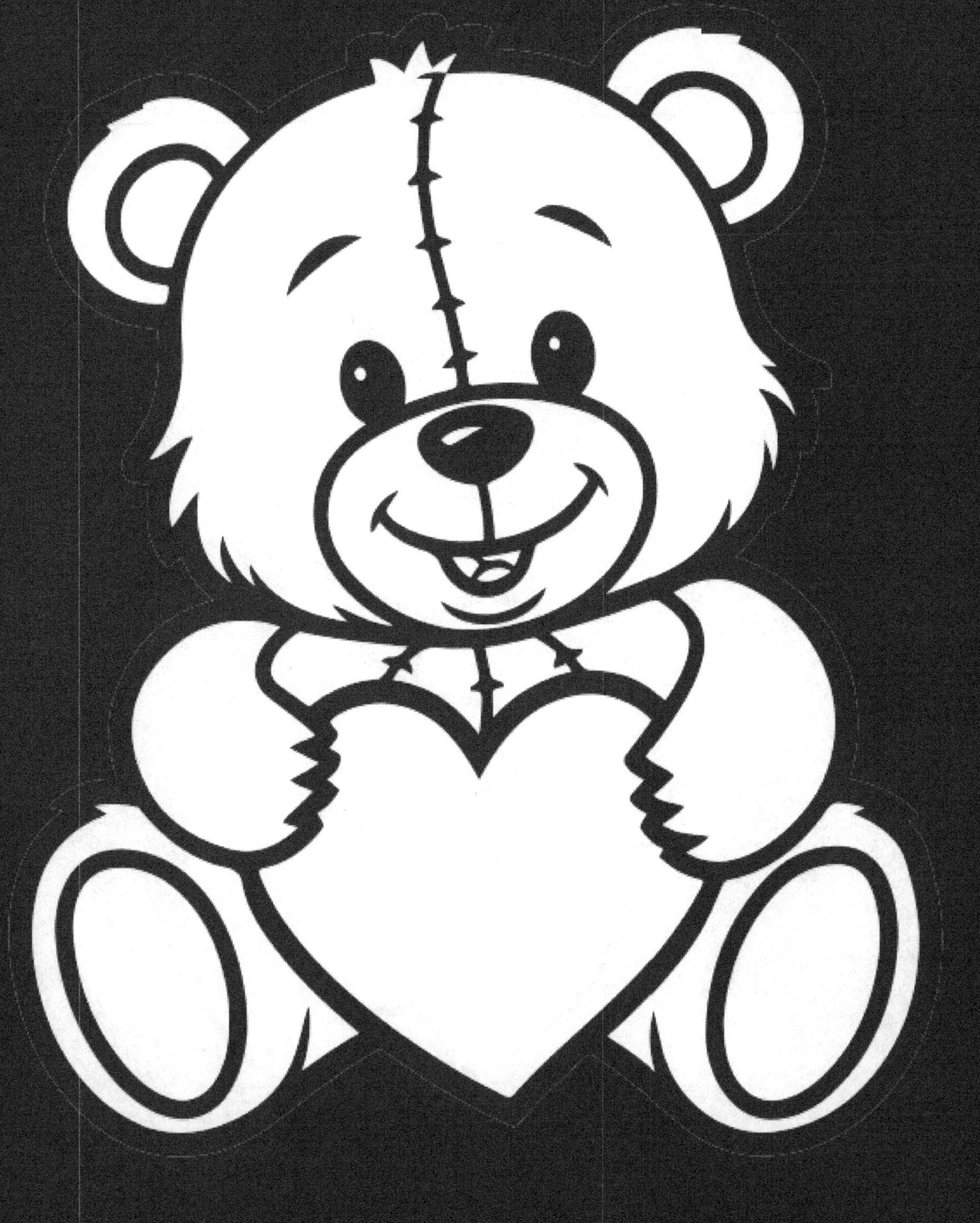

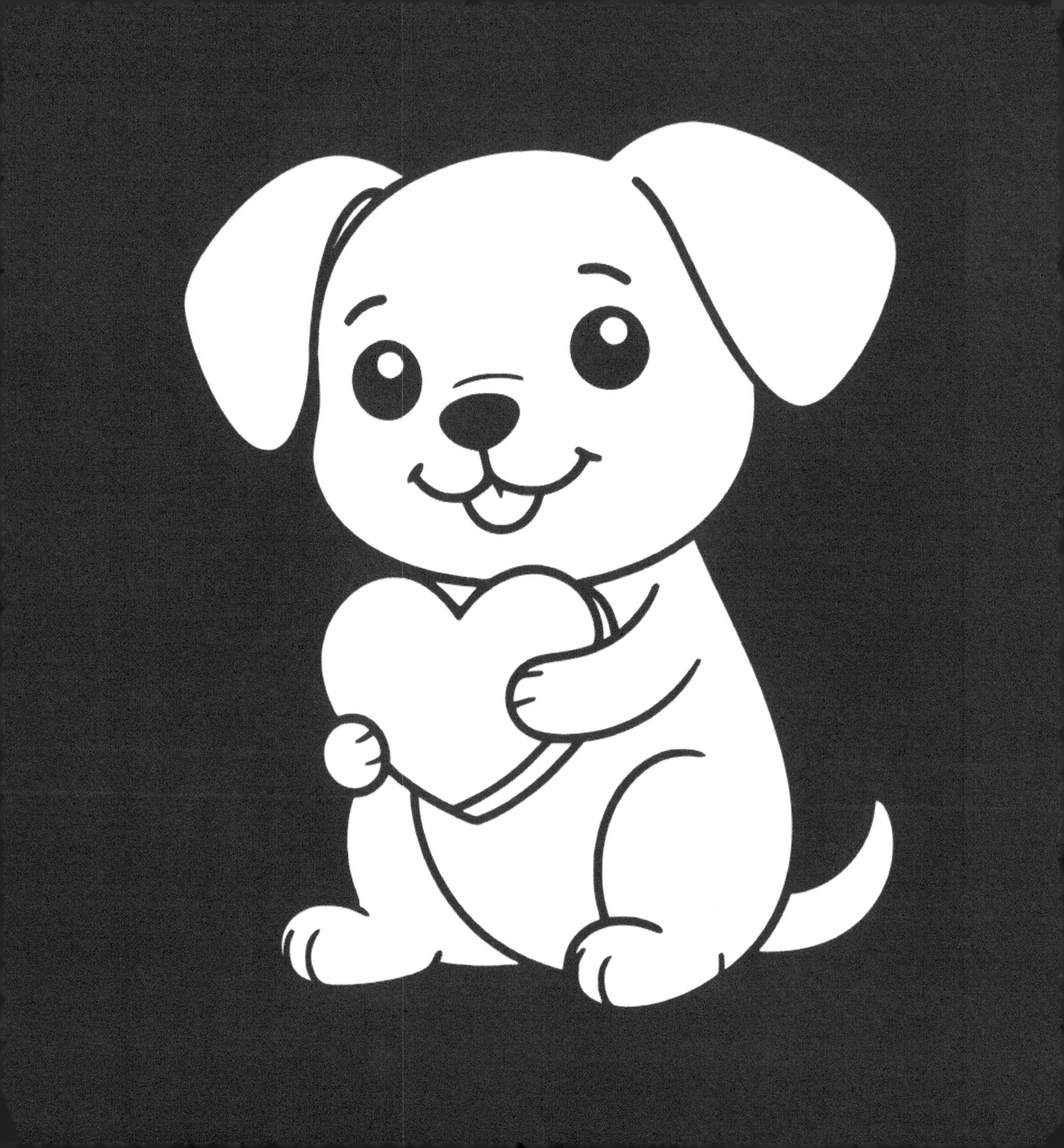

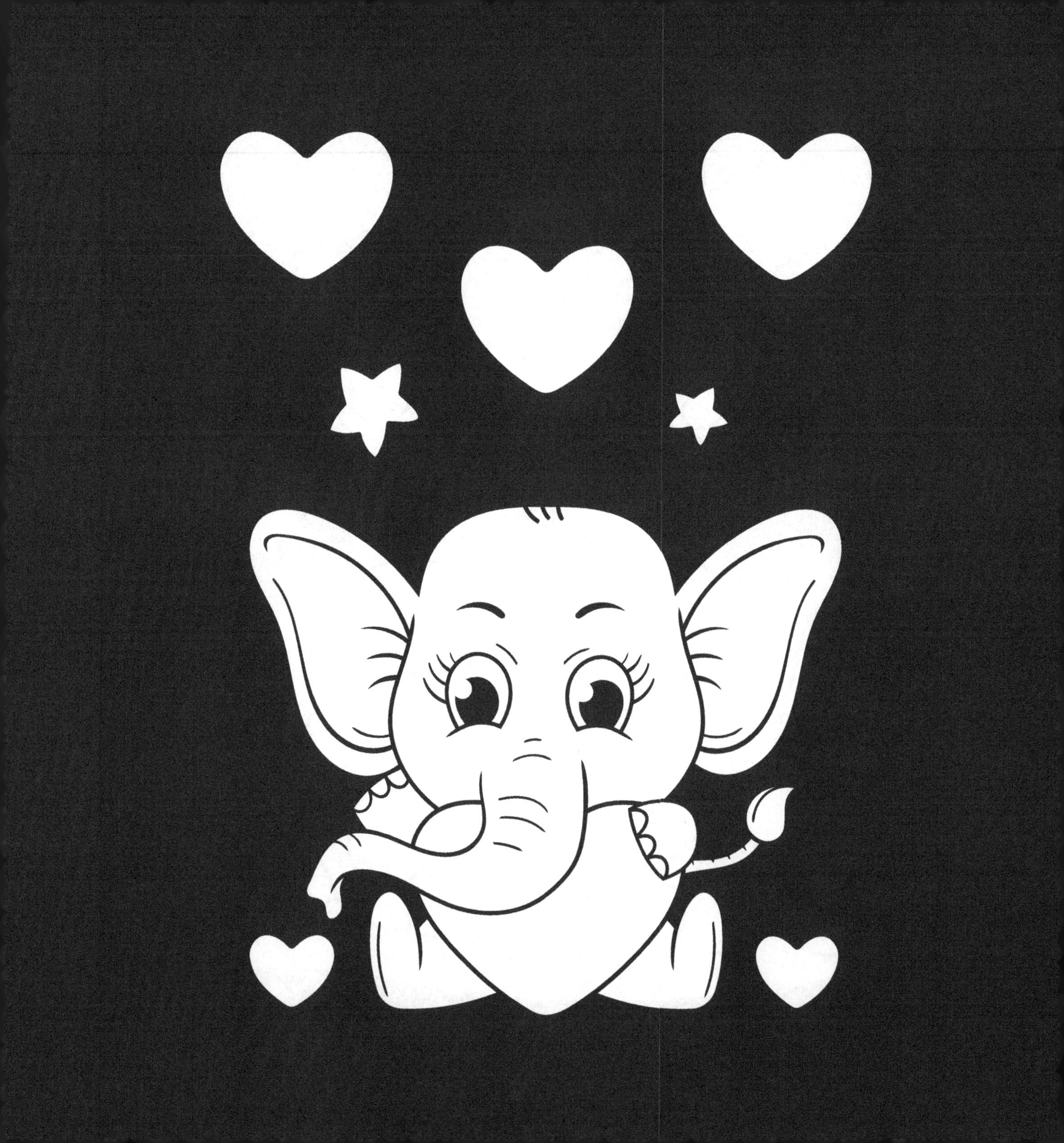

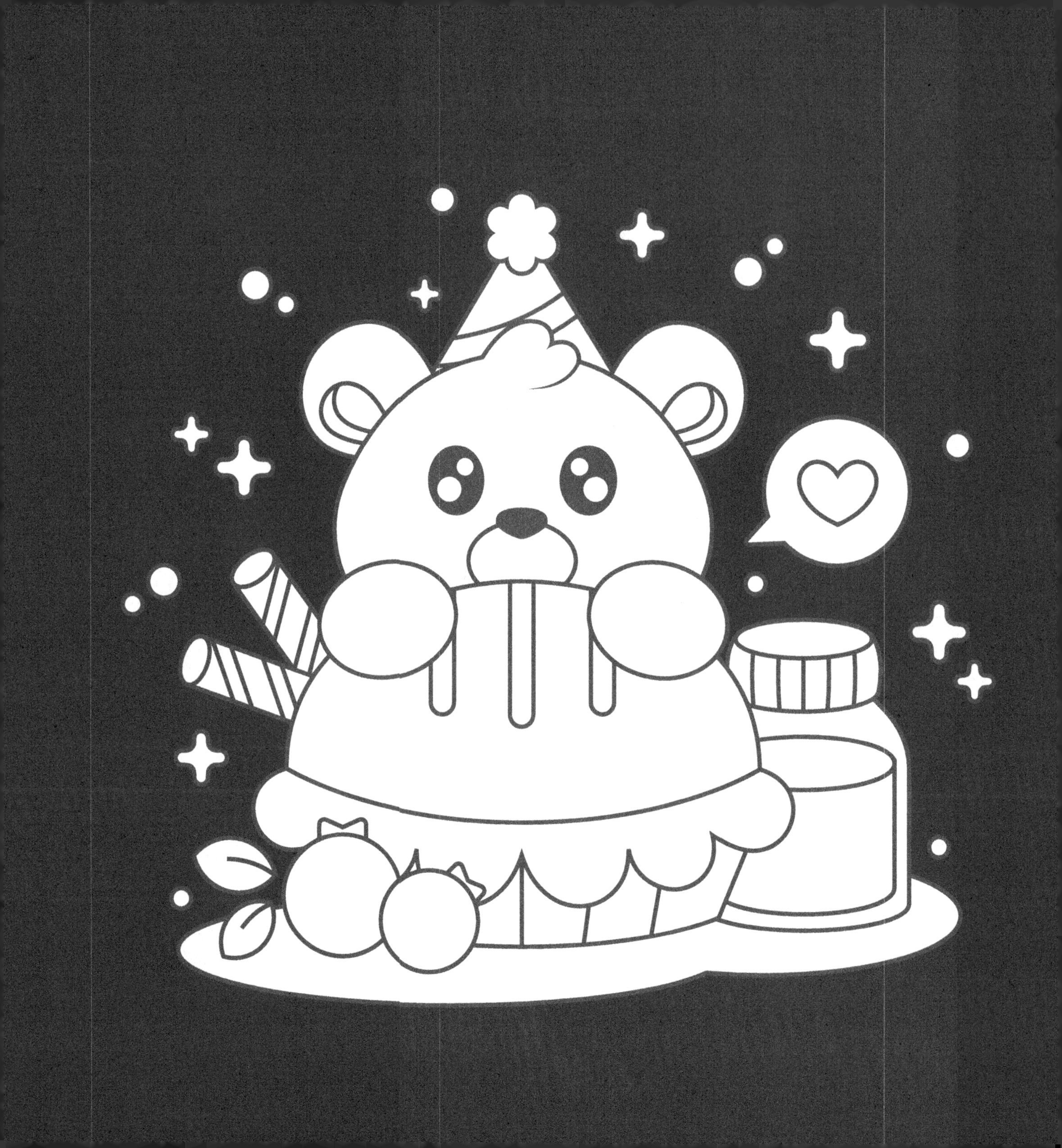

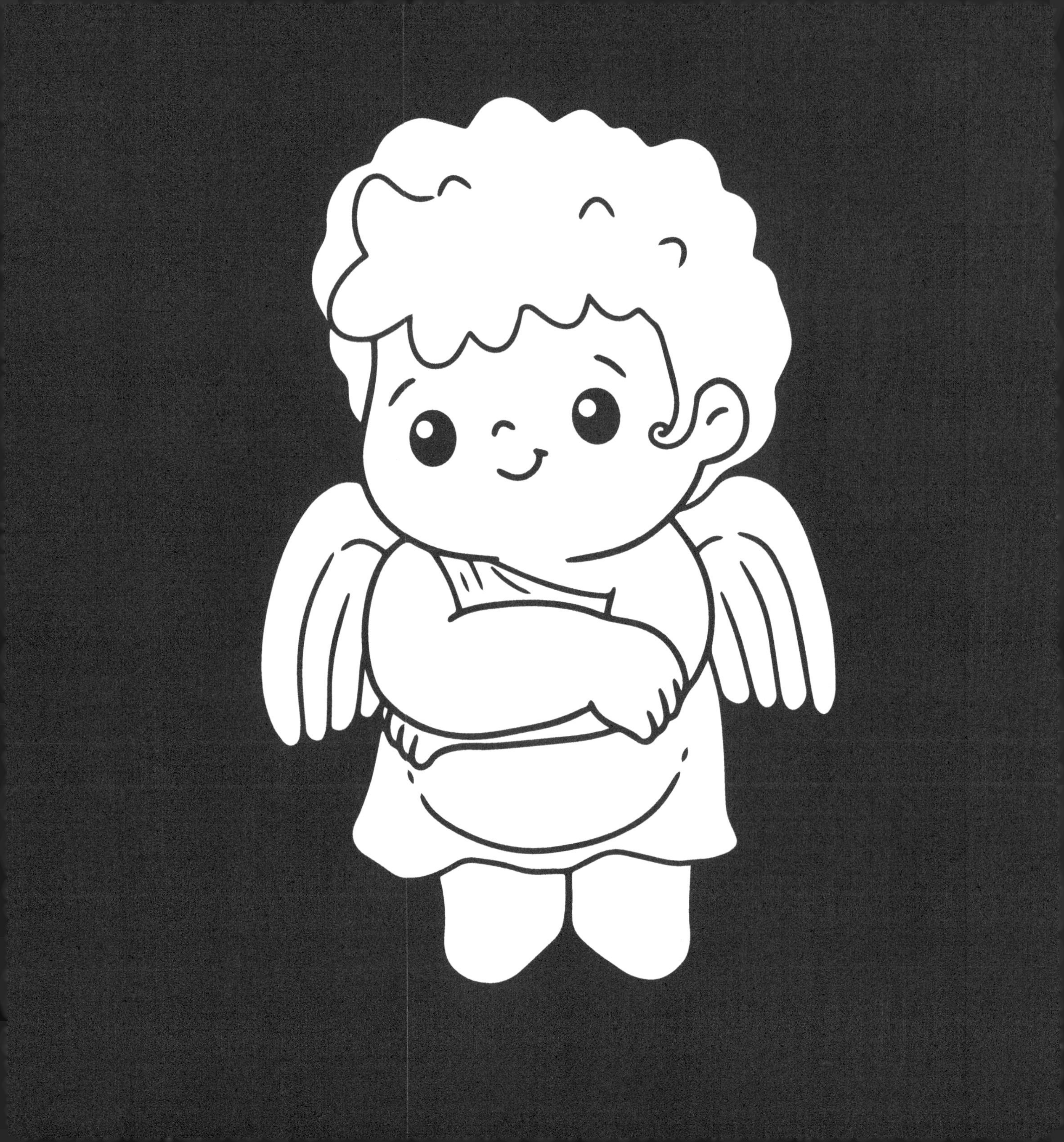

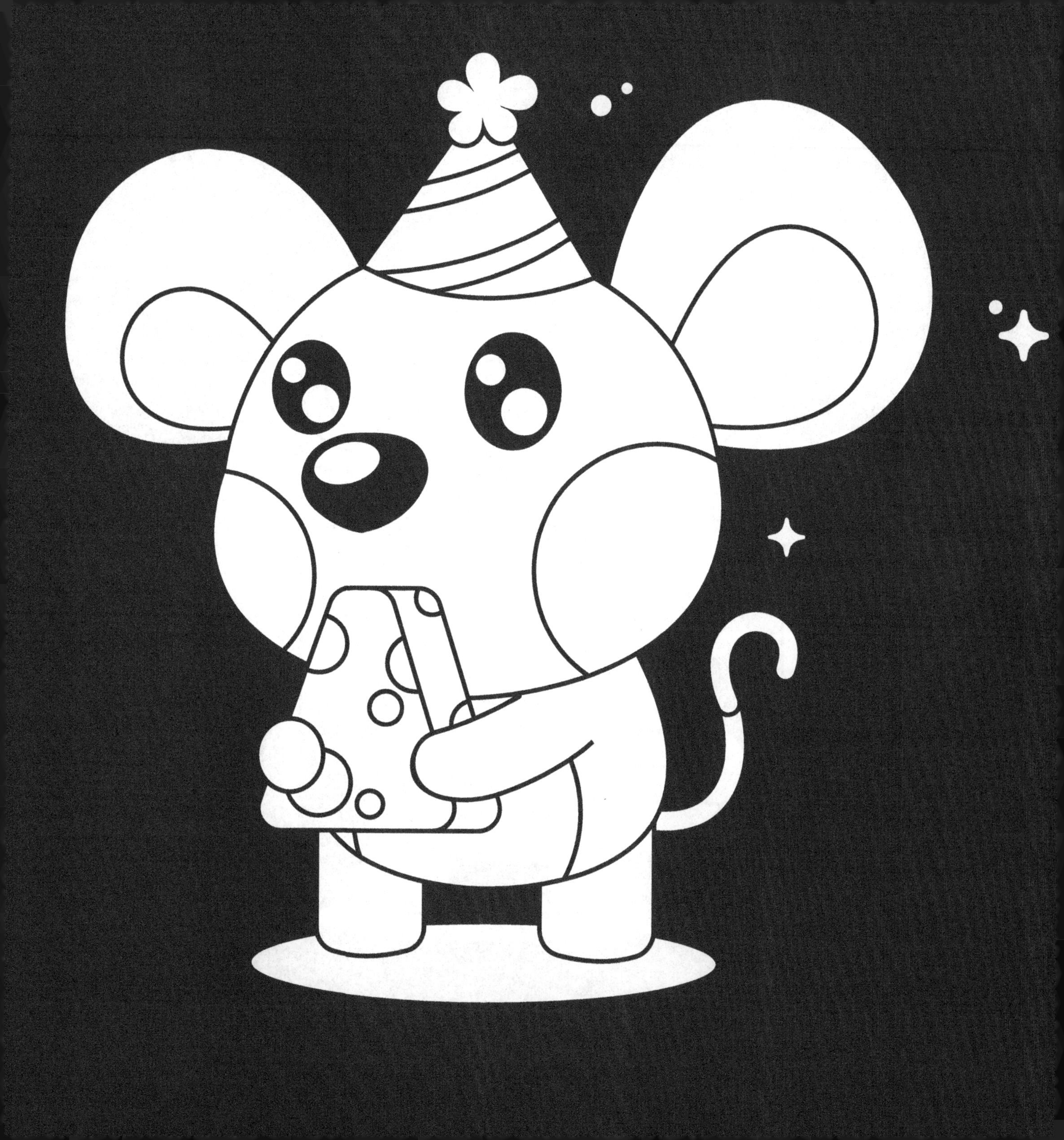

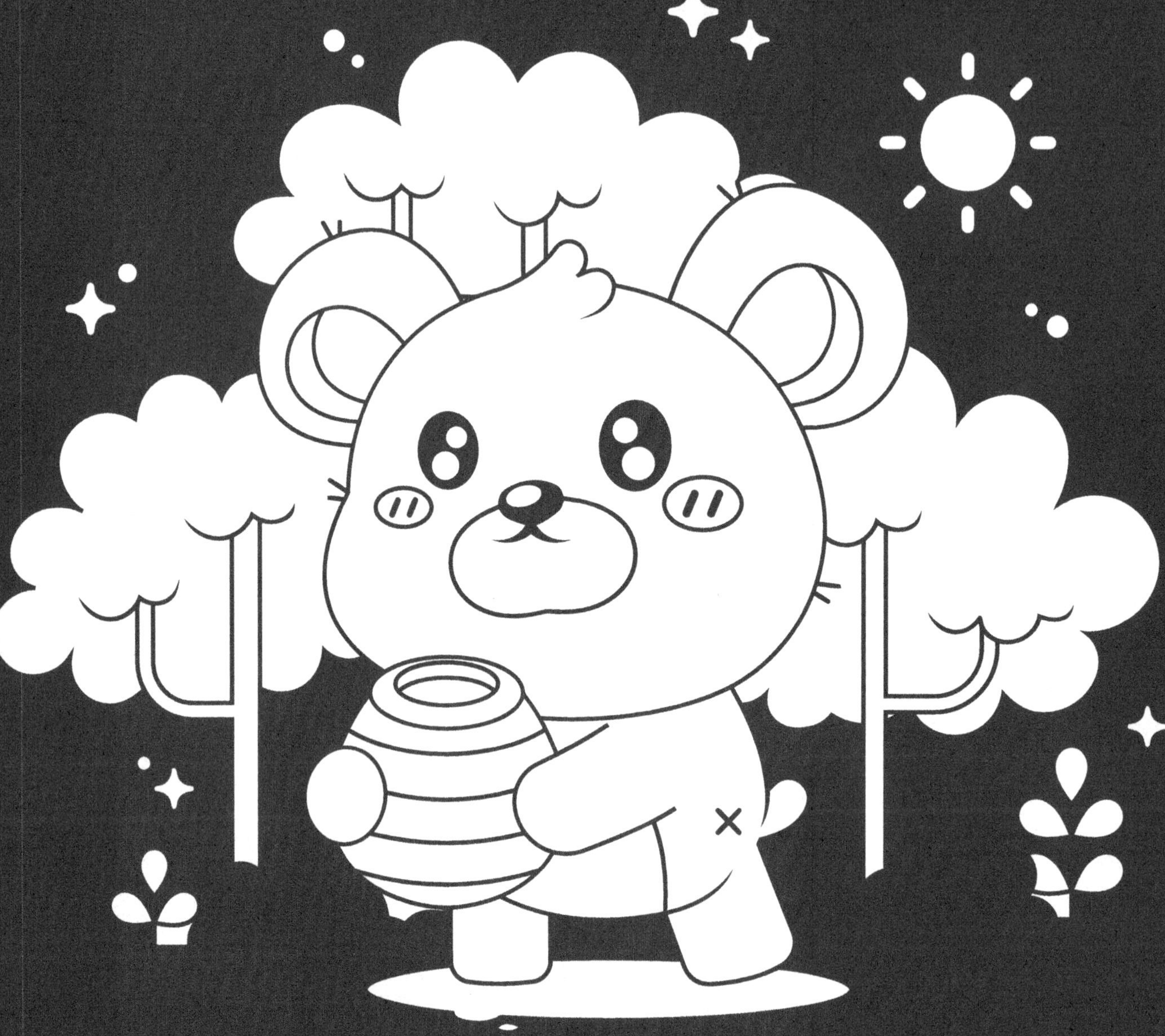

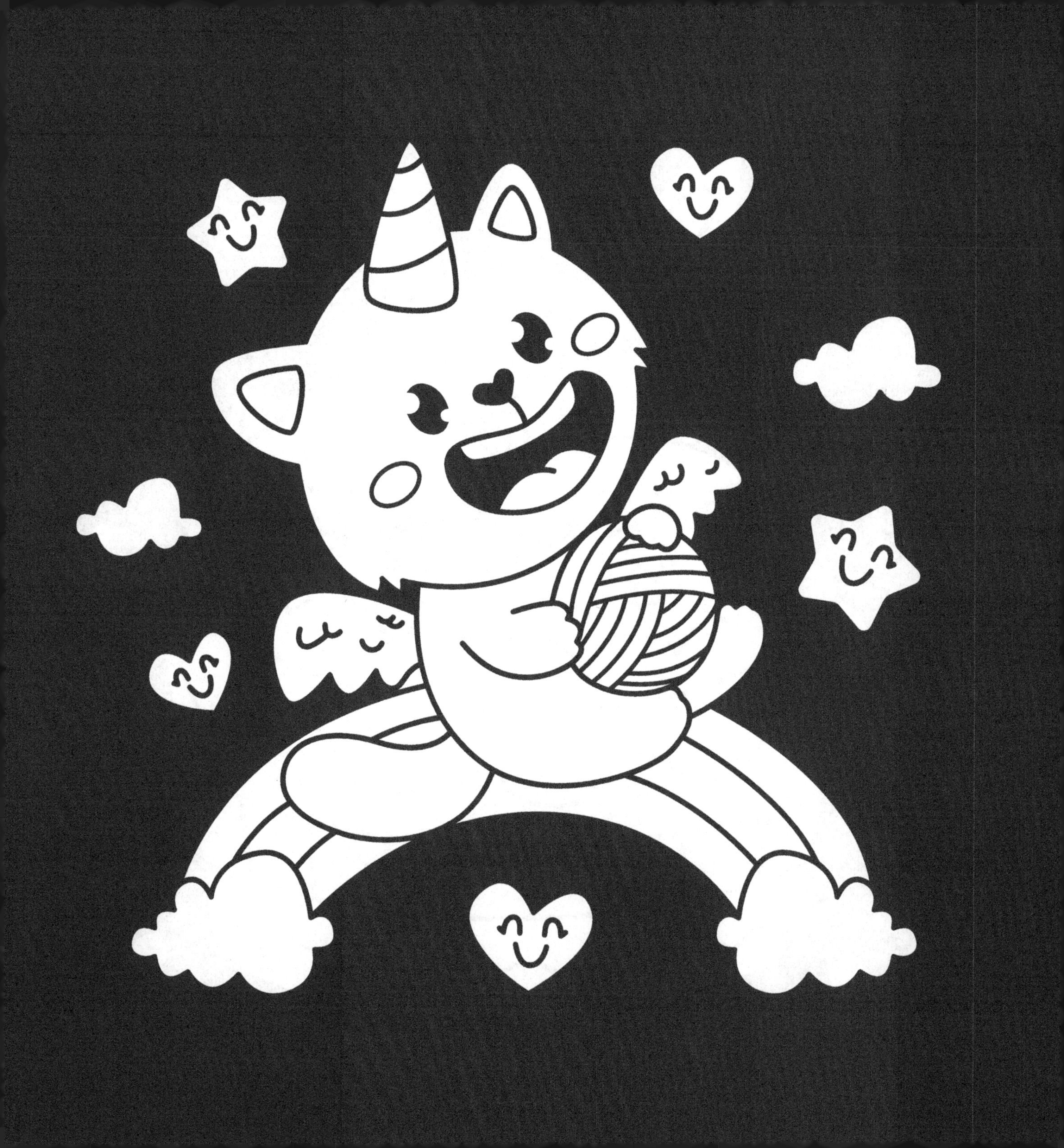

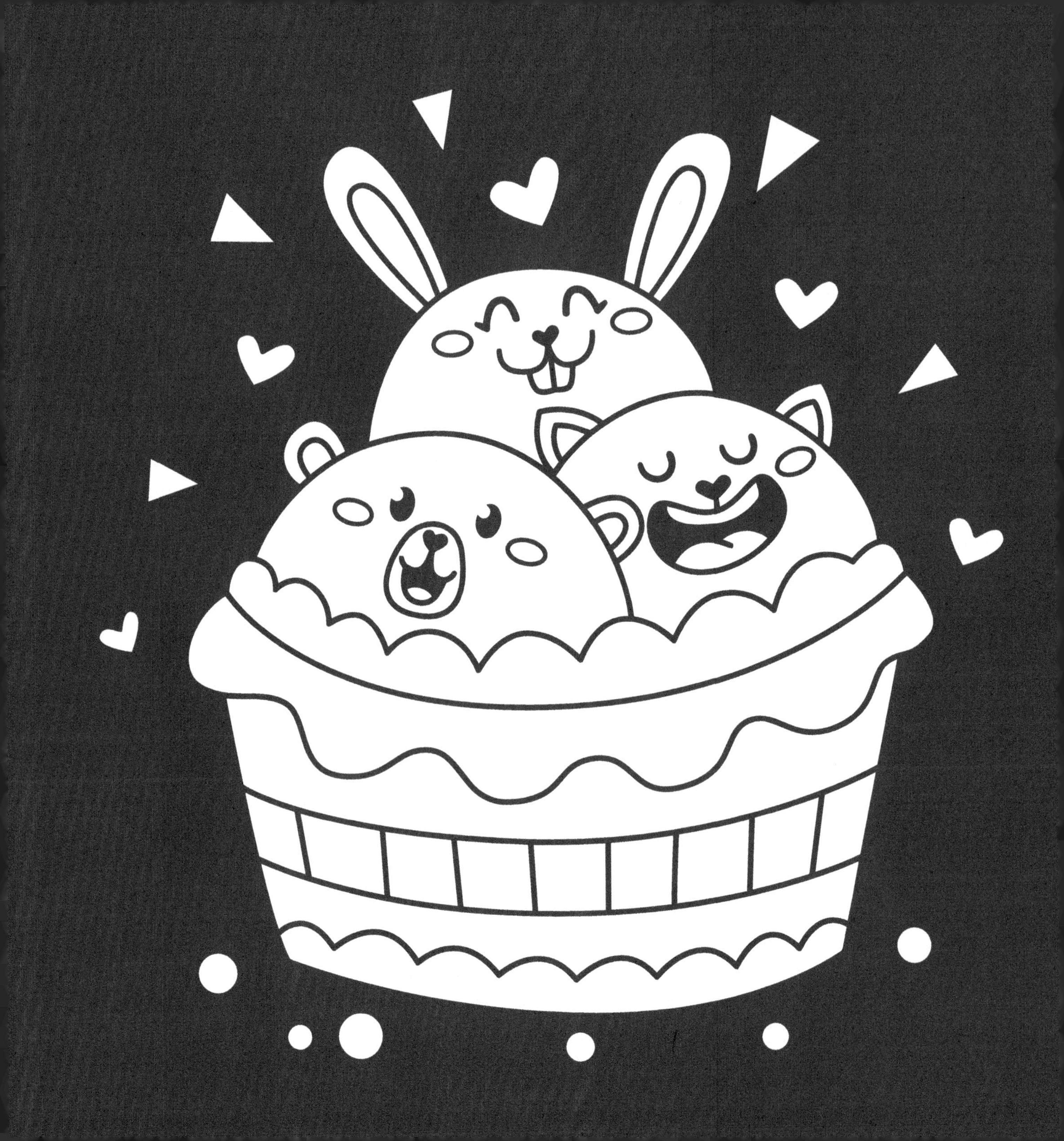

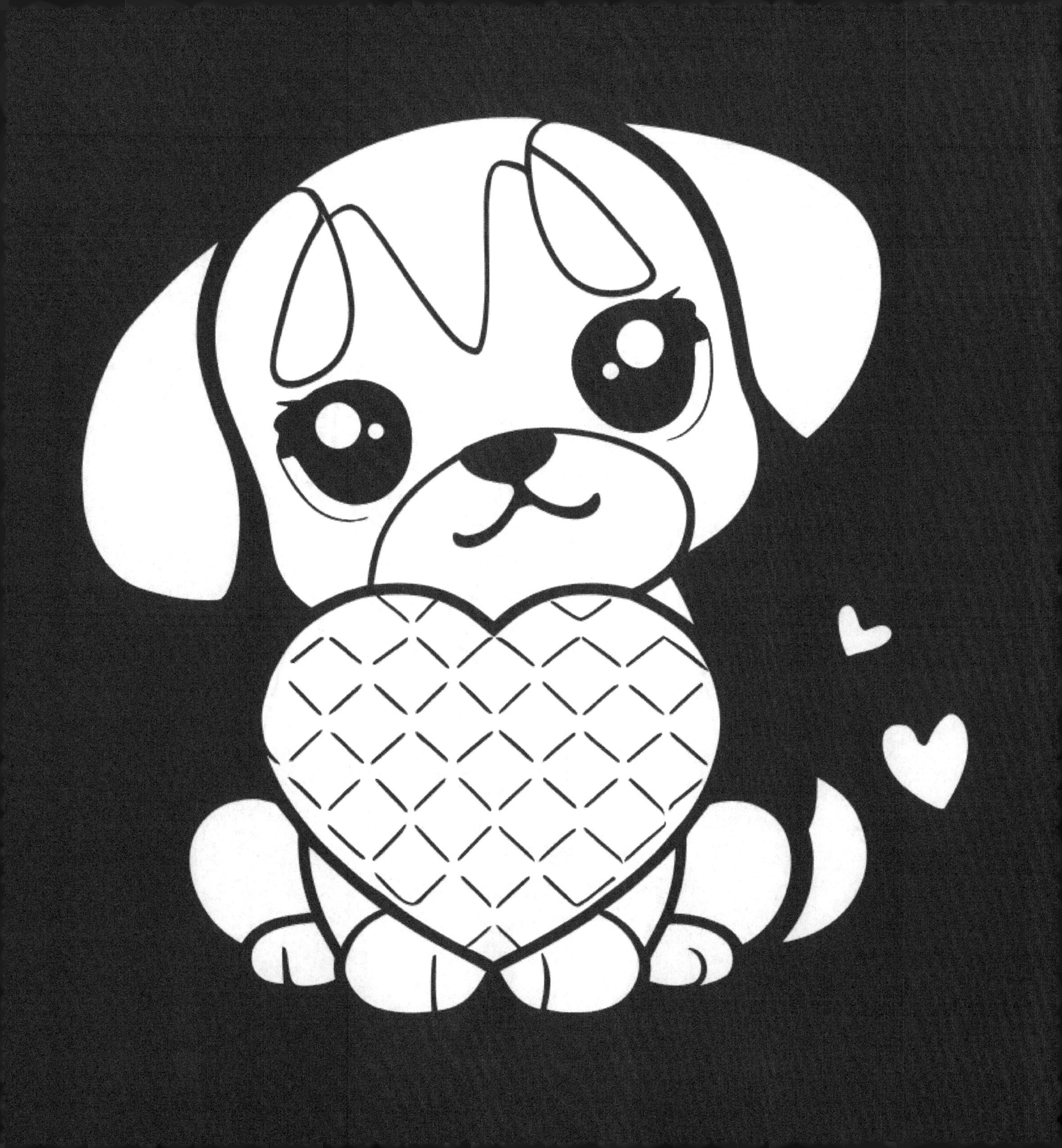

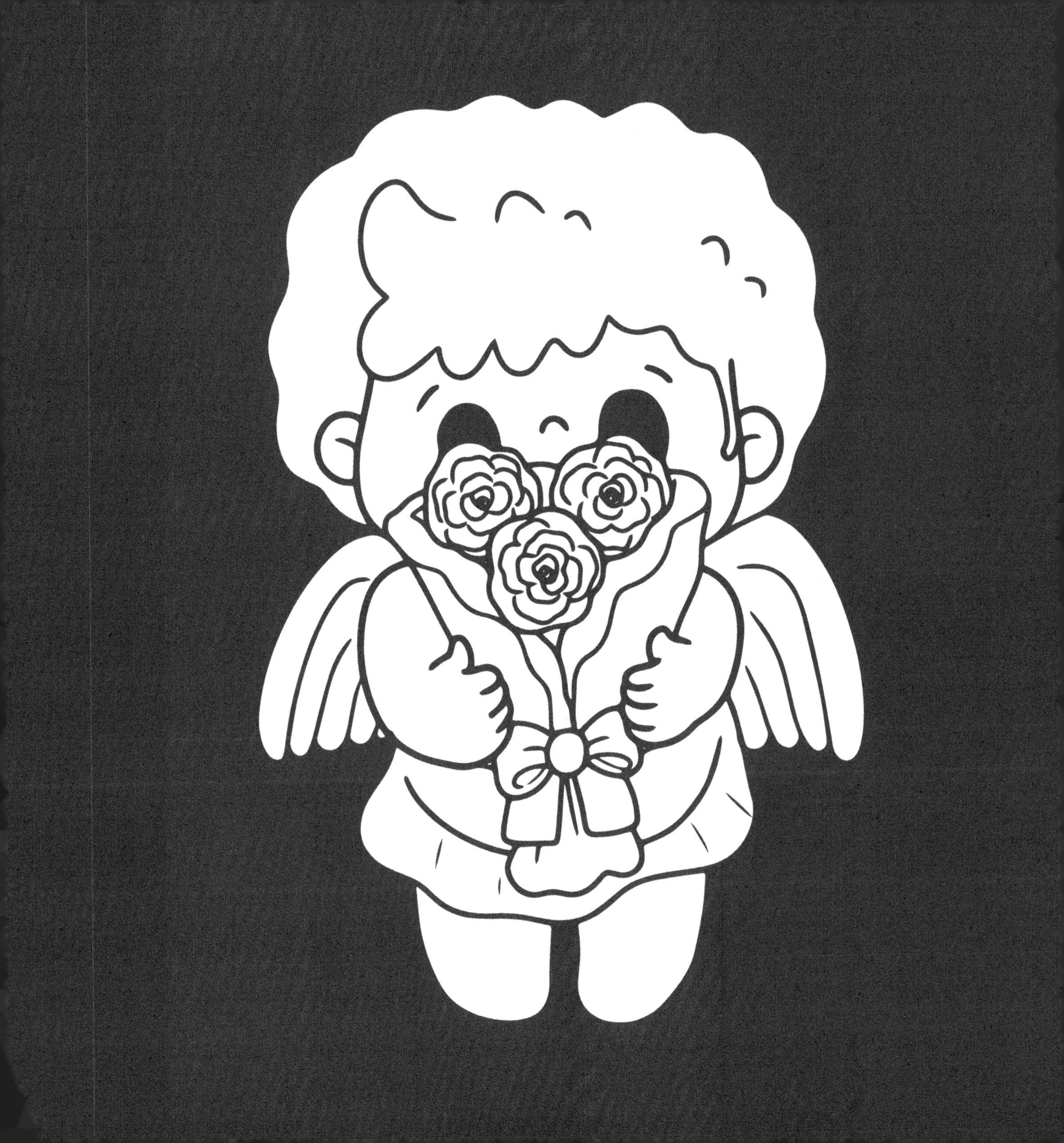

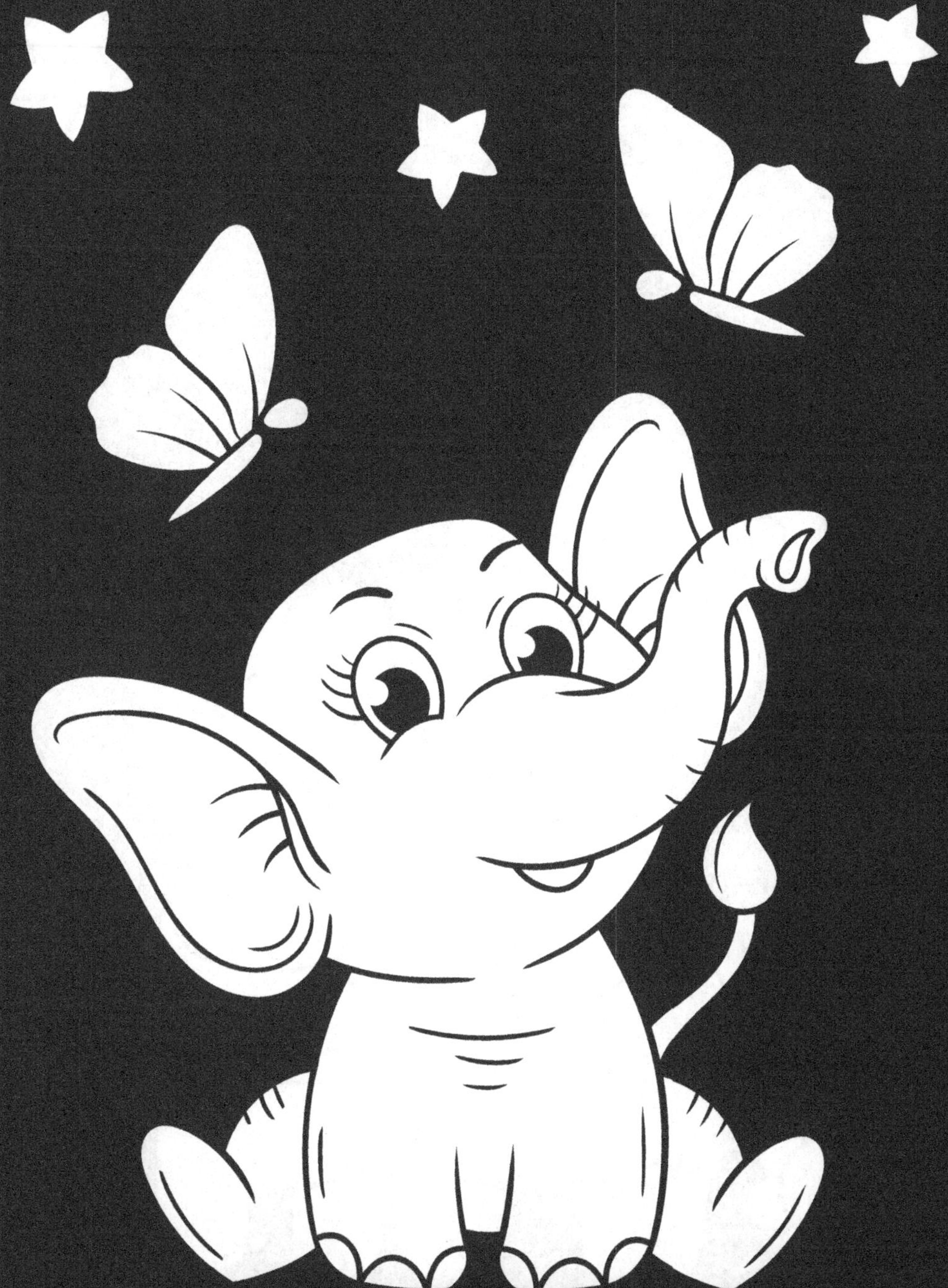

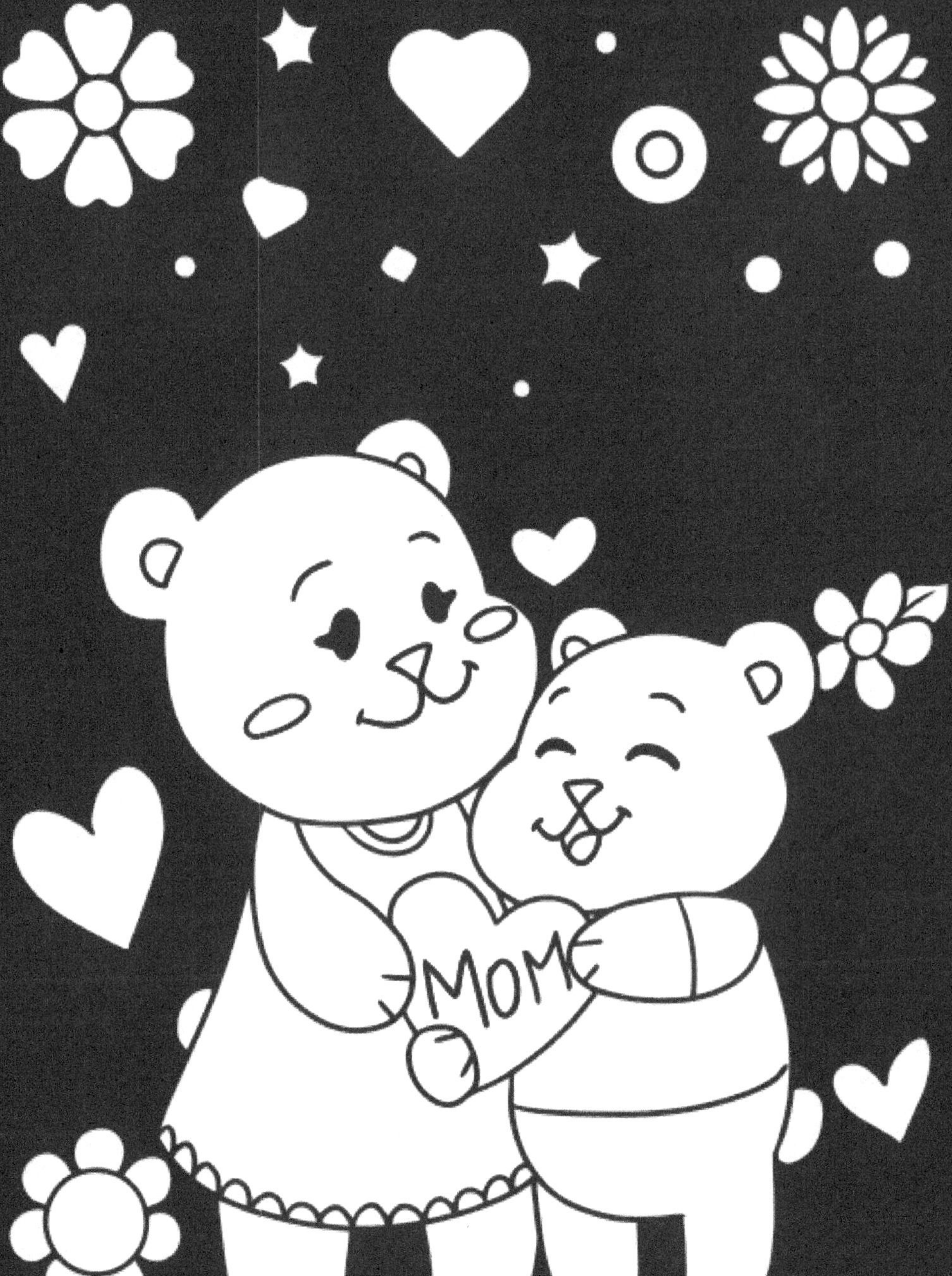
MOM

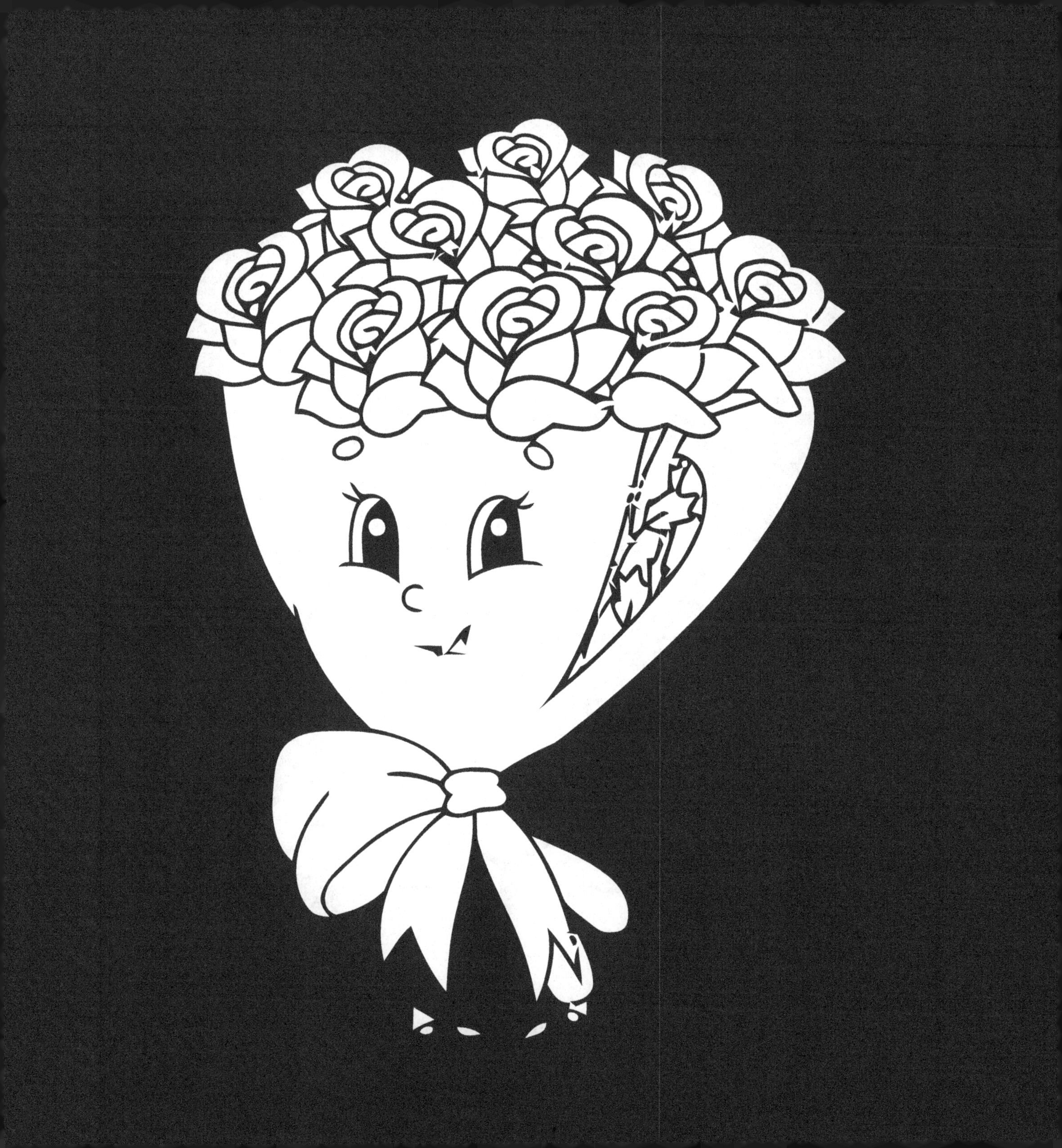

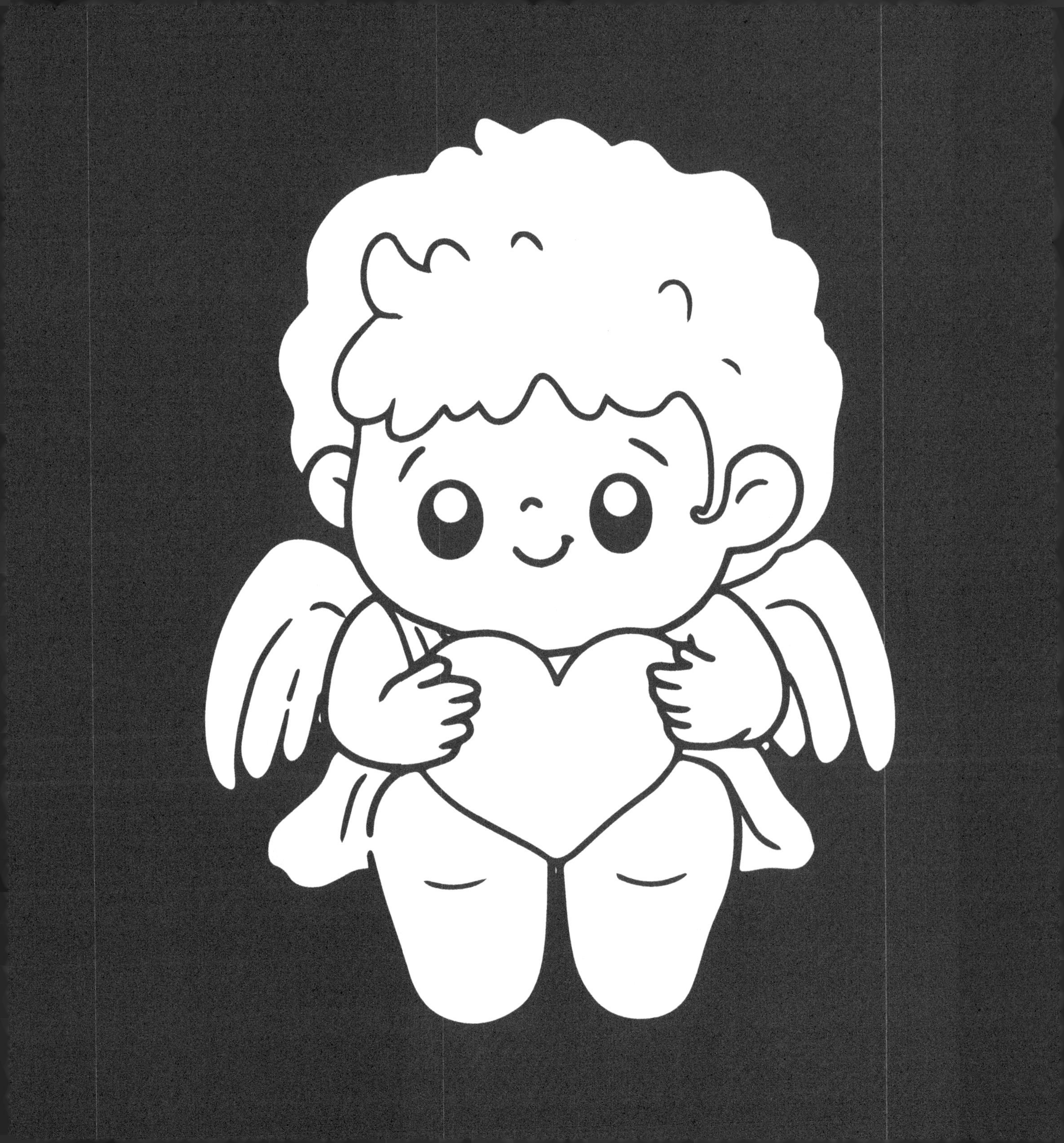

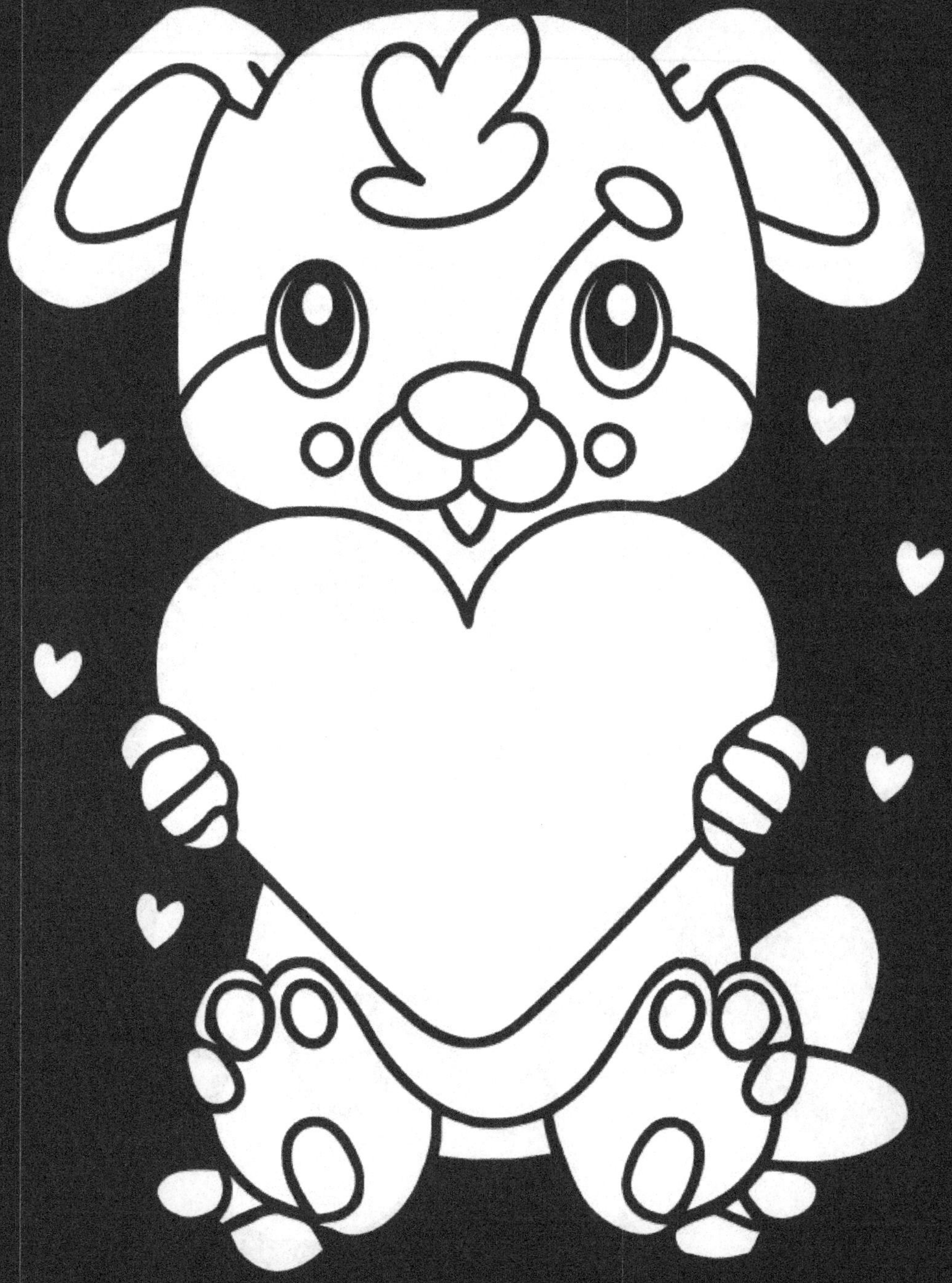

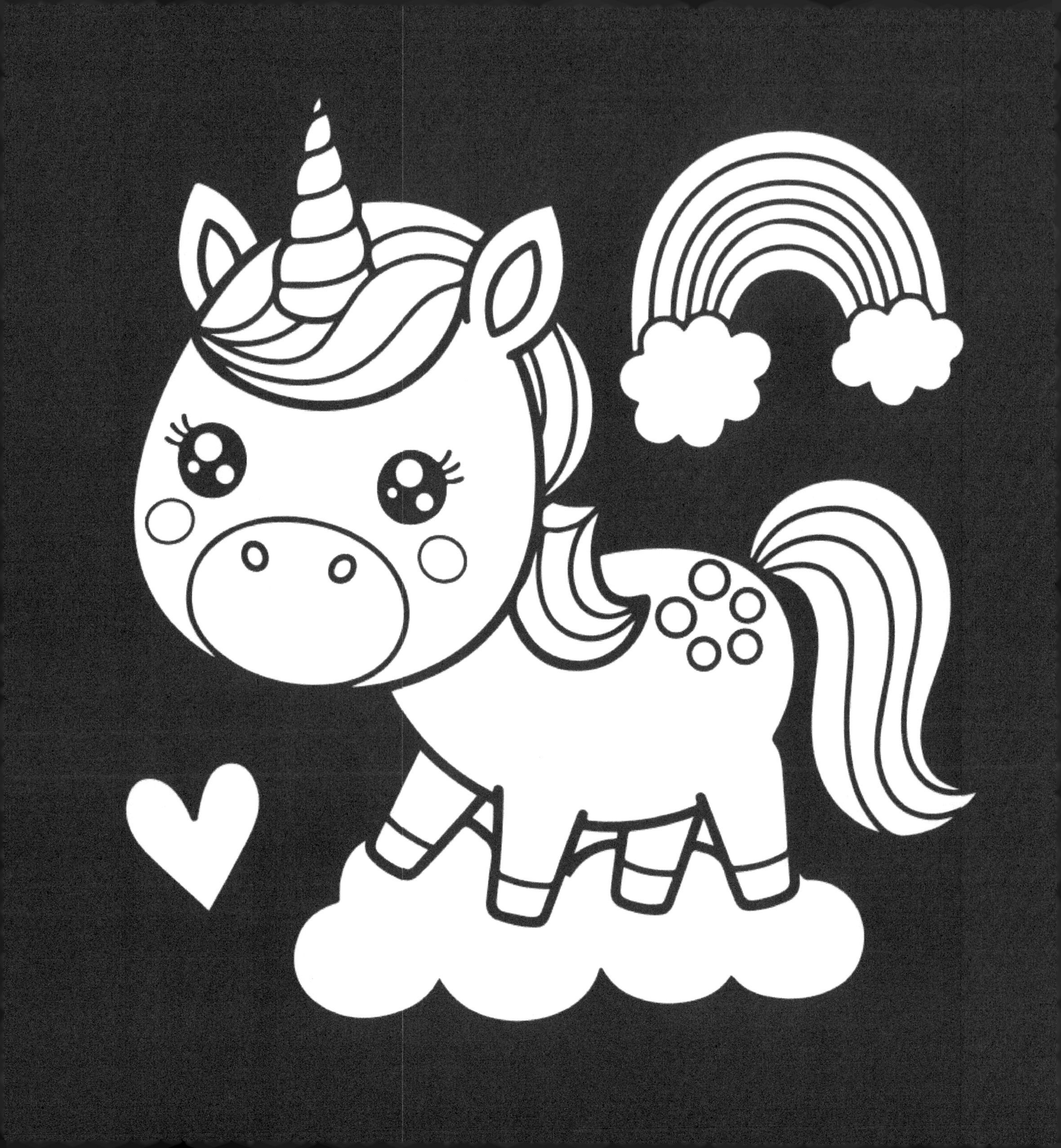

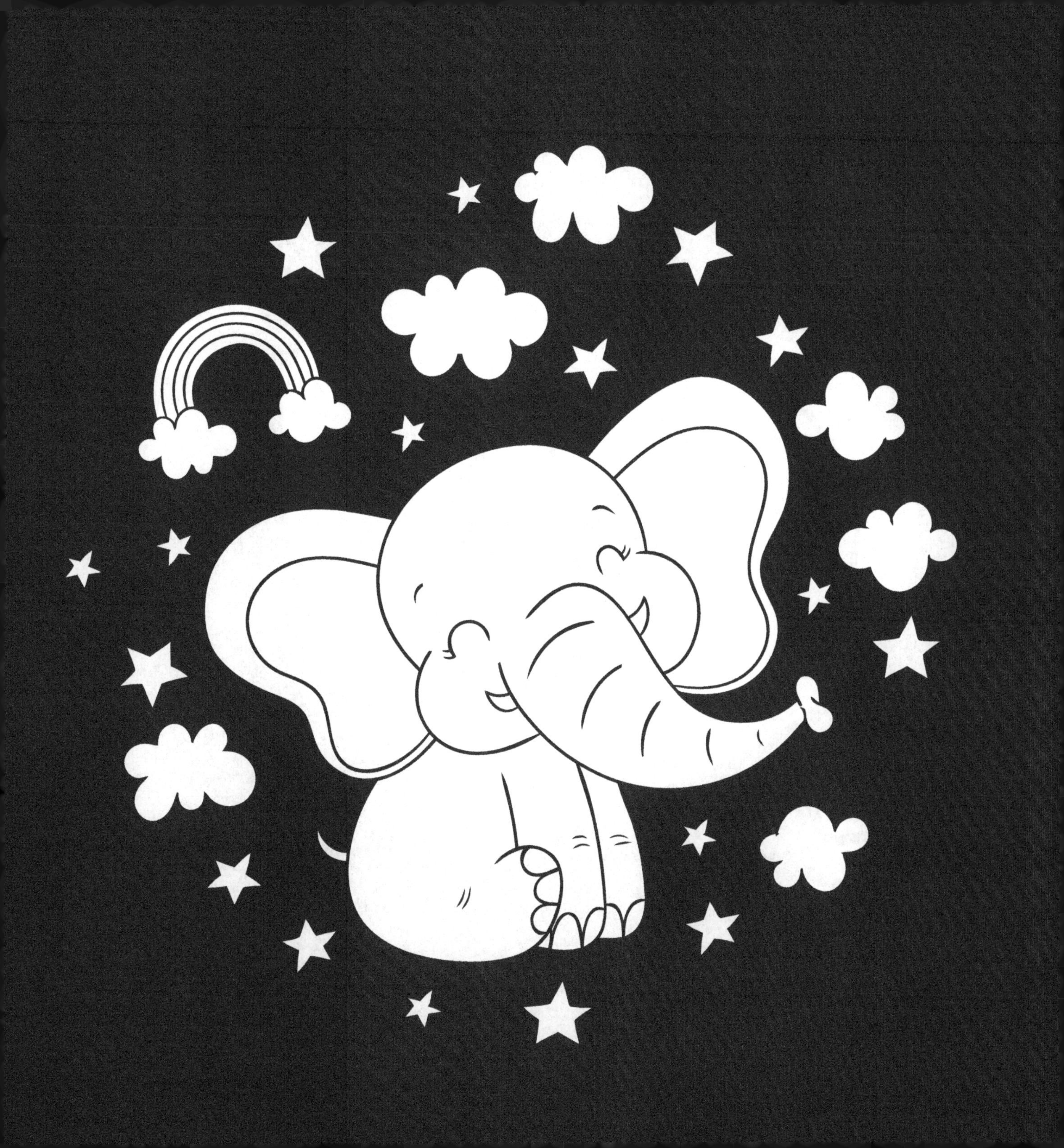

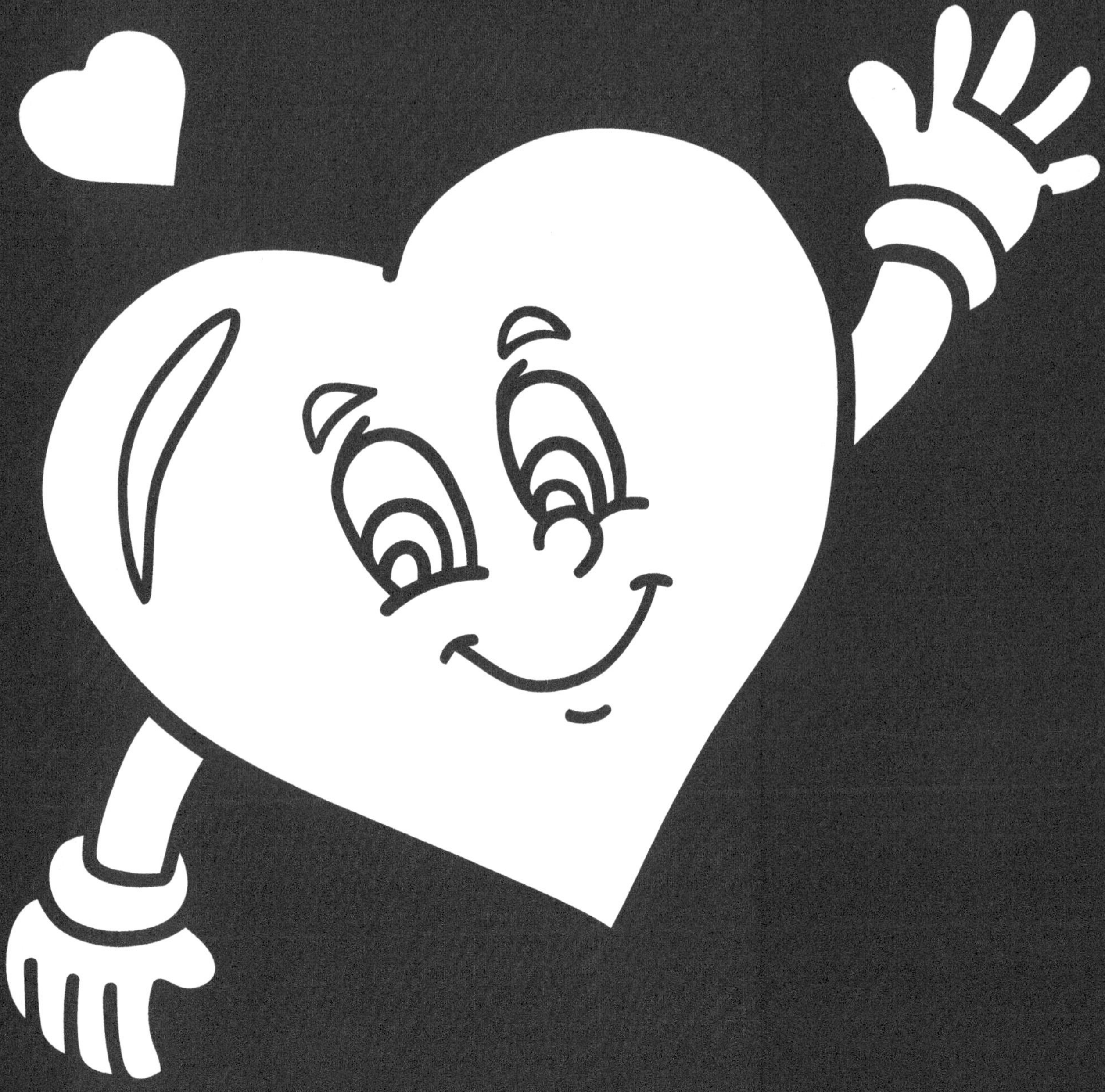

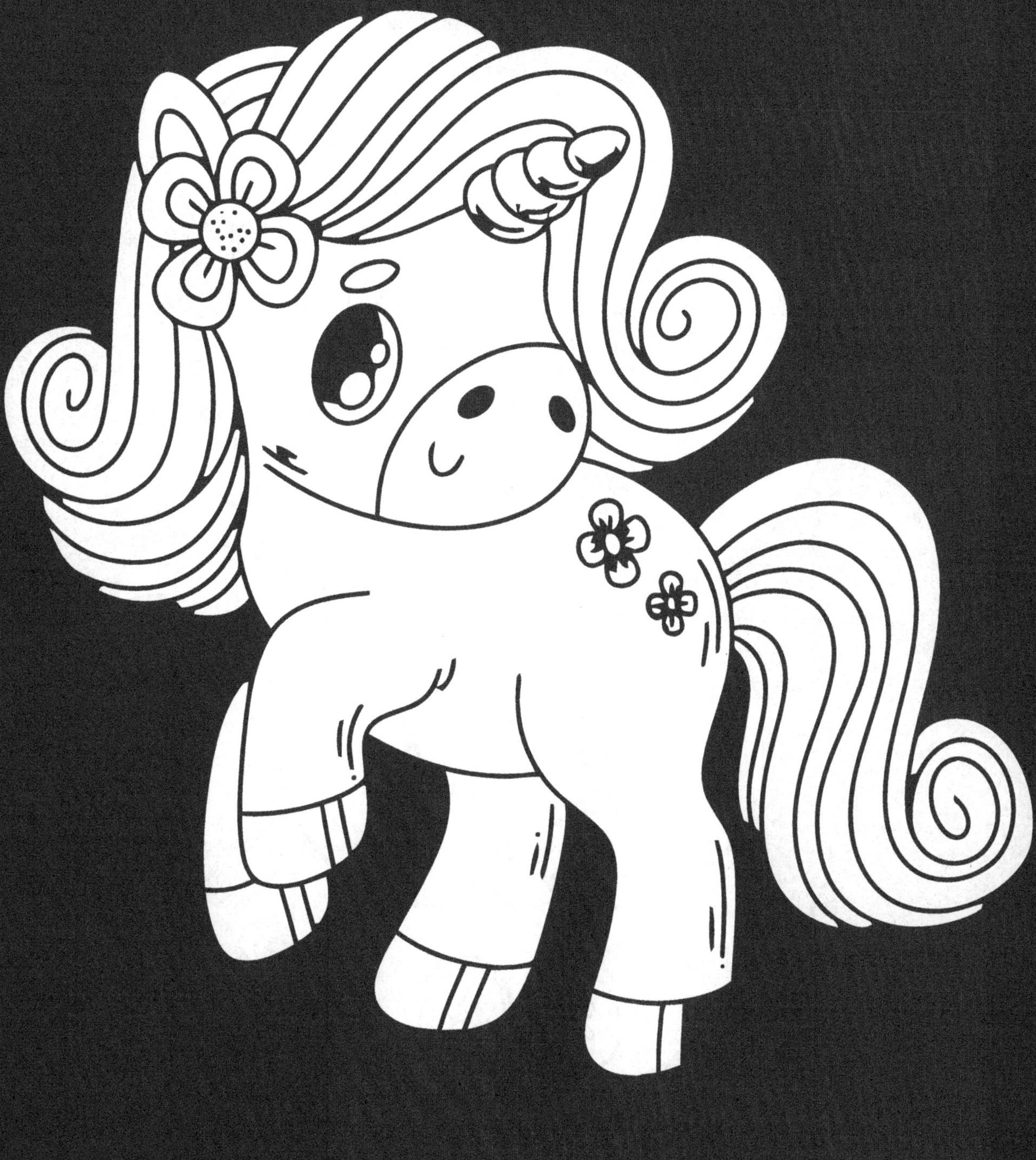

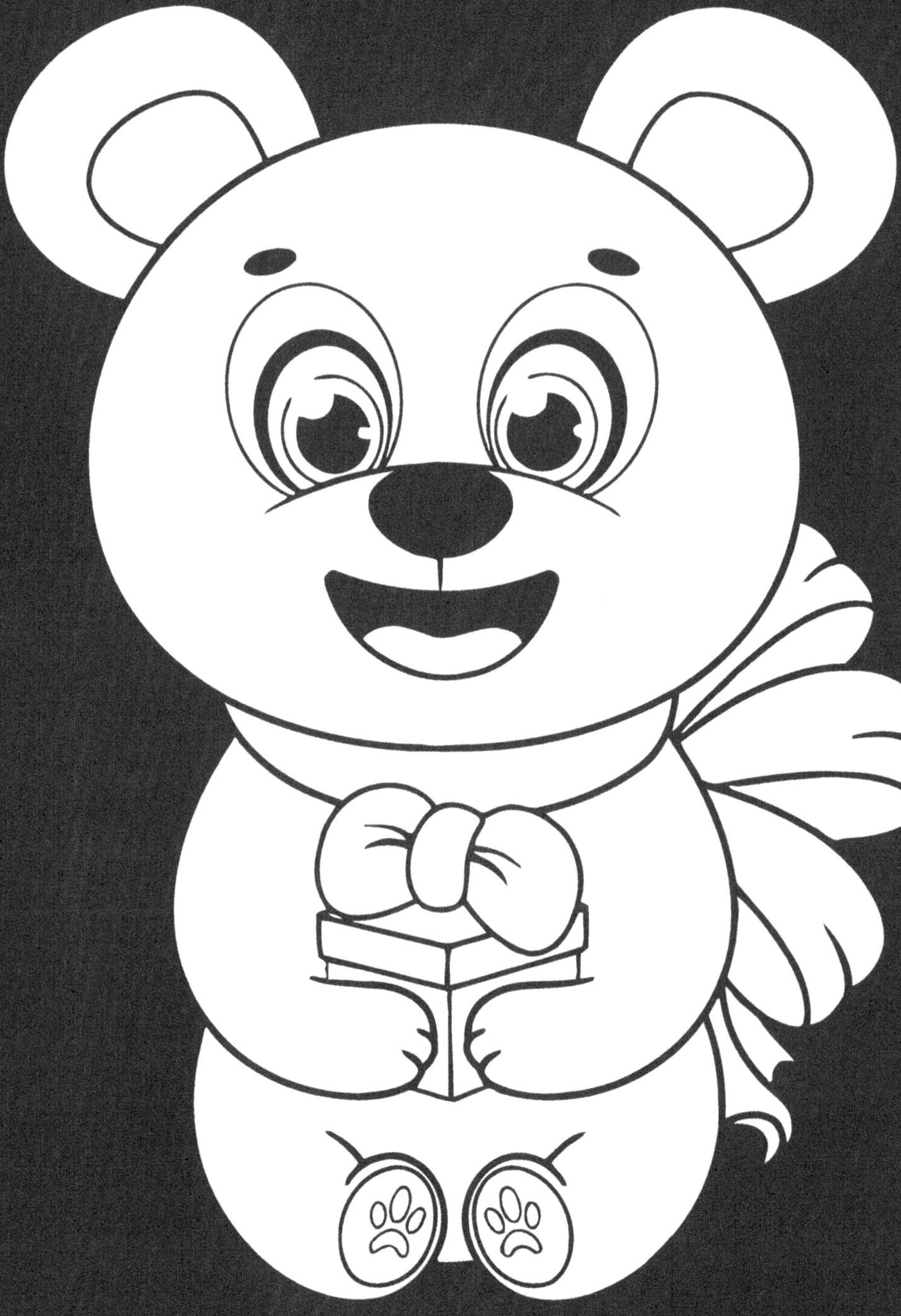

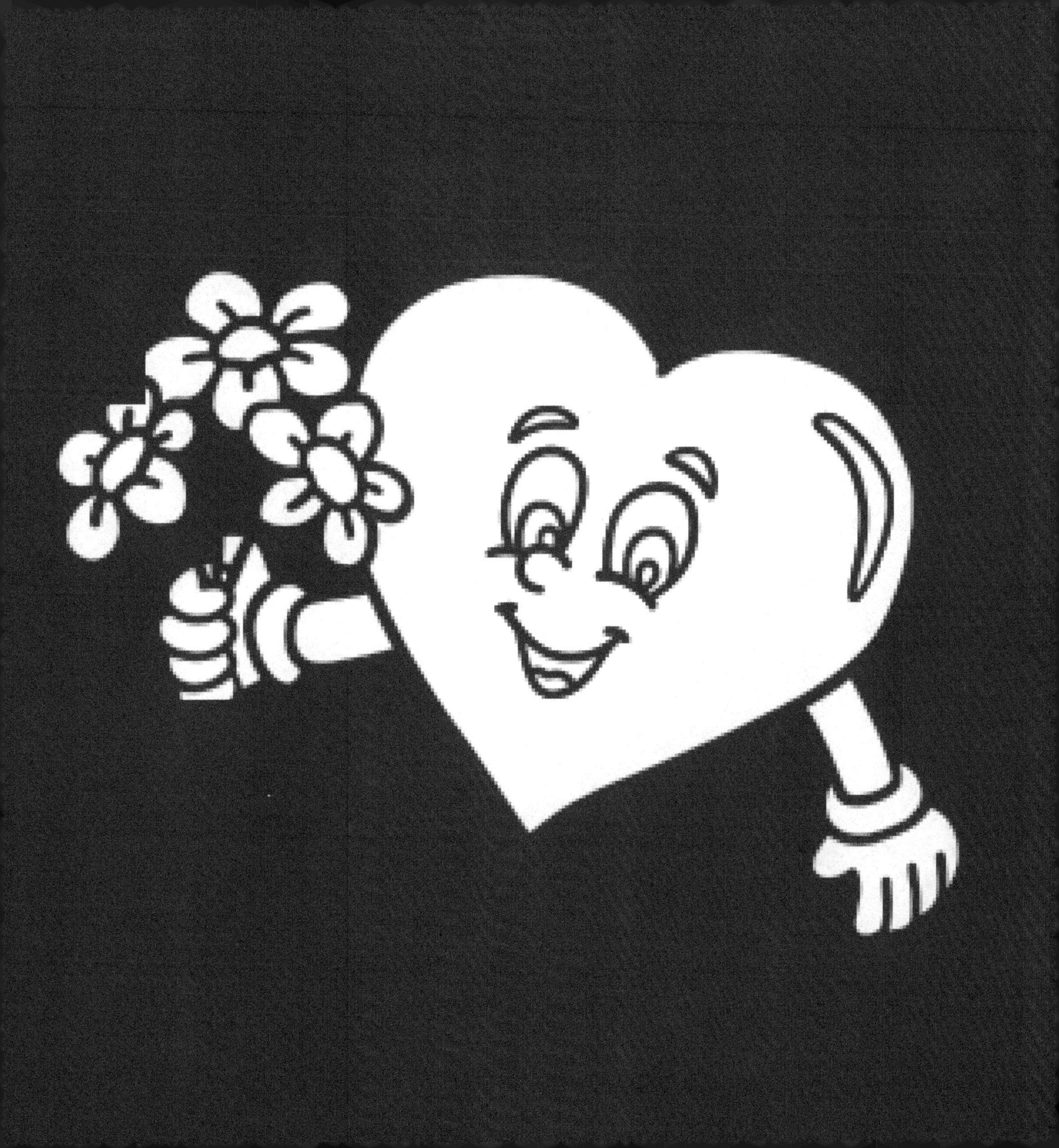

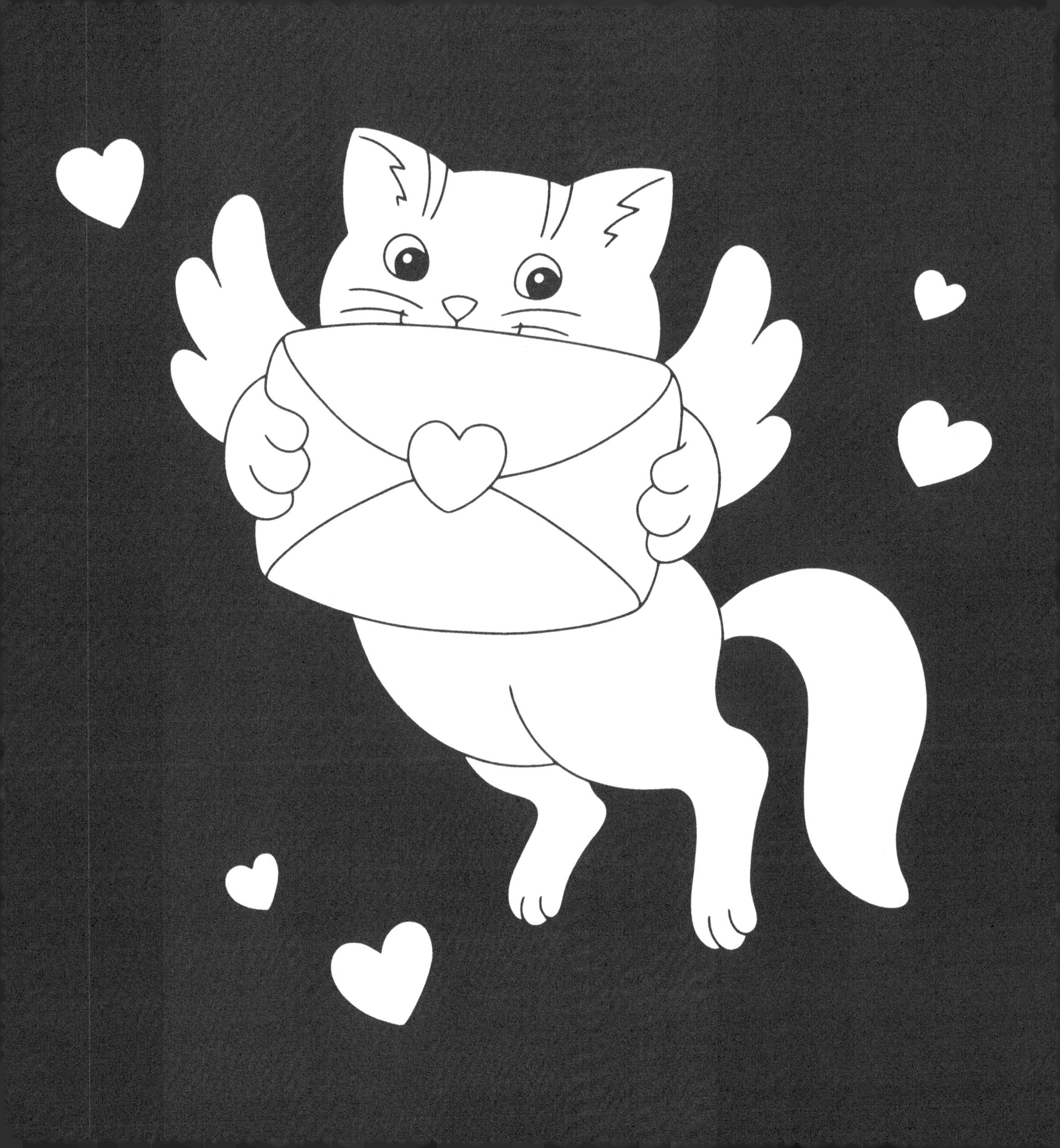

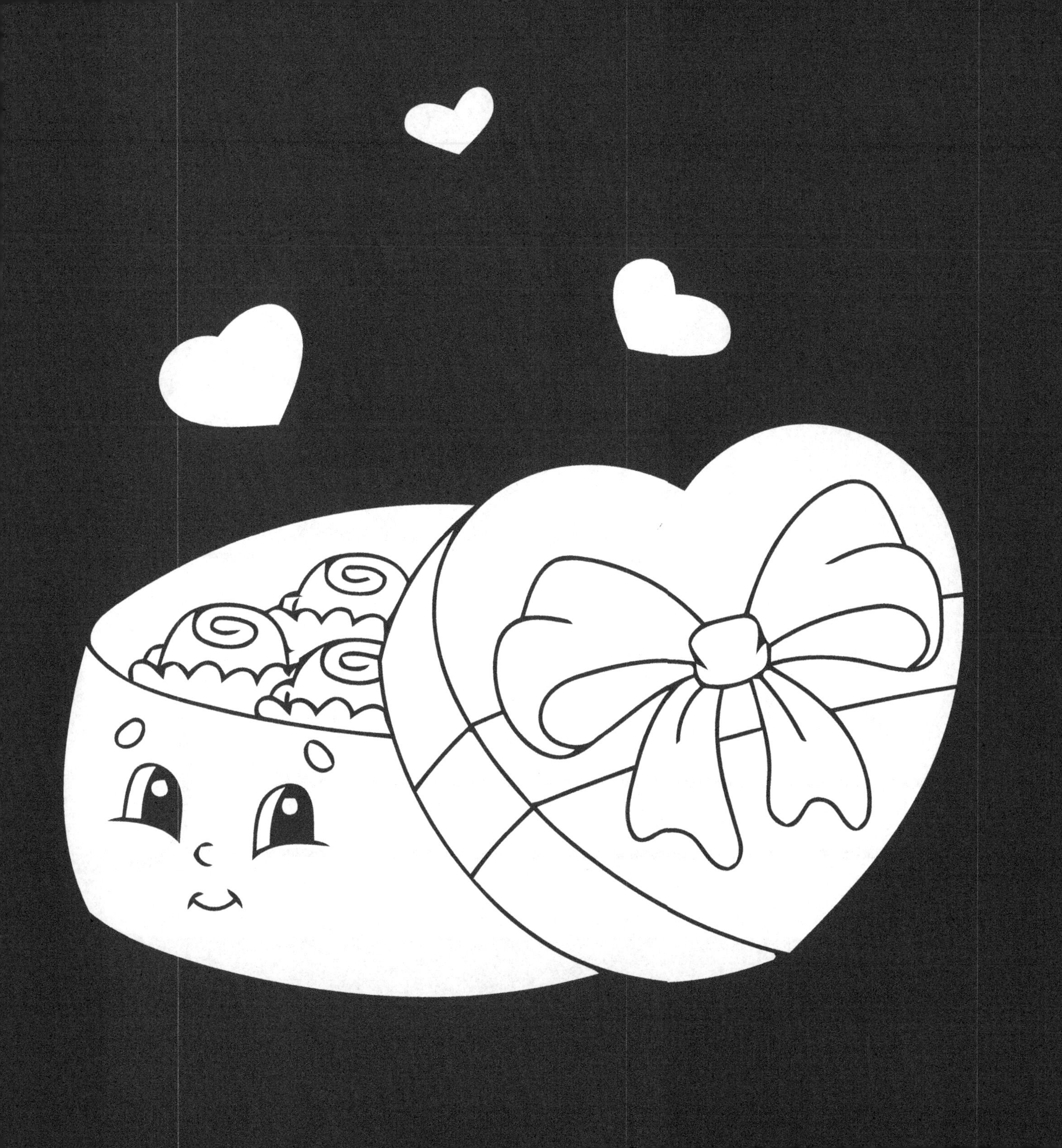

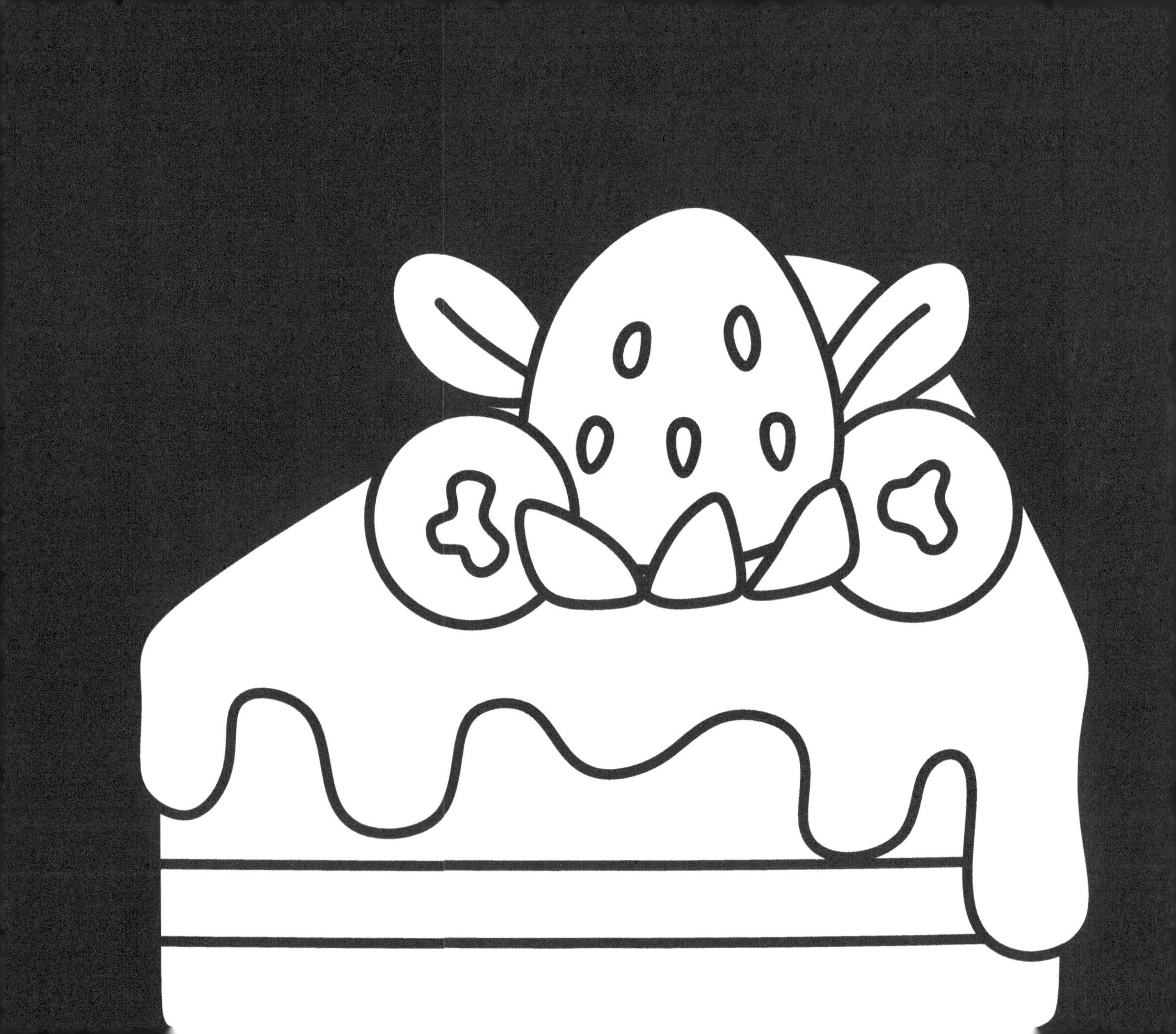

Made in the USA
Columbia, SC
29 January 2025

Pretty Little Psycho

M VIOLET

This book is a work of fiction. Names, characters, places, and incidents either are products of the author's imagination or used fictitiously. Any resemblance to actual events or locales, or persons, living or dead, is entirely coincidental and not intended by the author.

PRETTY LITTLE PSYCHO
M VIOLET

All Rights reserved. Except as permitted under the U.S. Copyright Act of 1976, no part of this publication may be reproduced, distributed, or transmitted in any form or by any means, or stored in a database or retrieval system, without prior consent and permission of the publisher.

Copyright 2023 by M Violet

Cover Design by ARTSCANDARE. All stock photos licensed appropriately.

Edited by Kat Wyeth (Kat's Literary Services)

Formatted by Champagne Book Design

For information on subsidiary rights, please contact the publisher at authormviolet@gmail.com

A Note From The Author

Pretty Little Psycho is a why choose, dark bully romance meant for 18+ readers only. It is a spin-off of the Wickford Hollow Duet. While you don't need to read that one first, I highly recommend it if you want to be fully immersed in this world. Extreme caution is advised before reading *Pretty Little Psycho*. There are many scenes that some may find triggering. Please see the full list of TWs below.

Trigger Warnings

Graphic sex
Graphic language
Graphic violence
Physical assault
Sexual assault
Extreme Bullying
Public humiliation
Kidnapping
Murder
Blood rituals
Cult practices
Sacrilege
Dubious consent
Non consent
Group sex
Sword crossing
Coercion
Manipulation
BDSM

Sex during menstruation
Stalking
Torture
Mutilation
Abuse by a parent
MFMM
MM

Kinks:
Choking
Spanking
Restraints
Sensory deprivation
Poison play
Knife play
Blood play
Praise
Degradation
Breath play
Gagging
Spitting
Anal sex
Double penetration

Playlist

ASK FOR IT (fritz-session)—Diana Goldberg
Psycho—EMM
Cannibal—Fae
Cruel—Jennalyn
All I Want—JEWLS
Good Enemy—PVRIS
Eat Your Young—Arankai
Far From Home (The Raven)—Sam Tinnesz
Sweet Karma (feat. Adam Woods)—Besomorph
I'm Jealous of Everyone—Grace Blue
I Sold My Soul—Gabbie Hanna
STRUT—EMELINE
Give—Sleep Token
Nameless—Stevie Howe
Love Is A…—PVRIS
Tattoo—Loreen
Slayer—Bryce Savage
You Can't Run From Love—Slaz
Pretty In The Dark—Ashley Sienna & Ellise
Guidelines—Masked Wolf
Call on Me (Stripped at SG's)—Tove Lo & SG Lewis
Bad Choices—Kode
Hangman (Villains Edition)—Arankai
Easy to Love—Bryce Savage
Crazy—DeathbyRomy
Take Me First—Bad Omens
What's Wrong—PVRIS
Do or Die—Natalie Jane
Bad Omen—FJORA
No Mourners, No Funerals—Victoria Carbol

*To all my naughty Vixens
This one's for you.*

"Darkness there and nothing more."
—The Raven, Edgar Allan Poe

Pretty Little Psycho

Prologue

Maureen

SOMETIMES THERE'S NOT ENOUGH LIGHT TO CHASE away the darkness. Not enough holy water to cleanse your sins.

I scrubbed the blood off my hands, but its metallic stench still lingers on my skin. That night still haunts me. Like a nightmare that begins as a pretty dream.

I still think about him. The masked man with the piercing blue eyes. He remains lost, nameless. But the memory of his fingers on my back, zipping up my corset in the bathroom at Wickford Mansion after those assholes defiled me, is fresh in my mind. I wanted to stay with him. But I had to go upstairs and murder a man.

I did the right thing…
Fuck.
Did I do the right thing?
Fuck it.
I'd do it again.

Chapter One

Maureen

TENEBROSE ACADEMY IS A BEAUTIFUL MONSTROSITY. It sprawls across the grounds, taking up most of the city of Raven's Gate. A mass of cold stone and pointed arches. It's ominous and sharp and stunning, warning you away. Drawing you in. It gives me breath and yet takes it away. A dark and stormy chaos seems to chant softly from behind its stained-glass windows. Whispers that flutter across my flesh, wrapping around my neck like delicate bony fingers, like twisted vines on iron spires.

"Are you going to stand there all day, or can I get inside before my balls freeze off?" a sharp gravelly voice barks at me from behind.

Breaking out of my trance, I spin around. Oh, fuck. My belly flutters as I meet his icy glare. With black hair and dark brown eyes I can get lost in, the most beautiful yet intimidating man towers over me.

I stumble back. "Sorry. Just taking it all in."

He steps into me, sending chills across my back. "I don't care if you like taking it in the ass, do it somewhere else, freshman."

My mouth drops open. I haven't even been on campus a full hour, and already some asshole, *albeit a gorgeous asshole*, is barking at me. The old me would have snapped back, but I am *trying*, for fuck's sake, to start over.

I can feel the heat rising to my cheeks as I step aside. "Gotcha. Won't happen again."

The beautiful asshole clenches his jaw and continues to stare down his nose at me. "Better not."

When he finally brushes past me, I blow out a deep breath. And I can't help but notice a few students snickering in my direction. *Fuck*. I'm off to a great fucking start.

"I'd stay out of his way, if I were you," a pretty blonde girl whispers next to me. I hadn't even noticed her standing there. She chews on her lower lip as I size her up.

"Oh? And why is that? *Who* was that?" I'd promised myself I would keep my head down here, but now I'm intrigued.

The girl wraps her arms around herself as if she wants to shrink into her own body. "Valentin Erebus. He's dangerous. They all are."

I look back toward the double doors he disappeared behind and my skin prickles. "They? What's so dangerous about—" As I turn back, my breath hitches. The girl is gone. *What the actual fuck?* I scan the front lawn but can't find any sign of her. And now I just look like a lunatic talking to myself.

I start for the doors when a loud squawk makes me jump and almost knock over my luggage. "Fucking hell." I look up to see a raven perched above the archway. Its glare seems to mimic Valentin's. "Well, screw you, too!" I hiss. A few more students whisper and laugh at me as they pass.

An uneasiness washes over me. As excited as I was to come here, something is off. I can't put my finger on it, but a creepy feeling began seeping into my bones the second I drove through those front gates.

I push on the double doors, and my jaw drops open when I enter the lobby. With dark wood-paneled walls, marble floors, and massive stone statues, Tenebrose looks like a museum. There's an iron staircases lined with ornate wall sconces that have actual burning candles in them. I look up to see the ceiling's painted as elaborately as the Sistine Chapel in a mural of runes, botanical elements, and alchemical symbols. I inhale a deep breath. Even the air smells and tastes different here.

The other students bustle around me seemingly unaffected by the visual onslaught of Victorian Gothic ambience. They don't even look up or around as they chatter with each other about their class schedules and their dorm room assignments. Am I the only one here who is blown away by all of this? It feels like at any second Edgar Allan Poe himself could come around the corner.

And then it dawns on me. These students are used to this. I'm a long way from Wickford Hollow—my sleepy small town where our idea of fun is breaking into abandoned houses, eating sweet potato fries at Ruby's Diner, and getting so drunk you forget your own name. Oh, and it's full of dead people walking around as if they are still alive. I understand creepy and weird, but this place is on a different level of macabre. How am I supposed to fit in here?

Hi, my name's Maureen. My mother hates me for being born, my father is the town Sheriff and also the town drunk. I've fucked half the football team, mostly while I was unconscious. Oh, and I did I mention my best friend is a ghost?

Fuck. I've only been gone for a day, and I already miss Bailey. She's my ride-or-die. Literally. Yeah, I'm sure people will be lining up to hang out with me. Ugh.

I make my way inside the admissions office, shuffling ahead of a group of girls who are prattling on about all the parties they can't wait to go to. The door swings open as I reach for it, and I walk straight into a wall of solid muscle. I gaze up only to lock eyes with the beautiful asshole from earlier. Fuck.

"You, again. For fuck's sake. Didn't anyone show you the proper way to walk through a doorway?"

I can feel that same heat rising to my cheeks again. His arrogance is astounding. "Seems like you walked into me."

Valentin clenches his jaw. His eyes darken while his nostrils flare. "Are you calling me a liar, freshman?"

The girls behind me gasp and stop talking. They are clearly afraid of him as much as the mystery girl from outside is. But I'd dealt with my fair share of monsters this summer. The things I've done…

I tilt my chin up. "I'm simply pointing out that maybe you should also watch where you're walking."

One of the girls behind me literally whimpers.

He cocks his head to the side and a strand of shiny black hair falls over his eye. It makes him look sexy and provocative and dangerous as hell. I hold my breath and wonder if I should have just kept my mouth shut. Fuck, I'm always taking things too far. Why can't I be more fucking docile?

When he takes another step closer, I almost stumble back. Looking up, I notice just how square his shoulders are, the flex of his chest as it stretches his T-shirt across his pectoral muscles. He's lean but strong, chiseled and carved like a piece of stone. And as my breath catches in my throat, I get a whiff of roses and cedar mixed with embalming fluid. When your best friend owns a mortuary, you become familiar with that scent.

Valentin licks his lips as his dark eyes flicker with something hungrier—feral. "I'll be watching a lot more closely now, freshman." He tugs on the hem of my skirt, and I bounce forward. Butterflies swarm my belly as he leans down and whispers in my ear, "I'll be watching your every move. No one disrespects me and gets away with it. *Not even needy girls with pretty mouths and hard nipples.*"

Holy fuck. I glance down my shirt to see that my tits have indeed betrayed me by way of two stiff peaks poking out from under my thin cotton blouse. But before I can fire back or even process what he said, Valentin Erebus has brushed past me, leaving me and the entire office speechless. And judging by the pale faces and looks of terror, I have a feeling that I just pissed off the one person I shouldn't have.

Fucking great. Off to a smashing start.

The line moves rather quickly and within minutes I'm at the front. "Maureen Blackwell." I shove my ID across the counter toward the pale lady with jet-black hair. She narrows her dark eyes at me while typing furiously into her computer. I avert my gaze to her name tag, focusing on the sharp letters that spell out *Miss Florian*.

"Here we go," she states. I flinch as the printer squeaks. *Why am I so fucking jumpy?* "This is your class schedule. Make sure you familiarize yourself with it thoroughly. Our esteemed professors do not tolerate tardiness, absences, or insolence." The lines on her face seem to get sharper the more she talks. "Here is a map of our campus. It would do you well to memorize it. It can be easy for one to get lost." She pauses and looks up over the rim of her glasses, her eyes narrowing. "Do not get lost, Miss Blackwell. The fog is thick, the shadows are dark, and the ground is hallowed. Not all who wander can be found."

I swallow down the lump in my throat as goose pimples tickle the backs of my arms. That eerie feeling I had when I first drove through the gates returns. Where I'm from, the dead walk around freely. It's the devil I know. But Raven's Gate is disorienting. I nod my head for her to continue because she seems to think I need to acknowledge her words before she'll go on.

Miss Florian sighs as her hand starts moving around the map again. "Dormitories are on the east end of the property near the Mourning Café and the campus bar. All paths are clearly marked, do not venture off them."

"Right, got it. Don't get lost in the woods." A larger structure catches my eye near the graveyard. I place a pointy, black-painted fingernail on it. "What is this place? It's unmarked."

Miss Florian snatches the map off the counter and stuffs it into a folder with my schedule and a few other papers. "A word of advice, Miss Blackwell—keep your questions focused on your studies and you'll get through this unscathed."

Get through this?

She smacks the folder into my hands along with a key which I assume is for my dorm room. "Good day, Miss Blackwell."

Before I can utter another word, I'm shoved aside by the group of girls behind me. Miss Florian throws me one more side glance but it's so subtle I wonder if I imagined it. I stuff the folder into my purse and spin on my heel, dragging my luggage behind me.

The rain's coming down hard by the time I make my way outside and back to my car. If I had known how big this campus was, and that I'd be driving to my room, I wouldn't have lugged all my bags out like an idiot. Another reason why people are staring and snickering at me, I'm sure. I load everything back into the trunk and let out a sigh as I look toward the main hall.

This place has secrets. I feel it in my bones. But so do I. And mine are dark enough to make the devil smile. But I came here to start over. To leave all that behind. So I need to keep my head down and take Miss Florian's advice—don't ask too many questions and stick to the designated paths. Because the last time I went wandering, I killed a man. A chill trickles down my spine. *No more murder, Maur.*

༄

I can barely see through my windshield as the rain turns into a torrential downpour. Through the thick fog, I inch along, praying my old clunker of a car makes it the last stretch. Bailey had insisted on loaning me her Mercedes, but I refused. She's already paying my tuition and giving me spending money. Best friend or not, I won't be anyone's charity case. And I have every intention of paying her back in full.

I pull up to the *dormitories* and my blood runs cold. *More like Dracula's castle.* I lean forward, straining to see through the violence of my windshield wipers at full speed. "*Fuck*," I mutter under my breath.

Its stone walls are covered in a thick layer of rotting vines and black roses. As if decay were a living thing and actively consuming the building, piece by piece. If it weren't for the flicker of lights from some of the windows, I'd think it was abandoned. I gaze up higher, following its sharp lines all the way up to the two points that threaten to stab the heavens. It has to be at least six stories.

A massive iron sign hangs between two posts: *The Nest*. I blow out a deep breath and pull into the closest parking spot I can find. By the time I reach the entrance, I look like a drowned rat. I'm kicking myself now for not allowing my dad to come along to help. Although, the last thing I want is for anyone here to find out that I'm a phony.

Even though I've never met my mother's family, I decided to register under their last name because they're fucking rich as hell. But they cut ties with my mom the second she got pregnant with me, so we never saw a penny of it. In Wickford Hollow, I'm just the Sheriff's daughter. But I can't be that here. They'll ask too many questions. Tenebrose Academy is the most expensive school in the country. And I don't want to have to explain how my dead best friend is footing the bill. Hence why I'm lugging all my shit through the rain by myself—so no one will find out that I don't belong here.

The main floor of the dormitory is cozier than I expect. On the farthest side of the room, there's a massive stone fireplace surrounded by brown leather couches. A few students gather around it, completely oblivious to my presence. A knot forms in my stomach. Everyone here seems to know each other already…

"Need a hand?" a tiny voice squeaks out.

I jump. "Jesus, where the fuck did you come from?"

The pretty but weird as fuck blonde girl from earlier smooths her hands over the purple and black lace of my largest suitcase. It's almost as big as her. "Sorry, I didn't mean to sneak up on you. Professor Erebus always says I'm too light-footed for my own good."

As I look closer at her, I notice her eyes are bright blue like a neon sign. But their intensity is masked by the dark circles under them. She looks like she hasn't slept in days. Her skin is pale with just a slight tinge of pink dotting her cheekbones.

"*Professor* Erebus? I thought that asshole was a student."

She purses her lips. "Valentin *is* a student. Julian, um Professor Erebus I mean, is his uncle."

I slump down onto my middle-sized suitcase, using it as a

makeshift chair, and whip out my class schedule. "Awesome. I have his Gothic Lit class first period and his nephew already hates me."

She studies my face, looking at me as if I'm the most interesting thing she's ever seen. "I think you can handle him."

I snort. "You don't know me."

Her eyes widen, and she shoves her hand toward me. "How rude of me. I'm Jessamine. But you can call me Jess."

I hesitate for a second before taking her hand and shaking it. "So proper, aren't you? I'm Maureen… Blackwell."

Jessamine's eyes widen again. "Oh, you're from Ever Graves?"

Fuck. I have to remind myself that I'm using a name that really doesn't belong to me. "Um, no not exactly. My mother is from there originally. But I grew up in Wickford Hollow."

She nods. "Well, it's lovely to meet you, Maureen." She grabs my key. "Follow me, I'll show you where your room is. We'll have to take the elevator. Looks like they put you on the top floor. You must be special."

I cock my head to the side. "Not sure what that means but if you say so." *Fuck, I thought Wickford Hollow was strange.* If I'm so special then maybe I'd have a room that wasn't the farthest away from the front door. Guess I won't be snoozing my alarm on Monday morning if it's going to take me twenty minutes just to get down here.

After helping me load all my crap into the elevator, Jessamine and I squeeze in, and she hits the button for the seventh floor. "The ravens keep watch on the roof. Don't feed them, though. Or they'll always expect it."

Is this chick for real? "Noted. Don't feed the birds." What in the actual fuck did I just sign up for?

"Don't call them that," she hisses. "They'll hear you… The ravens are so much more than just birds."

I'm starting to wonder if this girl even goes to school here. I might have just gotten into an enclosed space with a tiny deranged serial killer. My eyes dart to one of my smaller bags, remembering the knife Bailey tucked into it. "My bad," I mumbled.

Jessamine unclenches her jaw and smiles. "It's okay. You're new here. But you'll be one of us soon."

I nod, unsure of what else to say that won't elicit more of this bizarre rambling.

The doors open, revealing a lavish space, and my jaw drops. How can this be *my* room? I step inside to find myself in a small apartment with floor-to-ceiling windows, a sunken living room, and a small kitchen. I spin around in circles, taking it all in. "This must be a mistake. Are all the rooms like this?" I find it hard to believe that every dorm room has its own private elevator entrance.

Jessamine giggles. "No, silly. Only families of Ever Graves get these. Like I said, you're special."

My heart is literally pounding. Fuck. I don't belong here. How long before the school realizes that the Blackwells cut my mom off twenty-five years ago? I should have just registered under Maureen Gray. I came here to blend in with the crowd, not be the center of it. This *room* is anything but subtle.

I walk to the window and draw back one of the black velvet curtains. Peering down at the headlights below, a wave of nausea takes hold of me. I shake my head, my palms sweating. "I'll talk to them about this tomorrow. I can't stay in this room."

"Not up to your standards, Blackwell?" a girl's voice calls from behind followed by the sound of heels clicking across the marble floor.

I turn around to see a tall blonde girl with thick pouty lips and eyes the color of sea glass. Her slinky black dress hugs her curves like a lover's embrace, making me suddenly feel like I'm dressed in rags. "Who the fuck are you and where's Jessamine?"

She scrunches her eyebrows together. "*Jessa-who?*"

I sigh. "The tiny fairy-looking girl who was helping me bring my stuff up? She was just here."

She looks even more confused than I feel. "No idea what you're talking about. I hope you aren't always like this. Blackwell or not, I refuse to live with a weirdo."

My stomach drops. "*Oh.* You're my roommate… Sorry. I'm Maureen."

She snickers while looking at me up and down. "Yeah, I know. My name's Libra. Libra Thorn. And I can't wait to see the look on Riot's face when he finds out *you're* here."

I'm seriously starting to think someone slipped acid into my coffee this morning because this is all unreal. Like maybe I'm just having a bad trip in my basement back in Wickford Hollow. "I'm sorry, but you must think I'm someone else. I don't know anyone named Riot."

Libra shrugs. "Doesn't matter. Our names define us here at Tenebrose. You're a Blackwell. I'm a Thorn. How else do you think we got a whole floor all to ourselves?"

While a part of me wants to be excited, this whole thing feels wrong. Not to mention my other little blonde friend who keeps appearing and disappearing without warning. "Yeah, again, I think there's been a mix-up. I'll figure it out in the morning."

"Classes don't start till Monday," Libra hisses. "Now, go clean up. We have a party to get to. For fuck's sake, you look like you fell into the ocean."

The nerve of this bitch. Who talks like that to someone they've known for five minutes? But I'm not naïve to the fact that Libra Thorn is a spoiled rich girl. I can tell she's used to getting what she wants and she's not afraid to push people around to get it.

I look back toward the elevator, suddenly preferring the

weirdness of Jessamine over this bitchy beauty queen. "Look, I've been driving all day and just dragged all my shit through a thunderstorm. Not really in the mood to party."

I actually can't believe those words came out of my mouth. I *was* the fucking party in Wickford Hollow. But something about this place makes me want to curl up under the covers and cry myself to sleep.

Libra stalks over and glares down at me. "Listen, we don't have to be besties, but you will attend the parties. I've spent my entire life curating my image and part of that is having my own floor with a roommate who is equal in stature. Everyone expects us to be there tonight. If I go alone, the families will look weak. And if that happens, I will make your life a living hell."

Yep, should have just registered as Maureen Gray and told everyone I'm on financial aid or something. Fuck me. I tilt my chin up. "Fine. But threaten me again, and I'll stab you in your sleep."

Libra grins. "That's more like it. See, I knew you were a Blackwell."

I don't know who the fuck I'm supposed to be now. But the vibe in the air tells me I'm going to have to decide real soon.

Chapter Two

Riot

EYES LIKE BURNT HONEY… FUCK. EVERY TIME I GO TO sleep I dream of her. And when I wake, her essence lingers on my soul like an unholy stain. It takes every ounce of strength I have not to charge back to Wickford Hollow and capture her. Put her in a pretty cage so I can take her out and play with her whenever I want.

I don't even know her name… She's just my firecracker. *Mine.* But I can't leave Raven's Gate again. I'm weak when I'm away. So, I can only dream about her. I imagine her full lips wrapped around my cock as I stroke myself. The rose-scented bathwater splashes onto the floor as I grapple with my massive erection.

I don't even notice the bathroom door open. "There are plenty of girls waiting to fuck you, Riot. My cousin is one of them. Let me call her for you. Forget about the Wickford Hollow slut."

I glare at my friend with contempt. With white-blond hair and blue-green eyes, he truly resembles a Greek god. All of the Thorns do. "I prefer self-inflicted torture, Atlas," I grumble back.

He perches on the edge of the tub and watches me continue to rub one out. "Such a fucking masochist."

The pressure builds in my shaft as I throw my head back against the porcelain. "Fuck…" I rub my thumb over the tip of my cock and trace the edges of my latest sigil. A mark of virility.

Atlas reaches in and touches it as well. I shiver as the heat from his finger sends a tingle to my core. "It's healed nicely." He drags his fingers up and down my shaft, and I release a moan.

"You'll get yours soon enough," I murmur.

"Mmm… how about now?" He licks his lips and withdraws his hand.

I glare at him again. "Always so impatient. Take off your pants."

Atlas wastes no time taking off his black T-shirt and jeans. He smirks as he pulls a tiny vial of green liquid out from one of the pockets and takes a small swig. I watch as his veins turn from blue to green as the poison travels through him. His muscles clench and then relax.

I finish jerking myself off—moaning as my cum shoots out in thick white ropes. It paints the side of the tub before the water rinses it away. It's the release I need, but it's not as satisfying without my firecracker watching. I sigh and stand up as Atlas leans back against the red velvet sitting chair. He spreads his legs wide, offering his flesh to me.

I open a drawer and pull out my ritual box. The lid pops open with a snap of my fingers. My knife, *the blade of ravens*, gleams back at me, all shiny black and silver. I kneel down between his legs and get a firm grip on his cock. "Do you accept this mark?"

Atlas takes another swig of the green poison. Swirls of light dance in his eyes. "I do."

I press the tip of the blade to his abdomen. "In absentia lucis, tenebrae vincunt." *In the absence of light, darkness prevails.*

We pay with our blood. With our flesh. We make these sacrifices for our souls. For our lives. I begin to carve the rune into his flesh. He doesn't flinch but instead moans as his blood trickles down his shaft. I smear it in deeper, rubbing it in circles around the tip of his cock.

His eyes blaze with power as I finish carving the last line. A soft whimper escapes from his throat. "Mors tua, vita mea." *Your death, my life.*

I coat his entire cock with his own blood as tears spill from his eyes. The sigil burns bright, glowing red against his creamy alabaster skin.

Valentin comes through the door and rests his hands on Atlas's shoulders. He places a soft kiss on his cheek. "Mors vincit omnia." *Death always wins.*

Atlas throws his head back against the chair and releases a deep guttural moan. His silky white cum leaks out onto my fingers. I smear it into the blood and over his freshly carved sigil. "*For the raven,*" I breathe.

"For the raven," they both whisper back.

It *should* be the only time I don't long for my firecracker. When we are deep in ritual. But in fact, this is when I hunger for her more. I ache for it. To mark her with my power.

"You're thinking about her again, aren't you?" Valentin grumbles.

I watch the blood run down the drain as I wash my hands,

admiring the way it swirls against the porcelain, changing from dark red to pink. "No," I lie. I slowly glance up at myself in the mirror, wondering how much longer I can go without her. I run a hand through my black hair, tousling it between my scarred fingers. So many marks... I will soon run out of skin.

Atlas stands behind me, our eyes connecting in the mirror. "Tell us again."

I'd recounted the brief exchange to my two best friends a dozen times since Halloween. "I was bored and there was a party in Wickford Hollow. So I went."

Valentin hissed. "I still can't believe you went there by yourself. What if one of the Blackwells had been there?"

"Relax," I snapped. "I'm more than fucking capable of handling them on my own. Besides, there aren't any Blackwells in Wickford Hollow. I wore my ski mask. No one knew who the fuck I was."

Atlas fingers his freshly carved scar, dabbing at the blood that stains the skin around it. "And the firecracker?"

I sigh. Every time I tell them about her they both get hard as fuck. And they haven't even seen her like I have. "I stalked her through the house, watching the way her throat bobbed every time she took a drink. The way her sweat trickled down in between her tits. I watched as those bastards herded her into the bathroom..." I grip the edge of the counter, my heart racing from the memory. Atlas and Valentin each place a hand on my shoulder.

"Go on," Atlas murmurs.

"She was half-naked and covered in their cum." I inhale a deep breath as I remember the moment I looked into her jeweled eyes—honey-gold like she had two pieces of citrine in her sockets. "She wouldn't tell me her name. I didn't give her mine. I zipped up her bustier and it took every ounce of strength I had not to drag her back here with me that night..." I still wake up in a cold sweat and for a split-second think I see her dark brown hair splayed on the pillow next to me.

Valentin nods, his brown eyes seething with lust and darkness. "Tell us again how you killed them."

I white-knuckle the counter as a tiny drop of sweat trickles down the back of my neck. She was mine even before I saw her. *And no one touches what's mine.* Fuck, I enjoyed gutting them from neck to scrotum. "*Enough.* I'm done talking about this. Our little firecracker is better off far away from us…" *Wherever that may be.*

Atlas groans. "We need fresh meat to play with. I want to fuck something innocent tonight."

"They'll be plenty of pussy at the party later. Besides, I already think I found a shiny new toy to torture." Valentin's lips curl into a devious smirk. That's about the closest thing to a smile that will ever grace his flawless face. Even when he laughs, it's cruel and wicked, and it never reflects in his eyes.

I raise an eyebrow as I finish dressing. "Freshman?"

He nods. "She's got a feisty fucking mouth on her too."

Atlas's eyes light up. "Mmm, I love it when they bite back."

But they rarely do. All the pretty girls open their legs for us the minute we walk into a room. We take what we want and feed the rest of the school our scraps. It has been getting tiresome and boring, but it amplifies our power. It solidifies our place at Tenebrose—at the top of the fucking food chain. We are Nocturnus—an ancient and secret order that has been passed down through generations. Everyone fears us and desires us at the same time. But it isn't enough. I crave more. All three of us do.

Chapter Three

Maureen

"Keep up, Blackwell," Libra calls back to me.

This bitch.

I'm usually the bossy friend, not the other way around. And now here I am traipsing through the night, following a girl I've just met, in black stiletto heels and a short red dress that belongs to *her*. I can barely breathe in the form-fitting fabric and my feet are already aching. She had taken one look at the clothes I'd brought and announced she was taking me shopping next weekend. Ironic since I'm here at Tenebrose to study costume design.

I do have other clothes. Flashier pieces that I purposefully didn't bring. I don't want that kind of attention anymore. Fuck, I don't even want to go to this party. Well, technically I do *want* to go. But I decided before I moved here to not be *that* girl again. My stomach knots just thinking about all those drunken nights. Too many to count and mostly a blur. Besides, after what happened at the last party I went to...

My stomach lurches as the image of his contorted face flashes in my mind. My chest heaves. I look down at my hands and for a moment, I can still see the knife in my palm, the blood between my fingers. "Fuck." *Just breathe, Maur.*

"O.M.G," she spells out. "Pick up the pace. I wanna get there before those heathens drink all the expensive shit."

I can feel my cheeks heating. If I knock her out and hide her body in the woods, will anyone miss her? "Sorry, I didn't train to sprint in stiletto heels. How much farther?"

Libra hisses. "Nocturnus House is just up the road. Trust me, it's worth it. Wait till you see these guys."

"A frat house?" I groan and come to a dead stop. "Hell, no. Not my scene."

Libra whips around and throws me a glare that sends a ripple of chills across my skin. "Nocturnus is *not* a fraternity. And if I were you, I wouldn't call it that again unless you want to lose your tongue."

I shift my weight just as my left heel begins to sink into the soft dirt. "Well, what the fuck are they then? An astronomy club?"

"Very funny," she snaps. She looks me up and down, and I can't tell if she's admiring her own clothes on me or if she's finally starting to regret dragging me along. "You're really pretty, you know that?"

I swallow hard, unsure as to where she's going with this. "Thanks... I think."

It's fascinating to watch Libra's face change from scorn to delight in a matter of seconds. She runs the tip of her tongue over her bottom lip as she continues her assessment of me. "Nocturnus likes pretty girls. Especially new ones."

I snicker. "I don't really fucking care if they like me."

Her face falls, and she grabs my arm hard. "You better fucking care, Blackwell. Earning their favor guarantees your safety."

The memory of my best friend and I running through the woods while we were being chased by two psychos flashes in my mind. I rip my arm away from Libra and back up. "I can keep myself safe."

We glare at each other, daring the other to break first. Libra lets out a deep sigh, her features softening again. "Chill. It was just a metaphor. For fuck's sake, you need to lighten up. Come on, let's go."

Part of me wants to kick off these heels and stomp back to The Nest. I don't like or trust this girl one bit. But it's late and dark as fuck, and I remember Miss Florian's warning about straying off the path. Without my map or my bearings, I would for sure get lost out here.

I sigh as I walk past her. "Fine. But you need to find me a ride or a pair of slippers later. I'm not doing this again in these heels."

Libra giggles. "Deal." She slips her arm around mine like we're besties. "Now, when we get inside, I'll introduce you to all of them. I kind of have a thing going with Riot, so he's off limits. Not that I'm worried. *You* are so not his type. But you should go for Atlas. He's tall and blond with the body of a god."

I fight the urge to roll my eyes as I cringe at every word that leaves her surgically enhanced lips. "If Atlas is so amazing, why don't you go for him, then? Or is Riot just that much more smokin' hot?" *I literally couldn't care less.*

"Oh, Atlas is my cousin. We're close but not *that* close." She laughs.

Great. So Libra is rich, popular, and related to some super shady frat boy whom I'm not allowed to call a frat boy. The very thing I didn't want anything to do with this year—dangerous fuckboys. And here I am letting this bitch walk me straight into their den.

As we pass a creepy graveyard, *besides wondering why a prestigious academy has one*, I realize that we are headed toward the unmarked location on the map. The one that Miss Florian refused to speak about.

Through the trees, I spot it. Nocturnus House. A chill sweeps up my spine. Calling it a house is an understatement. This is a proper mansion. The lights glow from every window, staking it's claim to the space like a beacon in these dark shadowy woods.

As we get closer, I notice the paint is decaying on half the structure where other parts look freshly coated. The stairs leading up to the door are lined with flickering candles and fairy lights. With iron railings, twisting like branches, and black rose bushes as high as my chest, it's beautiful and horrific at the same time.

I'm drawn to its melancholy. The *Catherine and Heathcliff* of it all. The earthiness of the fresh soil it sits in, attempting to mask the putrid stench of rotting graves from just down the road. The cloyingly sweet traces of something I can't place, a scent that threatens to consume my every thought and desire. Like a two-way mirror with death watching me from the other side.

I grab my chest and stumble back. "What is this place?" I whisper.

Libra flashes me a grin. "The house that belongs to the night. Just like them."

I shake my head. "No, but what is that scent? It hurts to breathe."

"I keep forgetting you're not from around here." Libra laughs. "It's hemlock. You'll get used to it."

Poison? Fuck me. "They're growing hemlock? What the fuck for?"

Libra laughs again as she lets her blonde hair down from its tight bun. "Look, I know you grew up in Wickford Hollow, but I find it hard to believe that your parents didn't tell you *anything* about this place. But I love how you're totally owning this new girl naïve vibe."

My stomach twists in knots. Fuck. I might have made a horrible mistake coming here. And not just to Nocturnus House. But to Tenebrose. And I definitely never should have taken my mother's name. I regret not ever asking her questions about our family history.

If Bailey was here she'd tell me to be the fiery Maureen she knows and loves. And that's exactly what I'm going to need to do to survive this place.

I let out a deep breath and force the flirtiest smile I can muster. "A girl's gotta have some secrets. Am I right?" I make a mental note to research everything I can find on Ever Graves and Raven's Gate later.

Libra wraps her arm back around mine. "A lady never kills and tells. Come on, let's go get shitfaced."

If she only knew.

I follow Libra through the packed house, impressed by her prowess. As I watch her slither in and out of different groups, greeting various friends with air kisses on each cheek and giggling at all the right moments, I realize she's *me*. She's popular, admired, envied. I can see the way they look at her. They either want to fuck her or be her. Or both. Libra's the Raven's Gate version of me. Well, the old me, anyway.

After twenty minutes of being introduced to countless stunning girls and hot as fuck guys—all of whom I won't remember their names after tonight—we finally make our way over to the bar.

Before I can open my mouth, Libra orders a whiskey for herself and a gin and tonic for me.

I wrinkle my nose as the fumes from the drink hit my nostrils. "I hate gin."

Libra raises an eyebrow. "But it's your family's legacy."

I nearly choke on my first sip. "Come again?"

She snatches the bottle from behind the bar and shoves it in my face.

My stomach sinks. Splashed across the label is my last fucking name. Well, my mother's last name. I know her family's rich, but I had no clue that they are famous as well. Fuck.

I shrug, trying my best to recover from my obvious blunder. "Yeah, whatever. It doesn't mean I have to like it."

Libra freezes for a minute before bursting into laughter. "Yeah, fuck our families and their empires. I'm starting to like you, Blackwell."

I breathe a sigh of relief into my glass. It's too late now to come clean about not knowing them. It's not like I'm lying. Not completely. Just omitting *some* details. Okay, a lot of details.

A skinny blonde wearing glow-in-the-dark body paint roller skates past us, carrying a tray of jello shots. As I reach for one, Libra smacks my hand.

"What the fuck?" I bark.

"Only basic bitches drink jello shots, Maureen," she drawls. "Look around you. These people look up to us. This is Nocturnus House, and here… we are at the top of the fucking food chain. So you need to act like it."

A twinge of guilt wrenches in my gut. What would Bailey think of me hanging out with this bitch?

"Don't you mean you're *almost* at the top of the food chain?" a sexy voice chides from behind us.

M VIOLET

I spin around and my breath catches in my throat. With pale blond hair and those same blue-green eyes, he looks like the male version of Libra. And his body… *fuck*. He's at least six foot four and even through his black buttoned-up shirt, I can see the curves of his muscles.

She rolls her eyes. "Maureen, this is my cousin, Atlas. He lives here."

He winks and takes my hand, bringing it to his lips. His breath is hot, tickling the nerves on my fingers. "I bet you taste like sin."

I quiver as he places a gentle kiss on the top of my hand. His lips are thick and so fucking soft. I imagine what they'd feel like on other parts of me.

He chuckles, and I realize that my mouth is open. My cheeks flush. Fuck. I snatch my hand away. "I don't taste like anything."

Libra rolls her eyes. "My new roommate's been here for five seconds and you're already trying to fuck her? Give Blackwell some space, Atlas."

His body shifts back, his jaw muscles flexing as he narrows his eyes at his cousin, and then back to me. "Now I know you taste like sin."

"Excuse me?" His entire vibe changed the second she said my last name.

Atlas sighs and shoots Libra another tense look. She shrugs and puffs out a nervous chuckle. "What?"

He shakes his head. "I'm gonna go warn Riot and Valentin."

"Warn them about what?" I snap. *Someone better start telling me what the hell is going on here.*

"I'd like to know as well." His voice is deep and smooth. The kind of voice you want to read you a naughty bedtime story. As he steps out of the shadows, I inhale a sharp breath. His eyes widen as they meet mine. *There's something about him…*

All of a sudden Libra goes from loud and confident to shy and demure. "Riot, this is my new roommate, Maureen… Blackwell."

His blue eyes turn cold as ice. "Don't fucking play with me, Libra."

She swallows hard. "I'm not," she whispers.

Fuck, he's gorgeous. And terrifying. His jet-black hair is cropped short on the sides and long on top. He moves toward me and glares down. "If I had known then…" He points at Libra without breaking eye contact with me. "You've got some nerve bringing her here."

I can feel all the heat rush to my cheeks. The fucking audacity of this asshole. What the fuck did I do to deserve that comment? I grab hold of his arm as he turns to walk away. "Well, that was fucking rude. You don't even know me."

Riot flexes his arm, letting me know how strong he is. He glares down at my hand as if it were a snake biting him. "Listen, slut. *You* don't know *me*." He squeezes my wrist with his free hand, pinching it hard between his fingers as he pries it off his arm. "You don't know what I'm capable of."

My stomach twists in knots as he presses his lips to my ear and whispers, "You ever touch me again, *I will fucking destroy you.*"

As he releases me from his grasp, another figure emerges next to Atlas and a wave of sheer terror crawls up my spine. The beautiful asshole from this morning. *Valentin.* Fuck. Jessamine's warning, *he's dangerous, they all are,* echoes in my head.

He looks me up and down, licking his lips as he drinks in the sight of my slinky dress and stiletto heels. But when his dark eyes finally meet mine they harden. If looks could maim and murder, I'd be a pile of rotting flesh and bones.

"Why is the freshman here with Libra?" he snarls.

What the actual fuck is wrong with these people?

Atlas snickers. "She's Libra's new roommate. Maureen. *Blackwell.*"

Valentin clenches his jaw. "I knew you were gonna be a problem."

It's getting harder to breathe as the three of them glare at me. They look like a pack of feral wolves. My knees wobble as I take a shaky step back. "Look, I don't know what you think I did, but I swear I don't want any trouble."

Riot snakes a hand around Libra's throat. "There will be consequences for bringing her here."

She lowers her eyes and nods. In the few hours that I've spent with this girl, it's clear she's an alpha female. Not the kind of chick who gets pushed around. Until now.

"Hey, let her go," I snarl. I might not like the bitch, but I'm not going to stand around and let her get choked out.

Riot releases her and charges me, backing me up against a wall. "Get the fuck out of my house or there will be consequences for you too, Firecracker."

As I catch a faint whiff of coffee and tobacco, butterflies shoot through my stomach. I gaze deep into his electric blue eyes, and a fuzzy memory resurfaces. "Fuck… *it's you*," I squeak out.

"Get. Out." Riot slams his hand against the wall right next to my head.

The unfounded hatred he has for me mixes with a look of lust and desire. He presses in closer, our chests touching. His body caging me while his mouth yells at me to leave.

"You were wearing a mask, but I know it's you… You called me Firecracker that night too."

Riot pinches a strand of my hair between his fingers. "You know what I remember from that night? Hmm? All that disgusting cum." I fight the tears that well in my eyes as shame washes over me.

He winds my hair tight around his finger and yanks down, pulling my head. "It was all over your chest… your lips… fucking dripping down your thighs. I took pity on a drunk slut in a bathroom. That's all that was. All it will ever be."

Atlas and Valentin stand on either side of me now. "This is her?" Atlas asks.

"This is nobody," Riot growls.

"Fuck you," I snap back.

He pounds the wall again and grunts. "How fucking dare you."

Libra curses under her breath as she tugs on my hand. "Come on, let's go before they kill us both."

The three of them barely let me squeeze out of the little circle of hell they'd surrounded me in, but I manage to slip through.

I know I'm playing with fire, but I can't help but keep my eyes on Riot as Libra drags me away.

It was only my first day at Tenebrose and my dream of being here is already turning into a nightmare. I had felt so safe with him that night in the bathroom. The night he zipped me up after those frat boys had defiled me.

But Riot's no fucking savior. No. He's just like every other asshole. I want nothing to do with him or his douchebag friends. I came here to get away from my trauma, not create more.

Our walk back to the dorms is much quieter than the walk over. I'm grateful for that. All I want to do is crawl into my bed and forget this night ever happened.

But as the wind picks up speed, the shadows seem to be closing in. And I can't shake the feeling that this thing with Riot isn't over. It's just beginning.

Chapter Four

Riot

A S I LAY IN THE DARK, THE SHADOWS ENVELOPING me, the ground feels like a block of ice against my back. It's colder down here, but I welcome it. It eases the fever that consumes me, even as the sweat gathers on my brow. I can hear each droplet as it hits the hard cement underneath me. I can hear everything and nothing.

Maureen Blackwell.

She was my firecracker. My light in the endless night that I fixated on while the poison twisted through my veins. An obsession that has festered to the brink of insanity. But she is tainted, charred by the blood in her body like an ancient curse.

If I had known that night that she was a Blackwell, things would have gone a hell of a lot differently. She was sad and beautiful and covered in cum. I took pity on her. If I had known, I would have ruined her right then.

Instead, I got distracted by her thick pouty lips and amber-colored eyes. I had envisioned those lips wrapped around my cock. I imagined how those eyes would brim with tears as she choked on me. I thought she was special, but she's just another whore.

Just another traitorous Blackwell, sent here to spite me. Her blasphemous family got off easy after what they did to mine. But their little slut is in my backyard now. In my fucking web. All alone.

And I'm a hungry spider.

I stretch my legs and let out a deep breath. A sliver of the moon peeks into my vision through the skylight. The stars surround it like an army. This is what it feels like to belong to the night. To be one with it. *To command it.*

I pinch my eyes shut and curse under my breath. The rage I feel for my firecracker stings like the seven cuts on my chest. My fury festers as blood trickles down my stomach. I want to make her feel what I feel.

A surge of adrenaline courses through my veins, mingling with the poison as my sacrifice is taken by the raven. Its spirit rushes through me like a storm. I arch my back and cry out. The pressure smashes against my bones. My lungs fill with fire. I can taste the smolder on my tongue. I lick my lips and picture her face.

Fuck.

I slam my fists on the ground. It's not supposed to be like this. Not here in this sacred place. Not when I'm in ritual.

I hate her. I hate myself.

I release a quivering breath as I unzip my pants. The frosty cellar air hits my hard cock and I bite down on my lip so hard, blood fills my mouth.

"Mmm... fuck." I slide my hand up and down my cock, surrendering to its need. Her amber-colored eyes flash in my mind as I roll my thumb over the tip, smearing my pre cum around in circles.

I need this release.

The blood from my ritual cuts continue to ooze, sparking with power as I stroke faster, squeezing my dick harder with every thrust. I imagine my little firecracker, envisioning her swollen lips around my cock instead of my own hand. Picturing her tears and how I would lick them clean.

The pressure rumbles down my shaft, and I slap my inner thigh with my free hand. An explosion of tingles rolls through me. "Oh, fuck." My cum shoots out, sizzling as it marks the cold cement. I rock back and forth as my orgasm builds and threatens to suffocate me.

The last of it oozes out, and I take deep breaths, willing my heartbeat to slow. *Fuck, that's what I get for edging myself.* Ever since that night I saw her...

I had made offerings for her. *Sacrifices.* And the raven finally answered my cry. She came to Raven's Gate. To Tenebrose. But I should have been more careful of what I wished for. She could have been my queen...

Now I'll make her my slut. She'll be nothing but a toy for us to play with. And I'll take every ounce of my self-loathing out on her mouth and her cunt and her tight ass. There'll be no part of her that is unmarked or unscathed.

Two hooded figures tower over me, snapping me out of my revenge fantasy. The taller one eyes my dick. I lost track of their names. They serve Nocturnus like lap dogs. Their names and souls are inconsequential. Insignificant.

"Stare at it any harder, and I'll make you suck it," I snap. "Why are you bothering me?"

The one drooling over me, blushes. "You asked us for an update on the Blackwell girl."

The shorter of the two clears his throat. "We got you a copy of her class schedule."

Un-fucking-believable.

I leap to my feet, not bothering to tuck my dick back inside my jeans. "You came down to the fucking ritual room to give me a piece of paper I can get for myself?"

I enjoy the looks in their eyes, the way their faces twist in horror. I imagine what their insides look like curdling with fear.

The shorter initiate tilts his chin up. "Atlas said we should give it to you now."

I almost burst out laughing. Almost.

"Give me your knife."

He hesitates and looks at the taller one.

I rush into him, and he stumbles back. "Do I have to ask you again?"

He shakes his head as he fumbles for his knife. In one swift motion, I yank it from him and thrust it into the taller one's belly.

A gurgling cry wrenches from his throat as he keels over. Their eyes widen as I wave the knife over his head. "Never. Enter. The. Ritual. Room."

Blood spills from his gut and his face pales. The shorter one's mouth fills with bile but I arch my eyebrow at him, and he quickly swallows it.

"Am I understood?"

They both nod.

"Now get the fuck out of here. If he dies, bury him in the woods. Nocturnus is hallowed ground. Only the deserving get to rest here."

The whispers will grow again. Talk of the madness that takes place inside these walls will spread like wildfire. But they know better than to talk for too long or too loudly. They know what happens to those who get in our way.

As I put my dick back in my pants, another tremor trickles down my shaft. *I can't wait to show Maureen Blackwell what happens to those who get in my way.*

✥

The circular room we're in was built for punishment. A way for all who watch to get a good view. It's archaic, cold, and brutal from its stone walls and black cement floor to the steel table in the center.

I sit in a velvet chair with Valentin and Atlas on either side of me. I gaze around the room, taking stock of the initiates' faces. They must never get too comfortable. I have to keep these animals in their fucking places. The stunt Libra pulled last night was abhorrent. She fucking knew exactly what she was doing bringing Maureen Blackwell into this house. And now she will have to deal with the consequences. I can't have any of these fuckers thinking they can go around doing the same.

"Bring her in." I nod to the initiate by the door. I can hear her spoiled little voice whining as the door opens and she's dragged in by two of my largest initiates. They push her forward until she's standing between me and the steel table.

"Riot, I told you I was sorry. I didn't realize you hated the Blackwells *that* fucking much, okay?"

I spread my legs and lean back against the chair. "Don't be a cunt, Libra. Own what you did. I told you there'd be consequences."

The reality of what's happening is beginning to set in as sweat beads down her neck and chest. "Atlas," she pleads. "I'm your fucking cousin for fuck's sake. Do something."

He shakes his head. "I am doing something. Teaching you a fucking lesson. You know the rules, Lib. You've known them your whole life."

Tears stream down her cheeks. Fucking pathetic. This girl is the most manipulative chick I know. And she's done far worse to others than what I'm about to do to her.

"We can do this one of two ways, Libra. You can be compliant and own your punishment. Or… well you don't want to hear the other way."

She nervously glances around the room, looking at each of the twenty initiates that surround her. "I-I comply," she murmurs and lowers her head.

I nod at the two brutes who brought her in, and they step back, releasing her arms from their grip.

"Take off your clothes," I state without any desire to see her naked. No, this is about power. About making a statement to everyone here. Not even the cousin of a Nocturnus member is safe from punishment. If I'm doing this to Atlas's own blood relative, what do they think I'll do to one of them if they cross me?

Her hands tremble on each button of her designer cashmere cardigan. The electricity in the room sizzles as she unzips her skirt and lets it fall to the ground. I look around the room and see some of the initiates leaning forward now. Some adjust their cocks.

I let out a deep sigh. "Everything, Libra. Bra and panties too."

She starts to open her mouth to protest but thinks better of it. She keeps her gaze on the ground as she unhooks her bra. A few gasps ring out at the sight of her full breasts and hardened nipples. It's cold as fuck down here for a reason.

She shimmies out of her panties and starts to cover her pussy with her hand when I shake my head in disapproval. Her hands quickly go back to her sides.

"You brought this on yourself, Libra. Last night you made a fool of me bringing that Blackwell girl into my house. Who's the fool now?"

Libra whimpers. "I am. I deserve my punishment."

A surge of adrenaline rushes through my veins at her display of submission. I nod at the two brutes again and they return to her side. "Turn around and bend over the table, Libra."

As she does what I ask, one of the brutes secures her wrists in his, holding them down against the table. Her breasts smash against the cold steel. With her head turned to the side, I can see the tears that trickle out from behind her closed eyes.

"Spread your legs nice and wide for him."

The initiates around the room practically salivate as they watch her widen her stance. Her lily-white ass twitches even before the first lash is given.

The brute removes his studded leather belt from his pants, the look in his eyes feral. He folds the belt and brings it down hard against her ass.

"*Fuck*," Libra cries out.

The brute looks at me, and I nod. "Again."

His eyes blaze with hunger as he smacks the belt down harder. Libra jerks and twists. Red welts are already forming on her porcelain skin.

An initiate tries to stifle a moan as the brute teases her now, dragging the belt up and down her ass crack. She trembles and pinches her eyes shut tight.

I nod and he unleashes another lash with fury. Libra shrieks like a banshee. "Please, stop," she whispers.

But I'm not satisfied yet. A few spankings will only make her more defiant. No. I need to properly remind her of who we are.

"Turn her over."

The brute holding her wrists flips her over as if she weighs nothing.

Libra shakes her head. "Riot, I've learned my lesson. Please. I can beg if you want me to. Don't you want to hear me beg?"

"The only thing I want to hear from your cunt mouth right now are your screams," I snarl. "Now get completely on the table and spread your fucking legs."

The one brute drags her all the way on while the second one positions himself between her legs. He licks his lips as he eyes her pussy, and a sick and twisted idea is born.

I hold up my hand for him to wait as he taps the belt against his palm. "I'll make you a deal then, Libra. I can be somewhat merciful."

She's practically panting now. "Anything. Riot, please. Just tell me what you want."

Valentin snickers as he knows me too well.

I lick my lips. "You can get another lashing from the front, or… you can let him touch you. I know he wants to shove his fat fucking fingers inside that tight pussy of yours. It's your choice though, Libra. I'm not gonna force you."

It was her turn to snicker. "Some choice you're giving me."

"Clock is ticking. What's it going to be?" Judging by the way she's squirming, her ass is probably not feeling so great right now.

"Fine. He can touch me," she whimpers. "But only with his hands."

I smirk. "Fair enough." As I nod to the brute his eyes light up. He grunts and drops the belt to the ground.

The sexual tension in the room thickens as they look on. The brute doesn't even wait before he shoves a thick finger inside her pussy. She cries out as he thrusts another one in without coaxing. His tongue wags out of his mouth as he finger fucks her.

"Are you going to cum, Libra? Or are you so disgusted by all of this? I'm guessing there's a part of you that's turned on. Tell you what, I'm not going to let him stop until you cum for him."

She grunts and grinds her teeth. I can see her clenching from here.

"Give into it, Lib," Valentin coos.

The brute thrusts a third finger inside her and rubs her clit with his thumb. She bucks now, unable to control her own body's reaction. Her cries turn to moans as he rocks his hand against her.

I hear a couple of *oh, fucks* from a few of the initiates around the room. A few others have their cocks out and are rubbing one out.

"Pinch her clit between your fingers, my brother. Pinch it real hard and watch what happens."

He grins wide and does what I say. And the floodgates open. Libra arches her back and screams. I can almost see the orgasm rolling through her, traveling through every nerve in her body.

The brute works his fingers in deeper, pumping them faster as she cums all over him. It spills out and down her thighs, and then onto the steel table in puddles. He takes his fingers out of her pussy and sucks on them, licking every drop of her cream off. He closes his eyes and savors it like it's his last meal.

"Can I go now, please?" she begs.

Atlas snickers beside me. "He just let you cum pretty hard, Lib. I think you should be more thankful."

She sighs. The brute still eyes her pussy while she looks anywhere but at him.

"We're almost done here. But not quite." I motion to the initiate in the back row who's still stroking his cock. "You, come here."

He starts to put his cock in his pants, and I snarl. "Leave it out. I want you to finish on her." I point at Libra. "Finish on her face."

Her tears begin to stream again as the squirrely initiate stands over her. It doesn't take him long. He fists his cock a few more times and then his cum bursts out. He moans loudly.

"Don't spill a drop, brother. I want you to paint her fucking face with it. Get it in her fucking hair too," I bark.

And he does everything I ask. I'm mesmerized by the brutality of the scene. She coughs as it goes up her nose and down her throat. It oozes down her temples in thick white ropes, dripping into her ears and down her neck. This bitch will never fucking cross me again in her pathetic life. Never.

"You look like a stupid cunt, Libra. Now get the fuck out of my house."

She scrambles off the table and starts to put on her skirt when I stop her.

"I said go. Now. Right fucking now. This isn't a dressing room. You can put those back on when you're off my fucking property."

She looks at me like she wants to murder me. But the fear outweighs her rage. As I watch her scurry out of the room as fast as her legs will take her, the poison in my veins surges. I'm high on power. Addicted to it like a drug.

And soon I will have special things in store for Maureen Blackwell. Her punishment for stepping foot in this town will be far worse. The thought of *her* naked and bent over gets me harder than anything ever has.

Chapter Five

Maureen

I OPEN MY EYES TO THE RAIN DRIPPING DOWN MY windows in buckets. It takes a second for me to remember where I am. I glance around the room, willing my eyes to adjust to my new surroundings—the dark gray sheets and black comforter that envelop me, the black velvet curtains that frame the wrought iron barred windows, the sconce-lit chandelier that dangles just above my head threatening to impale me if it should ever fall. It's lavish and decadent and cold. Just like *them*.

A shudder rips through me as I remember last night. The looks on their faces... Riot, Atlas, and Valentin didn't just hate me... their eyes were murderous. All because of a name. My mother's cursed fucking name. And I have no clue as to why.

But I will fucking find out.

I throw back the sheets and flinch as my bare feet hit the icy marble floor. I thought Wickford Mansion was bougie, this place takes it to a whole other level. When I looked at the pictures of Tenebrose online last year, I knew it would be fancy, but nothing prepared me for *this*.

I wonder what the regular dorm rooms look like. *The one I was supposed to be staying in.* While a tiny part of me is elated to be surrounded by all this extravagance, the rational part of me knows it comes at a price—a target on my back, and the opening of a creepy can of worms that would rival Pandora's box. Not to mention the actual price. This isn't what I signed up for.

Bailey gave me plenty of money to cover tuition, room and board, and basic living expenses, but I don't believe that *this* apartment, which takes up an entire floor, is in my budget. There's no fucking way. I have to go and speak to someone about this on Monday. I'll explain the mix-up, that I'm not one of *those* Blackwells, and ask to be moved to a normal room with the rest of the regular students. I don't want the special treatment or the attention. In fact, I want the opposite of whatever this is. Then Libra and her psycho friends can forget all about me.

I barely spoke to Libra last night after the party. It was the quietest she's been since I met her. I didn't think she'd answer any of my questions truthfully anyway. She threw back another shot and then stumbled off to her room on the other side of the apartment while ranting on about curses and oaths. It was all very cryptic and vague. Just like my room assignment, the warnings about the woods from Miss Florian, the poisonous plants growing outside of Nocturnus, and the way everyone seems to stiffen at the name Blackwell. My mother had always told me that she left Ever Graves with my father because her family cut her off after she got pregnant with me. I'm starting to think there might be more to that story. *Maybe she was running from something else.*

And then there's Riot. The masked man kind enough to zip up my corset while I was covered in cum and alcohol in the bathroom of Wickford Mansion. Most of that night was a blur, up until I drove a knife through Chad's chest. I try not to think about any of it. But I could never forget Riot… his piercing blue eyes, the way he smelled like dark coffee and freshly rolled tobacco leaves…

If I hadn't already been defiled by those douchebags, I would have wanted him to defile me. There had been something electric between us. Something tethering us to each other for the briefest of moments. My fantasies since then consisted of him. But last night all that shattered. Riot, Atlas, and Valentin are nothing but over-privileged rich kids with control issues and a sick fascination with trying to intimidate freshmen.

Fuck them. If they think I'm scared of them, they have no idea who the fuck I am.

After taking a long hot shower, I throw on a pair of ripped jeans, brown leather riding boots, and a beige wool sweater. I crack open my bedroom door and breathe a sigh of relief when I realize Libra is nowhere in sight. Maybe she's still sleeping but hopefully, she's just out. I don't have the mental capacity to deal with her right now. That girl seems to have only two speeds—a lot and a lot more.

I throw my leather bag over my shoulder and head for the elevator. When the doors slide open I start forward then jump at the willowy figure standing inside. "Fuck. Jessamine, you scared the shit out of me."

The girl giggles. "Sorry, Maur. When I'm bored, I ride the elevator up and down. Did you know they sealed it off once? Because of the fire. They were trapped up here. I heard them choking. It's better now. No more smoke." She rocks back and forth on her feet, smiling like she's remembering a good dream.

Something in my gut twists. My skin prickles. There is something so off about this chick. And I don't like how casual she is with me. "Don't call me Maur. Only my best friend calls me that."

Jessamine's mouth gapes. Her eyes water. "I'm sorry," she whispers. "Professor Erebus always warns me about my manners." She drops her head down, and I feel like shit for snapping.

I let out a deep breath. "Fuck. It's fine. Sorry. Call me whatever you want. I just had a weird night. It's hard getting acclimated here."

Her smile returns, and she goes back to bouncing from side to side. "You should stay away from Nocturnus. The ravens might not let you leave next time."

I can't believe this girl is a student here. She is sweet but disturbed. She seems too young to be here and yet too old at the same time. "When was there a fire up here?" I find it hard to believe that my pristine apartment had been rebuilt recently. While the appliances and furniture were super modern, the windows and floors look antique.

The elevator doors ding open, and Jessamine hops out first. "Oh, it was a very long time ago. Like a century ago. I can't remember."

Um, what? "Wait. A hundred years ago? Jessamine, you're not making any sense. I thought you said you could hear them choking." I step out and look around at all the curious faces, their scrutiny aimed in my direction, and realize the strange little girl is gone. Again.

What the actual fuck? Now I look like a weirdo talking to myself again. She has got to stop doing that to me.

"I see you've met Jessamine. She must really like you." A striking girl with black hair and big brown eyes blocks my path.

"What makes you say that?" *I almost made the poor girl cry in the elevator.*

"She doesn't let everyone see her. But you can. Hence the liking you part," she teases. Her voice is warm and inviting. It makes me miss home. She sticks out her hand. "I'm Villette by the way."

I shake her hand, noticing how her flawless brown skin is make-up-free and gorgeous. How the hell does she keep that glow with all this rain and fog every day?

"I'm Maureen Bla—just Maureen." I shake her hand and cut myself off before I have yet another stranger look at me like they want to kill me. "I still don't understand what you mean about Jessamine."

Villette smirks. "I get it. My last name comes with baggage too. But, um, yeah so Jessamine is dead. She's you know, a ghost. Most of the students here think she's a myth but I've fed the birds with her on many occasions."

My stomach drops. Everything that has come out of Jessamine's mouth suddenly makes sense. "Fuck. How'd she die?"

Villette arches an eyebrow at me, a look of amusement in her eyes. "You believe me just like that?"

It was my turn to giggle. "Girl, I'm from Wickford Hollow. My best friend is a ghost."

Villette's grin widens. "I think I'm really going to like you."

A little bit of weight dissipates off my shoulders and for the first time since I arrived at Tenebrose, I'm excited to make a new friend. "Same. Wanna show me where the library is?"

Villette loops her arm through mine. "Be happy to."

Once we are outside, she tilts her head toward my ear and whispers, "Jessamine was murdered by the way. A long time ago. And she's not the only one."

A knot forms in the pit of my stomach. "By whom?"

Villette shrugs and quickens her pace, forcing me to do the same. "She says it was for the ravens. Some kind of sacrifice or something."

A tingling breaks out in my feet as my adrenaline surges. What the fuck was up with this town and their ravens? And did this have anything to do with the fire she mentioned earlier? "Did she tell you how she died?" I ask quietly.

She nods. "Poison."

Fuck.

Nocturnus.

A wave of nausea pans over me, and I stumble. Villette grips my arm tight, so I don't fall on my face. She giggles. "I got you. You'll get used to the uneven ground here. Some say Tenebrose was built on an ancient burial site and that the dead get restless. That they shift in their graves overnight."

Chills snake up my back. *No, I will not fucking get used to that.* What the fuck did I get myself into?

༺✦༻

The monstrosity in front of me seems to glare back like I'm insulting its space just by standing there. Graves Library takes Gothic architecture to another level. With sharp edges, black walls, and stained-glass windows, it looks like a church that the devil moved into.

A chill snakes up my back as I follow Villette inside. She twists her dark hair around her fingers as she looks all the way up to the pointed ceiling and then sweeps her gaze around the room. "For as long as anyone can remember, they've been calling this place the graveyard. A play on the name I guess. But the books in here have a hint of darkness in them."

"Creepy," I mutter under my breath. "Why Graves?"

Villette pulls me forward, guiding me down the first aisle. "A tribute to the Graves family. They donated most of these books when they came here from Ever Graves centuries ago."

I stop to finger a book with a soft velvet spine and notice that most of the books on this shelf are missing titles. "Where's the family now?"

Her grip tightens around my arm. "They're all still in Raven's Gate. One of them goes to school here. His name's Riot. And fair warning, he's hot as fuck, but I'm convinced that pure evil runs in his veins. I'd stay off his radar if I were you."

My stomach knots. Fuck. "Good to know. Thanks." I wasn't about to tell Villette that I'd already had a run-in with him and his band of assholes. I'd hate to lose my first friend here minutes after meeting her.

"Same goes for his two besties, Atlas Thorn, and Valentin Erebus. Nothing good happens when those three are around," she continues.

I nod. Yeah, definitely not telling this chick that I'm already on their shit list. She'll avoid me like the plague if she finds out. "I would like to avoid trouble at all costs so that won't be a problem for me."

We take the spiral staircase up to the second floor to find a cozy sitting area with black leather couches and a dark wood coffee table facing a large stone fireplace. A few students are studying at one end; a stack of books is piled up on the other.

A little tingle of excitement flutters through me. If there was any place I could possibly find out information about my family, this would be it. "Is there a genealogy or local history section here?"

Villette's lips turn up into a smirk. "You doing some snooping?"

A nervous laugh skitters out of me. "Um, something like that. Just want to know what I've gotten myself into."

She nods her chin toward a door that's sandwiched between

Gothic Literature and Victorian Poetry. "The archives are in there. But hey, I gotta run to the student store and pick up some more supplies for tomorrow. You going to Swallow later?"

Whoa. What? "Um, excuse me?"

She giggles. "Swallow. It's the campus bar."

Relief floods me, and I giggle back. "Oh, right. Yeah for sure. Meet you there later?"

Villette grabs my phone and punches in her number. "Text me when you're ready. I'll wait for you downstairs at The Nest so we can walk together."

I give my new friend a hug and watch in awe as she saunters away. Every student turns to watch her as well. She's stunning and radiates an energy that draws you in like a moth to a flame. What I would give to have even an ounce of Villette's confidence. I used to… But I lost it somewhere in between getting passed around at Billy's parties and everything that happened last Halloween at Wickford Mansion.

I shudder at the memory of steel pushing through flesh. I take a deep breath to try to quell the nausea that climbs up my throat. Ugh. It's bad enough that it haunts my sleep but during the day too now? *Fuck me.*

The door to the archives sticks when I push against it before finally opening with a loud creak. I look over my shoulder, expecting to see an onslaught of glares for being so noisy, but no one looks up from their books. I step into the sconce-lit room and close the door behind me, cursing under my breath as it creaks again.

The room is smaller than I expect. While the walls are lined with books, only a center island of shelves sits in the middle. I peruse some of the spines—more books without titles. Some have symbols etched into the binding. They look like alchemy symbols, similar to the ones painted on the ceiling of the admin building.

As I come around to the other side of the island, a figure moves in front of me. I shriek and drop my bag on the floor. My heart beats fast and I get ready to run until I see blonde hair and pale skin. *Fucking Jessamine.*

"Sorry, Maur, I didn't mean to scare you," she whispers.

I pick up my bag and wipe my sweaty palms over my jeans. "Dude, you just walked up on me out of nowhere in a creepy dark library room. What the fuck did you think was going to happen?"

She fingers the end of her braid. "I forget how quiet I am. Next time I'll be better. What are you doing here anyway? No one ever comes in this room."

I sigh. "It's fine. I need to find out more about my family. Was hoping there might be some Blackwell archives in here."

Jessamine gasps. "In here? That would be blasphemy. The Graves family took away anything with the name Blackwell on it decades ago."

Now, I'm annoyed. "Seriously? Why the fuck for?"

She looks around as if we aren't the only two people here before leaning in. "They committed horrible acts against the Graves. Unforgivable acts. You shouldn't have come here. It's not safe for you."

A cold draft tickles the back of my neck. I think about Riot's hatred of me. The rage in his eyes when he heard my last name. It's very personal and apparently dates back hundreds of years. I feel sick.

Fucking great.

I wonder how many times I can kick myself for not registering here as Maureen Gray. My stupid fucking insecurity wins again.

I palm my face, rubbing my temples as a headache starts to form. "So what's the story? Why is my family on Riot's shitlist?"

"I can't say."

"Jessa—"

"I can't say," she raises her voice. "I… don't remember. There's gaps in my memory. Sorry."

Fuckity, fuck, fuck. "Awesome. Well, at least point me to the books about *his* family then. I need to know who I'm dealing with."

She shakes her head, her eyes glassy. "Don't open that door, Maureen. You won't be able to close it if you do."

I am a lot of things, but a coward isn't one of them. "Classes start Monday, Jessamine. I only have twenty-four hours to prepare myself for what I'm walking into. I don't have time to sift through all of these. Please, for fuck's sake, show me which ones are about the Graves family."

She fists the sides of her white cotton dress, bunching the fabric in her palms. A wave of emotions seems to pass through her eyes before she shakes her head. "You won't find what you're looking for. This is *his* library, but he doesn't keep his secrets here."

I pinch my eyes shut as a searing pain shoots through my head. I grab onto a shelf as I lose my footing. "Fuck, I think I'm going to be sick."

Jessamine places a cold hand on my shoulder. "You need to leave this room. It doesn't want you here."

Don't need to tell me twice. My insides feel like they're cooking from within. I nod and dart out the door. Jessamine is gone again, and I'm not surprised. It's what she does. And she's also right. With every breath I take, the pain dissipates. *First time I've been rejected by an entire room.*

I rush into the nearest bathroom and brace myself on the sink. I suck on my lower lip and fight the last wave of nausea. But just as I start to feel better, it's snatched away. I look in the mirror to see Riot, Atlas, and Valentin staring back at me.

They glare daggers at me as I turn around. The edge of the sink digs into my lower back. I eye the door, calculating the distance between it and them. Fuck. I'm fucking trapped. Maybe another girl will walk in and call them out for being in here. As soon as I think that, Valentin bolts the door.

I sidestep slowly toward the door anyway as they surround me. Riot stands in the center like a beautiful monster, his blue eyes cold and vacant. "Going somewhere, Firecracker?"

My voice betrays me as I take another step back only to find myself up against the wall.

They close in.

Valentin threads his fingers through my hair. "I heard you like getting fucked in bathrooms."

"Go to hell," I cry out. My heart feels like it's going to explode. I'm sure of it.

"We're already in hell," Atlas counters. "And it's been less than stimulating. But now we've found something new to play with." As he towers over me, nudging my chin upward with his knuckles, I almost drown in his eyes. Almost. He's fucking gorgeous. All of them are. But I have to remind myself that they are predators.

My throat is dry. "No. That's not who I am anymore," I squeak out.

Valentin's grip tightens on my strands. "I disagree."

Atlas presses his thumb against my bottom lip. "I think she's going to let us play… isn't that right, darlin'? Unless you want us telling everyone all your dark and dirty secrets."

Fuck. What do they know? Riot was at that party last Halloween. He knows what those douchebags did to me in the bathroom. But did he see me go upstairs? Does he know what I did to Chad? My heart races as I struggle to keep my breath steady.

"Why are you doing this to me?" Fear mixed with anger twists in my gut like a knife.

Riot finally exhales, like a statue coming to life. He stalks forward and presses in close. That now familiar scent of coffee and tobacco envelops me. I want to breathe it in and spit it out in his face.

He pinches my hips hard between his fingers and gazes down at me with the ferociousness of a rabid animal. "Because we can."

"And because you share the blood of thieves," Valentin snarls.

Atlas yanks my lip down, forcing my mouth open. I gasp as he plunges two fingers deep inside. "And now we're going to get some payback."

My pussy, *that traitorous bitch,* twitches, and tingles as I taste the salt from his skin. I gag as he touches the back of my throat. But as tears stream down my cheeks, I glare daggers at them. *I will destroy them for this.*

"That's it, Firecracker. Look at me like you want to kill me." Riot digs his fingers into my hips while Atlas forces me to suck his fingers. "Give me all your pain. All your rage. Every fucking self-deprecating thought."

I can't move, pinned between the three of them. Riot wraps a hand around my throat and squeezes. He inches his other hand down my jeans and pulls my panties to the side. "*Give me all your violence,*" he rasps. A wave of dark euphoria ripples through me, pebbling my nipples as he thrusts two fingers deep inside my pussy.

Valentin nips at my ear, scraping his teeth across my lobe. "You like that, slut?"

I stagger back against the wall. A moan catches in my throat as I fight to keep quiet. I can't let them see the power they have over me right now.

Riot breathes heavily into my ear. "Your silence can't hide how fucking wet you are, Firecracker." He rolls his thumb over my clit and slowly kneads his fingers down into my core. "But I bet I could make you scream…"

Atlas pulls his fingers out of my mouth and licks them. "I bet you'd taste better with a mouth full of cum."

Fuck, I *hate* them. But my body is betraying me with every flick of his fingers. "Let me go."

Valentin snickers as he sticks a hand up my shirt and pulls my tit out of my bra. "Quit acting like you don't want this. I can smell how wet your cunt is." I bite my lip to try and stifle another moan as he pinches my nipple hard between his fingers.

Atlas lifts up my shirt and goes for my other breast. And I about lose it. The rage inside my chest burns like fire. But the trigger between my thighs is hotter. The pressure builds in my core as Riot thrusts his fingers deeper.

"You can play pretend with everyone else, but not us. We know who you really are," Riot mutters. He shoves a third finger in, and I buck. "Yeah, that's it. Be a good little slut for us. Ride my fucking hand."

I can't help it. Tears stream down my cheeks as the stimulation hits me from all sides. Atlas and Valentin roll my nipples between their fingers as I start to jerk my hips to the rhythm of Riot's fingers. I'm coming undone, a slave to my own selfish pleasure. Fuck. I'm not even drunk this time.

Riot's grip on my throat tightens as my hips sway faster. An orgasm grips me, rolling through me like a fucking tidal wave. I bite my lip hard, but I can't contain the deep moan that billows out of me. He squeezes tighter, and I can't breathe. "I could kill you right fucking now, Firecracker. And no one here would care. No one would stop me."

I claw at his wrist as my vision starts to blur.

"But I'm going to enjoy torturing you for a while first." He lets go, and I gasp for air.

"Get away from me," I hiss, my voice hoarse.

Valentin dips his head to my ear again and bites my lobe hard. "You'll never get away from us."

Atlas grins wide. "This was fun." He drags his finger across my stinging ear and holds it up. Just as I suspected, it's covered in blood. I tremble as he licks it off his finger. "Again, this would taste so much better with my cum in it."

Fucking assholes. And yet here I am panting between them, my nipples still rock hard and cream spilling from my pussy. What the actual fuck is wrong with me? Why am I like this?

Fists pound at the door. "I have to pee, assholes," a girl's voice shrieks from the other side.

Riot smirks and steps back. "You fucked up, Firecracker. This is *my* school, and you have no business being here. Your punishment will not be swift."

Valentin snickers as he unlocks the bathroom door. "I'd sleep with one eye open if I were you."

"Or both," Atlas adds, laughing as he leaves.

Riot looks back one last time. "If I were you, I wouldn't sleep at all." His eyes blaze with hate and malice. There's not an ounce of warmth or remorse for what they just did. For everything they are planning to do to me next.

Fuck.

Three girls brush past them, cursing as they enter the bathroom. They take one look at me and crack up laughing. "There's a reason they call them fresh meat every year," one quips.

Fuck these bitches. *They don't know me.*

Ugh. Who am I kidding? This is exactly who I am. And now

I'm royally fucked because they won't stop coming for me. Nope, guys like that never stop. Riot, Atlas, and Valentin are out for blood, for revenge, and for their own twisted psychotic fun.

But if they want the *slut in a bathroom* version of Maureen, then they'll be sorry as fuck. Because what they don't know is I can be just as fucking vengeful and psycho as they are.

Chapter Six

Atlas

"HE'S NOT THINKING CLEARLY," I MUTTER TO THE raven perched on my windowsill. It watches me, cocking its head from side to side as I pour liquid from one vial into another. This blend is my favorite—equal parts hemlock and nightshade extract. It's like a fucking aphrodisiac.

I take a tiny swig and clench my jaw as it singes the back of my throat. The sweet sting trickles through my veins like honey, slow and deliberate as it merges with my blood. "Riot's so blinded by his hate; he can't see the blessing that's been dropped in our laps. That spicy little firecracker. Mmm…"

The poison surges and wraps around my veins, twisting and

turning my insides. I take off my T-shirt and jeans and lie down naked on my bed. Black satin sheets caress my back, cool against my heated skin.

The raven flies away but I keep talking to it as if my voice will carry through the wind. "Her blood could give us so much more…"

I'm burning up. The more I think about her pretty mouth wrapped around my fingers, the more I want to cum inside her. I want to play with her. I fist my hard cock and slide my hand up and down. "Fuck…"

My bedroom door creaks open and Valentin struts in. "You talking to the ravens again, Atlas?"

"Mmm," I moan. "They like the sound of my voice." I slide my hands up, pinching the tip gently as the poison swirls inside my balls.

Valentin smirks as he sniffs the vial. "That cunt got you all worked up, didn't she?"

Another moan escapes me as I stroke faster.

He walks to the edge of the bed with the vial and takes a sip, his eyes blazing with need. "Close your eyes… Imagine she's here right now."

Oh, fuck. I shut my lids and let out a shuddering breath as Valentin pushes my hands away. "What would you tell her to do?"

"I'd tell her to wrap her lips around my cock," I stammer.

Valentin snickers. "Like this?"

I moan and jerk my hips as his soft lips work their way down my shaft. "Mmm, yeah just like that."

His tongue lashes over my balls, and I shiver as my blood rushes forward. He pulls up and scrapes his teeth against my tip. I grab a handful of his black hair and urge him back down.

He chuckles. "That's it. Show me how you're gonna make her choke on your huge cock. Let her drink some of your poisonous cum."

I yank him down until my cock hits the back of his throat. "Fuck," I cry out.

Valentin presses his tongue flat to the back of my shaft as I thrust in and out of his mouth. Every cell is on fire. I feel the poison and blood swirl together like a violent storm. It sends tremors like tiny electric shocks through my swollen cock.

He chuckles as I bury myself so deep down in his throat I can hear his breath quicken through his nose.

I let out a deep growl and fist his hair tight in my palm as my cum shoots forward and fills his mouth. "Fuck. Fuck. Yeah. Oh my fucking…" My words are lost as I grunt out the rest of my thoughts.

He cups my balls as he swallows every drop, rubbing them back and forth. I roll my hips into it, savoring the softness of his fingers.

"Mmm. You did so good. I can't wait to watch you fuck *her* mouth like that."

I open my eyes and grin, deliriously satisfied. "Only if I keep getting to practice with you first."

He leans down and licks the sigil on my abdomen. The new one that Riot carved into me before the party the other night. "Promise me you won't forget that she's just our toy. Nothing more. We get to benefit from Riot's vendetta but when he's through with her, so are we."

I nod. *She could be so much more.*

"Atlas, *promise* me. Say it."

I scoot off the bed, grab a towel, and clean off my dick before putting my jeans back on. "I promise. *For now.*"

He sighs. "I heard you earlier with the raven. Don't let Riot hear you talk like that."

I pocket the rest of the vial and go to my closet. "Yeah, whatever, Val." I feel like I'm about to lose it. My hands tremble as I push through my designer clothes, searching for my favorite black cashmere sweater. The comedown from the poison always hits me harder after I cum. "Riot is fooling himself if he thinks he'll be satisfied with Maureen Blackwell just being our toy. She's his firecracker from Wickford Hollow."

Valentin reaches past me and grabs the sweater I'm looking for. "That was before he knew her last name. The fact that he felt something for her in that bathroom makes him even angrier."

I shrug. "Whatever."

He places a hand on my shoulder. "Careful, Atlas. Remember what my father taught us about girls like her?"

How could I forget? I spent every summer with Valentin and his family at their country estate. I learned quickly that his father, Laurent Erebus, is a scary motherfucker.

"If they don't comply, then they must be silenced," I repeat his father's cryptic words through gritted teeth.

"Thatta, boy." He pats me on the back so hard, it would have made a smaller man topple forward. But I'm six-foot-four and two-hundred pounds of solid muscle. Not a fucking ounce of body fat on me. So I don't budge an inch.

I hear the flapping of wings just as the raven flies back onto my window ledge and squawks. The lingering poison in my veins surges. I pull on my sweater before pocketing a few more vials of some of the other special blends I made earlier.

"You heading over to Swallow with me?" I ask, hoping he isn't. He and Riot are my best friends but sometimes I need a fucking break from the brooding.

He winks. "I'll meet you there. Gotta handle a couple of things first."

"You mean jerk off in your car," I tease.

He feigns a look of horror. "I'm offended. *Mary Shelley* is not just a car. And you know I would never soil the interior with my cum… I'm going to jerk off *next* to my baby."

I burst out laughing. "You're a fucking freak, bro."

Valentin palms my dick through my pants. "As are you. That's why we're friends with benefits."

I grab my leather jacket and head for the door. "Nah, we're only friends cause our parents made us."

Valentin snickers. "You can go fuck *yourself* next time."

I shoot him a grin. "I'm too pretty to fuck alone. Make sure you lock up before you leave."

There are only two people I trust to be in my room when I'm not here—Riot and Valentin.

He gives me a half-ass salute before I turn to leave. Fucking Valentin. He's one of the smartest people I know. Loyal to the bone. He would do anything for me and Riot. But his father's ferociousness simmers through him. He lacks empathy and compassion for everyone. Even us. It's just who he is.

I'm greeted by a few initiates as I trot down the stairs, but I barely look up. Nocturnus House is like a game to them. A club that everyone wants to belong to. For me, Riot, and Valentin, it's so much more. I have zero interest in making small talk with any of these wannabe frat boys. I fly past them and out the front door, heading in the direction of the campus bar.

There's only one person who I want to get to know this year. *Maureen Blackwell.* Fuck, when I had my fingers down her throat, I expected her to choke. But that hot little firecracker took it so fucking well. I'm getting hard just thinking about it.

I want to make her scream and cum and squirt all over the fucking place. She's just as much mine and Valentin's now as she is Riot's. That sweet little pussy of hers has no fucking idea what the hell she's in for. But she will real soon.

Swallow is already buzzing with students by the time I get there. A huge grin spreads across my face as I glance through the floor-to-ceiling windows and spot our little firecracker inside. *Once a party girl, always a party girl.*

I go in to get a closer look and damn… *She's dressed to fucking kill.* Perched at the bar in a short black mini-skirt, fishnet stockings, stiletto heels, and a black off-the-shoulder crop top, she stirs her whiskey old fashioned with one of her pointy black fingernails. Her dark brown hair is down across her shoulders and practically begging to be wrapped around my wrist.

I start forward then stop as soon as I see who she's with. *Villette Crane*. She's not exactly an enemy but she isn't a friend either. The Cranes are neutral in the ongoing feud between the Graves and the Blackwells. But if Villette is cozying up to Maureen… Riot is going to lose his shit. He'll behave but only to avoid another brawl with her brother Bones. That motherfucker is a lunatic. And that's saying a lot coming from me. We could handle him if we had to, but Villette isn't worth the blood and sweat.

I scan the room for Riot but don't see him. Fuck it. I could give a rat's ass about the feud or the Cranes. I wanna go play with our new toy.

Maureen's eyes widen when she spots me walking toward her. I notice her crossed thighs clench on the bar stool. That's right, Firecracker. *I knew you fucking liked my fingers in your mouth.*

I wedge myself in between her and Villette and lean over the bar to order a drink. Villette rolls her eyes and moves back as if I have some contagious disease. But Maureen freezes, the vein in her neck pulsing. She smells of whiskey and vanilla, and I want to drink her like that fucking cocktail she's holding.

I lean in close and invade her space, blocking Villette from her view. Her breath hitches as she follows my gaze traveling slowly down the length of her body. "Not that girl anymore, aye?"

"Fuck off, Atlas." Even as she tilts her chin up, her lower lip quivers. She's trying so hard to play it cool, but I see right through the act.

"Oh, I'm not complaining. Far from it." I thread a finger through an opening in her fishnets. "I think you look good enough to eat."

Her throat bobs as she swats my hand away. "I'm not on the menu."

"Well, you should be." I don't need to touch her wrist to know her pulse is racing. I can see it in her dilated eyes. In the way her chest rises and falls in little bursts.

"I thought I told you to fuck off," she snaps.

"But I'm so hungry," I whisper in her ear. A tremor shoots through my cock as I hear her suck in another sharp breath.

"Hey, psycho Ken, my friend told you to leave her alone. *Twice.* Now back it up and give her some room. Fuck." Villette elbow-shoves me to the side, and I let her. Satisfied that our little firecracker is riled up and sweating from every crevice.

I grab my drink off the bar. "Relax, little Crane. Just having some fun with the new freshman."

When I turn back to Maureen, the look on her face is murderous. Her jaw ticks as she fixates on me, refusing to break eye contact. The longer she stares, the angrier she looks. And it excites the fucking hell out of me.

"What's wrong, Firecracker? Not used to only having one man's attention on you? Hmm?" She stiffens and sits up straighter. I laugh and take a sip of my drink before prodding her some more. "Don't worry. Riot and Val are on their way. Then we can all order a piece of you."

Villette opens her mouth to retort but is cut off by Maureen flying off the bar stool. In one swift move, she pulls a knife from her skirt and presses it to my throat.

Fuck.

I'm so turned on now I can barely breathe. "Don't threaten me with a good time, baby girl."

"*Then don't make me slit your fucking throat,*" she growls.

If I was capable of love, then this would be it. "Fuck, you really are a firecracker," I murmur.

Her gaze darts from my lips to my eyes. "That's the thing about firecrackers… we explode."

Chapter Seven

Maureen

I KNEW I SHOULDN'T HAVE LET LIBRA TALK ME INTO dressing in her fucking clothes again. But that bitch doesn't take no for an answer. If I didn't have to live with her, I would have blown her off. Now I'm wearing fishnets and a skirt so short I can barely sit down without letting the whole bar know what color panties I'm wearing. I guess the saying is right about history repeating itself.

Because here I am on only my second night at Tenebrose Academy with a knife pressed to her cousin's throat. But he's not just anyone. No. This act will have consequences. But right now, I don't care. I'm fucking fuming.

"I know you consider yourself a big deal around here, but I'm not like everyone else," I snap. "You have no idea who I am so don't fuck with me."

Atlas doesn't look the slightest bit fazed by the blade at his neck. In fact, the sick bastard looks turned on. I want to slice the shit grin off his face. But I make the mistake of looking into his eyes and almost get lost in them again.

Fuck.

Why does he have to be so fucking hot?

"It's cute that you think you're actually going to do something with that knife, pretty girl. Did your daddy give you that before you left? Hmm? You should put it away before you hurt yourself."

The fucking audacity.

Heat rushes to my cheeks, and I'm so close to blurting out what happened the last time I held a knife to someone's throat. But I don't. Instead, I withdraw the blade, step back, and look around. Other than Villette, no one has noticed our exchange.

"You have no idea who I've hurt," I mutter.

"Oh, look," Villette interjects, "one of your psycho friends is here. Go hang out with him and leave us alone."

Atlas laughs and blows me a kiss before stalking off to join his asshole friend.

Fuck.

My stomach knots. I don't have the energy to deal with Atlas and Valentin tonight. "Actually, Villette, I'm pretty tired. Plus, classes start tomorrow and I gotta be up early. I think I'm going to head to bed."

She pouts her lips. "Come on, just stay for one more drink. It's a Tenebrose tradition."

I shake my head and throw on my coat. "I can't be tired tomorrow. Sorry. Rain check?" I'm starting to feel homesick. Villette is a lovely girl, but I miss Bailey like crazy. She's the only one who gets me.

Villette nods but her lips are pursed. "Don't let those assholes bully you, Maureen. If you leave now, they will think they've won."

She's right, but I don't care. I really am exhausted too. "I'm not running away, I promise. I just need a good night's sleep."

She finally concedes and gives me a hug before I leave. As I head to the door, I feel eyes on me. I shouldn't look back, but I can't help myself. I throw a glance over my shoulder and see Atlas and Valentin are laser-focused on me. Fuck. I spin on my heel and storm out.

The air outside has dropped at least twenty degrees since sundown. I button up my coat, grateful that I remembered to bring it. An uneasy feeling settles into my bones. The path ahead is dark as fuck and the ground uneven. I take a deep breath and charge ahead, stumbling every few feet in my heels. *And I'm sober.* I can't understand how anyone could do this drunk. I guess the kids here are used to it. I really hope I don't twist my fucking ankle.

At least Villette was understanding. Libra is going to lose it when she finds out I left. I've barely seen her since the party at Nocturnus and then she just barges into my bedroom tonight with an outfit picked out for me. *That girl is something else.*

Oh, fuck. I'm not more than ten feet from Swallow when I see Libra barreling toward me.

"Nope, nope, nope. You're not bailing on me tonight, Blackwell." She grabs my wrist and spins me back around toward the bar.

I pull back, digging my heels in the dirt and almost topple over. "Whoa, slow the fuck down. And *stop* calling me that."

Libra whips around and her long blonde ponytail almost smacks me in the face. "There are rules here, Maureen. *Social standards.* Everyone parties at Swallow the night before the first semester starts. *Everyone.* I swear to god if you make me look bad—"

"All right!" I say a little too loudly. "Fuck. I'll go back inside. But I'm not hanging out with your cousin or his asshole friends."

Her breath quickens, and she tightens her grip on my arm. "Nocturnus is here?"

I resist the urge to roll my eyes at her referring to them like they're some famous boy band. "Atlas and Valentin are. I haven't seen Riot. Why do you seem surprised? You just said *everyone* goes to Swallow."

She lets go of my wrist and smooths her hands down her tight pink dress. "They just never show up this early."

I shrug. "I actually don't care."

She glares at me. "You don't care about anything, do you, Blackwell? But with your family's money and power, I guess you don't have to. Just remember you're in Raven's Gate now. We play differently here."

My mouth hangs open, stunned by her words. And then my anger kicks in. "Ever since I got here, I've been bullied, stalked, assaulted… and it's only been two fucking days. If this is how you all *play* here then I want no part of it."

"What are you talking about? I know I'm bossy, but I haven't assaulted you. Fuck, you're so dramatic," Libra quips.

I snicker. "Why don't you ask your cousin and his friends who assaulted me?"

Her cheeks redden. "Don't say things you can't take back, Maureen. They'll hear you."

I shake my head. This place is insane. "Who will hear me? The fucking birds? There is something seriously wrong with all of you." I step back and turn around. "Fuck this, I'm going back to the dorms."

"Wait!" she shrieks.

I stop but refuse to turn back around. "What do you want from me?" I sigh.

"I-I don't have any friends," she whispers.

What the actual fuck? I stalk back over to her. "Are you joking?"

Her eyes are glassy. "No. I don't have like *actual* friends. I mean, I know everyone, but no one wants to hang out with me."

My heart sinks, and I almost feel sorry for her. "Oh, stop. You're rich, gorgeous, and sometimes pleasant. Why wouldn't you have friends?" I imagine a whole scenario where dozens of girls follow her around like obedient little lap dogs.

Libra glances back toward the bar. "Everyone's scared of *them*."

My stomach flips. Fuck. "Libra… are *you* scared of them?"

She shakes her head. "No. Fuck that. They can be assholes, but they're all I know. I grew up with all three of them."

I nod and actually feel sorry for her now. "Let's go inside and get a drink."

Her face lights up. "Okay. Sorry, I was so bitchy before."

I grin. "It's fine. Probably just that dress cutting off all the oxygen to your brain," I tease.

She giggles and loops her arm through mine. But as we approach the doors she holds me back for a second. "I heard that Nocturnus cornered you in the bathroom… if they've marked you then they own you. They'll keep coming and there's nothing you can do about it."

I nod and stare straight ahead. My heart skips a beat when I lock eyes with Riot through the window. I remember the roughness of his fingers sliding inside me. The taste of Atlas's skin when I almost gagged on him. Valentin pinching my nipples… *I came so fucking hard.*

"Who did you hear that from? Thought you didn't have any friends." I try to mask the ache of remembrance in my voice.

Libra chuckles. "I don't. But I have plenty of spies."

Of course, she does.

Between being stalked by a dead girl, three hot psychos, and this unstable beauty queen who's quickly becoming a stage five clinger, I might have to do a little spying of my own. I get the feeling there's some really dark shit going on around here.

✥

I'm going to be good this year. Better than the me I was back in Wickford Hollow. But my anxiety is through the roof, and I need a drink. Besides, classes don't start till tomorrow. *I can be bad for one more night.*

I march over to the bar with Libra in tow and order another whiskey old fashioned. "So, are you ever going to tell me what's up with Nocturnus? Why do they hate me so much?"

Libra's gaze flickers over to Riot as she sucks down a big swig of her gin and tonic. "You'll have to ask him. I learned my lesson about getting involved with their business."

There's something different about her tonight. She's more uptight than usual. But then again, I've only known her for two days so maybe this is normal for her.

I nod and try to get lost in the music. The dance floor is more crowded than it was when I first came in. Libra sways beside me, humming along to the song. It's actually kind of fun when I'm not thinking about the three psychos who are watching me like a hawk from across the room.

With sparkling chandeliers, purple velvet couches, and marble floors, Swallow is fancy for a college bar. Everyone here is dressed like they just came from a red-carpet event. I think Bailey would love it. I wonder what she's up to back home. I pull out my phone, snap a selfie of myself at the bar, and shoot it off to her in a quick text.

Miss, you bitch.

Texting bubbles appear right away. *Miss you too, babe. You look hot AF btw.*

I smile and send her a kissy face emoji before slipping my phone back into my purse.

As I look back up, I come face to face with a gorgeous dark-haired guy with green eyes. He gives me a sloppy grin. "Hi. You're beautiful. What's your name?"

My stomach does a little flip. It's been ages since anyone's hit on me. I tilt my head to the side in an attempt to be flirty. "Maureen. What's yours?"

He takes my drink from me and sets it on the bar. "Zeke. Come on, let's dance."

I let out a giggle as he locks his fingers in mine. I'm suddenly nervous and have no desire to be on that dance floor with everyone's eyes on me. "Thanks but I think I'm just gonna hang at the bar."

Zeke laughs and snakes an arm around my waist. He pulls me flush against him. "Fine. We can dance here."

I glance over at Libra who just shrugs and turns her attention back to the guy hitting on her. A little warning bell goes off in my head. Zeke is tall, dark, and handsome, but a little too aggressive for my liking. "Whoa, easy there. Give a girl a little space," I tease.

"Relax," he whispers in my ear. His breath reeks of beer and weed. "It's just one dance." He wraps his other arm around my waist and locks me tight to his chest. I try to push back but he's got me in an iron grip.

"I'm flattered, but I don't want to. Let me go, please." My pulse starts to race as I realize he's got me pinned against the bar now. I could scream for help but then I'd look like a lunatic.

Zeke slides his hands down my back and cups my ass. "Don't be shy. Wanna take this to the bathroom? I heard all about what you like to do in there."

My cheeks flame. Fucking hell. *I'm going to kill Riot.*

I punch Zeke hard in the chest. "You don't know shit. Now get the fuck off me."

He laughs again and leans in for a kiss. I lurch back and push against his chest with all my strength. "Stop. Get away from me," I yell this time.

"All right, that's enough," a deep gravelly voice commands from behind.

Without looking back, Zeke tightens his grip on my waist. "Fuck off and go find your own slut."

Valentin steps around, so he's in view. "How do you know she isn't mine?"

Zeke's face pales, and he immediately lets go of me. "Fuck. Sorry, Val. I didn't know."

My heart's racing, pounding so hard in my chest, I can feel it in my ears.

"Well, now you do. Run along, little Zeke." I almost burst out laughing because Zeke towers over Valentin by at least a foot. But the sheer terror in Zeke's eyes lets me know that Valentin is the one to be feared.

Zeke doesn't even look at me again before he scurries off.

With my adrenaline still spiking, I turn on Valentin. "Thanks for the assist but don't ever tell anyone that I'm *yours* again."

His black hair is slicked back off his forehead, showing off his big brown eyes, long eyelashes, and radiant skin. Dressed in all black, he looks like he just walked out of a dark mafia romance novel. He narrows his eyes down at me. "Don't flatter yourself. I'd like nothing more than to never see you again. But Riot has plans for you…"

My breath hitches in my throat. *Riot.* Fucking prick. "Where is your dark lord and master, anyway? He and I need to have words before he disappears back into his coffin," I retort.

"Nice Dracula reference," Valentin grumbles. "But I wouldn't do that if I were you. Unless *you* want to end up in a coffin."

We'll fucking see about that.

I scan the crowd and spot Riot over by the other bar in the opposite corner. I thrust my purse at Libra. "I'll be right back."

Her eyes widen. "Maureen, don't. You'll regret it."

Fuck these people. They're about to find out who the fuck I am. I snicker at her and Valentin before stalking off. I pound the floor with my heels as I march over toward Riot in a fury.

He leans casually against the bar, sipping a glass of whiskey. He watches me stomp across the dance floor the entire time. Our eyes lock, and I almost lose my nerve. His stare is unnerving, piercing, deadly.

"How fucking dare you tell people about what happened in the bathroom," I hiss.

He shows no emotion or reaction as I stand there fuming, hands on my hips.

"Which time?" he replies coldly.

"Excuse me?" I am not even sure I'm making sense right now. He's got me so wound up I'm dizzy.

He nods to the guys surrounding him and they take off. "Was it when you got fucked by four frat boys in the bathroom at Wickford Mansion? Or when I made you cum in the bathroom at Graves Library? Or is there another one? It's hard to keep up with all of your indiscretions, Firecracker."

I fight the urge to slap him. Every cell in my body is on fire. I can feel the heat spreading to every inch of me. "*I hate you.*"

Riot straightens and hovers over me. "I hate you more."

I can't breathe with him this close to me. "Why?"

He clenches his jaw as his gaze falls to my lips. "Because you're the reason I'm in hell."

I tilt my chin, refusing to back down. "Maybe it's because you're the devil."

Riot steps in closer, invading my senses with his intoxicating scent. "And you're a filthy little sinner who needs to repent."

The tension between us is thick, fiery, electric. My heart beats out of control as we glare daggers at each other, our breaths mingling in the narrow space between our bodies.

"I don't understand," I cry. "I've done nothing to you."

He drags his fingers up my chest and then wraps his hand around my neck. "You insult me by existing. Your very presence wrongs me. *The blood pumping through your veins is blasphemy.*"

Fuck. He's talking about the Blackwells. I don't flinch as his grip tightens. I hate myself for liking the way his cold hand feels around my throat. "You're wrong. *I'm not like them.*"

Riot's gaze lingers on my lips so long that I think he might kiss me. Which is crazy because I'm pretty sure he'd rather murder me. He finally looks up again. "I wish… No. All you Blackwells are the same." He jerks his wrist and my head snaps forward. "You're going to get what's coming to you, Firecracker. The audacity of you to come *here*. You're going to pay for what your family did to mine."

That cursed fucking name. I have never wanted to take back something more in my life. I need to know what this is about.

As his hand slips away from my neck, I grab it. "I don't think you want to hate me. Ask yourself why that is next time you try to ruin me."

Riot snatches his hand away. "Watch your back, Firecracker. I'm coming for you."

My stomach flips, and I'm not sure if it's from fear or lust, or both. I want to kill him *and* fuck him. And I think that's the only mutual thing we have in common.

Chapter Eight

Valentin

As I watch Maureen stalk over to Riot, I feel every muscle in my body tense. She's a spoiled fucking brat that dangles her pussy between us like it's the last drop of water in a barren desert. I should've let Zeke do what he wanted with her but for some vile reason, seeing his hands on her made my jaw tick. The thought of some douchebag soiling her before I do pisses me the fuck off. Zeke can have our fucking leftovers when we decide we're done.

"She's not like us, you know?" Libra leans against the bar, following my gaze across the room.

Our families are rich, controlling, and toxic as fuck. It's all we know. I look at Libra. Not a single blonde hair is out of place on her head. With her elongated curves, full lips, and flawless skin, she's stunning. But when I look in her eyes, I see the resemblance to Atlas, and I'm reminded that she's like a fucking sister to me. If I look closer, I see the flaws. The arrogance and superficiality. Those full lips are pumped full of collagen. Everything about her is deliberate and curated. From her overpriced handbag to the designer dress that's tight enough to cut off her air supply. But none of it can change the fact that she's hollow inside. Just like the rest of us. Because money does buy happiness but it's fleeting. We always need more.

"Maureen's a Blackwell. She's worse than us," I retort.

Libra shakes her head. "I don't know... something is off about her. I've partied with Draven Blackwell. He's never mentioned anything about a cousin from Wickford Hollow. And she doesn't seem to know anything about them."

Women can be so cunning and yet so naïve at the same time. "It's an act. I don't know what she's doing here, but I promise you I'll find out. Keep your guard up around that one."

Libra nods but she doesn't look convinced as she lips her straw. "You never trust anyone, Val. Maybe you're wrong about her."

I'm fucking what? I clamp onto her wrist, and she almost drops her drink. "I noticed you haven't sat down at all tonight, Libra. Your ass still hurt from that spanking you got?"

Her eyes well up for a second, but she blinks any sign of sadness away. "Fuck you, Val. Hope you enjoyed the show cause that's the last time you'll see that again."

I snicker. "Unless you piss Riot off again. Which we both know is bound to happen. You just can't help yourself."

She slams her drink down on the bar. "Why are you like this? I've known you since birth and you just sat there and watched me get humiliated like it meant nothing."

My gaze flickers back over to Maureen and Riot and a little twinge of jealousy rips through me. I want to be the one she throws her fury at. I sigh and let go of Libra's wrist. "I don't fucking care, Libra. Just because I'm friends with Atlas doesn't mean I'm obligated to have any empathy for the rest of his family. You broke the rules and got punished. And you deserved every lashing that came your way."

Her eyes narrow at me as she snatches her purse off the barstool. "Whatever. I'm out of here. This bar is boring me."

Maybe if I was a different person, I'd feel some sort of remorse or compassion for her. But instead, I'm just annoyed. Girls like her expect the world to be handed to them on a silver platter. They take more than they deserve without lifting a finger. Riot, Atlas, and I keep everyone in their proper fucking place. If you mess up, there are consequences. Libra's just sour she got caught for once. But that bitch has been trying to manipulate Riot since we were kids.

She is right about one thing, though. This place is boring as fuck. More than usual. I only came to appease Riot and Atlas, anyway. All these people… they're pathetic sheep. We say jump and they ask, how high? The power doesn't get me off the way it does Riot. Nor do I care for the attention that Atlas so desperately craves.

Fuck all that. I need something else to fuel me. Something more depraved. And I know just who can give me that. My gaze flickers back to Maureen. She's stomping away from Riot toward the back door. Blood rushes to my cock, tingling and burning at the same time, reminding me of the poison that swirls through my veins.

I grab her purse, the one Libra was supposed to be watching, and follow her.

With every step, I move quietly and swiftly, careful not to alert her to my presence. She's so close I can smell her, almost taste her on my tongue. An ache grows in my belly as I stalk her through the darkened hallway, past the bathrooms, and out the back door.

This urge to hunt and trap screams at me. It lives in my bones and drives me to the edge of madness. It's been suffocating not having a worthy target. But now that Maureen has landed in Raven's Gate, I can finally have a little fun.

I catch her scent again on the path up ahead. She's naïve to think she can walk back to the dorms by herself at this hour. *She'll learn soon enough.* I'm practically salivating with each sway of her tight little ass. The way it moves under the purpose and guidance of her strut. I get an eyeful of her tattoos under the moonlight—flowers and lace and filigree that twist around her ankles, up her creamy white thighs, and then disappear under her skirt. I want to rip the fabric clean off her, so I can see the rest. Right before I stretch that tight pussy around my dick.

As we move deeper into the woods, she uses her phone flashlight to illuminate the path. But it's worthless. There are far worse things than not being able to see out here. She should be more afraid of looking decay in the eyes.

I hold my breath when her stiletto heel gets caught in the mud. "Fucking hell," she curses. I creep closer, my heartbeat and adrenaline racing at the thrill of being so close to her fire. She bends over and digs at the dirt with her fingers. I'm harder than a fucking rock now. Her skirt has inched up, giving me a slight peek at those pillowy ass cheeks.

She grunts and groans as she pulls on her heel to no avail. "Fuck it," she snaps. With her bare foot out of the shoe, she hobbles on the other one.

I slither up behind her and whisper in her ear, "Need a hand?"

A blood-curdling scream rips from her throat as she tries to spin on one foot and topples over. Her ass hits the ground with a sploosh and sends mud flying out in every direction. She glares up at me as I smirk. "Fuck. You scared the crap out of me, Valentin. What are you doing, stalking me?"

I kneel down next to her and drag a finger through the mud. She flinches as I smear a chunk of it across her cheek. "Yes," I state.

Her chest heaves. She's completely stuck in the mud with no way out. "What do you want?" There's a quiver in her voice that sounds more carnal than afraid. And it turns me on way too fucking much.

"For you to be a good little girl for me." I smear her other cheek with more mud and then pinch her trembling lower lip between my fingers. "We can help each other."

Her throat bobs. "How?"

I drag my finger down her neck. "You'll let me do whatever I want to you… and in return, I won't share your dirty little secret with the whole school. It would be a shame to be labeled a slut *and* a liar."

Maureen's eyes widen. "I have no idea what you're talking about." She tries to scoot away, but I grab her ankles and hold them down.

"I did some digging today. Turns out not a single Blackwell has ever heard of you. Riot already hates you, but he might actually kill you if he finds out you are pretending to be someone else." I lick my lips, satisfied with the way her face pales and her hands shake. "You'll lose your seat at the fucking table."

For a second she almost looks relieved, and I'm worried that she's going to call my bluff. "I didn't lie," she snaps. "I am a Blackwell. It's just… complicated."

I don't care if she is, or she isn't. But she clearly does. "Classes haven't even started yet, and you're already a fucking pain in my ass, Firecracker. A pain that I want to reciprocate. But you have made things a whole lot more interesting."

I inch my finger down her chest and finger the top of her shirt. "Perception is everything. The people here are fickle and vapid. They will turn on you in a second. Wouldn't it be a shame if you had to spend your entire time here alone with no friends?"

Her cheeks redden and her jaw ticks. "Why are you doing this to me?"

A little tremor pulses down my shaft. "Because I've been bored for so fucking long and now you're here to entertain me." I tug gently on the top of her shirt. "Do we have a deal?"

She closes her eyes for a second and takes a deep breath. "How do I know you won't go blab about me after you do whatever it is you're going to do to me?"

Mmm, here we go. I knew I had her by the fucking nipples. "You don't. But if you say no, I'll hang a sign on you and tie you to that tree, so everyone can come and spit on your lying face."

"I hate you so much." Maureen's fists are clenched, and it makes me even harder at the anticipation of her possibly punching me in the face.

I fist her shirt in my palm and pull her body in close to mine. "Good. Let's make no mistake about this. I will never care for you. All I want is to use you like the dirty slut you are."

Her nostrils flare. "Fine. I'll let you do whatever you want as long as you keep my business out of your mouth… How long will this little arrangement last?"

A sick and twisted idea takes shape in my mind. I shrug. "When you start to bore me. Could be a week or the entire time you're here."

Her mouth gapes. "I've enrolled for two years, Valentin. What the actual fuck? You are deeply disturbed."

"You have no idea. First thing I want you to do is watch that fucking mouth of yours." I pinch her jaw hard between my fingers. "Say, *yes sir*."

She rolls her eyes. "You've got to be joking."

Her feistiness sparks something so feral in me, I could cum without even pulling my dick out. "This isn't a game, Maureen. It's a deal that can't be broken. These are hallowed grounds, and you will soon learn that oaths are forever until the devil releases you. *Say it.*"

All sarcasm and grit leave her face. "Yes, sir," she whispers.

"Good girl. Now, open your legs for me."

She hesitates for a second before spreading her thighs apart in the mud. It takes all my restraint not to pounce on her. But I want to take my time and savor this. "You still have that knife on you, Firecracker."

Maureen huffs. "Yes. Would you like me to stab you with it?"

I snicker. "Give it to me."

"It's in my purse."

I give her a look, and she huffs again before pulling the blade out of her ridiculously tiny handbag. She slaps the blade in my expectant hand. "Is this where you cut me up into little pieces, you weirdo?"

This mouth on her. Fuck. "Not yet. Your clothes first." I grab the side of her panties and slip the blade underneath. "Let's start with these. Hold very still."

I press the flat of the blade against her slit and a little whimper spills from her lips. She's just as fucking turned on as I am. As I jam the tip of the blade through her panties and begin slicing through each lacy thread, her wetness pools against my fingers. *I'm not even touching her yet.*

"Look at that needy pussy, crying for me." I jerk the knife all the way down until her moist panties are split wide open. Her juices trickle down her legs.

I told her it wasn't a game but that's exactly what this is. And I am already winning.

Chapter Nine

Maureen

There are moments in life where you have to ask yourself, what did I do to deserve this? Oh, yeah, I murdered someone once. My karma is pretty fucked. But I've never been a liar. The fact that I'm being punished for something I didn't even do, makes it sting so much more.

But as I lay here in the mud with my panties ripped open, it doesn't feel like punishment. It's dark and dirty and Valentin is certifiably unhinged, but my traitorous pussy is loving every fucking minute of it. The fact that he knows it, pisses me off more.

He balls my panties into his fist and shoves them in his pocket.

"They say the soil here can wash away one's sins. It seeps with bone dust and the tears of angels."

Fuck, he's crazy. I shiver in the cold mud as we lock eyes. "It feels just like regular old mud to me," I hiss. And it's currently making its way up my ass as I sink farther into it.

Valentin rocks back on his heels. "Let's find out, shall we? I want you to paint yourself with it."

I snicker. "Fuck, no. I'm not rubbing dirt all over my body." I start to get up, but he shoves me back down.

"Do it or there will be consequences."

Fuck.

I sigh and scoop some up in my hand. "You really need therapy."

He leans forward, baring his teeth. "*This is my fucking therapy.* Start with your pretty pink nipples."

My hands shake as I pull my top down, the cold air instantly pebbling my nipples. I drop a glop of mud on my chest and begin smearing it around my breasts.

"Yeah, there you go. Get nice and dirty for me."

Something about the ache in his voice and the feral look in his eyes makes my pussy clench, sending a tingle to my core. Fuck. Why is this turning me on?

"You like that don't you?" He presses his palms against my thighs and spreads me wider. "Mmm, so wet. Fucking glistening. But still too clean. I like my pussy *filthy*."

Oh, fuck. A rush of spasms flutters through my belly as I watch him devour me with his eyes. Do I really care what these people think of me? Maybe I should just call it quits now and leave.

He arches an eyebrow at me. "Having second thoughts, Firecracker? Shall I drive you out of town so you can go back to your whore mom and alcoholic father?"

Rage billows inside me, hotter than fire. I scoop up another heap of mud and smash it against my belly. "You're disgusting."

His fingers start to burn my skin as he digs deeper into my thighs. *That's not normal, right?* It's like they're on fire. "And you like it," he sneers. "But you're close to severely pissing me off. Now fucking do it."

"Yes, sir," I hiss. I smear the mud down my slick pussy and thighs, rubbing it lightly so as not to actually get it inside me.

"Do you think I'm stupid?" Valentin barks.

I squeal as he flips me over onto my stomach and smacks me hard on the ass. As I try to push up, he digs a knee into my lower back. "Don't fucking move."

Oh shit.

He presses the side of my face into the mud. "I'm going to show you what happens to bad girls who don't do as they're told."

Fuck, I can't breathe. There's mud in my nose and my mouth. I hear what sounds like him sliding his belt off and panic rumbles in my chest. I try to cough out a plea but that just puts more mud in my mouth.

He yanks my arms behind my back and wraps his belt tightly around them. With his knee digging into my lower back, my anger starts to climb again. But it's mixed with something else. A carnal ache that's festering in my middle. Fuck. *I feel fucking rabid.*

Valentin slaps my ass hard, and it sends a tingle all the way down to my core. "I will leave a fucking permanent handprint on this ass as a reminder of our fucking deal." He slaps me again, even harder. And my pussy spasms through the pain. With each sting from his hand, my body sinks lower into the mud. I'm fucking covered now.

He yanks my head up and growls in my ear, "I fucking own you now. When I tell you I want *my* pussy filthy, then it better fucking be."

I nod as he flips me back over. Pain shoots up my arms as I land on them, still bound behind my back. His eyes glaze with hunger as they roam every inch of me. He swirls his fingers through the mud on my stomach, playing with it like he's painting a canvas. I guess I'm his fucking canvas now.

What the hell have I done?

His breath is shaky. He looks possessed. "You like the pain. I can feel it. You like it just as much as I do."

I swallow hard as he drags his fingers down, dangerously close to my clit. "Pain can make you feel more alive, I guess…"

He slaps the inside of my thigh, and I almost cum. My hips involuntarily arch, betraying me. His eyes light up at my reaction. "I'm going to use you up, Firecracker. And when I'm done, you will wish you'd never set foot in Raven's Gate."

I flinch as he slaps my thigh again. "You can certainly try," I snarl. He has another thing coming if he thinks I can be easily broken. "But I'm a lot stronger than I look."

Valentin smiles but it doesn't reach his eyes. "We'll see about that. Remember, I'm not the only one you'll have to deal with this year."

Fuck. Riot and Atlas. The three of them are determined to ruin my fucking life, and I've only known them for two days. Fuck me.

Valentin unhooks his belt and slides it back through his pants. He then snatches my phone and begins typing into it. "From now on, when I call, you answer. Rest up, Firecracker. You're going to need it."

I sit up and wiggle my skirt back down. I resist the urge to rub my sore wrists. I can't let him see any weakness. "Are we done for tonight, then?" I ask, annoyed. My ass and thighs are still tingling from his hand, along with my fully erect nipples. I'm exhausted and can't wait to crawl into bed.

He nods. "Don't even think about showering tonight. I want

you to sleep in your filth so you can remember what happens when you defy me. And trust me, I'll know. Your punishment will be even worse if you disobey me twice."

Is this a fucking joke? "Fuck you! I can't crawl into my clean bed like this. Are you insane?"

He flashes me a look so deadly it makes my insides coil. "Try it and find out. I fucking dare you."

Fucking bastard. And this is just the beginning. I can't even fathom what other twisted fucked up things he has planned for me. Not to mention the sick way that a part of me is excited by it.

I roll my eyes and stand up. "Yes, sir." I don't even remotely try to hide the sarcasm and disdain in my voice.

"You can shower in the morning. But tonight you'll pay your penance. And if you even think about breaking our deal, I'll show you who Nocturnus really is."

A shiver crawls up my spine and Libra's words from earlier echo in my mind. *If they mark you, they own you. Forever.*

🦋

I'm half-tempted to ignore Valentin's warning and jump in the shower, but an eerie feeling of being watched plagues me. He could have installed cameras in my room for all I know. I'm still picking leaves out of my hair when the elevator doors open to my floor, and I'm pretty sure I have twigs in my ass.

I was hoping to avoid my overbearing roommate, so when I see her perched on the kitchen counter, eating a tub of ice cream, I let out a frustrated sigh.

She takes one look at me and wrinkles her nose. "What the fuck happened to you?"

I feel my cheeks flame under her scrutiny. "I don't want to talk about it."

Her eyes darken. "They've claimed you, haven't they?"

I stare at her for what seems like an eternity, and I'm filled with envy. She's a slave to her money and her status but she's free to do what she wants. I will never have that here. "I'm not a piece of property, Libra."

She hops off the counter and puts the tub back in the freezer, licking her spoon one last time. "You don't get it, Blackwell. This town, this school… it all belongs to them. They'll never let you leave."

A raven squawks at our window. I flinch as it pecks the glass. Fuck. "We'll see about that. I'm going to bed."

Her eyes bulge out. "You're not going to shower first?"

I look down at the floor as the shame threatens to swallow me whole. "I'm… too tired."

"Fuck," she quips. "They won't let you. You're in so fucking deep."

"Goodnight, Libra."

I slam my bedroom door behind me and collapse against it. *I need to find a way to get the upper hand.* I can almost guarantee those psychos have some skeletons of their own hidden away. I refuse to be the broken girl they want me to be.

But for tonight, I'll play along. So, I peel off my dirty clothes and slide into bed, utterly disgusted that I'm sleeping in this filth.

As soon as I turn off my bedside lamp, my phone lights up. I groan when I see Valentin's name flash across the screen.

My stomach flips when I read his text. *Good girl.*

Fuck.

Can he see me? Or is he just so arrogant that he assumes I've obeyed him?

I hate myself so much right now.

I have to find a way to get out of this mess before I lose every ounce of self-respect I have left.

My phone lights up again, and I think I'm going to be sick. It's from an unknown number but I know exactly who it is.

If you had watched your back, Firecracker, you'd still be wearing clean panties.

Sweat beads down my back and it carries the scent of the woods in it. My fingers fly across the keyboard as I text back: *Fuck off, Riot.*

He texts back as soon as I hit send.

Meet me in the library tomorrow night if you want me to keep your dirty little secret.

What the actual fuck? Valentin said he wouldn't tell him anything.

I'll pass, thanks. I hit send and instantly regret it. I'm just winding him up even more.

The typing bubbles on the screen make me shudder as I wait for his response.

When two boys go missing on Halloween night
And a pretty little Firecracker is the last to see them alive,
On raven's wings, she takes a hurried flight.
And disappears by morning light.

Oh, that fucking secret.

Fuck.

It feels like the room is spinning out from under me. I clench the sheets, squeezing them until my fingers ache. How could he possibly know anything about that night?

I start to text and then erase it. Fuck. I don't even know how to respond. He could be bluffing.

Your silence is all the response I need. See you tomorrow night, Firecracker...

Fuck. I want to scream.

Chapter Ten

Maureen

AFTER TAKING TWO SHOWERS TO GET ALL THE MUD and grime off my body, I dress, grab my book bag, and head down the twisted path toward the main hall of Tenebrose Academy. I'm not more than a few feet away from The Nest when a willowy figure pops out from between the trees.

"Hi, Maur!" Jessamine shrieks, sending a flock of birds to scatter.

I jump and nearly twist my ankle on a piece of fallen dogwood. "For fuck's sake, Jess. You have to stop scaring me like that."

And in true Jessamine fashion, she shrugs, looking wounded and surprised all at the same time. I have to remind myself that she's a ghost from another century and has zero awareness of her ability to defy space and time. "Ugh, sorry, Maur. I was trying to announce myself louder this time, so you didn't think I was sneaking."

The trees are taller and closer together than I remember from last night. It provides an eerie blanket of darkness that creates more shadows. More places for creepy things to lurk. I sigh and start walking again. "Well, it had the opposite effect. Maybe next time, try just walking up like a normal person and saying hello."

She sticks out her lower lip in a pout. "Okay."

I feel bad. It's not her fault she's a ghost. "It's fine. I'll get used to it."

Her blue eyes sparkle, and she perks up again. "Are you excited for your first day of school? I remember my first day. At least, I think I do. Professor Erebus says I get my days confused."

What the actual fuck was up with that? "Jessamine, that's the third time you've brought him up. What's the deal with you two?"

Her eyes widen. "Nothing! We're friends. He's not like the others."

Oh, not like his psycho nephew who terrorizes girls he barely knows?

I'm about to press for more details when Villette calls my name from behind. "Hey, wait up!"

I turn to see her svelte figure jogging toward us. Her makeup and hair are flawless as usual. "Well, aren't you perky in the morning," I tease.

She laughs throatily. "The curse of having an insomniac for a brother. Someone had to be cheery in the morning."

As we walk, I catch traces of rose, hyacinth, and the faint trace of something familiar. Something I can't quite place. "So, are you from Raven's Gate or did you transplant in like my dumb ass?"

Villette scrunches her nose at me. "Already hating it here, I take it?" She shakes her head and laughs. "No, I'm from Ever Graves."

Jessamine skips around us as we walk. "Villette Crane," she chants. "The prettiest girl in Ever Graves."

I stop, making a decision that may make her wish she'd never befriended me. "I'm a Blackwell," I say abruptly.

Villette smirks. "I know."

"How? Oh, wait, let me guess, Riot and his hellhounds have told everyone." Fuck. I came here to start fresh and yet I'm once again the subject of drama.

Villette fumbles with the buttons on her black cashmere sweater. She shakes her head. "It wasn't hard to figure it out. Tenebrose only accepts students of a certain… caliber. I knew you weren't related to anyone from Nocturnus. Or me. Plus, you are sharing an entire floor with Libra Thorn. Only founding members of Tenebrose and Ever Graves get those rooms."

There's so much my mother has kept from me…

I dig my heels into the soft dirt. "Can you tell me why everyone hates my family?"

Her eyes widen. "You don't know?"

I sigh. "My mom was cut off from them when she got pregnant with me. I was raised in Wickford Hollow. I've never met anyone from her family, and she never talks about them."

Villette's face falls. She looks at me with what appears to be pity. Great.

Jessamine nods. "The ravens know."

I try hard not to roll my eyes. Because there's another part of me that senses something strange about these birds.

"Do you really not know anything about Ever Graves? About all of us?" Villette looks concerned now.

My stomach knots. We have gotten closer to the main hall without me even realizing it. With each step I take, more students appear. The front lawn is crowded with an array of the gothiest-looking goth people I've ever seen in my life. I feel like I've been dropped into an episode of a young adult vampire show where everyone is beautiful, intoxicating, and dangerous as fuck.

My head tingles a little as a burst of ice-cold air whooshes past me. "You catch on quick," I retort. "I know nothing, Villette. Please tell me." It's getting hard to breathe again. I can't figure out why. It's like there are these little airless pockets in the atmosphere that I keep slipping into.

Her eyes dart around the grounds. "Not here. Let's meet up after school."

I nod and try to swallow, but my mouth is dry.

Jessamine gives my pinky a hard pinch. *Don't get lost, Maur. Don't drown.*

I blink a few times and all the air rushes back into my lungs. Jessamine is gone and Villette is guiding me forward, her arm through mine.

"You've been marked," she whispers. "I'm so sorry."

What the fuck? Everyone is mad here. I'm sure of it. "Vi—"

She squeezes my elbow. "*After school.*"

Chills snake up my back to the sound of a large tower bell echoing through the grounds. *What is this place really?*

Villette gives me an air kiss. "Bye, girl. Enjoy your first day of classes. Text me if you need anything."

I need something right now, I angry scream in my head. I pull out my vape and inhale a deep puff. "See ya later," I say instead.

I pull out my schedule and the map and try to make sense of it. My first class is literally called *Appreciation of Melancholic Music*. Fuck me.

I follow the path around the main hall and shiver as I approach the spot on my map. The ominous black building with iron spires and purple stained-glass windows, resembles a church. Three black ravens perch on its highest point.

As I near the door, I notice a plaque on the side of it with the words, *Nephthys*, etched in gold. I trace my fingers over the warm metal and feel a surge of adrenaline spike in my bloodstream.

"It means goddess of death," a man's voice breaks through my spell.

I snatch my hand away and turn to see a handsome man standing next to me. His glasses sit low on his broad nose as he narrows his bright blue eyes down at me.

"Do people worship her here?" I ask like it's perfectly normal to hold a college class inside a creepy old church that has the goddess of death as their patron saint.

He sticks out his hand, avoiding the question. "Professor Harker."

So the teachers here are hot too…

I shake his hand. "Maureen Blackwell. You didn't answer my question."

He winks and runs a hand through his black hair. "I'm the teacher. I ask the questions."

I fidget with the zipper of my brown leather jacket. The way he looks at me makes me anxious. There is something about the men here. They all seem to have this underlying feral look in their eyes. Like they will snap at any given moment.

Students file past us, hurrying to get inside. A couple pat him on the back as they walk by. He smiles and nods back. I shake my head and start forward, not wanting to be the last person to go in. If Tenebrose is anything like a regular school at all, all the seats in the back will fill up first. No one wants to be head of the class on the first day. *Especially not me.*

Professor Harker steps in front of me, blocking my way to the door. "I'm sorry I didn't make it to your grandfather's service. Lionus was the epitome of stoic."

My mouth is dry again. It's one thing to know that I have grandparents in Ever Graves, but to hear one of their names out loud… It's like a punch to the gut. My grandfather is a man I've never met and now I never will.

I nod, concealing my surprise. "Thank you."

"Of, course. See you inside." He steps aside to let me pass.

As soon as I step into the drafty *goddess of death church*, I scan the room for my stalkers. Satisfied that they aren't in this class, I breathe out a sigh of relief and make my way over to an empty pew.

The doors shut with a bang and Professor Harker saunters to the front of the class. "Good morning everyone. Today we'll be listening to the ethereal music of the great Camille Saint-Saens, starting with *Danse Macabre* of course. But first, let's get that pesky roll call out of the way. I want to make sure you are all *accountable*."

His gaze lands on me and every inch of my body shivers.

Fuck me.

🦋

After agonizing through three more roll calls in Alchemy, Latin, and Poetry, we finally break for lunch. Still no sign of Riot, Atlas, or Valentin, so I'm relieved. But I also feel a strange sense of longing.

I avoid the cafeteria by finding a small café on campus. Tucked between two stone gargoyles, I almost miss it. A guy with blue hair and face piercings snickers from behind the counter when I walk in.

The irony that I first wanted to be known as a Blackwell here is sickening. Now I'd give anything to just be the poor daughter of a small town sheriff.

I look up at the menu, avoiding rude counter guy's snarky gaze. "I'll have a caramel latte and the chicken salad."

He raises a pierced eyebrow at me. "Are you sure?"

My annoyance builds as he continues to look at me like I don't belong there. "Um, yeah. Unless it's a bad choice."

"Your funeral." Blue-haired guy shrugs and punches in my order. "Have a seat, and I'll bring it over to you when it's ready."

Should I have ordered the soup instead? What the fuck was wrong with the chicken? I wonder if I'll have one day where something weird or creepy doesn't happen.

I pick a table in the corner and plop down. Only three more classes to go and then I can go back to my room and contemplate my terrible life choices. As I look around the sparse café, I don't see any other students. I'm grateful for the solitude but also curious.

Professor Harker walks in, making the hairs on my neck stand up. Fuck. I hope he doesn't want to sit with me. Although, maybe I can ask him more questions about my family.

I'm contemplating waving him over when the door swings open and in walks and the grown-up version of Valentin. That must be Professor Erebus…

His gaze lands on me and darkens.

Fuck.

He whispers something into Harker's ear and they both nod.

I jump as rude counter guy slams my food on the table.

"Thanks," I snap, emphasizing the s. I jerk my head toward the two teachers. "Don't they have like a faculty lounge or something?"

The guy snickers again. "This is the faculty lounge, genius." He laughs all the way back to the counter.

Ugh. Well, it's too late to get food anywhere else now. I'll just eat fast and then sprint out of here.

I shovel a huge bite of creamy chicken salad into my mouth

seconds before Professor Harker stalks over. "Miss Blackwell, breaking the rules already?"

I chew for what feels like an eternity while he expectantly taps his fingers on the table. "Not intentionally. I'm still learning my way around."

He nods and smiles, but his eyes remain cold and full of malice. "We'll let it slide for today."

I slump back against my chair, relieved. "Thank you, Professor. It won't happen again."

But just when I think I'm in the clear, Valentin's clone from the future strolls up. "Tenebrose is easy to get lost in, Miss Blackwell. I've tasked my nephew with being your guide for the day."

Oh, no. Heat floods my cheeks.

Professor Erebus smirks as he continues. "Valentin will be here shortly and walk you to your next class."

Fuck.

I grip the bottom of my chair. "Oh, I don't think I need a guide. Thank you, though. I can find my way around."

His eyes darken. "Nonsense. Valentin's great-grandfather, my uncle, founded Tenebrose Academy. He'll be an excellent guide."

There's no getting out of this. Fuck. I'm going to be stuck with Valentin all fucking day. I bet he'll make sure I don't stand Riot up tonight too.

I take a big gulp of my now cold latte and force a smile. "Sure. Can't wait."

But before I have a complete and total meltdown, Villette comes barreling in like a dark angel. "There you are!" She grabs my wrist and pulls me up from the chair. "Sorry, Professors, I was supposed to show Miss Blackwell the cafeteria."

Professor Erebus's eyebrows pinch into a scowl. "Very well.

I'm sure Valentin will be disappointed, though. He was looking forward to showing you around."

I bet he fucking was.

Villette drags me out of there so fast that I almost fall over outside. "Thanks for the save but please slow down."

She whips around. "Don't ever come over here again. The punishment…"

My skin prickles. "Okay, I promise."

Once we're back in front of the main hall, she lets go of my arm. "Sorry, if that was harsh, but there are certain rules you do not want to break."

I nod. "I'm starting to figure that out." Every sentence uttered in this place was subtext for something else. Every person here had something to hide. Their voices seem to be laced with sinister desire and craving. But they are so tightly wound, it gets stifled into something monstrous. I feel it in my bones.

I make it through the rest of my classes without running into Nocturnus, but only because they didn't show up for the last two. My stomach had clenched when their names were called. So when they didn't respond, I was able to relax and at least try to pay attention to the class.

But I can't help but wonder what they are up to.

As I wait by the path for Villette, three ravens fly at my face. I scream and lurch back just as they dive at me again. "Fucking hell." I cover my face and swat at them with the other hand.

"Leave her alone," Jessamine cries out.

The ravens squawk at her before taking off.

I feel my cheeks redden as two different groups of students laugh at me as they pass. "Yup, hilarious," I call out, which only makes them laugh harder.

Jessamine hands me the clip that must have fallen out of my hair. "They won't stop until you give in."

I huff as I pluck a few feathers out of my hair. "Give in to what?"

"I'm not allowed to say," she whispers.

I groan and brush past her. "Thanks for nothing," I call back.

Villette will understand. I hope.

The trees seem to cower away from me as I stomp through the woods. I'm fucking fuming so hard I don't notice until it's too late.

Fuck, I must have taken a wrong turn.

My chest tightens and I swallow hard as I find myself in front of Nocturnus House. The wind picks up. It tickles the back of my neck and sends goose pimples over my flesh.

I'm mesmerized by its vulgarity. In the light of day, I can see that its lines are sharper, the decay uglier, and the ground muddier than it was the night of the party. And the plants. Holy fucking shit. No wonder I couldn't breathe. The entire front of the house is covered in hemlock plants.

The iron gates open with a wail and Atlas stands there like a Greek god. He's so fucking beautiful it hurts to look directly into his eyes. They remind me of the ocean—soft yet dangerous. He's kinder than the other two. Just as psycho, I'm sure, but warmer. Or maybe it's just a trick to lure me.

He waves and a tingle floats through my body. "Come and hang out with me, Firecracker."

Moisture pools between my thighs. I lick my lips, thirsty all of a sudden. "I got turned around. Can you just point me in the direction of the dorms?"

He flashes me a devilish smile. "I want to show you something. Don't be scared."

Butterflies flutter my belly. I want to melt inside his voice, his chiseled arms, his thick thighs… Fuck. Not again. I need to stop bending over for these fuckboys. But I can't make myself leave. I'm captivated, drawn in, by all that he is.

I blow out a deep breath. "It takes a lot to scare me, Atlas."

He holds out his hand. "Is that a challenge? Nothing gets me more excited than making pretty girls scream."

I swallow hard and take his hand. "It's a fact."

As soon as our fingers touch, he laces them and pulls me through the gates. It feels ceremonious like I'm crossing a sacred threshold.

"You're turned on. Also a fact," he whispers.

I clench my thighs together as his scent envelops me. It's fresh and earthy like rain. "Don't flatter yourself," I quip back. The smirk on his face lets me know he's not buying my attempts to seem disinterested.

"This way, Firecracker." I let him lead me to a massive greenhouse behind the mansion.

"Plants? This is what you want to show me?" I scoff.

Atlas takes a vial from his pocket, pops the cap, and waves it under my nose. I wince as the pungent scent burns my nostrils. "What the fuck?"

"Foxglove." Without hesitating, he downs the whole thing.

"Are you crazy?" Oh, fuck. Did this asshole just off himself in front of me? Fuck.

Atlas rubs his lips. "Mmm. So good. I bet your pussy tastes like poison too."

I'm dumbfounded. Is this a joke? No, it couldn't be. I smelled it. He fucking just drank Foxglove and is not even breaking a sweat.

I hug my arms to my chest. "How are you not dead after drinking that?"

"You have a lot to learn, Firecracker." He brushes his finger across my chest, and I quiver. "And I'm going to teach you."

I clench my thighs together. His voice is deeper, raspier, more feral than the others. "I don't trust you," I murmur.

He runs the pad of his thumb up and down my collarbone. "Good. It's more fun when you don't."

I take the empty vial from him and smell it again. The fumes instantly send a searing pain through my head. He really fucking drank poison. "How are you immune?"

He inches his thumb up my neck and across my lips. I fight the urge to lick it. "I can make you powerful, Firecracker. Say yes, and I'll show you a world better than any fucking wet dream you've ever had."

I was close to passing out from tension and anticipation. There's no way in hell I can trust him but where's the harm in learning a few new tricks?

Besides, these plants grow all over the campus. I need to learn how to breathe around them.

I swat his hand away from my face. "What are you getting at, Atlas?"

He opens the door to the greenhouse and gestures for me to go inside. "I'll teach you how to be like me. Immune to all types of poison. But you have to do everything I say. Understand?"

My eyes dart between him and the door. "How do I know you're not just trying to kill me?"

Atlas laughs but it's not malicious. "Listen, pretty girl, if I wanted to kill you, you would have keeled over the second you took a sip of that caramel latte today. This isn't a trick. It's an invitation."

Fuck. Of course, he knew I was at the teachers' café today. He even knows what I fucking ordered. It's impossible to do anything discreet around here. That makes me really fucking nervous.

"Fuck it. Teach me." I instantly regret it as soon as I say it because I know this just pulls me in deeper with them. But I also can't pass up an opportunity to learn more about Nocturnus and the Blackwells. He thinks he'll be teaching me about poison while I'll be watching his every move. Sooner rather than later, I need to get some leverage on *them*.

Chapter Eleven

Atlas

I'm obsessed with her. She's not like the other girls. Riot and Valentin feel the same even though they won't admit it. But Maureen Blackwell has gotten into all of our heads. She's full of secrets and mystery. Like a puzzle I have to solve, or it will kill me.

The way her body reacts to me makes my cock so fucking hard. She wants us as much as we want her. But she's too proud to admit it.

I come up behind her as she's studying one of my plants. "That one's called deadly nightshade. Isn't it beautiful? It reminds me of you." I place my hands on her shoulders, and she flinches.

"Why do you drink poison?" Her voice is breathless and raspy.

I reach through her arms to snip a leaf off from the plant she stands in front of. Her body goes rigid against mine. "I need it. Some say it's a curse. But I fucking love it. It's like the best fucking drug you'll ever taste. You'll see."

She doesn't stop me when I lift up her shirt and caress her belly with the leaf. I draw circles around her belly button, obsessed with the way she quivers and shakes under my touch. While Riot and Valentin want to torture her, I'm going to make her my muse. A doll for me to play with.

I pull the edge of her shirt up higher, so I can look at the rise and fall of her breasts inside her black lace bra. Her pulse quickens as she leans back against my chest. "Atlas… I feel dizzy."

"*Good*," I hum in her ear. I take the tip of the leaf and drag it through her cleavage. "That's from the toxin. Don't be scared, pretty girl. Let it happen."

I move higher, dragging the leaf gently across her lips.

"Fuck… my mouth is tingling. It's starting to burn."

I smile into her ear as I remember my first time. "Relax… your body will build up a tolerance."

She bucks against me, and it takes everything I have not to bend her over my apothecary table and fuck her ass raw. I want to fill her up with poison and cum. But I have to be patient.

She lets out a little whimper as I slide the leaf down her chest again and slip it into her bra. I nestle it against her left nipple. "Oh, that stings. I don't know if I can do this."

The sight of sweat glistening down her belly makes my cock throb. I want to rip off all our clothes and grind against her body. "I'm going to edge the fuck out of both of us, pretty girl."

She clings to me as the toxin spreads into her pores. "I can't… breathe."

Fuck. I want to keep going, but she's not ready. I remove the leaf from her bra and spin her around to face me. Her eyes are glazed, hazy, like she's in a trance.

"Here, drink this." I place a cup of magnesium to her swollen lips.

Slowly, she drinks it down. I watch how her throat bobs and glistens under the pale sunlight. It's hot as fuck. She's drenched. Her hands shake around the cup, but she never breaks eye contact with me. Which makes me even harder.

I dab some of the magnesium onto a cloth. "Pull your bra down and let me tend to that pretty pink nipple of yours."

With a trembling hand, she slowly peels her bra back. I fight the urge to suck on her hard nipple. I want to watch her squirm as I lick the poison off. But I hold back.

"I-I can feel my lips again. What did you give me?" she murmurs.

I shake my head. "Don't worry about that, pretty girl." She shivers when I place the cool cloth against her breast and gently rub. "There... how does that feel?"

She tries to stifle a moan and it comes out like an adorable squeak. "Better. It doesn't sting anymore."

Fuck. I get just as excited with the aftercare as I do with inflicting the pain. "Good. We'll do more next time. It's time for you to go back to your room and get ready for Riot. He'll be pissed as fuck if you don't show up to the library tonight."

And like that, the spell breaks. Her brow furrows and her cheeks flush. "*If* I go. I fucking hate him."

No, she doesn't. She wants to hate him. To hate all of us. But she knows deep down inside, she's just like us. Riot knows it too. He just wants to take his vendetta out on her because she's the only Blackwell who was able to slip through the gate. A reminder of all his family has lost. A reminder of his curse.

I pull her shirt down and step back. Not touching her feels like death. "If you don't go, he will find you and punish you. This isn't Wickford Hollow, Firecracker. Riot isn't some overly aggressive frat boy. He's a monster. A devil. If you don't comply, he will torture you in ways that will scar you forever."

"And you're okay with that?" she snaps.

I shrug because she doesn't understand yet. "Of course, I am. I don't question his methods. Or those of Valentin either. We are all different, but we're loyal to each other. They have their reasons. Just as you have yours."

She grunts in frustration. "Fuck that, Atlas."

I pull her to my chest and look down into her golden amber eyes. It's like staring into the sun and all I want is for her to burn me. "When you stop lying to yourself, you will enjoy every second of our depravity. And you can come to me when their darkness suffocates you."

She shakes her head. "That's not what I came to Tenebrose for. You don't understand the things I've… I don't want to be that girl anymore."

So many nightmares plague her during the day, I want to fuck them all out of her. "This isn't a drunken night in the bathroom at a Halloween party, pretty girl. It's not a fucking game. You belong to us."

She sighs and turns to leave but pauses at the greenhouse door. "No. I need the three of you to stay the fuck away from me."

Her resistance makes me hard again. I charge forward and pin her against the door. "That's never going to happen."

She whimpers and stumbles back when I release her.

"Come to me after they hurt you, pretty girl. I'll be waiting."

Maureen is like a roll of the dice. She's impulsive, stubborn, and unpredictable. Which is why none of us are letting her go.

Chapter Twelve

Maureen

"YOU DID WHAT?" VILLETTE'S EYES WIDEN AFTER I tell her about me and Atlas in the greenhouse. My head is pounding, and my nipple is still tingling from the nightshade leaf. "Every time I get around them, something strange happens to me. It's like I'm under some kind of spell."

She flops down onto my couch and sighs. "That's because they've marked you. You have no idea what you're a part of now. If I were you, I'd leave town. Get far away from here."

What the fuck?

"She can't," Libra murmurs. I didn't even see her come in

My throat is scratchy like I haven't drank water in days. "Okay, one or both of you need to start talking right now."

They exchange a look between them that makes my stomach drop.

Libra goes to the kitchen and comes back with a bottle of wine and three glasses. After pouring one for each of us, she nestles down on the couch next to Villette. The two of them sitting side by side look like a designer perfume ad.

"Listen, Blackwell, I realize that your naivety is genuine, so I'm going to level with you. Your family is very powerful. They're fucking scary actually. When I found out that I'd be rooming with you… I'm not going to lie, I wasn't thrilled." Libra purses her lips onto her glass and takes a small sip of the pink rosé.

Villette rolls her eyes. "When are we going to stop paying for the sins of our ancestors? What happened to Riot's family is not *her* fault."

Libra groans. "Tell that to Riot. What I can't figure out is how she came through the gate."

"Um, hi. Still in the room. What the fuck are you both talking about?" I'm beyond frustrated. Everyone seems to know about my life but me.

Villette flashes me a look of pity. "Sorry, girl. There's bad blood between the Blackwells and the Graves. No one really knows how it started, but basically, your family drove Riot's family out of Ever Graves like a century ago or something."

"That's when Nocturnus was born," Libra adds. "They sold their souls to the devil, so to speak, and are bound to Raven's Gate forever. My brother, Aries, wants nothing to do with it, but Atlas… he got sucked in by Riot's spell just like the rest of us."

It feels like the room is spinning again. I'm no stranger to dark and spooky things, I come from a town full of fucking ghosts. *My best friend is a ghost.* But devils and oaths and sinister family feuds? That's not what I signed up for.

I take a hit off my vape and exhale slowly. "Are you saying they have powers or something? What is the deal with the ravens? Wait, why can't I leave?"

Villette jumps from the couch and grabs my hands, guiding me to the nearest chair. "Whoa, just breathe. You look like you're about to have a panic attack."

"She should have a panic attack," Libra hisses. "Blackwells aren't allowed in Raven's Gate. Yet somehow, poof, here she is. I had a feeling this year was going to be fucked."

I take a deep breath and glare at her. "Stop talking like I'm not right in front of you."

She shrugs and takes another big swig of wine. "Just stating the facts."

Villette shoots her a glare before turning back to me. "Yes, they have powers. When the feud started, all the families took sides. The Thorns sided with the Graves. My family, the Cranes, do our best to stay neutral. The ravens are hard to explain… Think of them as messengers, watchers, harbingers of darkness. They take more than they give. Nocturnus has served them for decades."

My fingers start to shake around the stem of my glass. I tighten my grip; afraid it will fall from my hands and shatter. "I don't think the ravens like me very much… Did they give them their powers?"

"Now, she's catching on," Libra groans. "For fuck's sake, Blackwell, do we have to spell it out for you? Nocturnus is untouchable. In over a hundred years, there's never been a coven like Riot, Atlas, and Valentin. Every day, they get stronger. Soon, the ravens will be serving *them*."

This can't be real. Ghosts are one thing, but covens? I can't.

"I'm hallucinating, right? The toxins from Atlas's stupid nightshade plant are clouding my mind."

Villette pours me another glass of wine. "Afraid not, girl. It's all very real. Nocturnus is out for blood. For revenge. And they want their town back."

"Ever Graves," I murmur.

Libra nods. "Yup. And then you walked in like a shiny new toy on Christmas morning. You're the first Blackwell to set foot in Raven's Gate since the feud started. Which means the ravens let you in."

Villette refills her glass. "Which means they want you here for a reason."

I feel my lip start to quiver. "But… I'm not from Ever Graves. My parents were cut off from the Blackwells when I was conceived. I have *nothing* to do with this fight."

The two stunning girls exchange another look.

Fuck.

Libra's throat bobs as she swallows down the rest of her wine. "That's because your mother was engaged to someone else… Her indiscretion caused a huge rift between the families and sent another clan here to Raven's Gate in support of the Graves."

I'm going to be sick. Should I really be surprised? She's cheated on my father my whole life. "Who?"

Villette shifts in her seat, hesitant. "Julian Erebus."

Fuck.

No. How could my mother let me come here not knowing any of this? She must hate me more than I thought. My dizziness fades as a surge of rage shoots through my body. "*Professor Erebus?* Fuck," I mutter as I look at Libra. "Earlier, you said I can't leave. Why not?"

"Because the ravens won't let you. Riot's made sacrifices to ensure that you don't." She says it so calmly as if it's perfectly normal to be held captive in a creepy town by a flock of birds.

"Sacrifices?" I ask.

"Blood oaths," Libra states.

The three of us jump as a raven squawks and pecks at the window. The nerves in my body are shot. "Well, fuck me. So Nocturnus is a cult. Great." I can't help but glare at the raven in contempt. *Fucking little asshole bird.*

Libra nods. "Pretty much."

As I get up from my chair, I try my best not to collapse. My knees are wobbly, and it feels like my adrenaline is sucking the life out of me. "So, I'm marked for what? Death? Riot kills me and gets his revenge? I still don't understand what I have to do with this curse."

Villette's eyes darken. "No one knows. But something big is coming. I can feel it."

Chills race up my spine. And yet a part of me still longs for the version of Riot I met in the bathroom on Halloween. The one who was tender and kind. The one I dreamed about for weeks. *But that's before he knew who I was.*

I finish the rest of my glass of wine and head for the elevator, my fury building with each step I take.

"Where are you going?" they both cry out in unison.

I push the call button and grit my teeth. "To go let Riot know that he's fucking with the wrong Blackwell."

I hear their pleas of protest as the elevator doors close behind me, but I don't falter. All my life I've dealt with people blaming me for my family's mistakes. I worked twice as hard to forge my own path away from my parents. It's time for Riot to see what I'm capable of.

Just before the doors open to the ground floor, Jessamine wooshes past me. *"If you play with fire, make sure you burn them first."*

I blink and she's gone.

Oh, I plan on burning it all down.

🦋

It's nightfall by the time I reach Graves Library. Aside from a few students lingering out front, it looks desolate. They side-eye me and whisper as I approach the doors. My belly flutters, and I fight down the panic that threatens to send my body into convulsions.

The lights are dim, far too dim to read by. The librarian behind the check-in desk, wrinkles her nose as she gathers her belongings and shuffles past me, avoiding eye contact. I pull the hood of my sweatshirt up around my head and scan the aisles for any sign of Riot.

A few more students close their books and scurry out as I pass them. It's like they're scared to be in here. I glance up at the massive clock that hangs between two iron railings to see that it's nine p.m. Closing time. Only those rules don't apply to Riot. *Not when he has his name on the fucking building.*

As I walk down each aisle, I can't help but peruse the stacks, running my fingers along the spines, almost forgetting for a moment that I'm being hunted. I turn down the next row and freeze as I notice a change in the atmosphere. My throat constricts from the heaviness in the air.

One by one, the lights hanging over each aisle turn off with a loud click. I breathe deeply through my nose and try to calm my racing heart. Fuck. Some light still trickles in from the moon and the outside lampposts so it's not pitch dark, but I can only see a few feet in front of me at a time.

I keep replaying my conversation with Libra and Villette in my head. *Coven. Blood oaths. Sacrifices.* I'd give anything to be back in Wickford Hollow right now, drinking jello shots with Bailey. I don't even want her to know about any of this. It's better if she thinks I'm having the best year of my life. She has enough of her own shit to deal with.

Shivers snake up my back as I glimpse a shadow dart past me. "Riot? Quit fucking around. I'm here."

Why in the hell did I come here alone? I should have asked Villette to wait outside for me. At least she'd be able to hear my screams.

"I'm right behind you," Riot yanks my hood down and snarls in my ear.

Fuck.

He spins me around and shoves me back against the bookshelf. Dressed in a black hoodie and black pants, his blue eyes stand out in the dark, glowing like a cat's. Like a fucking predator. I can almost taste coffee and tobacco on my tongue as his scent wildly consumes me.

"Hey there, Firecracker. Thanks for coming." He pins my arms over my head, against the stacks, while gazing hungrily at my lips.

For a minute, he almost sounds sweet, but his monstrous grip reminds me he's anything but.

"You say that like I had a choice," I snap. Despite the pain shooting through my wrists, I can't stop my hips from angling toward him. I shudder as I remember how soft his fingers felt against my skin that night he zipped up my corset.

Riot smirks and presses his hard body against mine. "You're our little slut now, Firecracker. No one else's. And you'll do what we say or else we'll ruin you."

My heart beats so fast, I'm afraid it might explode. "Listen,

Riot, please, I'm sorry for what the Blackwells did to you, but I had nothing to do with that. They kicked me out just like they did you."

He tightens his grip on my wrists. "You're a fucking liar just like the rest of them. But I have their pretty little girl in my web now. They have no idea what's coming for them."

I should be panicking but his breath on my skin is sending tingles straight to the center of my traitorous core. I clench my jaw. "*I'm not a liar.*"

A flicker of amusement flashes in his eyes. "Aren't you though? You've told the school you're a Blackwell but you're trying to convince me that you're not. Both can't be true so that in fact makes you a *fucking liar.*" The light leaves his eyes, and he looks like he wants to murder me.

But instead of scaring me, it turns the heat up in my body. "I never lied to *you.*"

He snickers and forces my legs apart with his knee. "Why would you lie at all, Firecracker?"

Moisture pools in the apex of my thighs as he presses his hip against my pussy. "You wouldn't understand. People like you never do."

He wraps his hand around my throat. "What the fuck is that supposed to mean?"

A small whimper flutters out of me. "Your last name is on the fucking building we're in. Figure it out."

"Ah, so this is about money. You don't strike me as the greedy type," he snickers.

He has no fucking clue. "It's not about money. Like I said, you wouldn't understand. Everything comes easy for you here. You have a whole fucking congregation of sheep who follow you."

The rage returns to his face, and he squeezes my throat. "Easy?

What the fuck do you know about me or this place? *Nothing.* So shut your mouth before I shove my cock in it."

Another wave of tremors pulses through the delicate flesh of my pussy. His touch is addictive, no matter how brutal it is. I lick my lips. "If you hate me so much, then why am I here? Why do you keep touching me?"

His grip around my throat tightens as he lets my other arm go. I tremble as he drags his hand across the waist of my jeans. "I touch you because I can. Because I relish in the fact that you despise me."

My stomach flips as he unbuttons my jeans.

"You're my penance. My reward for bad deeds. And I plan on using every inch of your body for my own sick pleasure." He unzips my jeans. "As payment for what your family has stolen from me."

I gasp as he slips his hand inside my wet panties. "You're a fucking bastard."

He snickers and pinches my clit. "Yeah. A bastard who gets to play with your pretty little cunt."

I moan as he slips his finger inside. "*Stop.*"

He chuckles and adds a second finger, stretching me open as he kneads at my tender flesh. "I'll never stop, Firecracker. You can scream, cry, beg… I don't fucking care. You belong to me now. To Nocturnus."

I roll my hips up as he thrusts his fingers in and out. Another moan waffles out of me. "No." I shake my head even though the last thing I want him to do is stop. He touches me like no one ever has. Not for his own pleasure, but for mine. Despite what he says, he wants me to enjoy this.

"*Yes.*" He hovers his lips over mine but doesn't kiss me. And fuck how I want him to kiss me. I want to taste him so bad.

He squeezes my throat even tighter while palming my pussy

with his other hand. He presses hard against the flesh, grinding his palm against my swollen clit, and adds a third finger inside.

I bite my lip so hard I break the skin. Blood trickles down my chin, but I'm lost in this ecstasy, so I don't bother to wipe it up. "*Fuck*," I whisper.

"This won't be the last time you bleed for me, Firecracker." His fingers curl up toward my G-spot and an explosion of stars and light cloud my vision. A wave of vibrations rocks my core like electric shocks.

I moan and cry out right before he cuts off the air to my lungs. I don't even care. The lack of oxygen does something strange and new to my body. Like all I can feel is this orgasm taking over. I feel every tremor, every tender flick from his fingers.

Tears stream down my cheeks, and I gag as he releases his hold on my throat. I cough and choke on my own saliva while my orgasm still buzzes through me.

Riot pulls his fingers from my pussy and presses them to my mouth. "I want you to taste what I did to you. That way you'll never question who you belong to again."

My knees tremble. If it weren't for his thigh between my legs, I'd surely collapse. I try to turn my face, but he pinches me hard on the chin, yanking it back. "*Open your fucking mouth.*"

I can barely part my lips before he presses three soaking wet fingers against my tongue. Another tingle shatters my core as I taste my own cum on his salty skin. He shoves them all the way to the back of my throat and something feral comes over me. I suck them clean.

"The next time you contemplate standing me up, remember this moment," he snarls.

Fuck. I can't do this again. I made myself a promise. Fuck him and his crazy threats. I don't believe in curses or magic anyway. But more importantly, *I don't want to crave this*.

I zip up and button my jeans. "As fun and weird as this has been, I'm not a piece of property to own. I'm truly sorry that my family has wronged you, but I can't—"

Riot slams me so hard against the shelves, a few books fall to the ground and the air wooshes out of my lungs. "Do you know why you were able to enter Raven's Gate, Maureen? Do you think anyone can just waltz in here? *Hmm*?"

All I can do is shake my head as I struggle for breath.

"The night I first saw you at Wickford Mansion… we both killed people."

Fuck. This can't be happening. Tears stream down my cheeks. "You don't understand."

Riot squeezes my wrists so tight, my hands tingle. "It took me a minute to put it all together. But it explains everything. While I was out front murdering your pathetic frat boys, you were somewhere in the house spilling blood yourself. Two blood sacrifices from a Graves and a Blackwell on Halloween night. The ravens saw and opened up the gates for you."

What the fuck? "You murdered those guys from the bathroom?"

Riot snickers. "That's the part you're focusing on? For fuck's sake. Yeah, it had nothing to do with you. They pissed me off later."

He's lying. I can tell by the way his throat bobs and his lip twitches. "It's my fault they're dead. Great."

He shakes me. "Everything is your fucking fault, Maureen."

I cringe at the way my name sounds on his lips. He says it like it's a virus that can't be contained. "So, you know all my dirty little secrets now, Riot. Congratulations. What do you want a medal?"

"What I want is for you to suffer like I have," he roars.

"Oh, is that what your fingers were doing inside my pussy? Making me suffer?" I bite back.

He lets me go and steps back. "Don't flatter yourself. That was me reminding you who's in fucking charge of your traitorous little body."

I slide away from him and back up toward the main doors. "*I'm in charge of my body.* No one else. And you can't stop me from leaving." Even as I say it out loud, I don't really believe it.

He clenches his fists but doesn't take another step. "Go back to The Nest, Firecracker. You're going to need all the rest you can get."

I laugh as a crazed sensation takes hold of me. "Oh, I will. But only to pack my bags. Fuck this school and everyone in it. I'm going back to Wickford Hollow in the morning."

A flicker of light bounces off his body. *Are his tattoos glowing?*

"We'll see about that," he whispers.

I don't walk but sprint through the forest. And I don't stop until I'm inside the elevator heading back up to my room.

When I walk in, Villette and Libra are both passed out on the couch amidst a mess of wine bottles, candy wrappers, and weed gummies. An ache twists in my chest. The scene reminds me of all my girls' nights back home with Bailey.

I throw a blanket over each of them and head to my room to pack. If I don't get the fuck out of here tomorrow, this place will ruin me even more than it already has.

Chapter Thirteen

Riot

I PACE AROUND THE PARKING LOT WHILE I WAIT FOR Valentin to finish tampering with Maureen's car. She can't leave either way, but this will send a clear message—*we own you, Firecracker, and we can do whatever we want.*

Atlas perches on the trunk, chuckling at me. "You all right, man? Looks like you're about to pop a vein in your neck."

I glare at him. "Am I all right? Fuck you, Atlas."

Valentin pokes his head out from underneath the hood. "Done. I cut the fuel line, so our little slut won't be going anywhere unless it's on foot."

Atlas hops off the car and pats me on the back. "Now, wouldn't that be fun? Stalking her through the woods… I'm getting hard just thinking about it."

Valentin clenches his jaw as he runs a hand through his jet-black locks. "If you really think her blood will end your curse, then let's get it and be done with her."

A little tremor slides down my shaft. I want to punish her. Torture her. "No. Not until we've had some fun. She's fucking aching for our cocks. I can smell it on her. Don't you want to make her cry and cum at the same time?"

Atlas licks his lips and lets out a little whimper. "Mmm, yeah. I want to play with her first before we get rid of her."

I look at Val, and I can see he's warring with himself. There's not an ounce of compassion in his bones. He was raised to be hardened, vicious, and cold. But he likes to stick his cock in tight wet pussy just like the rest of us.

His eyes darken except for the tiny swirl of light that dances around his pupils. A flicker of electricity skates up his arms, casting a glow against his tattoos. "Once I go down that road, there's no stopping me, Riot. I'll fucking break her and make her lose her mind."

"Good," I quip. "She deserves nothing less."

Atlas chuckles. "So, what's our first move?"

I slide my hand across the hood of Maureen's car, imagining it's the smooth of her back. I slam my hand down hard on the metal and the whole car jerks, immediately deflating all four tires. "We wait."

"Wait for what?" Atlas asks. "I'm horny as fuck. Why can't we drag her out of bed right now?"

"Because we need to give her the illusion that her bed is safe… for now." I can't help but smile as I say this.

Valentin nods. "She'll seek us out the second she sees her car. Like the perfect prey, she'll fall right into our laps, and we won't have to lift a fucking finger."

"Oh, I'll be lifting some fingers inside her fucking pussy," Atlas drawls.

We all will. There is something so addictive about hating her. The more my anger spreads, the more it turns me on. The other girls at Tenebrose bore the fuck out of me. They are always so eager, so fucking sweet and sugary. They bat their eyelashes and open their legs with a snap of my fingers.

But not our firecracker... She fucking hates us. And it fuels me. Her anger and resistance is what keeps me hooked. It keeps me in a constant state of craving that nothing can quench. Not even her. It's never enough. Every time I get around her, I'm consumed. I want to devour every fucking piece of her.

I look up at the full moon and release a deep breath. "Let's get back before its power wanes. We need to make a sacrifice for our new sigils."

Full moons are when our power peaks. Each sigil we've carved onto our bodies is a reminder of that. They are all different and hold their own power. But they require blood and ritual. Each one is like a little oath we made, linking us to the raven and to each other.

As we pile into Valentin's car and head back to Nocturnus House, I feel a surge of adrenaline rush through my veins. It's more than just the thought of tonight's sacrifice, *which always excites me*, it's that Maureen does something to my blood. Something dormant is awakening within me. And I feel like *her* blood is the key to ending this curse against my family once and for all.

The ritual room is dark when we enter except for a few sconces that flicker against the stone walls. We are deep underground below Nocturnus House, surrounded by empty graves and tortured spirits.

In the center of the circular room is our altar. The thick stone surface in which we lay our offerings. We've been down here a thousand times and yet its power grips me like it's the first every time.

We strip out of our clothes and form a circle around it. Valentin places a pair of Maureen's panties down first. He fingers the crotch, rubbing at the dried cream. "We mark her. We claim her. We own her. Maureen Blackwell's body, mind, and spirit belong to us."

I shiver as a surge of power shoots up my thighs, encircling my cock. I'm harder than these stone walls that surround us.

Atlas pulls out a vial of nightshade and passes it to each of us before taking the last sip. "Made from the leaf that I rubbed against her flesh."

The poison burns through my veins. It gets easier each time, but the pain is excruciating. I resist the urge to panic as my throat constricts and breath leaves my lungs. It can't kill me, but it feels like it might. But after a few minutes, it settles into my blood like an old friend. I draw in a deep breath and feel my lungs expand back to normal.

I glance over to see Valentin wincing as he struggles with the poison as well. Atlas just grins as his eyes light up from the toxin. The Thorns were born with it in their veins. He could drink an entire vat of poison and not even flinch.

I remove the silver dagger from its velvet cloth and hold it up. A flicker of candlelight bounces off the blade, our gleaming source of power. The raven's blade. I have carved countless sigils into my flesh and theirs with it. It's the key to unlocking the gate. But only if it has the blood of a Blackwell on it.

Soon.

I turn to Valentin and press the blade against an unmarked patch of skin on his thigh. "Are you ready to receive the raven?"

He nods and widens his stance. "I am."

I kneel down and run my hand up the inside of his leg. I nudge his cock to the side before pressing the tip of the blade to his thigh. My skin tingles as I let the raven move through me. It feels like a rush of every emotion all at once. My head swirls and pulses as my fingers tremble.

Valentin lets out a deep guttural moan as I begin carving into his flesh. "Fuck."

Blood spills down his leg as I mutilate his flesh, digging the blade deeper and deeper with each mark. "Can you feel its power?"

Valentin fists my hair. "Yes…" His brown skin is slick with sweat and blood. I feel his cock pulse against the side of my hand as I finish up.

Fuck. It's beautiful. I smear my fingers in his blood. "Ready?"

He grips the edge of the altar to steady himself. "Yes… I need it."

Atlas pulls out another vial and tips it into Valentin's mouth. "Drink it all."

As soon as he finishes the last drop, I wrap my bloody hands around his cock and stroke up and down. "There we go. Fucking throb for me."

Valentin throws his head back and moans. "Harder," he begs. "Make it fucking hurt."

I squeeze him hard as I pull down all the way to the tip. The sight of him like this destroys me. I yearn for his release more than he does.

"Fuck, I'm gonna cum." He flexes his arms as he grips the stone altar, white-knuckling it.

I stroke my hands faster now, making sure to smear his blood up and down his shaft. "In absentia lucis, tenebrae vincunt." *In the absence of light, darkness prevails.*

He cries out as his cum shoots out in hot white ropes. I pinch the tip of his cock, milking him against the altar. "Oh, fuck. Fuck."

"Let it all go," I murmur. I can feel his pulse quicken, his shaft constricting as each wave of pleasure grips him. "Give it all to the raven. Every single drop."

He cries louder as the last of his cum trickles out. I stroke him gently, tickling each ridge with my fingertips. "You did so fucking good."

As Valentin pants for breath, I trace my fingers around his newly carved sigil. "Mors tua, vita mea…" *Your death, my life.* Every sigil strengthens us. The raven gives us more power every time. Soon we will be in control of the ravens and not the other way around.

Atlas straightens and puffs out his chest. "I'm ready."

This new one is special for him. But it's also dangerous. The power he's asking for… it will seal his ability to see through the eyes of every raven. He'll become our tracker. And no matter where Maureen goes, we'll find her.

But the ravens have dark desires. Cravings of their own. It requires us to commit the most depraved acts. And the more we do them, the more we crave it too.

I walk behind him and rest my hands on his hips. "Are you ready to receive the raven?"

Atlas nods. "I am."

I take a moment to admire his physique. Every muscle is taut and smooth, chiseled like the stone in this room. He doesn't have a single imperfection. I press the tip of the blade to the back of his neck. "For the raven. For sight. No one can hide from us now."

Atlas clenches his jaw as I carve the sigil into the delicate flesh just below his hairline. The dark red blood looks like a painting as it slides down his back, a beautiful contrast to his porcelain white flesh.

I feel the power thrumming through my fingertips again with each stroke of the dagger. "Close your eyes. What do you see?"

"*Everything*," he whispers.

I rub my hands in his blood, spreading it all over his body. "The raven is hungry. *Needy*."

"Mmm… yeah. Take whatever you want." Atlas shoves Maureen's panties into his mouth.

I can't fucking wait to have a collection of her cream-stained underwear. I'll fucking hang them around this house like trophies.

I suck on my finger before slipping it inside Atlas's ass. Fuck. It's so hot and tight. "Damn…"

Atlas's wails are muffled through the cotton panties. He jerks forward as I wedge my finger deeper inside. Valentin reaches around and fists Atlas's cock. I need more. I want to be buried inside to the fucking hilt.

I pull my finger out and press my cock to his entrance. "This is going to fucking hurt."

Stars blur my vision as I push inside him. Holy fuck. I want more and more. We are one, the three of us. As we've always been. But now I need my firecracker. I need her fucking strapped to this altar like a pretty little rag doll.

A torturous rage fills me as I feel her absence. Atlas lets out a deep guttural moan and I tear through him, sliding my cock in and out of his ass like I want to rip it apart.

Pain is our pleasure. It's what bonds us. "Fuck, you are so perfect for me right now."

Atlas bucks his hips as Valentin strokes his cock with fury. "Good boy, Atlas. Let us fucking unravel you."

I pound him harder as tingles spread down my shaft, my blood pumping faster. "I'm about to fill you up. Fuck." I clench and release, slamming into him as my cum bursts out.

"Cum with me," I beg.

Atlas slams his hands on the altar and rocks his hips into Valentin's palm.

"Mmm, there we go. Fuck, yeah."

I'm still inside him as he releases into Valentin's hand, the three of us rocking against each other like one symbiotic unit.

I reach around and slowly pull the panties out of his mouth. "Did you see our little firecracker?"

He nods and bites his lip. "She's in her bed… naked. Her legs are spread open."

Fuck. I almost cum again. "Tell me what she's doing, Atlas."

His chest heaves. "She's playing with her pussy. Fuck… Her fingers… she's got them in so fucking deep."

I rest my damp forehead against his bloody back. My cock throbs against his ass, and I have to resist thrusting into him again. "Well, we'll have to punish her for putting on a show without us."

Valentin strokes my back. "Mors vincit omnia," *Death always wins.* "She's ours now, brother. We have given blood and cum and sweat to make sure of that. Let her play with her own cunt tonight. Her last night of freedom. Starting tomorrow no one touches her cunt but us."

Atlas spins around and grips my shoulders. He presses his forehead to mine. "For the raven."

For Nocturnus.

A surge of power spikes in my veins as we close the circle and seal the room behind us. Soon the raven will be serving us.

Chapter Fourteen

Maureen

"**Y**OU'RE NOT LISTENING. SOMEONE TAMPERED WITH my car." And by *someone*, I know that it's Riot, Atlas, and Valentin. I'm fuming as I stand in the dean's office, my cheeks burning, ready to punch someone in the throat.

The dean's assistant scrunches her pointy nose at me. "I'm sure no one would intentionally ruin your car, Miss Blackwell. Why don't we just call your parents and have them send you a new one?"

Fuck. "No. I don't want to bother them. Just forget it. Thanks for nothing." I get a few chuckles as I storm out of the dean's office with my luggage in tow. What the fuck am I supposed to do now?

As I march back to the dorms, I pull out my phone to check

my bank account. Maybe I can buy a cheap used one somewhere. There's gotta be a car lot in Raven's Gate.

"Hey, you okay?" Villette asks when I come to a dead stop in front of The Nest.

My hands start to shake as I scroll through my account. "What the actual fuck?"

"What?" She pinches her brows together, confused as all hell.

I hold up my phone and show her the screen. "That's a lot of fucking zeroes in my bank account."

She shrugs. "You're rich. So what?"

"Villette… I'm not rich. This deposit was made this morning by the Blackwell Family Trust. I don't know any of them. I don't want to owe them anything." I feel sick. Dizzy. I've never seen so much money in my life.

"It's probably an inheritance from your grandfather. He passed away this year. The more important question is what are you going to do about Nocturnus?"

An ache is kicking in between my shoulders and shooting straight up the back of my neck. I shake my head and massage my temples. "I'm going to get even. They want to fuck with me, I'll fuck with them right back."

Villette laughs. "You're not scared of them, are you?"

"Not much scares me, Villette. Not after the year I've had." If she only knew that I helped my best friend murder a man…

Something in my eyes must darken because she takes a step back and hugs her arms to her chest. "What are you going to do?"

An eye for an eye. The wind shifts and a chill creeps up my spine. The roar of an engine gets louder just as I lock eyes with Valentin driving by. He glares at me, and my stomach does a little somersault. "I'm going to get myself another car."

"Oh, fuck. You might be just as psycho as they are," Villette groans.

I can't help but laugh. "Girl, you have no idea."

After she helps me drag all my bags upstairs, I walk back to the main building for class. As much as I like Villette's company, I'm relieved when she tells me she's taking a sick day. I need some time alone to process everything.

The ravens squawk at me the whole way, and I do my best to ignore them. But the sound is unnerving, like nails on a chalkboard.

With each step I take, I try to focus my thoughts. I remind myself that I'm a fighter. That I don't run away. But I'm also drawn to them. As much as I protest, a part of me knows that I can't stay away from them. My body lights up like a beacon whenever they're near.

I keep replaying our conversations in my head. Riot killed those guys from the bathroom at Wickford Mansion. Was that for me? Or is he just a cold-blooded killer who murders without rhyme or reason?

Atlas has a few screws loose and it intrigues me. He's so beautiful that I lose my breath every time I see his perfectly asymmetrical face. Those blue-green eyes of his pull me in like the tide, striking and dangerous like the sea. I want to drown in them.

And then there's Valentin. He's so cold, he should be frozen like a block of solid ice. But he looks at me in a way that's so feral I can't help but imagine what his hands would feel like all over me. Would his touch be just as cold? Or would our bodies ignite and burst into flames?

They have a hold on me I can't explain. Maybe because our bloodlines have been connected for centuries. Tied together by hate and betrayal and deception. I wish I knew more. There are just these little bits and pieces, but I'm missing the whole picture. My mother never talked about Ever Graves or her family. But the vein in her neck would protrude any time they were brought up. It was definitely a sore spot.

Finding out that she was first engaged to Julian Erebus shocked me to my core. What made her leave him for my father when she clearly isn't happy with him either? I'll probably never know. That woman couldn't tell the truth if her life depended on it.

I'm so deep in thought that it takes me a minute to realize Jessamine is walking in step with me. She keeps quiet as if she knows I'm lost inside my own mind and can't be disturbed.

We walk in silence through the woods, and I relish the peacefulness of it. When she's not bouncing around shrieking, her presence is quite calming.

"Who killed you?" I blurt out without warning.

Her eyes glaze like her mind is in some far-off place. "It was an accident. He didn't mean to."

I glance at my phone to check the time. Class starts in twenty minutes, so I grab her elbow and pull her to a stop. I wait for a few groups of chatty students to pass us before launching back in.

"Who didn't mean to? I need to know what kind of danger I'm in."

Jessamine tucks a strand of blonde hair behind her ear and looks up at the sky, as if there's something actually up there besides clouds and stars. "His name was Silas Graves. We were in love. But we should have been more careful. We were playing in the dark. With the ravens."

A shiver races up my back. "You mean dark, like evil stuff? What did the ravens do to you?"

She looks to the sky again. "Up there, we have the sun and the moon and the stars." Her gaze averts down to the muddy ground. She points to it. "And down there… we have decay and death and ravens. Do you understand?"

Heaven and Hell. I nod and shiver again as the hairs on the back of my arms prickle. "But you exist somewhere in between. Why?"

She shrugs, her eyes filling with sadness. "Neither wants to let me in. I'm tied to Tenebrose forever. Alone."

My heart aches for her. I clasp her hand and lace my fingers through hers. "You're not alone, Jess… What happened to you? To Silas?"

Her lower lip starts to quiver, and she swallows hard as if she's physically trying to shove the pain down. "He made a sacrifice to the ravens. They promised him power, and we trusted them. He loved me, but he was a silly boy. There was a ritual, and we drank too much poison. We both died, but I woke up like this, and he was just… gone."

I gasp and throw my arms around her. "Girl, I'm so sorry. Fuck." I'm sick for her. What a freakishly fucked up thing to happen.

Her body is rigid, and she doesn't hug me back. "I'd do anything to get him back, Maur. Anything."

A cold wind blows around us, and my mind clicks something else into place. I pull away to look into her eyes and try to put it all together. *Her death. The timeline of it. The Graves family getting banished from Ever Graves. The curse. The ravens…*

Fuck.

Fucking hell.

I clasp my hand to my mouth. "You… you're a Blackwell. You're the reason the Graves are cursed."

She sighs. "I'm the reason Nocturnus exists. And the reason they are making your life a living hell. Our family blames theirs for my death. But it wasn't Silas's fault."

I'm in shock. I can't keep my mouth from dropping open. "Jessamine…" I don't know what to say. This girl is my blood. My ancestor.

She squeezes my hand back. "It's okay, Maur. Things will be different this time. But I have to go now. The ravens are listening. They don't like me talking to you. I'll find you later."

Before I can utter another word, she pulls her usual ghost disappearing act.

🦋

I walk through the rest of the day like a zombie. I try my best to pay attention in class, but I can't stop thinking about my connection to Jessamine. I try to wrap my head around what happened to her and what it has to do with me.

But the air around me changes as I waltz into my last class—Tragic Music. The most haunting melody fills the room as I grab the nearest seat and search for the source. My heart skips a beat when I spot Valentin in the corner, *playing the violin*. For fuck's sake, as if he wasn't already ridiculously hot and mysterious.

His jet-black hair is tousled with a few strands hanging over his eyes. He doesn't seem to notice as his fingers seem to fly over the instrument. Beads of sweat drip from his temples while he works the bow over the strings faster than the human eye can comprehend.

My whole body vibrates with each unearthly note he creates. As the music builds, his whole body moves like a force of nature. I can't look away. It feels like nothing else exists but this. Like he's playing it just for me. The chatter around the room is distant, muffled, and all I hear is Valentin.

And all I want is for him to play *me*.

He strums one last powerful note, drawing it out until I think I might cry or suffocate. And in those few seconds between the silence and the applause, he lifts his head and looks only at me.

My breath catches in my throat and for a brief moment, the

darkness in his eyes dissipates. A spark of light flickers around his pupils, and I have to resist the urge to go to him.

In a flash, the spell is broken by Professor Harker. "Excellent work, Valentin." He turns to the class. "The rest of us can only hope to have a sliver of that sort of talent."

I look back at Valentin and his face has hardened once again. He glares at me before returning to his seat.

We can go back to hating each other now. But in that moment, I had forgotten all about what he did to my car. What he did to me in the woods. He was just a beautiful boy with magic in his fingertips.

"*Miss Blackwell*," Professor Harker hisses.

Oh, shit. That didn't sound like the first time he's called my name. "Y-yes, sorry. I was um—"

"Please, don't ramble. While I'm grateful that you are now paying attention to me, I am wondering where your instrument is?"

Fuck.

I forgot the flute Libra left for me. I don't have a musical bone in my body, but this class is required so I figured I could fake it till I make it. But with everything that's been going on with Nocturnus, a wind instrument was the last thing on my mind.

My palms sweat as all eyes land on me. "I'm sorry, Professor. I forgot it in my room."

He shakes his head. "Unacceptable. Well, would you at least share with the class what you chose and what you were planning on playing today?"

My stomach turns. "I… um. I have a flute. I've never played one before. So yeah, no song lined up. Sorry."

Valentin snickers. "Well, how hard can it be? I mean just wet your lips and blow. Isn't that what you're best at?"

I feel my cheeks burn as laughter erupts throughout the class.

I slouch down in my chair, wishing I could disappear like Jessamine does.

Professor Harker raises his hand sternly, but he can't hide the smirk on his face. "Enough. Quiet down. I'll let it slide today, Miss Blackwell, but next time there will be consequences."

I nod and imagine shoving that flute up his ass. *All the teachers here are fucking assholes.*

As he continues on with the class, I feel Valentin's eyes burning a hole in me. When I finally muster the courage to look at him, all humor and teasing are gone. The look in his eyes is murderous and feral. It fuels my rage and only makes me more eager to get back at him.

When the last bell rings, I bolt for the exit before anyone else. I practically sprint across the grounds and through the woods. If I'm going to pull this off, I need every second to plan and prepare. There's a party at Nocturnus House tonight, and I have every intention of taking full advantage of it.

Chapter Fifteen

Maureen

I AM A BADASS.

I almost feel guilty about lying to Libra about my intentions but then I remember that she used me the first night I arrived here by throwing me into the lion's den. So, as we both shimmy through the woods in skin-tight dresses and stiletto heels, I pretend to be as excited as she is to party at Nocturnus House.

I'm hit with the scent of hemlock as soon as we approach, and I almost choke. If Atlas doesn't want to kill me after tonight, I'll take him up on his offer to start ingesting it. I'm not planning on staying in Raven's Gate forever, but I have to learn to acclimate for the time being.

I spot Valentin's shiny black car off to the side of the driveway and my belly flutters. *Don't chicken out, Maur.* Just as Libra and I pass it, my phone buzzes from a text message. Right on time.

I flip it open and fake a frown. "Fuck."

"What's wrong?" Libra asks.

I glance at the message from Villette and try not to laugh. *Does this mean I'm an accomplice now?*

"It's my mom. There's some kind of emergency or something. Let me give her a call really quick. I'll catch up with you inside," I lie.

Libra sighs dramatically. "Don't take forever, Blackwell, or I'll drink all the good booze as punishment for you leaving me by myself."

I actually do feel bad, and I hope that she doesn't get any backlash for what I'm about to do. "Yep. I'll be right there."

Fuck. I can't even look at her. To be fair, she's not been a great friend to me either, though.

I wait until another group of students passes by and goes inside before I slowly stalk over to his car and check the door handle. A little rush of adrenaline surges through me when it opens. *Of course, that egotistical maniac would leave it unlocked.* Who would dare break into Valentin Erebus's car?

This bitch. Me.

I scan the front drive one more time to make sure no one's watching before dipping my head under the steering wheel. One of the perks of being the Sheriff's daughter is you learn all kinds of crazy criminal shit at an early age. *Hot wiring a car is one of them.*

I yank on the wires, fuse them together, and after a few sparks, the engine roars to life. Yes! I almost have a fucking orgasm I'm so happy.

The black leather seats are smooth against my thighs. It feels dangerous and luxurious at the same time. I roll the window down and howl into the night as I step on the gas. "Thanks for the new car, fuckers!" Before I pull out onto the road, I stick my middle finger out the window at Nocturnus House.

I can't stop laughing. I feel like the real me tonight. The me I thought I'd lost here. Which is going to come in handy for phase two. Valentin's car hugs the road like a glove as I take the turns way too fast. Adrenaline courses through my veins like the wind whipping through my hair.

I follow the route that Villette mapped out for me and head into town. It's a few miles away from school so that gives me enough time and distance to really piss them off before I'm caught.

The tiny dive bar, Angel's Trumpet, is packed with people when I walk in. The men are less refined here. Not rich and polished like the ones at Tenebrose. But these are the kind of guys I'm used to—small-town bad boys who like to drink beer, smoke weed, and talk shit. They also like to buy pretty girls drinks.

Dressed in a black crop top and matching mini skirt, it doesn't take long to grab more than a few guys' attention. My long wavy hair swishes back and forth as I prance over to the bar. I notice how their gazes follow the length of my body, ogling my tattoos and curves. And it gives me a rush I haven't felt in a long time. Riot, Atlas, and Valentin are going to learn tonight that no one owns me. Especially not them.

Although, I can't lie that a part of me almost ditched this whole plan to go to the party with Libra. This obsession I have with them is fucking me up. This need I have to fuel their hate and their desire... It's fucking toxic. *Which is exactly why I have to resist it.*

I order a shot of tequila, but before I can reach for my wallet, a tall scruffy biker-looking dude leans over and throws a wad of one-dollar bills on the bar. He's muscular and smells like old leather. "I got this one, darlin."

I raise my glass to his. "Cheers to that."

After a couple more shots, I learn that his name is Willie, but his friends call him Spade. I only half-listen as he rambles on about his self-proclaimed poker skills.

"Wanna take a picture with me, Spade?"

I can't imagine it took long for Libra to bitch to the guys that I left her there. They have to know that Valentin's car is gone too. Time to drive the final nail in the coffin.

"With our clothes on or off?" Spade drawls.

I fight back the nausea and fake a giggle. "Smile for the camera."

He throws his arm around me while I snap a selfie of us. I quickly text it to Valentin with the caption: *Getting my lips wet so I can blow better.*

I chuckle to myself as I see the typing bubbles appear, then disappear, and then appear again. I can only imagine the look on his face right now.

"Wanna get out of here, beautiful?" I flinch as Spade rests his hand on my thigh.

Time to go.

"Sorry, but I have an early morning. Thanks for the drinks and the conversation." I stand up so abruptly, all the blood and booze rush to my head. I stumble back but catch myself on the chair.

"Come on now. Let's go back to my place and have some more drinks." He licks his lips as his gaze lands on my bare midriff.

I shake my head as I angle for the door. "Maybe next time, Spade. I really have to go."

The wind chills my skin as I step outside of the toasty bar. I stumble again and almost twist my ankle. *Fuck.* I'm more buzzed than I'd planned to be. I also regret parking in that desolate garage down the street. I was so set on hiding Valentin's car, that I didn't think about how fucking dark and creepy it is.

I hear footsteps behind me, so I pick up my pace, my nerves on edge. I tuck my hand inside my purse and feel around for my knife, exhaling as soon as I have the hilt tucked inside my palm.

The parking garage looks even darker on my way back in. I climb the stairs two at a time, desperate to get to Valentin's car before the man stalking me catches up. I'm sure it's Spade from the bar, but I can't be certain. Either way, I need to get away from whomever it is. Nothing good happens this late at night in a sketchy part of town.

As I get closer to the car, the footsteps grow louder behind me. Spade lets out a low whistle. "Slow down, beautiful. You forgot to give me a goodnight kiss," he calls out.

Fuck. My stomach knots. I break out into a jog to get to the car. And so does he to get to me.

Before I can open the car, Spade grabs the back of my neck, spins me around, and pins me to the hood. My purse spills to the ground and lands out of my reach.

"Get the fuck off me," I yell.

He grins as he leans over me. "I bought you drinks. The least you can give me is a little kiss."

Every cell in my body is on fire. I start to panic as my mind instantly flashes back to the night Billy and Chad held me and Bailey hostage at her house. "I don't owe you shit, motherfucker. Now, let me go."

His grip tightens around my wrists. "Shit, dressed like this?" His gaze travels over my midriff and thighs. "You came looking for trouble now, didn't ya? Well, you found it."

I start to flail and scream, but I know that it's no use. There are no other cars except the one I stole. There's no one around to hear me.

"Shh, just relax, baby. Let me show you a good time," he slurs in my ear. I almost puke from the stench of his beer-soaked breath.

My heart pounds as Spade inches his hand up my thigh. I think I might hyperventilate or pass out. Fuck. *Maybe it would be better if I blacked out.*

As his fingers move closer to the edge of my panties, the piercing screech of tires causes both of us to jerk our heads toward the sound.

Oh, please for the love of anything holy, let whoever's driving that car see me up here. *Please.*

The engine roars, echoing through the barren garage as it approaches. With each squeal of the tires, my pulse races faster.

Spade drags me off the car and grabs me by the hair. "Who the fuck is that?"

"I-I don't know." I breathe in through my nose and out my mouth, slowly, in an attempt to calm my heart. I am ten seconds away from having a full-blown panic attack.

A black sedan comes around the bend and slows to a stop in front of us. I can't see who's driving through the tinted windows, but as soon as the doors burst open, my blood runs cold. Riot, Atlas, and Valentin slide out from the back seat. None of them are smiling.

"Who the fuck are you?" Spade spits.

Riot waves at his driver and he takes off, leaving the three of them behind. He glares at the drunk creep who has a firm grip on my hair. "You have something that belongs to us, and we want it back."

"What? The car? Go ahead and take it, man. I got what I want right here," Spade snickers.

I try to shove him away. "Let me the fuck go, asshole."

Valentin's jaw is clenched so tight, I think it might shatter. "The car *and* the girl are ours."

"And if there's damage to our property," Atlas adds, his blue-green eyes murderous, "then we'll have to seek compensation."

Riot's eyes darken. "And we take payment in blood."

Spade pulls out a knife from his back pocket and presses it to my throat. "Nah, I think I'll take this one for a spin."

I look at the guys, who all avoid my gaze now, but I notice they've been subtly stepping closer with each second that ticks by. Without thinking, I elbow Spade hard in the gut. The tip of the blade grazes my neck as he curses at me. But before he can react, Riot yanks me out of his arms and shoves me into Valentin's.

I whip back around to watch Riot jam his fingers into Spade's eye sockets. "You think you can touch our girl and get away with it?" He roars in the man's face.

There's a wet stain forming on Spade's crotch as he starts to cry. "Fuck, I'm sorry. Please, don't kill me."

"It's too late for that," Riot states calmly. *A little too calmly.* He presses his palms to Spade's head and in one swift motion, jerks it to the side, snapping his neck. Spade's body slumps to the ground, lifeless.

I shake and stumble back against Valentin. "Oh, fuck…"

"Get in the back seat," Riot growls as he nudges me toward Valentin's car.

My throat burns from trying to swallow down the bile that's rising up. "I-I'm sorry I took the car. It was just a joke."

"Well, *that* motherfucker isn't laughing." He points to the mangled corpse. "Now, get in the fucking car."

I shrink back. Fuck. He's so fucking pissed. It wouldn't take much for him to snap my neck the way he did Spade's.

Riot grabs my wrist. "Don't make me hurt you, Maureen."

I can't stop my knees from shaking as I slide into the back seat next to Valentin. Riot follows in after, sandwiching me between the two of them.

"Drive," he barks at Atlas.

As the engine roars to life, my stomach knots. Atlas hits the gas hard and peels out of the garage. With the windows rolled down, the icy wind howls through the car, blowing my dark strands everywhere.

Riot digs his fingers into my thigh. "I think you owe Valentin an apology."

I turn my head slowly toward the black-haired Adonis and force myself to meet his icy glare. "I-I'm sorry I took your car. But you fucked with mine first to be fair."

Riot presses in close to me and whispers, "We don't want your words, Firecracker."

Valentin unzips his pants and pulls out his cock. "Get down here and show me how fucking sorry you are," Valentin snarls.

Oh, hell no. Not like this. "You can't be serious," I snap. "I'm not going down on you right here."

Riot fists my hair and shoves my head in between Valentin's thighs. "You will. Or I'll force you to suck that fucking corpse's dick back there. I wonder what dead cum tastes like."

My stomach curls at the thought. "You're all insane."

Valentin's slams his hand against the back of the driver's seat. "Atlas, turn this bitch around and go back to the garage."

Oh, shit. They're serious. "No! Okay, fine. I'll do it. Fuck."

Riot chuckles in my ear. "That's a good girl."

Valentin grabs the back of my head and yanks me down. "Open your mouth."

I can barely part my lips before he thrusts his cock inside. I almost gag as he fills my mouth, stretching me wide to accommodate his girth. My eyes water as he rams the back of my throat.

"Mmm, fuck. Such a tight little mouth. You better swallow every fucking drop, or I'll rip it apart."

Riot slides his hands underneath my skirt. "Let's see how wet you are."

I flinch and squirm as he rubs his fingers over my panties.

"Don't you dare fucking stop," Valentin growls and pulls my hair tight to his palm.

I hate them for making me do this. And because it's turning me on… *I hate myself.*

Riot peels my panties to the side and drags a finger up my slit. "Fucking soaked."

I can't stop the moan from rumbling in my throat. What they're doing to me is dirty and wrong. But it sends spasms straight to my core.

"Fuck this," Atlas grumbled. "I'm pulling over, so I can watch."

As the car slows to a stop, my heart beats faster. I can hear Atlas spin around in his seat and crush into the leather. "Pull her skirt up, so I can see what you're doing back there."

Valentin's cock throbs inside my mouth as he thrusts in and out. I can barely breathe. And I'm ashamed that I like it. *He tastes so fucking good.*

Riot yanks my skirt up around my waist. "Look at what we have here. A little string hanging from her pussy. Our little slut is on her period."

Atlas sucks in a sharp breath. "*Fuck.* You know how I feel about that. Pull it out."

"Let's get these panties off first," Riot urges.

Oh my god. I shake my head and try to pull up, but Valentin has me in a firm grip. "You're not going anywhere until every drop of my cum is in your belly."

Tears stream down my cheeks as he shoves his cock deeper down my throat just as the wind hits my bare ass after Riot slides my panties off.

"When you steal from us…" Riot circles my wet entrance with his finger. "We steal from you."

I can't help but clench as he tugs on the string. My traitorous clit spasms as he pulls the blood-soaked tampon out slowly. "Mmm, that looks tasty."

"Shit, yeah it does. Give it to me," Atlas grunts.

This was so fucking wrong. Fuck.

Riot hands it to Atlas and then pushes his finger deep inside my pussy. "Ohhh… fuck. It's like an oven in here. I just want to bury my fucking cock inside you… I want your blood all over me."

I let out another moan as he works his finger through my slick folds. I want more. Fuck. I need it. *What is wrong with me?*

"What do you say, Firecracker? Want me to bury my cock inside you?"

Valentin yanks my head up. "Answer him."

I gasp for air as I rock against his hand, desperate for release.

Riot slaps my ass. "Fucking answer me."

The pressure is building inside me. "No," I lie.

Atlas snickers. "She wants to feel all of us fill her. Dirty little slut."

I shake my head again. "No. Get off me."

Riot lifts my hips up higher and spreads my legs farther apart. "It was actually a rhetorical question, Firecracker. We own you. We don't need your fucking permission," he snarls.

I can feel my blood trickling down my thighs, and I want to scream. This is humiliating. And yet my body is on fire with the need for it. I try to prop myself up and away from Valentin when I feel a hard slap against my ass. "Fuck you, Riot," I cry out.

He grabs my arms and pins them behind me. "Yeah, that's exactly what's about to happen." I hear him slide his belt out from the loops of his jeans and my heart races. Oh, fuck.

He wraps it around my wrists and buckles it so tight I start to lose circulation almost immediately. "Keep sucking him off, Firecracker. You're about to have two cocks in you."

A flicker of fear flashes in my gut as a spasm rocks my core. My head is shoved back down onto Valentin's cock just as Riot unzips his pants. He rubs the tip of his cock against my entrance. "Fuck, that pussy is so wet. So fucking bloody. Mmm."

"Inch it in slowly," Atlas commands.

Riot pushes in, and I can't stifle the moan that escapes my throat. As he slides out, he lets out a deep moan. "Fuck, your blood looks pretty on my cock."

It feels amazing. The ease of how he slides in and out. I'm burning up, ready to explode.

"Yeah just like that," Atlas rasps. "Get nice and deep."

A violent rumble stirs in my core as he spreads my legs farther apart and thrusts in and out of me.

Valentin lets out a moan as my teeth scrape against his cock. "Fuck, get ready to drink."

His cock pulses and throbs right before his hot cum fills my mouth. Fuck. *Breathe through your nose, Maur.* But I can't concentrate on anything except Riot's thick cock buried deep inside me.

I start to gag and gasp for air, but Valentin pinches my jaw. "Fucking swallow all of it."

Riot laughs and plunges deeper into my pussy as I fight the urge to choke. I take slow breaths through my nose as Valentin's salty cum gushes down my throat. He lets out a deep guttural moan and digs his fingers hard into my skull.

"Don't let her fucking cum," he barks at Riot. "She doesn't deserve to."

Riot yanks my head up. "He's right. Thieves don't get rewards." He pulls out of my pussy and wipes his fingers across my cheeks before tossing my panties to Atlas. "They also don't get to wear panties."

After he rips the belt off my wrists, I shrink back against the seat and pull my skirt down. "Fuck you, Riot."

He wraps his hand around my throat and pins me to the seat. "Yeah, you did. And you liked it." He leans in closer to my ear and whispers, "You'll fuck all three of us whenever we want you to."

Shame fills me but also lust. I crave these things from them. As I sit between them with blood and juices running down my thighs, I feel rabid. Deranged. Unhinged. *Fuck, I want more.*

Atlas chuckles and turns back around. As our eyes meet in the rearview mirror, he proceeds to tie my bloody tampon around it. "Next time, I'll slide my tongue in there, Firecracker. I bet your blood tastes so fucking sweet."

Sick fucks. And yet the idea of Atlas's tongue inside my pussy makes my clit spasm again.

I start to reach for my seatbelt when Valentin stops me. "You won't be needing that."

I snicker. "The way he drives? Yes, I think I'll put it on."

Riot opens the car door and slides out, dragging me with him. "Thieves also don't get rides back to campus from the ones she stole a car from."

No. *They wouldn't.* My stomach knots. It's dark, freezing, and we're miles away from Tenebrose. And they have my panties. "Riot, please. You can't make me walk all the way back to campus. I'll freeze to death."

Valentin pokes his head out. "Should have thought about that before you fucked with my shit. Besides, I don't want your fucking blood all over my leather seats."

I knew Valentin was cruel and heartless but leaving me here is inhumane. "Guys… you have my underwear. You can't be serious. Riot… Atlas, *please*."

"You're lucky I don't take all your clothes and make you walk back naked," Riot snaps.

Atlas chuckles. "Fuck, yeah. I'll drive slowly behind her just so I can watch."

They are insane. All three of them.

"So, you did get your lips nice and wet for me. Just like playing the flute, right?" Valentin flashes me a sadistic grin before he ducks back inside the car. I stand there shivering as they drive away and leave me on the side of the road.

Fucking bastards.

Chapter Sixteen

Valentin

My cock throbs at the memory of Maureen's full lips sliding up and down it. The way she pressed her tongue against the tip and sucked while she was getting railed by Riot from behind. It was hot as fuck.

I'm still pissed as all hell that she stole my car but a little impressed. No one has the audacity to fuck with me except for her. Fuck, that turns me on more than I want to admit.

From the moment I laid eyes on Maureen Blackwell, I didn't like her. She was a fucking annoyance. From the way she gawked at Tenebrose, looking like trailer trash, to her feisty little mouth trying to big-time me in front of everyone in the admissions office. I couldn't wait to put that slut in her place. Well, I fucking shut her up good tonight.

But a fire thrums through me, a burning that lingers from her touch. Fuck, I hate her for that. So when she starts banging on my door at three in the morning, I'm secretly ecstatic to go another round with her.

"Are you trying to wake up the whole fucking house?" I growl.

Maureen stumbles into my bedroom, a disheveled mess. Blood stains her thighs and fingers, one of the heels of her stilettos is broken, and she has the biggest case of bedhead I've ever seen. She's fucking pissed. Feral. The sight makes my dick throb. I want to devour every inch of her.

"You tampered with *my* car first. How fucking dare you?" She shoves her finger hard into my chest.

I wrap my hand around it and squeeze, threatening to break it. "Listen, you little fucking psycho, you don't get to make demands. You're lucky we showed up when we did. You were about ten seconds away from getting fucked in the ass by your new bar buddy."

She smirks and tilts her chin up. "Aw, you didn't like my selfie? That made you real fucking jealous, didn't it?"

"Don't push me, Maureen," I warn. Seeing that asshole all over her struck a nerve. She's my toy to play with. *My fucking slut.* And now that I've had a taste of her, I want more.

"I like pushing you." She jabs me in the chest again with her other hand and I grab that one too. I take a step back and pull her with me. She grins and presses her breasts to my chest. "I like pissing you off." She backs me up against the wall, and I'm seconds away from ripping her clothes off.

I take her bottom lip between my teeth and lightly apply pressure. She trembles against me, releasing a slow quivering breath into my mouth. Mmm, fuck she tastes like the deadliest sin. I dip my tongue inside her mouth and we both gasp.

Fuck. I kiss her hard, our tongues swirling together in a desperate frenzy to consume. She moans into my mouth when I bite down on her lip again, harder this time. "I hate you so fucking much," I breathe in between kisses.

"I hate you too. You're such an asshole," she whispers back.

I wrap my hand around her neck, so I can feel her pulse race against my palm. "Why'd you really come here tonight? Hmm? Tell me what you want."

There was an ache spreading in my chest, *in my fucking core* for her right now.

"In the car earlier… I made you cum." She takes my bottom lip in her mouth and sucks before releasing it with a pop. "You owe me."

The balls on this woman. She fucking smiles when I tighten my grip around her neck. "You fucking stole my car and made Riot kill a man. I don't owe you shit."

She has no idea how close I am to crumbling. Something about this girl makes me feel alive in ways I never have. I've been taught to push this down my whole life. But I just had to go and kiss her. Fuck me. I'm so screwed.

An animalistic hunger stirs in my belly as she unbuttons my jeans and unzips them. "Didn't get enough of my cock earlier, Firecracker?"

"Don't flatter yourself. I'm going to use you like you used me," she purrs.

If she's trying to turn me on, it's working. The thought of her using me to get herself off makes my dick so fucking hard. I shove two fingers down her throat, forcing her head back. "Don't forget who's in control here. I'll make sure you can't walk straight for a week."

She moans and sucks my fingers like they're her favorite snack. I've never met anyone like her. The way her body responds to my every touch is enough to start a wildfire within me.

She wraps her hand around my cock, and I almost cum in it. "Finish what Riot started earlier… Hate fuck me until I forget my own name."

Fuck. I can't resist her when she talks so fucking dirty. I spin her around and bend her over my bed. I yank her skirt off and spread her legs apart. The blood circling her thighs and pussy gets me harder. *Fuck, I'm going to slide right in.*

"You thought you were gonna be a good girl this year, didn't you?" I slap her ass, making her buck and cry out. "But you took one look at us and couldn't wait to open your legs." I slap her ass a second time as I line up my needy cock to her entrance.

"Fuck," she whimpers. "No. It wasn't supposed to be like this…"

I snicker. "You're wrong, Firecracker." I inch just the tip inside her pussy. "This is exactly how it was supposed to be." I thrust in my cock, burying it all the way into the hilt. *Fuck.* She's so warm and tight, I have to still myself, so I don't cum too early. I take a deep breath before I inch out and then plunge back in. "No one can save you from us."

A deep moan erupts from her throat as she bucks back, urging my cock in deeper. "I hate you for doing this to me," she cries.

"You're a fucking liar," I bite back as I push inside her so hard her whole body bounces forward on the bed. Her blood stains my sheets, my fingers, and my cock as I fuck every ounce of self-respect out of her. "You hate yourself because you *want* to be our little slut. You fucking need *this* more than you need air."

I move my cock in circles inside her, desperate to penetrate every inch of her flesh. "I'm going to make you cum now. Not because I *owe* your little cunt anything, but because it needs reminding of who controls it."

"Oh, fuck. I hate you so much. Fuck," she screams into the mattress, her hands fisting the sheets. "Please, Val…"

I snicker and reach around till I find her clit. I give it a hard pinch as I thrust slow and deep inside her soaking wet pussy. I roll my hips up and down, taking us into an agonizing rhythm that threatens to unravel us both. "Yeah, you're taking every inch of me like a good little slut. So full. Fuck." She's so tight, it takes every ounce of strength I have not to release into her.

Her moan deepens as I play with her clit, rolling my thumb in circles around it. I can feel that she's close to the edge. I shove my other finger into her asshole and now I completely control her. Her body shakes and trembles as I press all of her buttons. "Oh yeah, there you go. Getting fucked so good. I'm going to fucking consume you."

"Oh my god. I can't… *Fuck*. I'm coming." A blood-curdling scream rips from her throat as I slam my cock back into her.

"Fuck," I yell. My cum is hot and thick when it shoots inside her. But her cream is thicker. I drill into her, moving in circles to ensure every inch of my cock is covered in it.

We rock back and forth as our orgasms grip us. It's like a fucking dam breaking. Like neither of us have ever cum before. It makes me angry and sick and fucking livid that she can do this to me.

I slap her hard on the ass as she grinds her pussy into the mattress. My fury builds when it only makes her moan louder. I need to hurt her but the more I try, the more pleasure she gets.

"Is that all you got?" she taunts.

My traitorous cock stiffens again as I thrust it in as far as it will go. I slap her so hard this time, it leaves a handprint on her ass cheek. "I warned you not to push me."

Maureen wiggles her ass while she rides my cock. "*More.*"

I slide my belt from the loops of my jeans and fold it in half. "Once I get going… fuck, I'm not going to stop."

Another whimper flutters out of her. "I stole your car. I let another man touch me. Punish me."

Oh fuck. She's trying to wind me up, and it's working. The thought of that douchebag touching her… pinning her up against *my* car… it unleashes something I can't undo.

I grunt and smack my belt across her ass so hard, it leaves a welt. I rub my hand over it. "You get off on pain, is that it? Let me show you some real fucking pain, Firecracker."

"*Yes.* Give it to me. I need it," she begs.

I pull out of her pussy and without warning, shove my cock inside her ass. It's so fucking tight I barely get an inch in when she clenches and screams, "Wait… *don't fucking stop.*"

"Mmm, my pretty little psycho, begging me to hurt her. You make me so fucking hard. Fuck. I'm going to cum again." I can't hold back this time as I fill her ass with my cum before I'm even all the way in. I slide in deeper as my cum helps ease me in another inch.

"Uhhh," she moans. "Fuck. *Valentin.*"

The sound of my name in her mouth does something feral to me. I squeeze her ass cheeks together and burrow myself all the way in and rail her with a fury, sparked from the darkest depths of my soul.

I grab the back of her neck and ride her like a fucking horse. "I will rip you apart, Firecracker. From limb to fucking limb."

Tears stream down her cheeks as she wails. But she doesn't tell me to stop. She raises her hips up and rocks into me, meeting me thrust for thrust. Fucking hell.

"Good," she moans. "It makes me hate you even more."

Yeah, baby. Fucking same.

Chapter Seventeen

Maureen

THE BIRDS HAVE BEEN PECKING AT MY WINDOWS FOR days. Ever since I left Valentin's room the other night. He left a chill in my bones and a fire in my belly. After I let him fuck me, *twice*, I couldn't get out of there fast enough. I hobbled all the way back to The Nest and went straight to my room without so much as a glance at Libra.

I'm thankful that she's left me alone. For once, her self-absorption is working in my favor. But Villette on the other hand won't stop blowing up my phone. I finally agree to meet up with her today.

Jessamine has appeared for the past three nights, but she's kept quiet and just sat in the corner and watched me sleep. I think she can sense my fear and frustration.

My emotions are tangled and twisted. I went from liking what they did to me in the car to being so angry when they left me there. It took me hours to walk back to Tenebrose in my stiletto heels. Three fucking hours. I was bruised and bloody and furious. I still don't know what came over me. What fucking possessed me to go to Nocturnus House. To bang on Valentin's door. I was just so fucking angry and yet so turned on at the same time.

This year is supposed to be different... I was going to study hard and hang out with nice people and make Bailey proud. But instead, I'm somehow in an ancient blood feud with three hot as fuck psychos who want to torture me as much as they want to fuck me.

It's sickening but it's all I can think about. I can barely pay attention in class. Especially the ones they're in. I can feel their eyes on me, taunting me, from across the classrooms. I've become their obsession and they're mine.

I want to tell Riot about Jessamine. I want to call up the grandmother I've never met and tell her that we can end this hatred between our families. But there is a darkness here that is getting harder to resist. A sinister energy that permeates around Riot, Atlas, and Valentin. It snakes around me every time they're near, tempting me to give in to it.

I hit the snooze button on my alarm for the third and final time before hopping out of bed. It's the weekend, so I don't technically have to get up early, but I also don't want to sleep the whole day away. If I wallow in here any longer, I'll never have the strength to go outside again. I need to face my fate.

"The shop is on the outskirts of town, so we'll have plenty of time for you to spill all the tea."

I groan as I slide into the passenger seat of Libra's sports car. "Nope. I don't want to talk about it."

The Winter Solstice Ball is next weekend, so Libra is insisting we go dress shopping today. Luckily, Villette is coming too, so she can balance the energy. Otherwise, I might end up knocking Libra out with a designer handbag or something.

"I have to admit I'm curious too, Maur," Villette chimes in from the back seat. "I was really worried when you didn't come out of your room for three days."

Libra snorts. "That's because she got railed so hard she couldn't walk."

"I don't understand… Don't you hate them?" Villette asks.

I close my eyes and sink into the leather seats, wishing I had just stayed in bed. "It's complicated."

I listen to the two of them go back and forth the whole drive and only chime in with a short response here and there to placate them. But what I'm really focused on is my phone. Riot has sent me a slew of messages since we pulled out of Tenebrose, each one getting increasingly aggressive.

Where are you? I need to see you.
You're not going to like what happens when you ignore me.
If I have to come find you, I'm going to be fucking pissed.
See you soon, Firecracker. Can't wait to pick out a dress for you.

Fuck.

Butterflies swim in my belly. He really will fucking show up at the dress shop. Do I care? I don't even want to go shopping anyway. Am I secretly turned on by this? Yes. Fuck me, I am. What the fuck is wrong with me?

"Who are you texting?" Libra snaps out of nowhere.

I let out a deep sigh. "I might have to cut out early today."

Villette whines in my ear, "You *like* them. Fuck. Have I not told you enough about how dangerous they are? They are already trying to control you."

I bite my lower lip in shame. I know it sounds crazy. That I shouldn't be so attracted to them. So drawn in. But I'm a hot mess and can't help myself. "I know what I'm doing, Villette. It's fine. I'm just…"

"Playing with fire is what you're doing," she retorts back.

"I am the fire." A surge of something protective and possessive reaches into my core and grips me. "They are the ones who want to play."

Libra white-knuckles the steering wheel and grits her teeth. "You have no idea what you're getting into with them. They will use you and humiliate you. Nocturnus controls everything and everyone at our school. Fuck, in this whole town. If you're one of the lucky ones who doesn't exist on their radar, then you just go about your business and stay out of their way. But people like you and me… we don't get that luxury."

I did my best not to gape at her but holy fuck. That was the most honest thing that's ever come out of her mouth. I didn't like a word of it, but it was her truth for once.

Yet despite the guys' brutality, I can't help but think back to how kind Riot was that night in Wickford Hollow. Then I think about Valentin stepping in when I was getting manhandled by Zeke that night at Swallow. And the way Atlas touches me like I'm a fragile flower.

"Maybe they aren't the monsters you think they are." I knew how stupid that sounded the second it left my mouth. *Why am I defending them now?*

She snickers. "Says the girl who got me whipped in front of all the Nocturnus initiates. They *are* monsters. But I bet that makes you want them even more, doesn't it? I had you pegged wrong at first. Thought you were going to be a fun party girl to get drunk and bang frat boys with. But after seeing the way you look at all three of them... they're right. They fucking own you, and you like it."

"For fuck's sake, Lib, you don't have to be so harsh," Villette chides.

What the fuck is she talking about? "*Whipped?* I'm going to need you to elaborate."

Libra lets out a dramatic sigh as she pulls into a parking spot outside the dress shop. "I shouldn't have brought you to the party that first night you got here. I knew that Riot hated your family. But I thought it would be fun to fuck with him. I didn't realize how deep it went... I got what I deserved."

I could feel my cheeks heating. "So they whipped you in front of their entire little cult? That's not okay, Lib. Fuck. Why didn't you tell me?"

"Because that's what we do, Blackwell. We keep their dirty little secrets. But I'm no angel. I should have known better. When I saw the way he looked at you... It's more than hate. He's obsessed with you."

Villette curses under her breath. "Fuck, Lib. Did you have a thing for Riot?"

She snickers and shakes her head. "I have a thing for a lot of assholes. But after what he did to me? Nah, you can have him, Blackwell. I'm not a fucking psycho."

But apparently, I am? Maybe she's right. But I can't help feeling a twinge of guilt at the thought of Riot taking his issues with me out on her.

I'm still fuming as we sprint into the dress shop just as the rain starts pouring down on us. The store looks more like a Halloween shop than a designer boutique. The walls are painted black with purple trim. There are shelves lined with skulls and most of the dresses on the racks are black. I wander off and start fumbling through them. I spot a couple I like, but my heart isn't in it today. I'm pissed at myself because I usually love shopping.

The store clerk points me in the direction of the dressing rooms. I have to walk down a long, black and gold-painted hallway to get to mine. As soon as I turn the knob, I'm yanked inside and pinned against the door.

I open my mouth to scream but nothing comes out as I meet Riot's icy glare. It's like my voice is lodged in my throat and no matter how many times I tell my brain to let it out, it won't budge.

He pinches my chin between his fingers. "You've been a naughty little slut, haven't you?"

Chills snake down my back and my heart races. He smells so fucking good I want to lick him. But a hundred thoughts rush to my brain at the same time. I think of the ravens, the feud, the way Libra and Villette refer to them as a coven… I clear my throat and feel my voice returning. "What did you just do to me? What are you?"

Riot pushes against me, pressing me hard against the dressing room door. "I'm the devil you will obey. The monster who terrorizes you until you lose your fucking mind. Until I own it completely."

I swallow hard as he wraps his hand around my throat. "I could snap your neck right now."

Something dark and disturbed settles into my bones at the thought of him crushing my lungs. "Then why don't you?"

His grin is sadistic. *Unhinged.* "Mmm, yeah, Valentin told me you like it rough. The threat of violence gets you so fucking wet, doesn't it?"

I look away, ashamed that he can see how turned on I am. "Get out, or I will scream."

He yanks my head toward him, forcing me to look into his eyes.

A flicker of light moves in circles around his dilated pupils. "No, you won't. Not unless I want you to."

Fuck. I feel dizzy. My limbs are heavy. "*What* are you?" I stutter out.

Riot presses his lips gently to mine. His breath is hot and heavy. "Powerful," he growls into my mouth. "You can't escape this, Firecracker. We are your fucking destiny. We're each other's curse. You think you came to Tenebrose all on your own? *I fucking summoned you.* You have no idea how many blood sacrifices I had to make. How many sigils we have burned into our flesh for you."

A wave of euphoria hits me, and I feel so strange. I should be terrified of this man. "I don't understand," I whisper.

His lips still hover over mine, so close we're almost kissing. "I know, but you will. Soon. But today, we've come here to pick out your dress. You know since you'll be accompanying us to the Winter Solstice."

My jaw drops. "You're a fucking psycho. I'm not going to the ball with any of you. I don't know who the fuck you think I am." I'm fuming again.

He fists my hair and gives it a hard tug. "You don't have a choice. Get that out of your head right fucking now. You're our little slut. You'll go where we say and wear what we tell you to. Now, take your fucking clothes off, and put on a good show."

A little light seeps into the dressing room and I almost have a heart attack when I see the two figures in the corner. Atlas and Valentin. Fuck, have they been here this whole time? There is only one way into this room so they must have been. *I feel like I'm losing my mind.*

I try to turn the knob behind me, but it won't open. "What the fuck? How is this locked? Let me out. I don't want to play anymore."

Valentin snickers. "You don't get it yet, do you? That door won't open unless we tell it to."

Oh, fuck. My stomach knots as I start letting my mind wander the possibilities. They could be fucking demons, devils, witches… I feel sick. "I'm not your dress-up doll." I can't keep my voice from shaking.

Atlas grins. "Yes, you are. You're our pretty little doll to mangle and fuck and ruin."

I flinch as he starts toward me. His eyes are glazed and wild. He pulls out a tube of red lipstick and applies it to my lips. I'm frozen, dumbfounded as he then takes his thumb and smears it around my face. "Mmm, look how pretty you are." He spins me toward the mirror and wraps his arms around me from behind. I draw in a deep breath as he starts unbuttoning my shirt.

"All three of you are deranged," I murmur. My pulse races so fast I can't contain it. I feel like I'm going to pass out or spontaneously combust.

He takes my shirt off and then unhooks my bra, pausing to grin at me in the mirror while they all watch. "Do I need to keep going or are you going to be a good little slut and take off the rest?"

Why does my pussy spasm every time they call me that? I turn around to face them and don't bother to cover my naked breasts from their view. This is what they want. And they will get it no matter what I try to do to stop it.

I unzip my skirt and let it fall to the floor. "Fine, hand me a dress to try on."

Riot saddles up behind me, and I can feel his cock harden against my ass. "Take off your panties, Firecracker. Naughty little sluts like you don't get to wear those anymore." He inches his hands across my belly.

Oh, fuck. Moisture pools between my thighs. With trembling

fingers, I push my panties down and step out of them. Riot coos in my ear, "Good girl. Now go sit on Atlas's lap while Val and I decide which dress we want you to try on first."

He nudges me forward and I stumble onto Atlas. He takes a deep breath, inhaling my scent before running the length of his tongue up my neck. "Time for another lesson, pretty girl."

My stomach flips when I see the tiny vial in his hand. Fuck. "I'm not ready for that, Atlas."

He pops off the top and holds the vial to my lips. "Just one sip and you'll feel amazing. It only hurts for a second."

I shake my head. Is he trying to kill me? "Atlas, no. I'm not drinking poison."

"Okay, fine. Then kiss me." He dabs some on his tongue, and his eyes nearly roll back in his head.

Fuck. "I-I don't know. I'm scared."

"Shh, relax, pretty girl. Open up for me."

I part my lips and let him kiss me. The second his tongue touches mine I feel a sharp sting. I wince and try to pull away, but he holds me firm and kisses me harder.

I whimper against him, caught between the erotic rhythm of his tongue and the fear of dying naked in a dressing room with three psychos who I can't seem to stay away from.

But as our lips smack against each other, the pain begins to fade like a distant alarm ringing far away. And I'm left with an ache between my legs.

Atlas chuckles and slides his hand down my belly. "There we go. Now do you see how fun this is?"

I forget where I am, who I am, and spread my legs wide across his lap. The poison is like a drug. Like an aphrodisiac. And I can't control myself. *I want more.*

"Mmm, that's my pretty little doll. Lean back."

I tilt my head against his shoulder and let him release a drop of the poison directly into my mouth. My insides feel like they are on fire, and I start to panic. "It burns… I can't breathe."

Atlas pinches my nipples hard, and it distracts me from the pain in my throat. "You're doing so good, Firecracker. Hold your nipples for me like this, so I can play with that pretty cunt of yours."

Oh. Fuck. I am coming undone, unbalanced. I want to give them everything they demand. All of me. Every dark and demented piece of my soul. I arch my back and grab hold of my raw nipples. A surge of tingles shoots down to my core as Atlas fingers the lips of my pussy.

Within seconds, Riot's standing over us, his hand around my throat. He looks down to watch Atlas's fingers thrusting in and out of me. "I want to see how wide that pussy can stretch for me."

I let out a moan and roll my hips back as Atlas pulls my thighs apart as wide as they'll spread and angles my hips forward. He pulls his cock out of his pants and forces me to sit on it. I shudder at the wide girth of him. I can't help but clench around his shaft as I slide down. "Oh, shit. Fuck."

"Mmm, you're so fucking tight for a little slut." He pushes all the way in. "Oh, yeah, pretty girl. Just like that. You're Daddy's dirty little slut, aren't you?"

I nearly cum at his words. Fuck this is hot and so fucking wrong. I slide up and down his thick cock while Riot has a stranglehold on my neck. He just watches silently, his icy blue eyes expressionless while Atlas fucks me hard.

Valentin pulls up a chair next to us and leans over. He inches his fingers slowly down the length of my body, across my belly, and down my wet slit before caressing my swollen nub. "You have three daddies now. Three vengeful and merciless daddies who will punish you when you don't behave."

Riot tightens his grip on my throat as if he can sense I'm about to cum. He wants to push me over the edge. "*Yes*," I utter hoarsely.

Atlas slaps my thigh as he thrusts his cock in hard and deep. "I'm going to fill you up pretty girl. Mmm, here we go. Fuck."

A burst of hot sticky cum shoots into me, and I cry out. The rush of it sets something off in me and a deep orgasm rumbles through me. Riot squeezes my throat until I see stars. I start to black out and all I can focus on is Valentin's fingers rubbing my clit back and forth until I think I might die from pleasure.

I buck wildly as I slide down Atlas's shaft, my pussy tingling over each veiny ridge. I am happy to die this way. I don't care about life or death or air. I will gladly sacrifice my body for this. For them.

Chapter Eighteen

Atlas

OUR LITTLE FIRECRACKER LOOKS PERFECT WITH my cum oozing down her legs. With my poison on her tongue. The fresh sigil on the back of my neck tingles. I rub my thumb over it and feel its power. I can be anywhere and everywhere now. All I have to do is close my eyes and allow the ravens to show me what I want to see. It's how we found Maureen today.

"Time for our pretty doll to play dress up," I sputter as Riot pulls her off my lap.

Her cheeks are flushed with a shade of pink so deep it matches her pebbled nipples. She's breathless and weak from the poison and my cum. There's no fight in her now as she allows Riot to slip one of the dresses over her head.

Valentin tightens the laces of her corset, pushing her breasts up till they are almost exposed again. The slinky black dress has a slit down each side, showing off our pretty little girl's thick thighs. He wraps his hand around her throat and shoves her toward the mirror. "This is the one. Look how fucking naughty you look."

Riot slips his hand inside one of the slits, eliciting a tiny squeak from her lipstick-smeared mouth. "They're all gonna want you, Firecracker. But you belong to us, and we'll murder anyone who touches you. Remember that the next time you try to tempt one of the local townies. Their blood will be on your hands."

"What have you done to me?" Her voice quivers with fear but there's an ache to it that is so satisfying. She has carnal cravings that only we can fulfill.

I stand behind her in the mirror. "We marked you… and now we've claimed you."

"A fair trade for the fate your family has bestowed upon mine," Riot snarls.

Maureen's eyes brim with tears as she whips around to face him. "All you care about is revenge and power. You disgust me. I hope you never get what you want."

Fuck. Now she's done it.

Riot's nostrils flare as he charges her, pushing her back against the mirror. The glass cracks on impact. "And I hope you never have a moment of peace again. In fact, I'll make sure you don't. Your body and mind will be so fucking broken when we're done with you…"

"Not if I break you first," she bites back.

I can't help but grin. Her fire feeds my fucking soul. I wrap my arm around her waist and pull her away from Riot before he actually kills her. "Come on, pretty girl. Let's get you cleaned up before my cousin throws one of her temper tantrums."

Libra and Villette have been pacing outside the dressing room door for the last thirty minutes. They both know better than to barge in, but I'm trying to make somewhat of amends with Libra for allowing her to get spanked in front of the entire Nocturnus House.

"*No*," Riot sneers. "Send them away. Maureen comes back with us tonight. We're going to teach her a little lesson."

Fuck. He's beyond furious that she insulted him. But he's also frustrated that she can get under his skin the way she does. I think it's hilarious but also disturbing. Maureen and Riot will destroy each other if they aren't careful.

I nod. "Fine. I'll go deal with my cousin and the Crane girl."

Valentin snickers. "I'll call a meeting at Nocturnus. Elder members only."

Riot bares his teeth at her, his grin twisting into something sick and depraved. "You want to know what I am? What *we* are? Tonight, you're going to find out."

Maureen backs away from him. "No. Let me go. I don't want to know anymore. Please, just let me leave with my friends."

"Too late for begging, Firecracker. You've pushed me too far this time," Riot snaps.

Libra is easy to send away but the other one, Villette, gets in my face in a way that rubs me the wrong way. She's lucky we don't want any beef with her family, otherwise I'd shove a bottle of poison down her throat and drop her body in the fucking river.

After Riot pays for the dress and gets Maureen back in her regular clothes, we have to drag her to the car kicking and screaming. Which fuck, I'd be a liar if I said that didn't make my cock hard again.

The drive back is eerily quiet. Maureen sits as far away from Riot as she can get in the back seat of Valentin's car. The ravens fly alongside us, squawking the entire way. They know they are getting fed soon. We all are. And our little firecracker is going to be the meal.

Chapter Nineteen

Maureen

I NEVER SHOULD'VE LEFT WICKFORD HOLLOW. RAVEN'S Gate… Tenebrose… is fucking cursed. Every nerve in my body stands on edge as Riot, Atlas, and Valentin ride in silence. All of my deepest fears resurface as they steer me closer toward their depraved world. I may not survive tonight. So why do I feel more alive than I ever have?

Nocturnus House has an ethereal glow about it tonight. Muted light flickers through its iron-barred windows. It feels different. *I* feel different approaching it. I can still smell the hemlock in the air but breathing it in doesn't hurt my chest as badly as it did the last time. Maybe Atlas's micro-dosing is already working.

My stomach flips when I see the hooded figures lined up in the driveway. What the fuck? They're all wearing masks. I want to run. I didn't sign up for this level of insanity. But Riot drags me out of the car before I can even think about bolting.

"If you run, I'll hunt you down like the fucking predator I am. Maybe I should let you try. Nothing gets me harder than the chase." He has a crazed look in his eyes. A look that means he's either going to torture me to death or fuck me so hard I won't remember my own name. Moisture gathers in the crevices of my thighs despite how terrified I am. It's a sickness. This addiction to their brutality. I hate that I crave it. That I need it.

The interior also looks different without the crowd of drunken students and full staff serving them whatever they desire. Now it's just me and the guys and their seemingly mindless initiates. Chills sweep up my back as they guide me down a staircase that goes so far down below the house, I wonder if I'll ever breathe fresh air again. It's dark and damp and musty. The humidity clings to my skin like burnt honey.

When we finally get to the bottom, I find myself in a circular room with stone walls lined with iron sconces. There's what looks like an altar in the center, stained with blood and other substances I can't place.

My stomach knots, and I have to breathe deeply through my nose to keep from vomiting. Fuck. I'm in so much fucking trouble.

"Riot," my words echo through the hollow room, causing me to jump. I lower my voice to a whisper, "Please tell me what's going on."

He nods at two of his initiates and within seconds they grab my arms and pull me toward the altar.

Oh fuck. *No.*

Panic spreads in my chest as I try to swallow and almost choke. "Wait, what the fuck are you doing?" I cry out. "Let me go."

My heart races as I feel the cool metal shackles enclose around my wrists. I try to pull away but it's no use. I'm alone with all of them. And I'm at their mercy, even though they have none.

"Atlas, don't let him do this to me," I beg.

"*We* are doing this to you, Firecracker. No one here is going to save you." There's a more sinister tone to Atlas's voice. It matches the others', so now I know I'm completely screwed.

Once the initiates finish chaining my wrists to the altar, they do the same to my ankles, before getting back into formation with the others.

Riot stands over me and glares down. He licks his lips as his gaze travels over every inch of my body. "Time for penance, Firecracker."

I can't stop trembling as I glance around the room. The fact that I can't see their faces is unnerving. I feel like I'm about to hyperventilate. Fuck.

Riot slowly unbuttons my shirt and pulls it back. It's deliberate and agonizing. I feel my chest heave with each flick of his wrist. One of his initiates hands him a knife and he uses it to cut my bra off.

"Riot, stop. I'm sorry I insulted you earlier," I plead.

He doesn't respond while he drags the tip of the knife down my belly, careful not to break the skin. He cuts through my skirt and flings it to the cement floor. I'm shivering now despite the humidity. Am I going into shock?

He grunts as he slices through the fabric of my panties, tearing them to shreds. "I want you all to bear witness," he addresses the room, "to the claiming of Maureen Blackwell. She belongs to Atlas and Valentin and *me*. You may look but never touch. Her blood has cursed us. But that ends soon."

Oh, fuck. Is he really going to kill me?

Tears stream down my cheeks. "Riot… *please*."

He strokes my cheek. "Shh. Relax." He leans down and whispers in my ear, "You're going to cum so fucking hard."

My traitorous clit spasms. "What are you going to do?"

"Feast on you in this sacred place. Your tears and cum will spill onto this altar. I'm going to have my pussy and eat it too."

I shudder as he pulls back the tender flesh, exposing me to the entire room. "If a single one of you initiates touch my pussy, I will kill you. If any one of you sees someone touch my pussy and you don't kill them, I will kill you after I kill them. Understood?"

A collective murmur of agreement breaks out in the room. What the actual fuck is happening to me?

Riot traces his thumb in circles around my clit, and I buck. "That's a good little slut. Open up. Show them how bad you want to cum for me."

I can't control it. Every touch from him sends my body into a state of ecstasy. I try to stifle a moan, but I choke, and it turns into a wail.

He leans over and licks the length of my entrance from taint to nub. "Mmm, taste that sweet cunt," he grits out while beckoning for Valentin and Atlas.

I'm unraveling, unafraid of them watching me now. In fact, it's starting to turn me on. I can't help it. The ache in my swollen nub festers as Valentin and Atlas take turns thrusting their tongues inside me. I rock toward it as much as my restraints will let me.

"Oh, fuck," I whisper as Valentin and Atlas's dive in together, their tongues entering me at the same time. They kiss each other passionately while they devour my pussy, their tongues crossing and twirling feverishly as they lap up my juices and each other's saliva.

Riot eyes me like a hungry wolf. "For the raven," he mutters. "The Blackwells may have cursed us but now we have one of theirs."

He grabs the knife and slices it into his own hand. He holds his open wound over my body and lets the blood splatter against my breasts. "This is my offering. My sacrifice. You are ours, Firecracker. *Our light.* And we are the darkness." He smears the blood on my chest. "In absentia lucis, tenebrae vincunt. *In the absence of light, darkness prevails.*"

Valentin takes the knife and does the same thing. "Mors tua, vita mea. *Your death, my life*," he murmurs with my juices still dripping from his lips.

I'm covered in blood and about to cum just as Atlas follows suit by cutting his hand and holding his open wound over my chest. "Mors vincit omnia. *Death always wins.*"

A buzz thrums in the room like a pulse. The stone altar is suddenly hot against my flesh. I glance between them to see their eyes glowing. My core spasms like it's been jolted with electricity. Fuck. I grind my hips against the stone as something deeply carnal comes over me. What is happening?

The initiates begin to chant so loud my ears ring. Fuck. I want it to stop but the three of them are touching me again. Their fingers pinch my nipples and circle my nub. I close my eyes and surrender. I don't want to fight it. It feels too good.

An orgasm tears through me as the humming gets louder. I feel like my ears will explode at any moment. But I don't care. I open my mouth and scream as an onslaught of spasms grip my core. "Uhhh," I moan over and over again. I can't stop. Their hands move faster, pressing harder on every erogenous part of me. Everything is a blur. My back is raw from rubbing against the stone altar. I don't stop, though. I need to keep chasing this high. I can't get enough.

And right when I think I'm going to die, Riot kisses me hard on the lips. He kisses me like he cares. Like he wants me… like he needs me. I kiss him back and lose myself in his breath.

It's dark when I come to. I have no idea how long I've been asleep. I'm not in the altar room but in a bedroom, wrapped in soft sheets. My body aches. Every muscle hurts to move. But I roll over and see Riot's back. It's covered in markings. They're not like tattoos, but raised, scarred, symbols that almost look like they're alive.

By the way he breathes, I can tell he's awake. "Why did you bring me here?" I whisper in the dark.

"I told you last night. To show you what we are," he mutters.

I want to reach out and caress his back. But I don't because it's quiet and peaceful, and I don't want to disrupt it.

"No, I mean here. In your bed. Why did you bring me *here*?" I ask.

The silence is so loud it's deafening. It goes on for what seems like an agonizing amount of time. Endless quiet as the tension between us begins to climb and then seemingly fizzles out.

He turns onto his back and glares at the ceiling. "You're mine. You sleep in my bed."

My heart flutters for a moment. His voice is soft and achingly beautiful. "I thought you said I belong to all three of you…"

He turns his head to look at me, and I almost cry when his blue eyes meet mine. "Yeah, but you were mine first. Before…"

"Before you knew I was a Blackwell," I say sadly.

He sighs and looks back to the ceiling. "I was raised to hate you."

I wait to see if he'll elaborate but when he doesn't I'm filled with grief. Remorse for a life that was thrust upon us without our say. "Yeah, well, I was raised in the dark. To not know anything about you or my own family. I know you think I'm lying, but it's the truth. I grew up in Wickford Hollow, the daughter of the town's alcoholic Sheriff and his cheating wife. My best friend is a ghost and after you zipped me up in the bathroom that night, I went upstairs and killed a man."

Riot rolls over to face me. "Why did you kill him?"

I pull the sheet up around my body as I shiver at the memory. "Because he and his friend tied us up and threatened to do horrible things to us. And they would have if we hadn't gotten away. Because they'd been taunting us since we were kids. Because they used to spike my drinks and make me suck their cocks. Because his friend killed my friend. An eye for an eye."

"A soul for a soul," Riot whispers back and a wave of chills trickles over me. Those had been Bailey's exact words.

I nod. "When I stuck the knife in his neck, I didn't feel shame or guilt… just relief."

"If those bastards weren't already dead, I'd kill them myself." Riot cups my face in his hands, and I want to melt. To drown in his icy blue eyes forever. "I don't want to hate you," he rasps. "Especially after that night…"

Butterflies swim in my belly. I remember seeing his eyes through the ski mask that night in the bathroom. I was drunk and sloppy and a hot fucking mess. But I remember how he looked at me. The same way he's looking at me now.

My lip trembles as I stifle a sob. "Why did you really kill those guys from the bathroom?"

He breathes in another deep breath and presses his forehead to mine. "Because they didn't deserve to touch you. They were bragging about spiking your drink. About fucking you like you were a piece of trash. *You're so much more than that, Firecracker*. And no one gets to hurt you but me."

I don't know how to respond to that. His words confuse me. I know he struggles with this lifelong vendetta of hating my family, but I can see he's torn between it and the way he feels for the version of me he met back in Wickford Hollow. So I don't say anything back. I just let him hold my face in his hands. We fall asleep like that I think.

And when I wake again, I'm back in my own bed, wondering if it was all a dream. Until I turn my head to see a black rose on my pillow attached to a note that reads: *In absentia lucis, tenebrae vincunt.*

"In the absence of light, darkness prevails…" I murmur, remembering their chant from last night in the altar room.

I shudder and burrow myself in the blankets, wishing I was still in Riot's arms.

Chapter Twenty

Maureen

"We're worried about you," Villette says after taking a long sip of her peppermint mocha. Libra scrunches her nose over an egg nog latte and scoffs. I almost laugh because I know that showing concern for others is not one of her strengths.

I gaze out the window of the coffee shop and get lost for a moment in the view. The brown and gold autumn leaves are almost gone as winter slowly approaches. It makes the trees look naked and lonely. It invokes old memories. Good memories of Bailey and I getting ready for the holidays in Wickford Hollow. We'd go gift shopping together and then spike our coffee with rum for the walk home. Those days are gone now, and I can't ever get them back. We grew up too fast. *Lived too hard.*

I hover my nose over the steaming cup of pumpkin spice coffee, probably my last one for the season, and breathe in those nostalgic scents of cinnamon and nutmeg. And I think it's nice that two girls I barely know care enough to worry about me. "Thank you," I murmur.

Libra rolls her eyes. "Um, you're welcome? What the fuck, Blackwell? That shit in the dressing room last week was crazy. I know how they can get, but they are obsessed with you with a capital O."

Villette throws her a warning look. "What she means is, are you okay? Is this whole thing with them… consensual?"

How do I even answer that? "It's complicated…"

"So, that's a no then. Have they brainwashed you?" Libra snorts.

Villette shakes her head in protest. "Lib, we talked about you not blurting out every thought that enters your head, remember?"

"It's fine," I concede, but my shame threatens to drown me. I can't admit my darker tendencies to these girls. I'm still dealing with the guilt from what I did last Halloween. I don't know how to explain to them that Riot, Atlas, and Valentin's brutality brings me to life. I crave it so much that it makes me question my own sanity.

"I feel safe with them. I know that must sound strange, but there's a connection between us that grows every time we're together… I don't know why." I feel my hands start to shake around the cup as I try to explain our twisted relationship.

"They're dangerous," Libra says.

I nod. "So am I."

"They'll just keep hurting you," Villette groans.

"Then I'll hurt them back," I reply.

Libra chuckles into her drink. "You're just as psycho as they are."

"Lib!" Villette hisses.

"It's okay," I chime in. "I've done some really fucked up things in my life. It's not the first time someone has called me psycho. I'm not offended. I probably deserve that."

Libra sighs. "Sorry, I shouldn't have said that… Are you going to the Solstice with them?"

As much as she annoyed me at first, Libra is growing on me. She's unapologetically herself—bitchy and bat-shit but she owns it.

"Yeah, they didn't give me a choice." There are things I can't tell them that happened that night after we went dress shopping. Things that neither of them would understand. Libra might, but she'd still scoff at it. That night in the altar room was terrifying *and* hot as fuck. Maybe that was my sexual trigger. *I need to be scared out of my fucking mind to cum hard.*

Villette leans back and crosses her arms. "Yeah, I don't get it. How can you be so calm about being forced to go to the ball with them? I didn't take you for a pushover, Maur."

"I'm not. It's just a game we play. I act like I don't want them, and they chase me down and… make me do things. I guess I'm a glutton for punishment. The more I hate them, the more I want them. I've wanted them since the moment we met."

"I take back my apology. You *are* a fucking psycho," Libra quips.

Villette bites her lip. "Um, yeah you kind of are, Maur."

I feign a gasp and then burst out laughing. Within seconds, they both join in, and we are giggling like a bunch of teenagers. It's been so long since I had girlfriends, it reminds me of how much I miss it. We spend the rest of the afternoon chatting about the other boys at Tenebrose, mostly whom Libra is planning on seducing, and making plans for a girls' night before everyone goes home for the holiday break.

I agree to catch up with them later and head across campus for my Gothic Literature class. My good mood is instantly ruined when I walk in. Professor Erebus is huddled at his desk with none other than my *freaking mother*.

Fuck me.

My stomach knots and my palms dampen. What the fuck is she doing here?

Their conversation looks light and playful until she spots me. And that familiar look of disappointment washes over her face. She sticks a pointy pink nail out and curls it back, beckoning for me to come over.

Now would be a really good time for the guys to pull one of their let's kidnap Maureen games.

I groan as I shuffle over. "Why are you here?" I snap.

She purses her lips. "That's a very rude way to greet your mother, Maureen. Aren't you happy to see me?"

Professor Erebus snickers, clearly enjoying my discomfort. "I'm sure she's just tired from all her *extra-curricular* activities."

Oh my god. I want to scream. My cheeks burn so hot, I might pass out.

My mother arches her eyebrow. "Oh? Back home all she did was hang out with that Bishop girl in her weird mansion. I'm glad to hear she's being more active."

"That she is indeed," he drawls.

Fuck my life. This is the most awkward conversation I've ever had. I make a mental note to strangle Valentin later for talking about me with his dirty uncle.

I force a smile. "Well, I learned from the best." I motion to my mother. "How do you two know each other?"

The amusement fades from both their faces as they get a taste of their own medicine. Yeah, I can play this game too, asshole.

My mother averts her eyes the way she does when she's trying to look bored. "We both grew up in Ever Graves. But we didn't really know each other that well, did we Julian?"

Right. Keep telling yourself that, liar.

He clenches his jaw through a fake smile. "Well enough... anyhow, I must get class started. Lovely to see you as always, Shana."

I wait for him to walk over to a bunch of students before I turn on her. "What in the actual fuck are you doing here? Haven't you embarrassed me enough in my life?"

She grabs my wrist hard. "Watch your tone, young lady. I'm still your mother. I could ask you the same question. Why did I get a call from *my* mother, asking me why you're using the Blackwell name? I haven't spoken to that bitch in twenty years."

Wow. She never ceases to amaze me. "Well, seems like the apple doesn't fall far from the tree."

Her eyes narrow, and she lowers her voice. "Come with me right now." She gives Professor Erebus a look and as soon as he nods back, I'm being dragged out of the class and into the empty hallway.

I yank my wrist away and step back. "What is wrong with you? I'm about to start class. You can't just come in here and fuck everything up like you always do."

The fury in her eyes is unmatched. Without my father here to act as a buffer, I get the full psycho Shana Gray in all her devious glory. She backs me up against the lockers. "Listen, you little brat, you had no right to use *my* family name. Those people didn't want us. I left Ever Graves and never looked back. But now you're stirring something up that will only bring us all trouble."

She really has managed to hit a new low. "Sounds like they didn't want you after you cheated on your fiancé, *Julian Erebus*. Maybe if you weren't such a whore—"

Her hand hits my face before I can get the rest out. I hold my head as the sting of it makes my ears ring.

"You ungrateful little bitch. I gave up everything for you. My life, my friends, *my money*. And I regret it every day. I never should've had you." Her eyes are wild, crazed.

I want to cry, but I won't let her see my tears, so I swallow them down. And in this moment a part of me does wish I'd never been born. "Well, I'm never going back to Wickford Hollow, so you get what you've always wanted."

She lunges for me again but stops as Valentin walks over. "Hit her again, and I'll break your fucking hand."

Where the fuck did he come from?

My mother lifts her chin to look up at him. "How dare you threaten me? Do you know who I am? I'm a Blackwell."

Valentin's eyes darken as he takes a calculated step toward her. His shoulders tense. "No. You're the cheating wife of an alcoholic who has nothing better to do than take out her sad pathetic life choices on her own daughter. *She's* a Blackwell, not you."

She looks like she's going to burst a blood vessel in her neck. "You're not going to tell me how to discipline my own daughter, young man. Now step aside before I call Professor Erebus out here to make you."

Oh, fuck here we go.

Valentin snickers. "My uncle has far better things to do than involve himself in a matter that is clearly over. Maureen is no longer yours. She belongs to Nocturnus now. You're lucky I'm letting you off with a warning."

I'm in shock as I stand behind Val, my cheek still throbbing. "Just go, mother. Go and never come back."

She glares at me. "Nocturnus… you've really done it this time, Maureen. No one can save you now. Enjoy your servitude."

I let out the breath I'd been holding as soon as she spins on her heel and stomps off. I can't help myself from slightly collapsing into

Valentin. His body is warm and strong and just acted as a barrier between me and the devil herself.

He gently traces his fingers over my bruised cheek. "Are you all right?"

I nod. "Thanks for that. No one has ever stood up to her for me before."

The look in his eyes is tortured. He squeezes my hand in his. "Come on, let's get out of here."

I look back toward the door. "But what about class?"

"Don't worry about my uncle. I'll make sure you're excused," he quips.

We dash across the campus and hop into his car. I feel wild and free and alive with the windows down and my brown hair blowing all over the place. I stick my hand out to feel the cold wind against my sweaty palm and close my eyes. I can't believe how calm I feel after what just happened.

When I open my eyes, Valentin is staring at me. His face is more relaxed than I've ever seen. He smiles at me. Holy fuck. A real genuine smile that makes him look more boyish. "What are you looking at?" I ask playfully as I grin back.

He runs a hand through his black hair and his throat bobs. "You're fucking beautiful."

A flurry of nerves tingles my belly. His brown eyes are framed by long black lashes that almost touch his cheeks. I hadn't ever noticed because he's always so angry. I was afraid before to look too deep into them but now I want to fall into their abyss. "So are you," I murmur back.

The road we're on twists and turns up and away from town. The sky gets darker as mountains surround us the higher we climb. "Where are you taking me?" I ask.

The muscles in his arm flex as he shifts gears. I'm seeing his body with fresh eyes. The perfection of it takes my breath away.

"To my family's cabin," he replies. "No one uses it anymore. I come up here when I want to get away from everything."

My jaw nearly drops. *Now he's taking me to his special place?* This is a whole side of Valentin I didn't even realize I'd been longing for. "It sounds perfect."

I watch him drive, unafraid. I like looking at him so much I never want to stop. He glances back and forth between me and the road every few minutes. We are silent for the rest of the trip. No music, no talking, just the sound of the engine and the wind.

It fills the ache in my chest, soothing my untethered emotions and grounding me in ways I've never felt. My mother was the storm that tried to drown me today, but Valentin was the anchor that kept me afloat. I chuckle as I think of the absurdity of it. This man hates me the most out of all three of them. But today he saved me.

He chuckles back as if he can read my thoughts. As if he knows that he and I are the most unlikely pair. And yet I feel in my soul that we are more alike than we realize.

As we reach the highest peak of the mountain, the trees narrow and create a path for us to drive through. The house at the end of the road is a French chateau with brown shutters, bougainvillea-draped arches and a stone walkway leading up to a beautiful oak door. We park in front, and I am awestruck. "Holy fuck, Val. This is massive. I think my idea of a cabin and yours is very different."

He shrugs. "That's just what we've always called it."

I nod and follow him inside. The house is bright and airy and looks nothing like what I pictured. Valentin is a gloomy guy. He's practically the poster child for dark and Gothic. But this place is pretty in a way that fancy delicate things are.

We enter the spacious kitchen, and he motions for me to sit

at the table by an open window that overlooks the garden. I take a deep breath and inhale the scent of roses, jasmine, and honeysuckle. "No poison," I murmur.

"No, not out there. There is a small patch of hemlock on the other side of the house." He hands me a glass of white wine.

I arch an eyebrow as I gladly take it from him. "Day drinking, are we?"

"Well, you did just get smacked in the face. I think it calls for it, don't you?" he teases.

I snort mid-sip and a little spurt of wine comes out my nose. "And you're a comedian too. What other secrets are you hiding?"

He smiles but some of that pain starts to creep back into his eyes. He pours himself a glass of the tart white wine and sits across from me. "My father used to hit me too," he says softly.

My heart sinks. I reach across the table and squeeze his hand. "Fuck… I'm sorry."

"Don't be. It's not your fault." He flashes me another grin. "It's an Erebus family tradition. My uncle Julian tried his best to shield me but even he was terrified of my father. So when he stopped spending the summers here, Atlas came instead."

I swallow a big gulp of wine down. "He wouldn't hit you in front of outsiders…"

Valentin rubs his jaw. "He was less violent in front of my friends, yeah. Atlas had his own family shit to deal with, so he couldn't wait to spend his summers here. But the abuse wasn't just physical. He said we couldn't trust women. That the only thing they were good for was fucking and servitude to us. That if you don't control them, they'll leave like my mother did. But I always knew why she left. He beat the shit out of her too. I just wish she would have taken me with her…"

This is why he's the way he is. I want to wrap my arms around him and hold him forever. He looks so broken, so fragile right now.

"Maybe she didn't have a choice," I murmur.

He snickers and shoots back the rest of his wine. "There's always a choice, Maureen."

I nod, my heart breaking for him. "You're not your father, Val."

He lets out a deep sigh. "Aren't I? I don't know. Sometimes I think violence is ingrained in my blood. But I try not to be. I'm just so fucking angry all the time."

I grab his other hand from across the table. "Ditto. I stifle it and push it down so deep until I snap. Then I do some crazy shit I can't take back so that everyone will hate me. My mother blames me for her shitty life. She was engaged to your uncle, and she left him for my father. The Blackwells cut us off and banished us to Wickford Hollow. Now my grandmother is probably pissed that I'm here, using their name, and… well… hanging out with her sworn enemy."

Valentin pours us more wine and holds up his glass to toast. "Cheers to your mother *not* marrying my uncle because then we'd be cousins, and I'm really not into that sort of thing."

I burst out laughing as I clank my glass to his. "Same. I'm not really into kissing cousins either."

"Do you want to stay the night here with me?" he asks, his voice hoarse.

A shiver races up my spine. In the midst of all this new bonding and playful banter, I almost forget about the night we fucked each other like crazed animals. My cheeks flush as I think about the way he bent me over his bed and defiled me while I was on my period. The way he made me choke on his cock in the car…

Something in my eyes must have changed because his gaze darkens and that carnal hunger returns.

"You don't have to drink, or fuck me, or even stay… if you don't want to," he adds nervously.

I've never seen him look so shy before. So gentle. *It's everything.* "What if I want to? What would we do?"

A flicker of light swirls around his pupils. "We can drink, fuck, read poetry under the stars, fall in love… whatever you want, Firecracker. I'll give you anything you want."

I lick my lips and swallow hard. My heart races under his seductive gaze. "Yeah, I want to stay."

He smirks and leans back in his chair. "Good. Let's finish this wine, so we can open another bottle."

Chapter Twenty-One

Valentin

I'VE NEVER BROUGHT A WOMAN HERE BEFORE. I WAS ON my way up here when I decided to stop and let my uncle know I was going. He always worries about me. I needed to get the fuck away to deal with my demons alone. But when I saw Maureen's mother smack the shit out of her, something protective and possessive came over me. It triggered all those memories I had of me cowering from my father when he was on one of his rampages. The look in Maureen's eyes, the fear mixed with rage and hate… it was like looking into a mirror from the past.

She sits across from me now in my family home, which no one except Riot and Atlas are privy to. It was an impulsive decision, but

I couldn't let her go back to class after that humiliation. A switch ignited at that moment. And now I can't stop looking at her and seeing how fucking beautiful she is. With her bruised cheek now turning a shade of yellow that matches the gold flecks in her eyes, she is addicting to look at it. To be around. I don't want the moment to end yet. And I want to show her how she can move past the pain. I want to show her dark and dirty things that lessen the ache in my chest.

I open a third bottle of wine and gaze in amusement at her lopsided grin. She's giddy and relaxed. Most women aren't that way around me. I make people nervous and keep them on edge. But not this one. Even when I'm at my most brutal, she's not afraid of me, and it's fucking refreshing.

When I roll up my sleeves, I watch as her gaze lands on my sigils. "Go ahead, ask me anything you want."

She curls her legs up underneath her. "What are those markings? Riot and Atlas have them too. Why do you have them?"

"They're alchemy symbols. They offer the bearer great power. Riot is the conduit. The cursed one. So he marks our flesh during rituals, and we are granted new abilities from the ravens." I watch as her eyes widen and then come to the realization that she probably already knew.

She nods. "That's how you locked my dressing room door… I've seen your eyes glow before. Riot's too. And you all drink poison… Is Nocturnus a cult? Or are you like a coven or something?"

I chuckle. "All of the above. Neither. I don't know. Something like that, yeah. There is no definition that can be explained with words. It just is. And we exist in it. The more sigils we have, the more powerful we become."

She looks even more beautiful as she tries to wrap her head around the truth about us. The fact that she hasn't bolted for the door, lets me know I was right to bring her here. And that she's ready to fall even deeper into our dark void.

"And you need me for more power? To break the curse?" she asks, her voice breathy.

Smart girl. Now she's starting to get it. "We need you to be the fourth. So there's balance and strength from the blood bond of four of the most powerful families in all of Melancholia. Erebus, Thorn, Graves, and Blackwell. I'm air, Atlas is earth, Riot is water and you're—"

"Fire," she murmurs.

I nod. "We don't know if the curse can be broken but the more sigils we have, the more power... the less hold the ravens have on us. So maybe one day we'll be free."

Maureen fidgets with the sleeves of her sweater as she looks down. "You know it was all a mistake. A misunderstanding. Jessamine told me. Her death was an accident."

Ah. I suspected she'd latch onto Maureen. They are blood after all. "It doesn't matter anymore, Firecracker. The Blackwells have hated the Graves for too long. It's become part of their DNA. Atlas and I are guilty by association. Our families have abandoned us too now. Raven's Gate may be cursed but *we're* in charge here. So they can all go fuck themselves."

She lifts her chin and almost looks like she might cry. "Well, I hate them too now. I don't want their name anymore."

Her admonition sends a spark straight to my core. I want to hold her in my arms until I almost crush the breath out of her. She invokes a different emotion from me every second. She's mine. Fucking hell, she's perfect and she's mine.

"You can take any name you want, Firecracker. Erebus, Graves, Thorn. All three. But the pain and agony of what has happened to you never goes away fully."

"How do you deal with it?" she asks. "How do you keep the pain from eating you alive?"

She leans forward and I realize that we've been talking for hours, and I haven't even touched her. But I catch a whiff of her sweet scent and my hunger for her kicks in. "Sensory deprivation."

Her eyes widen. "Like breath play?"

Fuck, I can't wait to show her everything. "That's one aspect. But I have other methods that I prefer more… would you like to try one tonight?"

The base of her throat bobs and a tiny trickle of sweat runs down her forehead. "I think so. Yes. Show me."

I pull her up from the table and resist the urge to bend her over it. "We're going to go to a really dark place tonight. Are you sure?"

Her eyes light up as she nods but her fingers are trembling in mine. "I love the dark," she whispers.

˜

As we stand in the cold crypt underneath my house, in front of the open coffin, Maureen's face pales. "You want me to get into that?"

I want to show her how fucking hard she can cum when she's in a state of panic. When it's dark and confined, and she has no control over her own body.

"Take off your clothes and lay down on your back for me, Firecracker. Let me show you true fucking darkness." I grab her hips and pull her flush against my chest, so she can feel how hard my cock is through my pants. I take her lip between my teeth and lightly nibble. *"You're going to cum so fucking hard. I promise you."*

She lets out a little whimper. "Fucking hell. The girls were right. I'm just as fucking psycho as you are if I get in there."

This sends a deep rumble to my chest. "Yeah, you're my pretty

Pretty Little Psycho

little psycho. Show me how good you can be for Daddy. Be a naughty little slut in the pitch dark with me tonight."

I can't tell if she's afraid or excited or both, but she steps back and peels off her sweater. My breath hitches as I watch her take her time with each piece. Her pants come off next, then her bra, and finally her panties. "Mmm, you're fucking perfect."

She hesitates for a moment before climbing into the coffin and lying back. "How long will you keep me in here?"

I take her wrists and secure them above her head with the metal restraints that she didn't notice. "Shh, relax. I got you. I'll let you out when I think you're ready."

"Val... I don't know. I'm not good in enclosed spaces." Her breathing is already starting to quicken. Which makes all of this so much fucking hotter.

"That's the point, pretty girl. You'll see." I drag my fingers down her legs until I get to her ankles and restrain those as well.

I then pull out the gift I'd been saving for her. A remote-controlled vibrator designed to fit snugly inside her wet pussy. "Remember, the more you scream, the more oxygen you'll use. Try to conserve your breath."

"What the actual fuck? Wait you're actually going to close the lid on this thing? No. Let me out. I'm done." The panic in her voice deepens my arousal and sends a tremor down my shaft.

She moans as I peel back the lips of her pussy and slide the vibrator deep inside her. It has a lip on it that clasps to her clit, so she can get outer and inner stimulation at the same time. "Mmm, there we go. So fucking snug. You're going to feel every pulse."

Her nipples pebble and juices begin to drip down her legs despite her resistance. "Fear is an illusion, Firecracker. Pleasure and pain are real. Give in to this and you will never be afraid again."

Chapter Twenty-Two

Maureen

RIGHT BEFORE VALENTIN LOWERS THE LID OF THE coffin, I take a deep breath and close my eyes. The vibrator inside my pussy remains motionless, the anticipation threatening to completely unhinge me.

It's so quiet, all I can hear is my own heartbeat. I think it might explode out of my chest. Sweat pours down my naked body as the heat increases inside the coffin. I make the mistake of lifting my head and it hits the lid. *Fuck*. Now I know just how tight this space really is.

"Valentin," I cry out. "I changed my mind. I can't do this." Tears stream down my cheeks.

Fuck. Fuck. Fuck.

What if he left me here to die?

The panic spreads to my limbs, and I'm afraid I'll hyperventilate. No. I'm not ready for this. I try to get my wrists free, but the more I flail, the tighter the restraints get. If I move another inch, I risk my circulation being cut off.

Just breathe, Maur. Nice and easy.

I try to think about anything else than the fact that I'm tied up in a coffin. I try not to think about the fact that no one knows I'm here.

Another wave of panic flutters over me just as the vibrator in my pussy buzzes. I clench and thrust my hips up as it pulses and throbs inside me. *Oh, fuck.*

"Relax, Firecracker…" Valentin's voice somehow breaks through the steel of the tomb I'm trapped in.

It strangely brings me comfort and is the only thing tethering me to reality. I exhale slowly and unclench my muscles.

The vibrator kicks up a notch, and it sends a deep spasm to my core. "Oh, shit," I murmur.

It feels so fucking good, I forget where I am. It makes me feral as I ache for him to be in here with me. I need his hands on me. Want to feel his hot mouth sucking on my swollen nipples.

The lip on the vibrator buzzes against my clit, and I almost scream from the torture of being overstimulated in the dark. I can't see or move so these spasms in my pussy are all I can focus on. There's nothing else.

I arch my back as the speed and pressure increase. "Uhhh,' I moan. It pulses hard against my insides, flicking and grinding back against my G-spot. I want to tear my wrists out of these ropes, so I can shove it in deeper. Fuck.

"Valentin… please. I need you," I whine.

I hear him chuckle and the vibration increases yet again. I roll my hips so hard I almost tip the whole coffin over. My belly tightens as the pressure in my core climbs. Spasms spread through my pussy in waves that I can't control. I can't breathe as I clench and throw my head from side to side.

My cream gushes out, soaking my thighs. I'm drenched in my own cum as the toy inside me continues to pulse and flick against all my most sensitive spots.

"Fuck," I cry out. My chest heaves as every nerve in my body tingles. I gasp for air, whimpering while I ride out my orgasm.

I feel wild. Feral. I feel fucking alive and dead at the same time. Fearless. With every breath I take, a calm settles over me. I want to drown in the darkness, lose myself in the silence.

I lay here without any concept of time or space, escaping into the recesses of my mind. Remembrance fades like a crutch I no longer need to cling to, releasing the weight that has rested on my shoulders for too long.

My muscles twitch, aching from the onslaught of pain and pleasure. But I'm not afraid.

The lid creaks as it's thrust open. I blink my eyes a few times to adjust. Valentin hovers over me, looking like a dark angel in the muted light.

His lips quiver as he gazes down between my thighs. "Firecracker... you did so fucking good."

Heat floods my body, and I almost cum again when he pushes his fingers inside me and pulls the vibrator out. I release it with a heavy sigh. "Valentin... I've never cum like that before."

He unties me and lifts me out of the coffin. I feel his heart beating fast against me as he holds me close. "I'm going to lick every inch of cream from your cunt. And then I'm going to fill it back up with my own."

I let him carry me up the stairs to the bedroom. He sets me on the bed before taking off his clothes. I can see more of those sigils carved into his body. They sweep across his chest and down his torso, through his legs and down his shaft. They seem to pulse with energy as he nears me.

"What does this one do?" I point to the strange symbol embedded in his abdomen.

He climbs onto the bed and spreads my legs apart, nestling himself in between them. "Some of our power stems from our core. Our libido. This one is connected to that. I feel everything more intensely."

He is the epitome of intensity.

I lick my lips as the heat between my thighs sends a flush over my skin. Everything tingles. "Fuck, I want one of those."

Valentin's eyes glow as his gaze lands on my wet pussy. "You're going to have all sorts of marks when we're done with you, Firecracker."

I buck as he lashes his tongue against my swollen clit. I jerk my head back and release a guttural moan. He licks me slowly, lapping up every drop of cum I released. His urgency creates a spasm in my core, restimulating me all over again. I want to cry it feels so fucking good.

"Mmm, I love the way you taste. Knowing I did this to you gets me so fucking hard," he breathes in between licking and sucking the raw flesh of my pussy. "Open yourself wider for me."

I slide my hands down and peel back the lips of my pussy, offering myself up to him on a platter. "You've ruined me, Valentin," I clamor. "All three of you have ruined me."

He hums softly against my heated flesh. "Oh, we're just getting started, pretty girl." The force of his tongue thrusting inside makes my whole body contort.

I cry out as he burrows in deeper. He takes all of me inside his mouth, his lips stretching wide to cover every inch of my throbbing flesh. As if he wants to swallow me whole. He hums louder, rocking my core in a violent assault of vibrations so jarring that stars twinkle and pop in my vision. I scream and writhe against him as my cream bursts onto his tongue.

Valentin moans as he drinks. He digs his fingers into my flesh, bruising me with his brutality. I want his marks on me. *I need them.*

"Mmm," he comes up for air and angles his face toward mine. "*Tastes like sin*," he purrs before he kisses me, my juices still on his tongue. *Fuck.* It's so hot, I can't get enough. I kiss him back hard, desperate to consume all that he gives me.

"That's my naughty little slut, tasting yourself on my tongue," he rasps. He flips me over onto my belly, yanks my hair back, and shoves his finger into my mouth. "Suck that cream off. Taste how fucking good you are for me."

A deep guttural moan wrenches from my throat as he gags me.

"I'm not just going to ruin you." He squeezes the tip of his cock inside my ass, and I buck. "I'm going to tear you the fuck apart."

I scream as he drives into me. It feels like I am being torn open. The first time he did this, I was slippery from all the blood. I was angry and on the edge of madness. This time… fuck. I can barely take it. "Valentin, wait. It hurts."

He snickers. "That's how you know it's good, Firecracker." He digs his fingers into my flesh and spreads my ass cheeks apart as he hammers his cock farther in. "Fuck, you're so warm and tight. I'm going to cum in fucking seconds."

Tears stream down my cheeks. My insides are raw, burning from being stretched by his thickness. But I don't want him to stop. I roll my hips and rub my pussy against the mattress.

He lobs a glob of spit down my entrance. "Mmm, yeah. Now you're opening up for me. Fuck. I can't hold back much longer."

As he slides in and out slowly, I can feel every ridge rubbing me raw, but the tingling in my nub increases with every inch.

"Val… fuck, it's too much."

He kneads my ass cheeks while he rides me in an achingly slow, agonizing rhythm. "It will never be enough… My. Dirty. Fucking. Girl… *Fuck.*"

An unkindness of ravens squawk and peck against the window just as he cries out and his hot cum fills me to the brim. He slaps my ass cheeks over and over again as he thrusts like an animal, burying himself so far in, I think he might actually destroy me.

🦋

The front of the dorms are all abuzz when Valentin roars his car in the parking lot with me in the passenger seat. The rumors of me being claimed by them were already flying but on this gray drizzly morning, all their suspicions are confirmed.

"Do Riot and Atlas know I was with you all night?" They make it no secret that I'm to be shared between them, but they had been uncharacteristically absent for a couple of days.

Ever since the night Riot opened up to me.

Valentin's jaw is back to being clenched, and it's as if last night never happened. "Of course. We don't keep secrets from each other. Besides… they were occupied with something else."

An unexpected tinge of jealousy grips me. And it suddenly dawns on me that I never asked them if I'm the only one they fuck with. "Occupied with what?" I snap.

He snickers as he glares at a group of students walking by who can't seem to take their eyes off us. The vein in his neck starts to twitch. "Nothing for you to worry about. Now run along. I got shit to do."

His dissonance irritates me. How can he be so sweet and charming all night and then flip his asshole switch back on by morning? Fuck that. I hop out of the car and slam the door. But before I stomp off, I stick my head in the driver's side window, causing him to flinch.

"I have shit to do too," I grumble. "Remember that the next time the three of you decide to whisk me away without asking."

I try to make a dramatic exit, but he catches my wrist and pins it to the door. "The man I was last night… I can't be him all the time. You'll be sorely disappointed if you think otherwise."

I sigh. ""Like you said last night, Valentin, there's always a choice…"

He blinks and for a second the boyish gentleman from the cabin is there, haunting the body that holds him captive. But the darkness wins out, and I'm back to gazing into his empty void.

"Not for me," he mutters.

I have to jump back to avoid getting run over when he steps on the gas without warning. What the fuck? I'm more confused and twisted than ever now. This obsession we have with each other is depraved and sick. It's born from hate and evil. But I can't help myself. I want to push them so hard they snap.

As I head toward the elevator, I hear footsteps sprinting behind me. "Hey, hold the doors," a guy calls out.

Fuck, I'm not in the mood for chit-chat.

Without looking up, I hold one hand through the doors to keep them from closing and punch the button to my floor with the other.

"Floor?" I ask.

"Aren't you gonna say hi, beautiful?"

An uneasy feeling washes over me as I look up and see Zeke staring back at me. I shudder as I remember the way he tried to manhandle me at Swallow. Until Valentin scared him off. *Ugh, fucking Valentin.* Why did he have to ruin our perfect night this morning?

I step sideways away from Zeke. "Hi. What floor are you on?" I ask again, curtly.

A devious grin takes hold of his lips. "Oh, I actually don't stay here. I just saw you and wanted to say what's up."

Under the bright lights of the elevator lift, I size him up, taking better stock of his build and mass. He's at least six-foot-three and made of hard solid muscle. He'd actually be kind of hot if he wasn't such a fucking creep. My stomach knots as he leers at me.

"So, you stalked me all the way into my building?"

"Well, when you say it like that, it makes me sound like a pervert. You don't really think that about me, do you, Maureen?"

There's a crazed look in his eyes. Like if I say or do the wrong thing he's going to pounce. I shake my head and try to calm my racing heart. "Of course, not. I'm just teasing."

He licks his lips and backs me into the corner. "Yeah, you are a fucking tease. We never got to finish that dance the other night. How about now?"

Fuck. I look over toward the elevator buttons and my stomach drops as I realize we're not moving. His finger is firmly pressed against the button that keeps the doors from opening. "Look, I'm sorry if you misread my intentions that night, but I'm already seeing someone."

He glowers down at me. "I heard you're seeing *three* dudes. One cock ain't enough for you?"

The fuck? I shove my hands against his chest, but he doesn't budge. "That's none of your business. But if any of them find out about what you're doing right now, they will murder you."

Zeke chuckles. "I think you overestimate your pussy, darling. Riot was just in the locker room the other day talking about how you let all three of them finger bang you at Nocturnus House."

My blood chills and it hurts to breathe. "What?"

Zeke presses his body against mine, boxing me into the corner of the elevator that still isn't fucking moving. "Yeah," he continues. "But I didn't need him to tell me. *I was there*, beautiful."

My head spins as the weight of his words threatens to suck the life out of me.

He takes a strand of my hair and twirls it around his finger. "That's right. I was there watching you get your pussy mangled. You were so eager. So fucking willing. I like that about you."

He's a fucking Nocturnus initiate? No. This can't be happening. I swallow and lick my lips to will moisture back into my mouth. "Well, then you remember when Riot warned you all what would happen if anybody touched me."

Zeke laughs. "Who's gonna tell him? You? Like he's going to believe a nasty little whore over one of his own members. *He doesn't fucking trust you*. He said so himself."

Lies. Riot would believe me. Wouldn't he? Moments flash through my mind. That night he found me in the bathroom, the way I flirted with Zeke at Swallow, stealing Valentin's car, and taking selfies with the guy at the bar… Fuck. I haven't given Riot a single reason to trust me.

I look up at his smug face and fight the urge to cry. "I need to get ready for class. Please let me go."

Zeke places a hand on either side of me, caging me in tighter. "If you recall, he said I can't *touch*. He never said anything about not looking."

I start to hyperventilate. "Please, just let me out. I won't say anything."

"Shhh, it's okay. I'm going to let you go. Yeah, but first I want you to play with your pussy for me."

I shake my head and try to slip out of his grip but he's too strong. "No. I don't want to," I yell.

Zeke slams his palm against the elevator wall, barely missing my cheek. "Yeah, *you do*. If you don't fucking do it right now, I'll tell everyone that you seduced me to get back at them. That you came to me and begged to ride my cock all fucking night. And they'll believe it. I saw that little argument between you and Val just now. You're a feisty little bitch who wants to make her daddy jealous."

Fuck. What if he's right? I stomped off after getting possessive over their whereabouts. I'm unpredictable and Riot still isn't convinced I'm telling the truth about my past.

"You're disgusting," I snarl as I lean back against the wall. I close my eyes before reaching down and unzipping my pants. I can smell his hot breath on my face, and it makes me want to vomit.

I start to slide my hand down my panties when the elevator doors ding open. "Get the fuck away from her!"

My eyes fly open to see Libra holding a baseball bat, primed like she's ready to swing.

Oh, thank fuck.

Zeke shrinks back laughing. "Calm down, Lib, I can fuck you too after. No need to get jealous."

"Oh, fuck off, Zeke. No one wants to fuck you," she snorts.

I scurry past them both and sprint to my room, grab my knife, and hurry back. I nudge Libra out of the way and stalk toward him, waving the blade in the space between us. "If you ever come at me again like that, I will fucking gut you."

Jessamine's willowy figure appears next to him. "Do it now, Maur," she whispers. "Kill him so he can't hurt us."

"Oh, now you show up? Thanks a fucking lot!" I yell at her.

Zeke raises an eyebrow. "Who ya talking to, psycho?"

Libra shoves him hard against the elevator and smashes the down button. "Don't ever come up here again, Zeke. You might be an initiate, but Atlas *is* Nocturnus. And I'm his blood. So don't think for one second you have more power than me."

Zeke laughs hysterically as she sends the elevator back down.

"Are you okay, Blackwell? Fuck, that guy is a prick. Where have you been all night anyway? Villette was sick with worry when you didn't show up to meet us at Swallow."

My head pounds as I try to stave off the nausea. And then the fury settles into my bones. The fucking rage I have from what Zeke said. The fact that he was there in the altar room, that he was one of the masked hoods watching as they defiled me, makes me want to smash all their faces in. But I need a fucking shower and a stiff drink first. I don't even care that it's barely noon.

I ignore Libra and charge into the kitchen to pour myself a whiskey. She watches with arms crossed as I shoot it back. "*Maureen,*" she protests.

"Wow, you called me by my first name for once. You feeling okay?" I snicker.

She snatches the whiskey bottle out of my hand before I can pour another. "If you want to get drunk before breakfast, I'm all for it. Hell, I'll even join you. But you have got to start trusting someone. If not me, then at least call Villette. You're in way over your head, *Blackwell.*"

She's right. I hate to admit it. I actually like Libra. She's tough and confident and takes zero shit. She reminds me of how I used to be before all that shit happened in Wickford Hollow.

I hold out my glass. "Fine. Have a drink with me and I'll talk."

She smirks, satisfied with herself. We grab the bottle and head to the living room. I spend the next two hours telling her everything. I start at the beginning, all the way back to meeting Riot in the bathroom, and all that happened after. *All of it.*

Chapter Twenty-Three

Riot

I PACE AROUND THE LIVING ROOM WAITING FOR ATLAS and Valentin. There has been a fucking breach in our home, and I'm about to fucking murder everyone.

"Where have you two been? I've been texting you both for hours," I bark out as they saunter through the door.

Valentin looks disheveled. His hair is damp and messy around his face. He leans against the doorway in wrinkled jeans and a T-shirt that looks like it shrunk in the wash. "I went for a drive after I dropped Maureen off at The Nest. What's going on?"

"And you," I point to Atlas who has that shit grin on his face that he wears when my anger amuses him. "Don't tell me you got distracted talking to ravens again. I told you to use your sigil to keep an eye on our firecracker."

He shrugs. "She was with Val."

Fucking hell. "Someone is running their mouth about what we do here. Specifically the night Maureen was on the altar."

Valentin's eyes flicker with rage. "The fuck?"

Atlas's smirk falls as he flexes his arms. "Who? I'll cut their fucking tongue out and feed it to my snake."

"I don't know. But it wasn't any of us, or her. It had to be an initiate," I say.

"About to be a dead fucking initiate," Valentin snaps.

One of the most sacred vows we take is silence outside these walls. Whatever happens here is for our eyes and ears only. The thought of one of our own airing our secrets all over campus makes me fucking sick. And murderous.

"I've called a meeting to get to the bottom of it. And after tonight, no one enters our sacred room except us three. Not until we know our secrets are protected." I grab my case of knives before heading down to the altar room.

Valentin and Atlas follow me down the stairs, their footsteps heavy as our anger collectively builds. I can feel it buzzing off of them. I imagine it must be the way they felt that night I murdered those douchebags in Wickford Hollow. They could feel my anger through our sigils all the way from Raven's Gate.

With the three of us walking in step, our rage and fury is palpable, explosive, and all-consuming. I wrench open the iron door. It makes a loud screech as it scrapes across the cement floor. From the second we enter; I can practically taste the fear that bounces in between the initiates. They know I don't call impromptu meetings unless I'm fucking pissed and about to kill someone.

I stalk to the center of the room and slowly make eye contact with each one of them. "I demand loyalty. Obedience. *Secrecy*. All three have been violated in one single act." I take my knives out from their case and arrange them by size on the table. "Everyone in here swore an oath. And you know if you break that oath, the consequence is death."

They all stare straight ahead, afraid to look at the vengeance in my eyes. I pick up the largest knife and begin circling each initiate. The blade is almost as long as my forearm. I relish the way the worn leather hilt feels familiar in my palm as I twirl it around.

Atlas picks up one of the smaller knives and without warning, charges toward one of the larger initiates. He grabs him by the collar and looks him dead in the eye. The man begins to shake. Atlas and he are the same size, but Atlas is actually crazy.

He jabs the tip of the blade into his cheek. "Was it you? You have the balls to spill our secrets?" The man shakes his head furiously and whimpers. Atlas waves the blade in front of his face. "Maybe I'll cut out your eyes. Can't talk about what you can't see."

"P-please, no. It wasn't me. I would never," the initiate sputters out.

Atlas smirks and drags the tip of the blade down to his mouth. "Or maybe I'll cut out your tongue so you can't fucking talk no matter what you see."

With the group hyper-focused on Atlas, a young initiate doesn't have to time react when I come up behind him. I yank his head back and hold my knife to his throat. "Or maybe it's this one. What do you think, Val?"

Valentin has a knife in each hand when he comes toward us. "I say we kill all of them just to be sure."

The whimpering turns to full-on crying from a handful of them. While others lift their chins higher in a pathetic attempt to look brave. Too bad for them, I can see the puddles of piss pooling at their feet.

"Who's going to break first?" I taunt.

Atlas moves to the next guy and smacks him in the forehead with the flat of the blade. "There's a traitor in this room. Is it you?"

This one doesn't move a muscle as he stares straight ahead, his head held high. He's also the only one who hasn't pissed himself. I circle him. "Your name's Zeke, right? Weren't you harassing our girl at the Swallow a few weeks ago?" I glance over at Valentin while waving my knife in the guy's face. "This is him, right?"

Valentin nods. "That's him."

"I didn't harass anyone," Zeke snaps with a little too much bark for my liking.

Atlas smacks him on the forehead again. "Are you calling Valentin a liar?"

He shakes his head. "No. Sorry. I didn't know she was your girl."

There's an uneasiness about him. He's one of the newer initiates and has been nothing but obedient. He keeps to himself and follows all the house rules. But there's a nervous energy bubbling below his calm exterior.

"When Val relayed what you did, I let it go because I truly believed you didn't know she belonged to us. But now one of you is running your mouth about our girl. About what they witnessed. But you weren't there, so you're off the hook."

I turn back to address the group as a whole again. "In fact, there were only ten initiates in the altar room that night—the oldest and most trusted. And yet not so trustworthy apparently." I point to the ten new initiates, including Zeke. "You're all dismissed. But if I find out you know something and aren't talking, there will be a fucking reckoning."

They shuffle out, nodding and mumbling promises as they exit the room. I snicker and turn back toward the remaining initiates.

"Which one of you thinks it's okay to talk about our girl's pussy, hmm?" I tap my knife on each of their shoulders as I stalk behind them.

Valentin rears back and slaps a short chubby initiate across the face. "Someone start fucking talking," he screams into his ear.

The betrayal is sickening. It casts a shadow on Nocturnus, unlike anything I've ever seen. The stench is putrid and stains our souls. "Some of you have received the rare privilege of a sigil. The ravens have accepted you as we have. And this is how you repay them?"

Atlas sucks in a sharp breath and slashes his knife across the face of the initiate closest to him. "Fuck this. Let's kill them all and start over. I'm sure there are plenty of eager souls who would gladly take their places."

Valentin nods in agreement and grabs the guy on the end.

"Wait," he begs.

I motion for Val to stand down as I walk toward them. "Do you have something to confess?"

He looks down at the ground, his lips trembling. "I-I wasn't there that night."

"Then why the fuck are you speaking?" Atlas growls.

My stomach knots and a chill snakes up my spine. "But there were ten elder initiates. *You* are one of them. What do you mean you weren't fucking there?"

I feel like I'm having an out-of-body experience as my worst fucking nightmare comes true.

He swallows hard and keeps his gaze on the ground. "I-I couldn't find my phone anywhere that day. I never got the message about the ritual. Someone must have… replaced me."

Fuck. I knew it.

I exchange a knowing look with Valentin and Atlas before giving them a nod. A collective gasp rings out when the blood splatters on the remaining nine initiates' faces as Valentin slices open the missing initiate's throat.

I glare at all of them. "Find out who did this and bring him to me."

"And clean up this fucking mess," Atlas snarls. He's never been so unhinged before. But our firecracker makes all of us crazy. He's just as obsessed with her as I am.

We leave them there to deal with the body and head back upstairs. Taking a life isn't frivolous, just necessary at times. We give and we take. The ravens demand it. But once we have Maureen's sigil bond… we'll be the ones truly in charge.

"Maureen's not returning any of my texts," I hiss.

"I think I pissed her off earlier. She'll get over it," Valentin replies.

"She better," I snap. "I think we should do the claiming ritual after the Winter Solstice tomorrow night."

"I'll go find her and make sure she's okay." Atlas smooths his pale blond hair back off his dampened forehead. He really did get worked up down there. Fuck, this girl has got us all spinning.

Maybe I don't hate her as much as I hate her family. But I can't let my cock cloud my judgment. There are liars all around me and she could still very well be one of them.

But once she takes the mark of Nocturnus, once we brand her with our sigil… I fucking win and get justice for every Graves man and woman who came before me. I will spread their curse like a fucking disease and make sure that the Blackwell bloodline is forever tainted.

Chapter Twenty-Four

Atlas

I use my sight to track Maureen. I see her sitting on the floor between two aisles, a pile of books surrounding her. I hop on my bike and within minutes, I'm blazing into the parking lot of Graves Library. I ignore the stares and murmurs from various groups as I storm past them. Ever since Maureen got to Tenebrose I haven't been able to focus on anything else. I deleted all the random girls' numbers from my phone and ghosted all of them.

My father would keel over if he saw how I've been acting. And all because of one girl. Nah, he'd think I've lost my fucking mind. The Thorn men were not loyal to their women. Not in the sexual sense

Sure, he'd take a bullet for my mom, but then he'd turn around and fuck the first hot piece of ass who offered to nurse him back to health.

While Valentin's father raised him to hate women, mine taught me to love them all. Literally. My cousins, Aries and Libra, had a similar upbringing, but their dad had a daughter to worry about. He eased up on the *bachelor for life* rhetoric a lot. But I am the only son of Pisces Thorn and he'd be damned if he saw me chasing after one girl.

I lean against the stacks, my arms crossed. "Hey, pretty girl. I've missed you."

To my surprise, she glares up at me. "Fuck off, Atlas. I'm busy."

A snort escapes me. "Oh, we're back to this now, are we? Don't make me bend you over right here and spank you. You know I will."

She scrambles to her feet and starts gathering her books together. "Yeah, I'm sure you'd like everyone here to see that. Since humiliating me is what gets all three of you off."

Fuck.

I run a hand through my hair. "You heard about the breach… we're handling it."

She spins around and gives me a hard shove. "Breach? Handling it? Fuck you. You tell everyone they're not allowed to look at me, but then go around bragging about fucking me to the whole school. I'm tired of your games. Just leave me the fuck alone."

What the fuck is she talking about? I grab her wrist. "We've done no such thing. Who told you that?"

Her cheeks flush and she looks down at the floor. "It doesn't matter. I thought the three of you might be different. That despite all your psychotic tendencies, I meant something to you. Even Riot. I know he hates my family, but I thought maybe he didn't hate me anymore. I guess I am just a stupid slut."

I cup her face in my hands. "You're *our* little slut. But you're also our firecracker. Our... mate. We would never shame you like that. Someone is lying to you. Tell me who."

This has to do with the breach at Nocturnus. I can feel it in my fucking bones. I can't wait to find this fucker and feed him to my snake piece by piece.

Maureen's eyes well with tears. "I don't know what I am to any of you. I shouldn't care. You, Riot, and Valentin are all a bunch of entitled assholes. The only things that matter to you are power and control."

"That's not true. You matter to us," I quip back.

She snickers. "Yeah, my blood matters to you. Valentin told me you need a fourth for your twisted little coven. You need a Blackwell, so you can get payback. I should have known you were just using me from the start."

I blow out a deep breath. I wish Val had waited to tell her until we were all together. She doesn't understand the significance of the bond. I want to explain it, but she's in no mood to listen. "Come with me, please. I want to show you something. Let me prove to you that you're wrong about us."

She looks at me like she wants to slap me. "Are you for real? I don't trust you."

"You will. I swear it. Just come with me," I plead.

A surge of power shoots through my veins as I gaze into her exquisite, amber-colored eyes. I know she can't resist me, though I feel her trying. But her fate and ours are tied now. We are connected by ancient feuds, bad blood, and now... poison.

"Give me *something* to believe you," she commands.

I nod. "The poison. It's my family's legacy. And other than them, there are only three other people I've shared it with."

Her breath hitches as she realizes the weight of my words.

I hold three fingers up and count them down. "Riot, Valentin, and *you*." I brush my thumb across her lips. "You're the *only* woman I have ever shared it with. You're not a fool, Firecracker. Look into my eyes and see for yourself if I'm lying."

"Fuck," she mutters. Her resistance is weakening even more as she lets herself drown in my eyes. I have her. *I've always had her*.

I hold out my hand. "I'm asking this time. No more kidnapping plots."

She stares down for what seems like forever before finally slipping her slender hand in mine. "Okay. But don't make me regret this."

I guide her gently outside and hand her a helmet. She hops on behind me, and I almost melt when she slides her arms around my waist. Her body feels so warm and soft against mine. I can't wait to devour every inch of her. But first, I need her to believe me. We can hate fuck each other all we want but none of this works if we don't have trust.

༺༻

"Atlas, you said I could trust you. I don't want to see Riot or Valentin right now." Maureen leaps off my bike and throws the helmet at me.

"No one is here. We sent all the initiates away, and I told the guys to bounce as well. It's just us, Firecracker. I promise."

She crinkles her nose toward the house, and I can't tell if it's an aversion to its monstrosity or just the hemlock getting to her. "What are we doing here?"

I grin, satisfied that my pretty little psycho responds so well to me. She thinks I'm the sweet one, and I find that adorable. Little does she know… I lace my fingers through hers and pull her with me. "Come on. I'll show you."

Her shoulders tense when we enter the house. After taking

a few lingering looks around, she releases her breath. "I've never seen it so quiet."

I smirk. "See, I told you it's just us. I'm a lot of things. A liar isn't one of them."

Her face lights up upon entering my room. I'm not bothered by the fact that it's cluttered and messy. That's me in a nutshell. I have hoodies and jeans strewn over chairs, stacks of books in misshapen piles on the floor, overflowing candle wax that's stuck and hardened to my bedside table. She scans over it but the thing her gaze fixates on is the island in the center—containing beds of poisonous flowers actually growing inside this room.

I grab a remote to click on my Bluetooth speakers and Arankai's version of *Eat Your Young* starts to play. I watch as she moves closer to the toxic plants and then stops. She looks around the room again. "I like it in here. It's… inviting."

She's fucking *inviting*. Fuck. I want to taste every inch of her fiery skin. "I like how *you* look in here. You fit."

I walk toward her and fondle the belt loops on her jeans. She takes a deep quivering breath when my fingers skim her bare midriff. I lean down and nestle my nose against her neck. "You smell good enough to eat, Firecracker."

The vein in her neck throbs. "What did you want to show me?" She asks nervously.

I love how I can unnerve her. I drag my fingertips up her spine all the way up to the back of her neck. When I get to her nape, I tangle my fingers in her hair. I tug her head back and press a light kiss to her lips. Fuck, so soft. So fucking sweet.

"Do you trust me?" I ask.

She lets out a little whimper after each peck I give her. "No… not yet."

I smile against her lips. "Good. It's more fun when you don't."

I walk her back toward my bed and nudge her onto it. Her eyes blaze with lust and ache as she watches me take off my shirt and pants. A flicker of amusement rushes through me as I watch her eyes widen when she sees my cock. It's been inside her before, but it was from behind. It's much more intimidating when it's staring her right in the face.

I slide my hand slowly down my shaft. "Look how fucking hard you make me."

She licks her lips. "You're so fucking pretty, you know that?"

I chuckle. "No one's ever called me that, Firecracker." I unbutton her pants and slide them off. She doesn't attempt to stop me. "I wanna share something really special with you. But I need you to promise me you'll stay calm."

She arches her eyebrow. "You got a forked tongue or something I don't know about?" She teases.

I almost fall over laughing. "Not exactly." I slide her panties down and the hunger in her eyes turns feral. She's fucking perfect. I love how her appetite matches mine. "Scoot back and open your legs nice and wide for me."

She leans back against the pillows and moisture starts to pool between her legs. It trickles down her thighs like sweet nectar.

"Good girl... You might not trust me, but I need you to know that I won't let anything bad happen to you. Okay?"

Her breath hitches. "What the fuck are you up to, Atlas? You're starting to freak me out with all this cryptic talk."

I place a gentle kiss against her thigh, and she twitches. "I'm going to need you to stay really still, Firecracker. Zeus doesn't like any sudden movements."

"Who the fuck is Zeus?" Before she can fully allow herself to panic, I run my finger down her wet slit. She shudders and rolls her hips. "Atlas… you're fucking insane. But how can I not say yes to your crazy when you touch me like that?"

I chuckle and slide off the bed. "Because you're just as fucking crazy as me, pretty girl."

I go to the center island and reach deep inside the case that hides below it. As soon as I stick my hand in, I feel Zeus wrap around my arm and tighten. "It's okay, killer. It's me," I coo.

When I turn around to face her, she scurries back against the headboard, her eyes as wide as saucers. "What… what the fuck is that?"

I stalk toward the bed with Zeus slithering around my arm, the length of him hangs down to the floor. "This is how we establish trust, Maur."

Chapter Twenty-Five

Maureen

A FUCKING SNAKE? NO, NOT JUST ANY SNAKE. A fucking poisonous king cobra snake. Of course, Atlas would keep one of the deadliest predators as a pet. I seriously need to rethink my life choices.

"Please, put him back, Atlas," I beg. I can't stop my legs from shaking. Its black and white scales seem to glow as it slithers around Atlas's naked body. How he isn't afraid is beyond me. That thing could kill both of us in seconds.

Atlas takes another calculated step forward. "Don't move, pretty girl. He doesn't know you yet."

How can I not move? I'm fucking trembling. "Why are you

doing this?" I whisper, afraid that even my voice will startle the feral reptile that clings to his arm.

Atlas climbs onto the bed slowly. He's only inches away now. The snake's body is so long it touches the ground. "In about twenty seconds, he's going to latch onto your thigh and bite you. Do not panic. It will hurt a lot, but it will be worse if you freak out."

Um, what? I'm dead. Atlas is certifiable. He's lured me up here to feed me to his pet snake. Fuck. I want to run but the cobra fans out his neck as he eyes me. I won't get away in time. "No. I don't want this. What the fuck? You think this is going to make me trust you?"

"I control Zeus, not the other way around. He's a predator like me. But the venom in his fangs is rare. I haven't let anyone have a taste. Not even Riot or Valentin. After he bites you, I'll coax him off, put him away, and suck the poison out." Atlas's arm flexes as Zeus snaps forward.

I flinch and curse under my breath. "I don't understand the point of this."

Atlas smiles. "I want this bond with you. There's nothing more intimate than this. To be at our most vulnerable and trust each other completely."

Fuck. He looks so beautiful holding that snake. I don't know what it is about these guys that make me do things I'd never do. I always want to give in to them. "I'm scared," I whisper.

"I know." When he lowers his arm, Zeus hisses and slithers down onto the bed. "The poison will paralyze you for a moment. But I promise, I'll suck it out before it's too late."

Not the most reassuring sentiment I've heard. Fucking hell. Why am I doing this? I inhale short steady breaths as I watch his snake make its way toward me. When its scaly body rubs against my leg, I almost lose my entire stomach. I suck in a deep breath and secretly wish I could just black out.

"You're doing so good, Firecracker. Just relax," Atlas whispers. He still holds onto part of Zeus, but I seriously doubt how much power he really has over him. Will he really be able to stop this creature from eating me alive?

Zeus jerks his head a few times and it takes all my willpower to keep still. He flaps his neck and lets out a loud hiss. *Oh, fuck.*

I buck my hips as his sharp fangs sink into the inside of my thigh. A stifled scream unleashes from my throat. The pain is excruciating. My insides burn so hot I can't breathe. I'm going to die. I'm such an idiot.

Through my blurred vision, I glimpse Atlas leaping off the bed with the snake. At least I think I do. I can't hear anything. My tongue feels like a weight I can't lift. Fuck. My life is in his hands.

When Atlas returns, he's on me in a flash. I don't feel his lips at first, but I can see them pucker around the fresh snake bite. It makes my skin tingle and sweat.

"I got you, Firecracker," he murmurs. The grooves of his tongue feel like sandpaper against my raw flesh. I can't tell if I'm crying but my face feels wet. Or maybe I'm bleeding from my eyes.

Atlas doesn't seem alarmed. The harder he sucks, the more feeling returns to my body. I blink a few times and the room is sharper. Clearer. I take a deep breath and release it slowly while he laps at my wound and all around it.

"Mmm, so fucking good." He drags the tip of his tongue up my thigh and across my abdomen. "I want you to fuck my mouth, pretty girl. Rub that sweet pussy of yours all over my face. You did so good. You deserve to cum."

I let out a moan as he flicks his tongue between my pussy lips. "*Fuck me hard,*" he begs.

The room seems to spin as he thrusts the entire length of his rough tongue deep inside my pussy. I grab onto his head and thread my fingers through his blond locks.

He hums inside me as he digs his fingers into my ass cheeks and pulls me taut against him. I let him rock me up and down. Oh, fuck. The pressure in my core builds, my insides tingling and spasming with every flick.

He peers up at me with those piercing blue eyes, and I moan louder. There's something about him watching me unravel from his touch… I buck wildly as he lifts my legs up over my head, pinning me back as he devours my pussy.

"Atlas… what are you fucking doing to me?" I rasp.

He grabs a hold of my clit and pinches it. "*Cum for Daddy.*"

I gaze up at him, unhinged. His perfectly chiseled body glistens with sweat as he thrusts two fingers inside me. "Oh, fuck. I'm cumming."

"You're so fucking filthy. Fuck." He slaps my pussy and something feral comes over me.

I cry out as an orgasm rips through me, and my cream becomes a projectile. "Oh, shit. I can't stop."

"Fuck yeah. Squirt all over me," he pants as he adds a third finger inside and pushes all the way back to my most sensitive spot. "So fucking naughty, aren't you?"

He wraps a hand around my throat and squeezes. I arch my back into it as the pressure from him holding me down sparks another spasm in my swollen nub. I don't remember the pain or the fear from Zeus's bite anymore. All I feel, *all I know*, is this otherworldly pleasure that he's giving me right now.

He shoves two fingers down my throat, and I know I'm in trouble. The kind that makes your toes curl and your nipples pebble. This man wants to do despicable things to me, and I'm going to let him.

"Yeah, give me all those pretty tears while I choke you," He presses down on my tongue, and I gag which only makes me cum harder on the three fingers he's thrusting inside my pussy.

I moan louder as he controls my body like a marionette. Like I'm his toy to play with. I want him to use me up until there's nothing left.

He licks the tears off my cheeks. "Do you like being my pretty little doll?"

I'm addicted to the torture he inflicts. It's a toxic obsession that I crave because he rewards me with so much more. I clench around his fingers, my cum still dripping out as I ride the last of my orgasm. "Yes, Daddy," I moan. *A thousand fucking times, yes.* My body is on fire, wet with sweat and cum and tears. *I need his brutality.* His own weird fucking brand of psycho.

A devilish look flickers in his eyes as he drags me off the bed and bends me over the center island. I freeze when I notice the cubby carved into it. *Zeus's habitat.* And it doesn't look like it's enclosed. "Atlas, your snake is right fucking there," I stammer.

Atlas wraps something around my wrists, securing them behind my back. He holds my head down against the table and the stench of hemlock and oleander invades my senses, making me dizzy. "Shhh, don't startle him. He just wants to watch."

My arms ache behind my back, but I don't move or take my eyes off the deadly cobra. "You're a psychopath," I whisper.

He strokes his hands across my ass cheeks, chuckling as I tremble. "I want to see you cry when your tight little hole tries to stretch around my cock." I shudder at the way he gently pulls my ass cheeks apart. "And then I'm going to lick your tears and swallow them down with all that cum."

I clench as the tip of his cock nudges against my entrance. "But first, lets get you lubed up."

In my peripheral, I see him reach for a vial of poison. I squirm and try to lurch away from him. "You're *not* putting that inside me, Atlas."

"Yes, I am. You're ready, pretty girl. It will only burn for a second."

The liquid sizzles when it hits my flesh. My cry becomes a muffled gargle with his hand clamped over my mouth. "Shhh, pretty girl. You'll scare Zeus."

Fucking fuck my ass is literally on fire. It burns and tingles at the same time. But despite my fear, the poison loosens me up.

"Oh yeah, you're nice and slick now." He grabs my bound wrists, using them to anchor him, as he pushes inside my ass.

"*Uhhh*," I cry out.

"Damn, you're so fucking tight. Let me in, pretty girl. Let Daddy get nice and deep." His cock throbs and swells against my walls. My clit responds with a spasm and moisture instantly pools in my core. It leaks out and onto my thighs as he forces himself farther in.

He grinds against me, thrusting in circles. "Cry for me, Firecracker." He smacks his hand down hard against my ass while ramming his cock all the way in.

It feels like he's ripping me apart at the seams. His snake hisses when I unleash a bloodcurdling scream. Atlas slaps me again, harder this time and my knees buckle. "Mmm, there we go. Now I can see a couple of tears on your pretty face."

Holy fuck this man is depraved. *Un-fucking-hinged*. And I am disgusted with myself because I need it like I need air. My insides are raw from his thick cock rubbing against my walls, but it feels so fucking good. It's hot and fucked up for so many reasons.

I'm starting to relax when Zeus flaps his neck and hisses at me. "Oh fuck, Atlas…"

But it doesn't faze him. He chuckles and slams into me, tugging on my bound wrists like the reins of a saddle. "Fear is the best aphrodisiac. Give into it."

I hold my breath as Zeus slithers closer to us. "He's coming at me, Atlas."

"Aw, he just wants a closer look at my pretty girl."

Fuck. There's something wrong with me. The closer this deadly snake gets to possibly sinking its poisonous fangs back into me, the more my pussy throbs and aches. The harder I want Atlas to fuck me.

I go completely rigid when Zeus slithers over my back. "*Atlas*," I squeak out.

"Relax, pretty girl. Doesn't the threat of danger make you wet?" He groans.

I'm fucking soaked. "Yes," I pant.

My heart pounds in my chest as the snake slowly slithers over my body. Atlas slows his rhythm as he rocks into me more gently. "Fuck, so deep. I'm cumming, fuck."

I feel the warm gush of his cum shoot forward and it sends a ripple of spasms to my tender nub. I cry out and rub my pussy back and forth against the table. Zeus slithers across my lower back and down around my thigh.

"Just let him do his thing, pretty girl. He wants to feel your skin," Atlas quips as he pulls out of me and backs up, leaving me bent over the table with my wrists still tied.

The fear in my belly makes my pussy spasm harder. I never knew I could feel so terrified and turned on at the same time. I shiver as Zeus slithers over my raw ass cheeks and up my back before disappearing back down into his habitat.

"Trust is a beautiful thing, Firecracker." He rubs some kind of ointment on my ass cheeks, and it instantly soothes the burn. "Seeing you in pain right before you cum makes me feel so fucking alive. Your tears are my trigger. Do you like being my pretty little doll?"

I let out a quivering sigh. My soul is already black. There's no redemption for me. I'm a killer, a slut, and a glutton for punishment. I turn my face to the side to look up at him. "Yes, Daddy. I like letting you play with me."

Chapter Twenty-Six

Maureen

THERE IS AN EERIE CHILL ON MY SKIN. I FEEL LIKE something is coming. I didn't plan on spending the night with Atlas at Nocturnus House, but I couldn't keep my eyes open. My blood mixes with small traces of poison now. My veins have made room for it. It's like a drug. I crave more of it.

When I wake, I find myself draped across Atlas's naked body. Riot and Valentin sit across the room by the window. I wonder how long they've been watching us sleep.

I lift my heavy head and lock eyes with Riot. He glares possessively at the way Atlas's arm rests on my lower back. "You've unsettled this house," Riot seethes. "Ever since you got to Raven's Gate… it's been chaos."

Still sound asleep, Atlas rolls over and mumbles something incoherent. I sit up and pull the sheet up around my breasts. "I never asked for any of this," I murmur back.

"I know," Riot replies softly.

Valentin leans against the floor-to-ceiling window and looks down at the hallowed grounds below. "We've all been played. By the Blackwells, the ravens, our own initiates, and even the Graves. We can only trust each other now."

My voice cracks, and I almost cry. "So, you believe me now? That I had nothing to do with your curse. Or do you still hate me?"

Riot stalks toward me. His hand feels like ice as he caresses my hot cheek. "I think a part of me will always hate you. But I will not allow anyone to touch you but us."

My breath catches at his sudden gentleness. His power over me grows, and I practically crumble at the slightest praise. "So, you didn't brag about fucking me to anyone?"

His eyes darken. "Fuck, no. You're ours."

I'm more confused than ever. I don't understand the way they are. "But you let them watch…"

Valentin sighs and walks over to the bed. "That was a sacred ritual. It's different. But someone betrayed us. Someone else was in the room that wasn't supposed to be."

Atlas yawns and stretches out, then freezes when he sees his friends. "Good morning to you too, fuckers. You just couldn't wait to get in here, could you?" He laughs.

A sick feeling churns in my gut. "I think I know who," I whisper.

Riot's fingers tighten around my neck. "Tell me right now."

"Go on, pretty girl. Let us know so we can take care of it," Atlas urges.

Fuck. The second I say his name, he's dead. But would that be so bad? He's tried to assault me twice now. I might not get so lucky if there's a third time. I blow out a deep breath. "It was Zeke. He cornered me in the elevator the other day after Val dropped me off. He knew things about the ritual. About what you did to me..."

"Mother fucker," Riot roars. He pulls me from the bed and pins me up against the wall. As the sheet falls to the floor, he gazes over every inch of me. "Did he fucking touch you?"

I shake my head. "No. But he wouldn't let me out unless I touched myself in front of him. I—"

Valentin reaches for the blade inside his pocket. He pulls it out and brandishes it. "Atlas, find him. Right now."

Atlas leaps from the bed and throws on his pants before downing a vial of poison.

"Hold on," I cry. "I didn't have to do it because somehow the elevator got up to my floor and Libra busted in with a baseball bat. I think Jessamine must have intervened or something because Zeke had his finger on the button that keeps the doors closed."

Riot clenches his jaw and throws Valentin a dangerous look. "We get him tonight. At the Winter Solstice. And we let everyone know what happens when someone fucks with what's ours."

Oh, fuck. More murder. Great.

I'm starting to think that this is just my life now. "Isn't there another way to handle this?" I ask.

Atlas laughs. "Sure. We'll invite him over for dinner and ask him nicely to stop harassing our girl. I'm sure he'll be super agreeable."

I roll my eyes. "Very funny. I just thought it would be nice to not murder the problem away for once." They look at me like I have two heads.

"Zeke is more than a problem, Maur," Valentin snaps. "He's

an initiate who's betrayed the oath. He knows our secrets. *Your* secrets."

"We have to make an example out of him or there will be anarchy," Riot commands.

I know they're right. I think back to the promises I made and kept to Bailey. The blood I spilled for her. For myself. I nod. "Okay. Fine. But I want to have fun first. The last party I went to wasn't exactly my idea of a good time."

Riot throws me a knowing look. I will tell Valentin and Atlas eventually but right now one of them knowing is enough.

Atlas chuckles. "I don't think these two know what fun is, pretty girl. We're going to have to show them."

Valentin snickers. "Oh, is that how you convinced her to let Zeus take a chunk out of her leg? You tell her it'd be fun?"

My cheeks burn. Of course, they know everything. There are probably fucking cameras in here.

As if reading my mind, Riot snaps his fingers and a swirl of light trickles out. "We have gifts, Firecracker. Power that we share. It connects us."

Valentin clears his throat as he glances down my naked body. "You also have a very visible snake bite on your thigh. So there's that."

It was my turn to chuckle. "Right. Forgot about that."

"You want to go to this ball and drink and dance under the stars, Firecracker?" Riot asks as he throws Atlas's furry blue robe around me.

I nod. "Yeah. I want one magical night where I can feel like a fucking fairy princess. Is that okay?"

His eyes soften and a smirk plays at the corners of his mouth. "All right. Done. But then we kill that fucking bastard."

The mud underneath my boots is as thick as the fog surrounding me. The ravens circle overhead as I try to make my way back to The Nest. Apparently, there was a storm last night and it did a pretty good job of fucking up the path. Between Atlas sucking poison from a snake bite out of my thigh and him fucking me from behind on his apothecary table, it was hard to notice the lightning and thunder going on outside.

    The Winter Solstice ball isn't till later tonight, but I have to get back to the dorms before Libra and Villette send out a search party for me. With my phone dead, I can't even text them to let them know I'm okay. Although, they're not stupid. I'm sure they figured I went to Nocturnus House. Still, I want to get back to shower, change, and drink mimosas with them before the ball tonight. It was something Bailey and I used to always do before a big dance or event.

    I don't know exactly how close I am to the dorms at this point. I'm not lost, just a little disoriented. I pick up the pace but walk carefully enough, so I don't fall or trip over all of the wet foliage.

    I'm deep in the woods when I hear the roar of a motorcycle. Its headlights illuminate the ground in front of me. I freeze just as the rider whizzes past, slams on the brakes, and then circles back.

    A knot grows in my chest as the driver skids to a stop mere inches away from me. The force of the wind blows my hair back and sends chills up my spine. My heart races as I strain to see who the mystery rider is through the mist and fog.

    He snaps open the face of his helmet and my heart skips a beat when we lock eyes. Ice-cold, neon-blue eyes that pierce me and always send a sea of butterflies to the pit of my stomach. I exhale a deep breath. "Riot…"

"You shouldn't be out here alone," he shouts over the engine. He offers me a helmet. "Get on."

I take it without hesitating and climb on the bike. These woods are getting darker by the second, and I don't know what the fuck is lurking out here. At least Riot is the devil I know.

"Hold on tight, firecracker."

I wrap my arms around his waist and press my chest against his back. Fuck, his body is as hard as a rock. It dawns on me that I've never touched him like this before. In the car, he fucked me from behind, and in the library, he had me pinned against the stacks, but there was still space between us. Even when I woke up in his bed that night, we kept our distance.

My heart swells with an ache I didn't know was there as I hug him from behind. I breathe in his familiar scent of tobacco and coffee like it's my favorite drug. I wish I could bottle it up or make a candle out of it.

Riot hits the throttle, and I almost lose my breath. He takes the turns at full speed, knowing exactly where he's going. I should be terrified of being wrapped around a tree or crashing into a ditch. But I feel safe with him. He knows these woods like the back of his hand. And something tells me that the headlights are only for my benefit. *This man's eyes fucking glow in the dark.*

When we fly past The Nest without stopping, I squeeze his arm. "Hey, where are we going? You just passed the dorms."

He shakes his head but says nothing as he accelerates, and the world becomes a blur around us. I pinch my eyes shut to stave off the nausea.

I try to focus on the roar of the engine, the feel of his pulse beating against mine, and the scent of the rain-soaked soil that we race across. A warmth spreads through me, caressing my thighs and tickling my lips. It makes my ears buzz and my head spin. I feel our momentum slowing, steadying to a calmer pace.

"Open your eyes, firecracker," Riot calls out. His silky voice penetrates the noise of the bike, carrying over it as if it were a distant rumble.

As I open my lids, I see a precipice in the distance. A sign saying *Welcome to Raven's Gate* perches between two wooden posts. He slows the bike to a stop in front of it and kills the engine.

He takes off his helmet, then mine, before I hop off, confused and over-stimulated. "What's going on, Riot?"

"This is the end of the road. The border that separates Raven's Gate from the rest of Melancholia." He slides off the bike and faces me. *Fuck, he's gorgeous.*

"But why are we here? Neither of us can leave, right?" I ask. There's a part of me that's tempted to try. That rebellious streak in me that wants to see how far he'd go to hunt me down. The sick part of me that relishes in the chase. In the thought of being caught.

His eyes harden as he looks out across the threshold. "I can leave. But the second I do, my body starts to slowly decay. My powers weaken. The curse keeps me this way. After I left you in Wickford Hollow, I was sick for days. It almost killed me. I lingered too long."

There's a longing in his eyes. A longing I feel too. Deep in my gut. "Because of me?"

He nods. "I didn't want to leave you. You have no idea how close I came to stealing you away that night."

He has a nervous tick I've never noticed before. He looks at me, then the ground, and then back, each time flexing the muscle in his jaw like he's grinding his teeth.

"It hurts to look at you," he says softly as if reading my mind.

I take a cautious step toward him. "Why?"

He leans against his bike and looks me up and down. "Because you're beautiful and I'm… damaged. Because I want to own you, destroy you, and protect you all at the same time. Because you're the only woman I've ever wanted to hate and love with every ounce of light and darkness that I possess. You ruined me, firecracker. You fucking ruined everything."

In this moment, I feel the same way. I know exactly what he means even though it's fucked up and doesn't make any sense.

I take a few more steps toward him until I bridge the gap between us. The air seems to sizzle with electricity. His muscles twitch as I press my palms to his chest. "It's not your fault, Riot. Any more than it is mine."

He draws in a quick breath as I slide my hands down to his belly and lift up his shirt. His skin feels smooth and soft against my fingertips. "I'm damaged too. Our scars make us beautiful."

"No one has ever looked at me the way you do. Why?" he asks.

I unbutton his jeans and slide the zipper down. My heart races as I take control of his cock, relishing in the way it throbs in my hand. "Because I see you, Riot. The *real* you. And you see the real me. But I won't let you claim me unless you're willing to be claimed too."

His eyelids flutter, and he lets out a soft moan as I caress him gently. "Fuck… you've owned me since the moment I laid eyes on you, firecracker. Every depraved fucking piece of me."

I press my lips to his, urging him to kiss me. "Hate *them* for what they did to you. For what they did to me. But hating me is pointless, Riot. You and I are end game. So let's get revenge together."

"Fuck, I can't keep my hands off you any longer." He grabs my face and kisses me hard. We both gasp as our tongues lock and swirl together in a frantic state of lust and need. The desperation to consume him overwhelms me. He's my elusive monster. My demon who can't be slayed, only tamed.

I stroke his cock faster as he pulls my hair, forcing my head back, so he can devour my neck. He nips at my flesh with his teeth in between kisses and licks. "I wanna mark every inch of you. I want everyone to know you're mine." He bites down hard on my shoulder, and it sends waves of euphoria through my whole body.

The sensations of pain and pleasure are inseparable. I crave them both. I need every vile and depraved act he wants to thrust upon me. "I want you inside me," I murmur.

"Fuck," he whines and pulls me down to the ground. "Do you want me to fuck you in the dirt, firecracker? Hmm?" He pins my arms over my head. "Like a fucking animal?"

My clit spasms as moisture drips out of my aching pussy. I thrust my hips toward his. "*Yes*," I roar. "I need you to fuck me. Right. Fucking. Now. Or else kill me and be done with it."

He gazes down at me, fixated on my lips. "So, you have a death wish, is that it?"

The weight of him threatens to crush me, and I welcome it. My adrenaline spikes, sending shivers over every inch of me. The pounding in my chest is so loud it's almost deafening. "There's no fucking torture you can inflict that is worse than the kind I've been inflicting on myself. Except the torture of not having you inside me. I need it, Riot. But if you don't want me like that, then let death take me."

His eyes widen and his throat bobs as he swallows hard. "Maur…" He releases my wrists and angles up, straddling me on the dirty ground. He slides his palms under my blouse and rests them on my belly.

I arch my back, urging him to keep going. His touch feels like fire despite his icy flesh. "Don't make me beg, Riot."

"Fuck. You have no idea how bad I've been wanting you." He yanks my jeans down and off in one quick motion. "No fucking clue how every second I'm away from you is like starvation."

I shiver as the wind dances between my thighs. He fingers the edge of my panties, gazing hungrily at them. "You don't have to beg, firecracker. I need your pussy like I need air."

A whimper escapes me as he jerks my panties off and lines up his cock. I arch my back against the dirt and spread my legs wide for him. "Use me."

His lips quiver as he pushes the tip of his cock inside my pussy. "Fuck, you're so tight. Oh, my—" He loses his words in a moan as I stretch around his shaft. I can feel every inch of him throbbing against my walls as he pushes in slowly, savoring every second.

"Fuck, don't stop, please," I beg.

His movements are firm but slow and agonizing as he draws it out, forcing me to feel every ridge as he slides in deeper. Forcing me to feel his girth and how my pussy has to expand to accommodate it. It fills me up, sending pressure all the way up my spine. Like I might explode.

I cry out as he burrows all the way in and presses against my G-spot. We don't break eye contact. There's something more feral about the quiet way he penetrates me while never taking his neon-blue eyes off me. This feels different from the day in the car when he fucked me from behind. That day was about anger and hate and ownership. This right here is all of those things and none of them. Because now… he's fucking me like I own *him*.

He rolls his hips, and I almost cum. "Do you want to be our queen, baby girl?"

The angle of his cock, the torturous rhythm of it, elicits a deep guttural moan from my throat. "Yes," I cry.

He slows his pace, fucking me so softly that I'm shaking all over. "Will you let me brand you with my sigil? Will you wear it proudly?"

A flutter of spasms ripples through my clit at the thought of him marking me. I arch my hips, desperate for his brutality. The gentleness hurts more. The ache is festering. I want him to suffocate me. To break me. And he knows it. He's fucking edging me into insanity.

I lick my lips and nod. "Yes. I want to wear your marks like scars. Like tattoos. Ruin me, Riot. Ruin my flesh and remake it in your likeness."

His pupils dilate, and a ring of light swirls around them. He stills his cock inside me and I almost panic. I can feel him throbbing, pulsing against my walls and it's fucking torture. I take quick shallow breaths as I rock my hips back and forth, urging him to keep going.

"Relax, firecracker. Don't worry. I'm going to let you cum. But I want to relish being inside you for a while. If I unleash everything I have, I'll explode too quickly." He begins his slow agonizing rhythm again.

The tingling builds back up, and I feel like I'm on the edge of having a nervous breakdown. I can't fucking take it anymore. "Please, Riot," I beg.

He smirks and leans over me. He wraps a hand around my throat, applying light pressure. "I told you not to beg, firecracker." He pulls back, teasing my entrance with just the tip. "But I love it when you do." I scream as he slams back into me.

Oh, fuck. I am fucking rabid. Our hips bang together as he pounds my pussy harder and faster. He rubs my clit raw, violently, crushing it under his thumb until it swells. A fire burns in my veins as the deepest pleasure I've ever felt erupts in my core.

I scream out his name as I cum. I scream it over and over again until my throat hurts and my voice breaks. He squeezes my throat, stealing the air from my lungs as my body spasms.

"That's my girl. *Mine*," he growls as he rides me. "This is your salvation, firecracker. Your reckoning. And your rebirth." He grunts as the ridges in his shaft flex and constrict. He buries himself all the way in and unleashes an unearthly cry as his hot cum fills me up.

We grind against each other, riding out our orgasms until his cum and mine become one. With his hand still around my throat, he yanks me halfway up and presses his sweaty forehead against mine. His blue eyes blaze with lust. "*And I'm yours.*"

Chapter Twenty-Seven

Maureen

I'VE BEEN DEFILED IN THE MUD, FORCED NOT TO SHOWER, locked in a coffin, and bitten by a poisonous snake. I've been pulled and pushed and dominated in the most depraved ways. I should be disgusted. But as I stand here looking in the mirror, dressed in the exquisite black gown they picked out for me, I am willing to do it all again. I crave each of them in a different way. And I will walk through the fires of hell if it means that I end up right back here in Raven's Gate with my three deranged psychos.

The bustier is covered in lace with ribbon strings holding it together. I slip into a pair of black satin heels and twirl for them. The tulle skirt billows down to the floor but the two slits up the sides show off my tattooed legs. Libra and Villette both let out an excited squeal.

"You look stunning," Villette says.

Libra hands me an ornate mask. "Yeah, you look hot as fuck."

"What's this?" I ask as I take the mask from her.

"The Winter Solstice is a masquerade ball. So we got you a mask. Those are real raven feathers."

I smooth my hands over it before tying it around my face. I look back in the mirror and my stomach does a little flip. "It's perfect."

"Where are they? I thought you were going together." Villette can't hide the concern in her voice.

That eerie feeling snakes up my neck again. "I'm meeting them there. They have some Nocturnus business they need to handle."

Libra snorts. "I'm surprised they let you off your leash."

I chuckle. Nothing is going to ruin tonight for me. Not the promise of murder, or even Libra's snarky comments. "Maybe I like my leash." I press my lips together after applying another coat of lip gloss.

Villette chokes on a sip of champagne. "Damn, Maur. You've been hanging out with *them* too much."

I smile and take another look in the mirror. Butterflies dance in my stomach. My first ball, and I get to go on the arms of Riot, Atlas, and Valentin. I'm their pretty little psycho, and they're my nightmare. The dark spark that ignites my fire. They are the nocturnal haze I exist in. The tangled web I don't ever want to be free from.

We clank our glasses together in a toast. "Cheers to a wicked night, ladies. May we all find what we're looking for," I say.

"Yeah, let's hope the rest of us get fucked as hard as you tonight," Libra drawls. "I've been bored out of my mind."

Villette flinches as if her words physically assaulted her. "Calm down, Lib. It's a Tenebrose ball, not a sex club."

Libra shrugs. "That's a matter of perspective."

I burst out laughing. "You're growing on me too, Thorn," I tease.

The three of us finish getting ready and head downstairs.

Fireflies flicker past us as we cross the lawn to the path that leads to the Erebus Ballroom. Paper lanterns light the way as far as the eye can see. It's like a page out of a fantasy novel. Others gather in groups and join us in their tuxedos and gowns on the walk down.

The night is beautiful. Magical. The moon is bright and full, illuminating us like ethereal goddesses. Libra wears a baby pink satin dress that invokes old Hollywood vibes. And Villette is the picture of class and elegance in her emerald-green silk gown, the skirt covered in sparkly beads. The three of us look unstoppable tonight. A trio of devious vixens stalking through the woods like night sirens.

"I bet those boys just needed extra time to get ready. I swear they are more high-maintenance than any girl I know. Including myself," Libra jokes.

That was part of it. But I didn't have the nerve to tell them that they were lagging behind because Atlas was using his raven sight to track down Zeke. Villette and Libra aren't naïve to what Nocturnus is or does. They knew before I did. But they are just as excited as I am to drink and dance the night away. I don't want to spoil the mood with talk of murder and betrayal. Not yet. That will come later…

I laugh as the two of them go on and on about how boys are secretly more obsessed with their looks than girls are. "Yeah, I don't think I've ever seen a single hair on Atlas's head out of place. And don't even get me started on Riot and his perfectly pressed black T-shirts."

Villette snorts. "Don't forget about Valentin's obsession with suits. I swear he's been wearing them since we were kids."

I'd forgotten how long they've all known each other. I should have been picking their brains about my guys from the start. "What were they like as kids?" I ask. "Were they always so…"

"Depraved and disturbed?" Libra pipes in, laughing. "Yep. Atlas and my brother, Aries, started playing with poison in junior high."

Villette giggles. "Yeah, pretty sure Valentin was the reason all the graves in Raven's Gate Mortuary were dug up that summer. He watched a bunch of George Romero zombie movies and was convinced that the dead were going to reanimate."

A warm nostalgia sweeps over me even though these aren't my memories. I feel closer to all of them at this moment. "What about Riot? Was he always so… angry?"

Libra and Villette exchange a look before my beautiful, yet snarky friend opens her mouth to speak. "His house was not fun. The Graves family is fucking intense. This *curse* as they call it, consumes them constantly."

I almost trip as the path gets rockier. I stumble and catch myself. "You don't think it's really a curse?" I'm confused by her nonchalance.

She shakes her head. "No, it's not that. They really did get banished from Ever Graves. If Riot leaves Raven's Gate, he will age quickly, and then die. His power, his lifeblood, is forever tied to this place now. To the ravens. I can understand why his family is angry, but it's *all* they ever think about. Like fuck, accept it and move on."

"Riot never had a childhood, Maur. He has been on a mission since the day he was born to consume as much power as he can," Villette adds. "That's his family's legacy."

It suddenly hits me. "Because he wants to be able to go back to Ever Graves?"

Libra and Villette exchange another look that makes my skin crawl.

"What?" I ask, unsure if I really want to know.

Libra slows to a stop and turns toward me. "Because he wants to take back the power your family stole... and then destroy them."

Riot's made it no secret that he hates the Blackwells. I don't know how I feel about him wanting to murder all of them. I don't even know any of them and they shunned me since birth. But do I want them all dead? No. *I don't think so...*

I take a deep breath and keep walking. "Thank you for telling me."

Villette grabs my hand. "Maur, Riot has hurt every living thing that's ever crossed his path. Except you. I'm not his biggest fan, but I see how he looks at you. He's obsessed. He cares for you more than anyone thought he was capable of."

Libra nods in agreement. "He's a bastard. All of them are. But yeah, she's right. It doesn't matter what your last name is. I think they're all in love with you."

A tiny flutter of nerves swirls in my stomach. *Love?* Obsessed, yes. In lust, absolutely. But love just doesn't seem like something any of them are capable of. Especially Riot. From what they've just told me and from what I've seen myself, love isn't something that was shown to Riot, Atlas, or Valentin.

But then again, what the fuck do I know about love? My mother ignored me, and my father was too drunk to care. The only one who's ever loved me is Bailey. But she has her guys now. I shiver as I stifle a sob.

Villette squeezes my hand. "We got you, girl."

Libra rolls her eyes and grabs my other hand. "You're all right, Blackwell. Don't start getting mushy on me now."

On the verge of tears, the absurdity of my life makes me laugh instead. "We are the most ridiculous fucking freaks that Tenebrose has ever seen, aren't we?"

We all burst out laughing. "Pretty much," Libra says.

By the time we approach the ballroom, our mood has lifted. We take turns sipping on the flask of whiskey Libra smuggled in her purse. The stars glitter the whole sky, invoking something out of a fairytale.

We lock arms and strut inside like the badass bitches we are. I glance around at the spectacle that surrounds us. The ballroom is glowing with fairy lights, swinging chandeliers, and drippy candles. White-gloved servers float around the room carrying trays of frosted cakes and bubbly elixirs. But underneath this sparkly dream, lies a winter nightmare. A sinister energy that permeates every hushed whisper and masked face.

I feel them before I see them.

A draft blows a chill across my back. I spin around and look toward the entrance. Wearing tailored black suits, and ski masks, Riot, Atlas, and Valentin command the room. All eyes are on them. But their eyes are only on me.

I lose my breath as I meet each of their violent gazes.

They are mine.

"The devils of Raven's Gate are here," someone whispers. I spin around but can't tell who's talking through the masks.

"Ignore them," Libra groans. "They're just jealous."

I look back at my guys. They don't take their eyes off me. "I thought you hated them, Lib. After what they did to you…"

She scoffs. "Hate is a fragile concept, Maur. This is *my* world. I've been living in it my whole life. Our families do things differently than everyone else. You're lucky you didn't grow up with us."

Am I though? My whole life I've wanted to belong to something greater. They all grew up with darkness and hate, but I was raised in a blur of booze and adultery. Was I really that much better off?

I hold my breath as my three psychos stalk toward me. "They're coming over," I whisper.

Libra nods. "They're coming for you."

Villette sighs. "Well, that's my cue. I'm going to find something to drink. Meet up with you in a bit?"

"Hell yeah, bitch. We're going to get Libra to do a jello shot later," I snort.

Libra shrieks, her face twisting in horror. "I will do no such thing."

I giggle. "I love that your entire family drinks poison but it's jello shots that freak you out."

She flips her hair off her shoulder. "Is that a rhetorical question?"

"I didn't ask you a question." Villette and I burst out laughing.

"Whatever. Sorry, I'm classy," she mumbles as she walks away.

Villette shrugs and laughs again before following her.

I smile after them. They are so different and yet they tolerate each other in a way that truly impresses me. And they actually like *me*. I never thought I'd make friends here. No one can ever replace my bestie, Bailey, but these two are definitely starting to fill the void.

Riot offers me his hand. "Ready to dance the night away, Firecracker?"

My belly flutters. "You dance?"

"Don't look so surprised. I'm classically trained." He winks.

"We'll keep watch until it's our turn," Valentin adds.

They look so out of place with their ski masks and yet they are the most beautiful things I've ever seen.

The crowd parts for us, and all eyes are on me—the outsider girl with the three deadliest men in Raven's Gate.

Riot spins me around and dips me as the music slows. The

lights dim, and it's like we're the only two people in the room. He places his hand on my lower back and pulls me in close. "You look stunning. Fucking perfect."

The heat in my body rises. "Well, I had a little help," I tease.

His breath quickens in my ear. "It's not the dress. It's you. You're the most beautiful creature I've ever seen. You took my breath away from the first time I saw you."

I press my cheek to his, and I can feel the heat from his skin through the ski mask. "Riot… I dreamed about you ever since that night. You've been haunting me…"

He twirls me around again and pulls me back hard against his chest. "You'll never be free of me, Maureen. I will haunt you forever."

A breath lodges in my throat. "I don't want you to hate me anymore."

He pulls me to a stop as he lifts the bottom of his mask. I watch his jaw twitch as he gazes down at me. "Firecracker… *fuck*. I've never hated you. I've hated myself for not being good enough to love you."

My eyes dart back and forth between his ethereal blue eyes and his full lips. A sense of urgency comes over me. A feeling I've felt since that night in the bathroom. I slide my hand up his chest and wrap it around his throat. His eyes widen as his throat bobs in my grip. "You're good enough, Riot." I tilt my head up and inch my mouth closer to his. *"And you're mine."*

His lips quiver right before he kisses me and when our tongues meet, it feels like an explosion of fire and sin.

Chapter Twenty-Eight

Valentin

Riot spins Maureen again and sends her flying straight into my arms. I catch her and pull her close. She smells like vanilla and burnt honey, sweet and smoky. I grab her hips and move her with me in step to the music.

"Are you scared, Firecracker?" I slide my fingers up her spine.

She smirks. "Fear is just an illusion, right? The only thing I'm afraid of is not ever knowing what this could be."

The beat picks up and the fairy lights start to flash like strobe lights. I grind my hips against hers. "We've got you, pretty girl. No matter what happens with the ravens or the Blackwells, or with Zeke. You belong to us, and no one will hurt you ever again."

She whimpers and her eyelids flutter as she gazes shyly up at me. "I won't let anyone hurt you either."

My stomach flips. Just when I thought I couldn't fall any harder for this exquisite creature, she goes and says some powerful shit that makes me melt. I've been carved out of stone, hard like a diamond, and rough like the rock it sprang from. But this little bolt of electricity softens all my edges with just one look.

I tuck her in tighter and my cock throbs. "You're going to cum so fucking hard tonight," I whisper.

She pulls my hips hard against her as the bass thumps louder. "*Yes, Daddy.*"

I almost pull her off the dancefloor and drag her into the nearest bathroom when Riot gives me a nod. His eyes are dark and hard. I take a deep breath and feel the raven's power surge through my veins.

Trouble isn't coming.

It's here.

I hand Maureen off to Atlas and follow Riot outside.

We come face to face with our initiates. They wear skull masks and dark hoods. And an unkindness of ravens flock around them.

Fuck.

I pull out my phone to warn Atlas, but it's too late.

The doors creak open behind us, letting out a flood of music from the ball.

"What the fuck is all this?" Atlas barks.

Riot growls like a fucking wolf. "*Anarchy.*"

Chapter Twenty-Nine

Maureen

THE GUYS HAVE BEEN GONE TOO LONG. I CAN'T FIND Libra or Villette and I'm starting to feel like I did on that night in Wickford Hollow—scared, alone, and feral. I don't trust anyone else but them. And I can't find any of them. *What the fuck is going on?*

A soft hand grabs mine and I jump.

Jessamine.

"What the fuck?" I yell over the music. "We talked about sneaking up on me, Jess."

Her eyes widen. "He's coming for you, Maur. *Hide.*"

My stomach knots. "Who?"

She pushes me toward the front doors. "Zeke. Run, Maur. Run and hide in the woods."

Oh, fucking hell.

I shake my head. "No, not without the guys. They'll protect me. I need to find Libra and Villette." The panic is rising in my chest, threatening to suffocate me.

Jessamine hisses. "They're all in trouble. Zeke is going to kill you for your power. You have to hide. Please, Maureen."

What in the hell is she talking about? "Jess, I don't understand. I don't have any power. You're not making sense."

I realize how fucking strong she is when she drags me across the dancefloor. "You're the only one who can be their fourth," she calls back. "You're their firecracker. Zeke doesn't want Nocturnus to control the ravens. He wants that power for himself."

I pull back on her grip. "Jessamine, *stop*."

She whips around, her face twisting in horror. "Zeke is a bastard."

"Yeah, no shit," I snap.

"No, Maur, you don't. He's the bastard son of Holden Graves. He's Riot's *half-brother*." She purses her lips so hard I think she might shatter her own jaw.

I shake my head. "No. Riot would have said something."

Jessamine tightens her grip on my wrist. "Not if he doesn't know for sure."

That eerie feeling from earlier is back and spreading through my core. "How do *you* know?"

"Because I see and hear everything," she whispers. "Zeke is a Graves. He's turned all the initiates against Riot, Atlas, and Valentin. He wants Nocturnus power for himself. But he needs a Blackwell to do it. *You*."

It feels like the room is spinning and the floor is falling away from my feet. My knees start to tremble as the realization of what's happening finally sinks in. "Fuck. Okay, shit. What do I do?"

"You need to go to the woods, Maur. Soon the time will come for Nocturnus to join you. You'll be safe until they do." Her blue eyes glow under the chandeliers, ethereal and haunting.

Nothing feels right. I don't want to leave my guys... "I don't know, Jess."

"Libra and Villette are out there. They need you too," she murmurs.

Wait, what? "They were just here a second ago, Jess. Why would they go out into the woods?"

She tugs on my wrist again, but I don't budge this time. She lets out a frustrated sigh. "*Because I told them to.*"

Fuck. I can't let my friends put their lives in danger because of me. I nod. "Where do I go?"

She loosens her grip on me. "Follow the path past the old cemetery. That's where they'll be. And be careful, Maur. Don't get lost. Not all who wander can be found."

A chill snakes up my back as I remember those exact words from my first day here. Except they came out of Miss Florian's mouth. I don't have time to process the coincidence because Jessamine is shoving me out the front doors. When I look back, she's gone.

Fuck.

It's freezing now, and I don't have my coat. I wrap my arms around my body and shuffle forward. The ground is covered with a thick blanket of fresh snow. I curse as I try to muddle through it in my four-inch stiletto heels.

I try calling Riot, Atlas, and Valentin multiple times but none of them pick up. So I keep walking into the dark and creepy woods by myself during the winter solstice—the longest night of the year.

Libra and Villette don't answer my calls either, which makes me even more concerned. Maybe there's no reception by the cemetery... I hope they're okay. Fuck. I hope I'm okay.

As I walk, my thighs brush against each other, and I'm somewhat comforted by the cool smooth steel blade that's strapped inside my garter. After what happened to Bailey and me last summer, I try not to leave the house without it.

The stillness feels ominous. Like something is holding its breath and watching me, stalking me through the dark. There isn't a single soul around. Every student and professor is back at the ball dancing and drinking the night away while I'm stuck out here. Just once it'd be nice to go to a party without someone trying to kill me.

My feet ache in these shoes, but I pick up the pace. I'm half-tempted to run but with my luck, I'll end up breaking my fucking ankle or something. I take slow deep breaths and try to still my pulse. I use the flashlight on my phone when the path twists deeper into the woods, leaving all the lanterns and fairy lights behind.

The cemetery gates creak in the fluttering wind and my stomach knots. "Libra? Villette?" I call out.

A raven squawks, shattering the silence. Fuck, I hate these birds so much. I check my phone again—still no calls or texts from anyone. What the fuck is going on? Am I an idiot for coming out here by myself? I shudder as I pass a row of unmarked graves.

A branch snaps behind me. I spin around, my heart racing. "Guys? Are you there?"

"Hey, beautiful." A hooded figure steps out from behind a tree.

Zeke. No.

My teeth chatter and my knees shake. I try to step back but stumble onto a cold headstone. "Leave me alone, Zeke. I don't want any part of this."

His smirk is evil and sadistic. "But you are a part of this,

Maureen. I'm sick of chasing you. Tired of you always getting away. Thanks to Jessamine, I finally have some alone time with you."

Bile climbs up my throat. I swallow hard to force it down. This can't be happening. "She... set me up," I whisper.

Zeke chuckles. "She understands what I'm trying to do. Nocturnus should serve the ravens. Not the other way around. Silas Graves understood that. Every Graves did until Riot came along."

I can't believe that scrappy little ghost girl has been playing me this whole fucking time. I've been so blinded by my past, so desperate to make connections that remind me of home, that I didn't even see the truth right in front of me. Jessamine was always there, watching, stalking every move I made. She told Zeke I was at Nocturnus House that night. And when he followed me into the elevator, *she* told him I'd be there at that exact time. And now... she tricked me into coming out here by myself. All while pretending to help me. *If she weren't already dead, I'd fucking kill her.*

Zeke walks toward me. "You're seeing it now, aren't you? The ravens have promised to return Silas to her. But only if she delivers you to me. It's an eye for an eye, beautiful."

I wince. "*A soul for a soul.*"

"I assumed control of Nocturnus tonight. You belong to me now, Maureen. And I have so many plans for us," he sneers.

I shudder and dart out of his reach, putting the headstone in between us as a barrier. "Riot, Atlas, and Valentin will never let you get away with this. They will come for me."

He laughs. "If they aren't dead yet, sweetie. While Jessamine was distracting you, your psycho boyfriends were dealing with their *former* initiates."

Fuck.

I shake my head in denial. "They'll win. You have no idea just how *psycho* they are."

Zeke closes the distance between us, his eyes feral as he glares down at me. "They can't protect you *and* themselves. And after I carve a hundred sigils into your flesh, no one will be able to stop me."

I open my mouth to scream for help but it's too late. Zeke slaps his hand over it and drags me over to a tree. He wraps his other hand around my throat. "Time to give me that show you promised me, beautiful. Show me how you play with your tight little cunt."

Tears stream down my cheeks. I shake my head and try to scream but his hand is clamped down tight around my mouth.

"You *will* do it," he roars. "You belong to Nocturnus. And I am Nocturnus now." He lets me go for a second, only to tear the skirt of my gown down the middle. "Ahhh. No panties. You really are a dirty little whore, aren't you?"

I turn my head to the side and close my eyes, my cheeks burning with shame and disgust. The wind flutters against my bare pussy like it's taunting me. Telling me, *you stupid girl thinking you could trust anyone ever again.*

Zeke kicks open my legs. "Before I fuck you against this tree, I want you to get yourself wet for me. Get those fingers in nice and deep."

"No," I whimper. A fury from deep down in my bones rises, and I wrench away from him. "Get the fuck away from me," I wail.

He lunges at me, and in stiletto heels, I'm not quick enough to dodge him. He grabs a fistful of my hair and slams me back against the tree again. I start for the blade strapped to my thigh, but he catches my wrist before I can reach it, pinning both of my arms above my head. I look up and my insides curl with fear as I notice the rope dangling from the closest branch.

He wraps it around my wrists. His eyes fill with sadistic amusement as he retrieves a knife from his breast pocket. "After I'm done mutilating you, I'm going to let every single initiate have a turn inside your needy little cunt." He presses the tip of the blade against my clit, and I sob.

Zeke erupts into a fit of hysterical laughter. "Not so tough now, are you?" He presses the blade flat against my pussy. "Oh, I can't wait to make you my pet. I already have your cage and collar ready for you."

This man is a lunatic. Fuck. I'm starting to hyperventilate as he holds the blade firmly against my flesh. One wrong move, one tiny flick of his wrist, and he'll tear me to shreds.

"Please, don't do this," I beg. I can't stop the tears from gushing out.

He unzips his pants and pulls out his cock. "I want you to be nice and quiet for me now." He presses the knife to my lips. "If you scream, I'll cut out your tongue."

I close my eyes and pray for death.

Tires grind against the forest floor, followed by headlights illuminating our faces in the dark. Zeke jumps back as the car screeches to a halt only inches away from him. He turns toward the car and snarls as Riot, Atlas, and Valentin hop out.

Relief fills me when I glimpse their blood-stained faces. Their eyes are cold, vacant, monstrous. They look me up and down, noticing my torn dress, my bound wrists, and naked pussy. The rage coming off them is palpable. Their eyes glow like embers, and their sigils seem to come to life, lighting up the dark. No more masks. No more mercy.

Zeke's gaze darts around frantically. "What… how are you…?"

A madness awakens inside of me. I laugh. "Because they won," I yell in his face.

Zeke hisses and backhands me. "Stupid, cunt."

Riot charges forward and knocks him to the ground. "You think you can touch our girl? Did you forget who we fucking are?" he roars.

I shudder as the past comes back to haunt me. Remembering how small and weak and angry I felt the night Bailey and I were assaulted.

Atlas and Valentin cut me free before yanking Zeke to his feet. My whole body trembles as visions of blood flash in my mind. Memories that haunt me still.

Riot screams in his face, "You're the stupid cunt for thinking you could beat us."

My adrenaline surges as I twist the hidden knife out of my garter. My pulse steadies as I wrap my hands around the hilt, comforted by its weight in my grip.

Valentin slams his fist into Zeke's jaw. "And for thinking you could touch what's ours."

As I shuffle forward, I don't care that I'm naked from the waist down. Or that I'm hyperventilating. No. All I care about is protecting myself.

A bloodcurdling shriek escapes my throat as I lunge forward. Startled, they're too late to stop me.

Zeke's eyes widen as I plunge my knife into his chest. He squeezes my wrist as I twist it in deeper. But I won't let him stop me. He's just another fucking Chad. Another predator. His cries are muffled by the onslaught of blood in his throat.

I curl my lips into a smirk as Riot, Atlas, and Valentin stare at me speechless. I've been dangling between two versions of myself for so long, but now I'm finally free. I'm embracing my true nature.

I'm a killer. Just like them. Their pretty little psycho.

As the light from Zeke's eyes burns out, Riot curses under his breath. "*You* didn't have to do that, Firecracker."

I wrap my hand around the hilt and give it a hard yank. Blood spurts out as I wrench it free. "Yes, I did."

"This will forever stain your soul," Atlas murmurs.

I smile softly and look up at the sky just in time to see a shooting star.

Valentin sighs. "You've done this before."

I don't take my eyes off them as I sheath the bloody knife back into my garter without wiping it off. "Yes, I've murdered someone before. There's no redemption for me. Only darkness."

Riot pulls me to him, gently by the back of my neck, and the three of them surround me. "We are your darkness, pretty girl."

"We are your mercy and your redemption," Valentin adds with a growl.

Atlas takes off his jacket and ties it around my waist to cover me. "We will protect you."

Riot pinches my chin between his fingers. "We're the fucking devils you serve now. The only heathens who get to touch you. And we will leave our marks on you so that no one fucks with what is ours again."

His blue eyes burn bright like the base of a flame. My belly flutters. I don't want to run from this anymore. I have never felt more alive, more wanted than I have when I'm with them.

I lick my lips and tilt my chin up to his. "Then I will lay down at your altar tonight."

Chapter Thirty

Maureen

There is no after-party tonight. No celebration of the solstice. Only the silence of our sins as they hang in the air, threatening to consume us.

Libra and Villette had also been duped by Jessamine. She locked them in the ballroom basement and smashed their phones. No one could hear them cry for help over the music of the ball.

The guys had fought and beaten their initiates into submission—ostracized them from Nocturnus forever. They were physically stripped of their sigils and are currently fighting for their lives in the Tenebrose infirmary.

We will find new initiates. Ones we can trust this time.

After freeing my friends from the basement, we go back to my dorm, so I can change and wash the blood off my hands and body. It's a satisfying cleansing when I watch Zeke's essence get swept down the drain.

I put on a fresh pair of panties while Atlas picks out a short black dress for me to wear back to Nocturnus House. I like it when they dress me. It makes me feel cared for and treasured. I like the way they look at me when I've done something that pleases them.

Libra and Villette are still skeptical, but I know Bailey would get it. Someday, I'll tell her everything. When there's time to. But tonight the moon is full, and the night is the longest it will ever be all year. So we have to get moving.

Atlas constructs various threads of hemlock and winds them around the doorways and windows of my dorm room to keep Jessamine from getting in and harming Libra and Villette.

"That's why we surround our property with it. It keeps the restless dead out," Atlas says.

The ravens are quiet now. I don't hear them squawking as we pull out of The Nest. But I feel them watching.

"Nocturnus House was built over an ancient burial ground," Riot explains. "It's a place of power. We draw from it. Our sigils are conduits that funnel that power to us. There is a place like this in Ever Graves too. But your family sealed us off from it when Jessamine died. The second you took my half-brother's life; the score became even. It reset."

I hadn't even thought of that. "So, you knew Zeke was your brother?"

Riot nods. "I suspected it, which is why I let him get away with being such a fucking bag of dicks most of the time. My father is a private man, and my mother fucking hates him even though she won't leave his side. I'm sure I have many more half-brothers and sisters out there roaming around."

"I think we all do," Valentin grumbles.

An image of my mother fucking the pool cleaner flashes in my mind, and it makes me laugh out loud. "Sorry, I um, think I'm in that boat too."

It's so sad all I can do is make fun of it.

Valentin squeezes my leg. "She will never lay a hand on you ever again."

Riot whips his head around toward the back seat. "She fucking hit you?"

I swallow hard. "It's fine. Just let it go, please."

Atlas steers us into the driveway and parks in front of the door. "None of that matters now. After tonight, the four of us are untouchable."

Riot nods but there's still so much longing and ache in his eyes when he looks at me. On the way to the door, he pulls me close and whispers, "Just say the word, Firecracker. You know I won't think twice about killing for you."

Is it a sweet sentiment or the deranged words of a psycho killer? I care too much about him and us to get distracted by past transgressions. I shake my head. "She's already living her worst nightmare. That's punishment enough."

I'm surprised when they don't lead me to the ritual room and instead take me to a lavish bedroom upstairs. A fuzzy memory replays in my head, and I realize we're in Riot's room.

"I thought I was getting a sigil tonight." I plop down on the bed and a warmth fills my belly as I remember the night Riot brought me here.

"That room has been tainted by Zeke," Valentin says. "He violated you and us that night."

"Oh," I stammer. "I thought we had to be there."

Riot sits next to me and gently pushes me back onto the bed. "That was for the ravens. This is for us."

Atlas hands me a vial of poison. "Drink so we can start anew."

I tilt my head and let the toxin drip down my throat. My veins burn and my breath gets lost in my throat.

Atlas strokes my hair. "That's it, pretty girl. Surrender to it."

The three of them surround me on the king-size bed. Riot unzips my dress and pulls it off. I lie there in only my panties, on his cool black satin sheets, my skin feverish and aching to be touched by all three of them.

Riot holds his knife over me. "Do you trust us?"

Three weeks ago, I would have laughed and said no. Even three days ago, I would have been hesitant. But after tonight, after they came for me… I trust them more than I trust myself.

"Yes," I rasp.

My nipples pebble under Valentin and Atlas's touch. They stroke each of my breasts in slow agonizing rhythms.

"Hold her head still," Riot orders.

Atlas has my wrists pinned while Valentin tilts my head to the side, exposing my neck.

Riot straddles me with the blade in his hand. "No one will question who you belong to ever again."

I am theirs. No matter how fucked up they are. I belonged to them the second I stepped foot in Raven's Gate. Maybe even from the moment Riot zipped up my corset in the bathroom at Wickford Mansion last Halloween. With every moment and every breath, they claim another piece of me.

"And we show no mercy to anyone who touches our property," Atlas adds.

I blink back tears as Riot carves their sigil into the side of my neck, the tender spot just below my earlobe.

"The first one goes here, so I can see our mark when I look down at you sucking my cock."

The sharp tip of the blade burns like fire as he drags it through my flesh, molding his design. I take deep breaths and try not to cry. *The pain is only temporary. My soul is theirs forever.*

He sits back. "There. It's done."

Valentin loosens his grip on my head. I wince as he strokes a finger across my mutilated flesh and sucks in a sharp breath. "*Mors tua, vita mea.*"

Atlas bends over and plants a soft kiss on my forehead. "*In absentia lucis, tenebrae vincunt.*"

Riot licks his lips as he looks down at my belly. He fingers the edge of my panties, taking his time to roll his thumb across the lacy fabric before yanking them down. "*Mors vincit omnia.*"

One by one they take the dagger and cut an incision in each of their fingers. I watch them in wonder as they each press a bloody finger against my wet pussy and rub in slow, agonizing circles.

Their words repeat in my head as they take turns thrusting their fingers inside me.

Mors tua, vita mea. *Your death, my life.*

In absentia lucis, tenebrae vincunt. *In the absence of light, darkness prevails.*

Mors vincit omnia. *Death always wins.*

I arch my hips up to meet their rhythm. My clit spasms with every twitch of their slick fingers.

Valentin licks the blood from my neck as he pushes farther inside my core. "Do you like being owned by us?"

"Yes," I murmur.

Atlas slides his palm up and down my slit, pushing Valentin's finger deeper inside me. "Say it. Pledge yourself to us right now. Make your oath to serve only us."

I can't breathe with their hands between my legs. With the pressure building in my core. My clit swells as they rock against me. "I swear. I'm yours and no one else's."

Valentin threads his fingers through my hair and pulls my strands tight inside his palm. "Do you give us your body?"

"*Yes*," I moan.

Riot licks the inside of my thigh, lapping up my spilled juices and blood. "Do you give us your life?"

They were my salvation and my damnation. My cursed devils. "Always."

Riot's eyes blaze with a feral hunger. "Then make it binding. *Cum for us, Firecracker.*"

An explosion rocks through me as I surrender fully. I cry out as the most intense orgasm I've ever felt ripples through me. My body twists and contorts as I breathe through the ecstasy like it has a mind of its own.

And then the power surges through me. I arch my back and cry out as an array of sensations assaults me. It goes from tingling to burning to what feels like being flayed alive. Sparks like electric currents shoot through my veins. And when I look back at each of them, my vision is sharper. Clearer. I feel their love. Their need. I feel it in a way that I can't explain.

Riot's face lights up. "Eyes like burnt honey, glowing like gold resin. You're one of us now, Firecracker."

My fingertips crackle with energy. *Their energy*. It skates down my arms and legs, binding itself to my blood and my bones like a magnet. "What happens now?" I ask.

Riot lets his finger linger on my clit, rubbing it back and forth. "That was the first of many sigils I'll give you. With each one, we'll grow stronger as a coven."

His touch stimulates me again, leaving me wanting more. "Mmm, don't stop. I want all three of you inside me. Together."

Valentin removes his clothes and lays back on the bed. "Get on top of me, firecracker."

I smooth my hands over his chest as I straddle him and lower myself onto his thick cock. "Oh, fuck. You're going to make me cum again," I moan.

Riot is already naked behind me. He grabs a hold of my hips as I slide up and down Valentin's shaft. "Fuck, you're such a good little slut. Relax and open up for me."

I bite my lip hard as Riot slips his cock inside my ass. "Fuck," I cry out.

The pressure from both of them feels like I'm being ripped apart at the seams. Riot and Valentin take turns thrusting, bouncing me back and forth between them like a see-saw.

"Open wide for me, pretty girl," Atlas coos. He kneels before me and shoves his cock into my mouth. "That's my naughty girl. Taking us all so well."

Each agonizing thrust from Riot pushes me farther down onto Valentin's cock. The stimulation is everywhere. Every nerve on my body is raw and sensitive, aching for more.

Riot slaps my ass while Valentin pinches my nipples. Atlas pulls my hair and shoves his cock all the way to the back of my throat, forcing me to breathe through my nose. I purr like I'm an animal in heat as I'm rocked bath and forth between them.

"You love being fucked like this, don't you?" Riot demands.

He slaps my ass and buries his cock all the way in. I take deep breaths and try to nod but Atlas is thrusting hard into my mouth.

Valentin yanks my hips forward. "Yeah she does. Look how fucking eager she is."

I'm on the verge of blacking out from pleasure.

Atlas grunts. "Swallow for me, pretty girl." His cum bursts out like a fucking rocket, filling my mouth so full I almost choke. He strokes my lips. "Thatta girl. Fuck. Damn you do that so well. Don't spill a fucking drop."

Riot pulls my ass cheeks apart and thrusts in hard. "Mmm, fuck. We're filling you so fucking good." Another burst of thick hot cum enters me as Riot grinds into my ass. His moans are deafening, feral, like a wild animal.

And it sets Valentin off. He wraps his hand around my throat and lets out a deep guttural moan. His pupils widen as a silver light encircles them. He slams into me, unleashing his cum inside my pussy while Riot still rides out his orgasm in my ass.

Fuck. I'm filled to the brim. Soaked. The tingling in my clit quickens as a deep spasm rolls through me. Riot fingers my taint, urging me to lose complete control. Stars stud my vision as I cum onto Valentin's cock.

"Oh, fuck," I cry out. "*Uhhh.*"

Atlas sticks two fingers in my mouth, and I bite down on them. "Yeah, fucking take it out on me, pretty girl. Break my fucking skin."

And I do. The taste of his blood in my mouth makes me cum again until I have nothing left to give. Until my muscles won't hold me up any longer.

We collapse on the bed together, a sea of tangled limbs, cum, sweat, and bloody sigils.

The students at Tenebrose Academy don't look at me anymore. Not since the Winter Solstice ball last weekend. Not after the authorities had to cut Zeke's mutilated body down from the tree. And especially not after nine Nocturnus initiates were admitted to Absentia, the Raven's Gate mental institution, for observation.

But no one has questioned us. No one is speaking about that night. Not even the professors. Although, Professor Harker and Professor Erebus keep side-eyeing me when they think I'm not looking.

"You seem different," Villette says. She sits across the table from me and Libra at Swallow.

"That's because she's Nocturnus now," Libra quips. "Don't think I didn't notice that sigil on your neck."

I am different. And it's not just the sigil. I took another man's life. One who deserved it, but still… the weight of that sits with me. I made an oath to Riot, Atlas, and Valentin, binding myself to them for life. We serve each other now.

"A lot has happened." I shrug and take a sip of my whiskey.

Libra gives me a pained look. "Are you going home for winter break? Now that the curse is lifted?"

An uneasiness washes over me. The thought of going back to Wickford Hollow makes my skin crawl. But only because I don't want to face my parents. I do miss Bailey, though. And it would be nice to tell her everything in person.

"We haven't decided what we're doing yet. We're still talking about it." I can feel them judging me with their eyes. Neither one of them is a fan of my guys. Even Libra, who used to adore Atlas, has nothing nice to say about him now. I can't really blame her after they humiliated her in front of all the initiates.

Villette grabs my hand and squeezes it. "You have a lot to figure out. Lib and I are both here for you if you need us."

I nod and force a smile. "Riot's family wants to see all of us, so we'll most likely go there first. Thanks for not totally hating me."

Libra rolls her eyes. "Oh, don't be so dramatic, Blackwell. I've had worse things happen to me than getting locked in a basement by a ghost."

"We could never hate you," Villette adds. "Nocturnus is clearly your destiny. It has been since you were born. One way or another, you were always supposed to end up here."

A chill trickles up my spine. I never really believed in destiny before. I didn't believe in much of anything. But that's all changed now.

My phone buzzes. I look down to see a text from Riot and it sets off a flurry of nerves in my stomach. I give them a look and start to speak, but Libra cuts me off.

She waves her hand like she's shooing me. "Yeah, we know. They've summoned you. When they call, you go."

A twinge of guilt gnaws at me. I am not like them. Not anymore. The old me would have blown off boys for a girls' night without batting an eyelash. But what I have with Riot, Atlas, and Valentin is serious. Sacred. And the longer I'm away from them, the more it hurts to breathe.

I give them each a hug before I leave and do my best to lighten the mood with a joke about how they should change the name of the bar to Choke instead of Swallow. They laugh with me but I can still see the worry in their eyes.

When I step outside, the guys are already waiting for me. The three of them lean against Valentin's black sedan. A flood of emotions hits me like a tidal wave as soon I lock eyes with each of them. And I can't stop the grin from spreading across my face.

"Feel like taking a little drive, Firecracker?" Riot holds the door to the backseat open for me.

Butterflies dance in my belly as I gaze back at all three of them. They are torturously sexy. "Only if I get to drive this time." I quip back.

Valentin narrows his eyes at me for a second before flashing me a devious smirk. He towers over me, his gaze hungry and wild. "Only if I get to sit next to you and play with your pretty little pussy."

I'm instantly wet and tingling. I swallow hard. "Fuck."

Atlas howls with laughter. "I hope we don't crash."

Valentin hands me the keys and we all climb in, laughing.

I turn the key and flip on the headlights. The snow is coming down hard and the road is icy. Maybe it's not such a good idea for Val to finger fuck me while driving through this.

I shudder and check the mirrors. "So, where am I taking us?"

"To Val's cabin," Riot murmurs. "We need to regroup and figure out our next move."

I nod and pull out of the parking lot. As we sail through the wintry countryside of Raven's Gate, away from Tenebrose, my uneasiness dissipates. I'm safe now. I have my three psychos with me, and nothing can hurt us as long as we're together.

As if they can read my mind, Atlas and Riot each grab one of my shoulders, squeezing them gently. Valentin rests his hand on my thigh. "We got you, firecracker. No one will ever hurt you again."

It's a promise I'd like to believe, but I know our world is uncertain, and evil is everywhere. But at least for now, we're safe. We're together.

As we round the last bend before reaching Valentin's cabin, an unkindness of ravens flies past and settle into the treetops. A chill creeps into my bones under their watchful glares.

Ugh, these fucking birds.

I shake it off and turn up the music. *No Mourners, No Funerals* by Victoria Carbol blasts from the speakers. Valentin inches his hand up my thigh. "Shall we play in the crypt tonight?" he asks with a smirk.

I arch an eyebrow at him. "Oh, you want to lock me in a coffin again?" I tease.

"A coffin? What the hell did the two of you get up to last time you were here?" Atlas blurts out.

Valentin snickers. "At least I didn't try to feed her to my fucking snake, asshole."

The three of us burst out laughing. I lock eyes with Riot in the rearview mirror and he gives me the first genuine smile I've ever seen from him. I smile back. He leans forward and whispers, "Welcome to the family, Maur."

My heart swells. His words send a ripple of tingles across my flesh. It doesn't matter where we are or where we go. With them, *I'm finally home.*

We'll figure the rest out later…

And murder anyone who tries to come between us.

The end… for now.

MORE BOOKS BY M VIOLET

Good Girl (Wickford Hollow Duet Book 1)

Little Fox (Wickford Hollow Duet Book 2)

Wickford Hollow Duet (includes Good Girl, Little Fox, and an exclusive bonus chapter of Riot and Maureen)

Wicked Midnight
(A Dark Why Choose Romance Retelling of Cinderella)

Unholy Night (A Dark Why Choose Holiday Romance)

Acknowledgements

Thank you for reading *Pretty Little Psycho*! If you enjoyed diving into Maureen's world of hot AF psycho bullies, then you'll be happy to know that there will be a book 2! Riot, Atlas, and Valentin are just getting started.

Thank you to all my Vixens! I love each and every one of you! You are the best and most loyal readers an author could ask for. This book would not have been possible without all of your love and support. XOXO

Thank you to my beautiful and amazing friend Cara Lyn (AKA: Cassie Fairbanks)! Your friendship means everything to me. I'm so proud of you and can't wait to continue this author journey with you! Love you, girl!

I want to thank every ARC reader, reviewer, and blogger for reading *Pretty Little Psycho*. Whether you've been with me since Good Girl, or you're just joining my dark chaos now, your support means the world to me!

Thank you to my editor Kat, of Kat's Literary Services. You did such a fantastic job with Pretty Little Psycho. I am beyond thrilled to have you on my side!

Thank you to Artscandare for another dark and sinful cover! I'm so obsessed with this one!

Thank you to Stacie of Champagne Book Design for sprinkling your magic formatting fairy dust on another one of my books. I cannot express enough how much I adore and appreciate you.

Thank you to my awesomely bad-ass PA Darcy Bennett! I'm so happy I found you. You've definitely kicked my author game up a few notches. XOXO

Thank you to all of my family and friends for being supportive and understanding. I love each and every one of you so much.

And last but not least, I have to give a special shoutout and thank you to my Smutven ladies! Your friendship, camaraderie, recipes, rants, raves, memes, and Gifs give me life. Can't wait to meet all of you IRL.

About the Author

M Violet is a dark romance author with a flair for the dramatic. She likes whiskey, rainy nights, and writing by the fire. When she's not creating scorching hot villains for you to fall in love with, you can find her eating chocolate and binge watching her favorite shows.

Facebook: Authormviolet
Instagram: Authormviolet
Tik Tok: Authormviolet

Printed in Great Britain
by Amazon